Law and Piety in Medieval Islam

The Ayyubid and Mamluk periods were two of the most intellectually vibrant in Islamic history. Megan H. Reid's book, which traverses three centuries from 1170 to 1500, recovers the stories of medieval men and women who were renowned not only for their intellectual prowess but also for their devotional piety. Through these stories, the book examines trends in voluntary religious practice that have been largely overlooked in modern scholarship. This type of piety was distinguished by the pursuit of God's favor through additional rituals, which emphasized the body as an instrument of worship, and through the rejection of worldly pleasures, and even society itself. Using an array of sources including manuals of law, fatwa collections, chronicles, and obituaries, the book shows what it meant to be a good Muslim in the medieval period and how Islamic law helped to define holy behavior. In its concentration on personal piety, ritual, and ethics the book offers an intimate perspective on medieval Islamic society.

Megan H. Reid is Assistant Professor of Religion at the University of Southern California.

Cambridge Studies in Islamic Civilization

A list of books in the series can be found after the index.

Law and Piety in Medieval Islam

MEGAN H. REID
University of Southern California

CAMBRIDGE
UNIVERSITY PRESS

CAMBRIDGE UNIVERSITY PRESS
Cambridge, New York, Melbourne, Madrid, Cape Town,
Singapore, São Paulo, Delhi, Mexico City

Cambridge University Press
32 Avenue of the Americas, New York, NY 10013-2473, USA

www.cambridge.org
Information on this title: www.cambridge.org/9780521889599

First published 2013

Printed in the United States of America

A catalog record for this publication is available from the British Library.

Library of Congress Cataloging in Publication Data
Reid, Megan H.
Law and piety in medieval Islam / Megan H. Reid.
p. cm. – (Cambridge studies in islamic civilization)
Includes bibliographical references and index.
ISBN 978-0-521-88959-9 (hardback)
1. Islam – Customs and practices. 2. Spiritual life – Islam. 3. Muslims – Conduct of life 4. Islamic law. 5. Muslim scholars – Biography. I. Title.
BP188.R45 2011
297.5′70902–dc22 2011008594

ISBN 978-0-521-88959-9 Hardback

This book is dedicated to my father,
Watson Day Reid

Contents

Acknowledgments *page* xi

Introduction: Devotional Piety and Islamic Law 1

1. The Persistence of Asceticism 21
2. "Devote Yourselves to Deeds You Can Bear": Voluntary Fasting and Bodily Piety 56
3. Charity, Food, and the Right of Refusal 97
4. The Devil at the Fountain: Problems of Ritual 144

Conclusion: Beyond Transgression, Beyond *sunna* 197

Glossary 215

Bibliography 219

Index 241

Acknowledgments

This book benefited first of all from Marigold Acland at Cambridge University Press, who expressed enthusiasm for my project and was a pleasure to work with. She encouraged me patiently through challenges, as did Helen Wheeler and Mary Starkey. Mary did far more than copyedit this text; engaging with someone of her caliber was immensely rewarding, and I know that not many authors have this privilege. Both readers for Cambridge drew my attention to issues large and small, particularly Marion Katz, who caught some "egregious errors" (to use Ibn al-Najjār's expression) and was generous with her detailed, insightful comments.

I want to express my deep appreciation for the support I received from a number of institutions and foundations. At the University of Southern California I have benefited from Faculty Development Grants, and I want to thank especially Deans Dani Byrd and Kathleen Speer, who have shown great kindness and were instrumental in allowing me time to work on this project. A fellowship from the USC–Huntington Early Modern Studies Institute provided me a semester in which to reconceptualize parts of the book. I traveled to London with a grant from the Center for Feminist Research at USC that allowed me to undertake several weeks of follow-up archival research.

The book was built upon earlier research and writing conducted with the help of Foreign Language and Area Studies Fellowships, the Ora J. Bretall Fellowship in Religion, and other generous support from Princeton University. A Fulbright-Hays Doctoral Dissertation Research Fellowship allowed me to spend a year in Egypt and France; and the Charlotte Newcombe Doctoral Dissertation Fellowship was crucial during the final year of writing.

I am happy to acknowledge never-to-be-repaid debts to several teachers and mentors. Michael Morony at UCLA encouraged my interest in writing about a model of piety rather than a social type. My dissertation advisor, Shaun Marmon, brought an entire world to life through her excitement about the field and the Arabic sources. I still miss the pleasure of her intellectual rigor and her good company. I am proud to have been her first graduate student.

Discussions with Peter Brown encouraged me to look for and appreciate the strange, the puzzling, and the humorous in the lives of people in the medieval period. His belief in my project was a great source of comfort. My years at Princeton were enlivened by a friendship with Oleg Grabar, with whom I had wandering and scandalous conversations about many things, including wanderers and scandalous piety. I thank Avram Udovitch, under whose tutelage my love of Islamic legal texts blossomed, and also Patricia Crone, who was a marvelous interlocutor. I thoroughly enjoyed the year I spent as her research assistant at the Institute for Advanced Study.

I feel lucky to have chosen a field filled with colleagues whose ideas I admire and whose companionship I have enjoyed so much: Ali Ballouti, Jonathan Berkey, Anne Broadbridge, Sandra Campbell, Dani Doueiri, Brian Edwards, Daphna Ephrat, Jason Glenn, Molly Green, John Iskander, Tariq al-Jamil, Nasser Rabbat, Jennifer Roth, and Brad Verter. Before I met any of these, the door was opened by Emile Durzi, to whom I will always be grateful.

Tamer el-Leithy and I worked on our dissertations together, and there is much of our delightful friendship in this book. Lisa Bitel has had the least fun role to play, but she cannot know how much her support, her intellectual engagement, and her irreverent sense of humor have meant to me. She and Peter Mancall have brought much joy to my life in Los Angeles.

The most important thanks of all must go to Paul Cobb, who every year has provided yet more steady friendship and super support as a comrade, colleague, trouper, reader, mover, shaker.

At the last stages, and thus last in these acknowledgments, my loving thanks and unending gratitude go to my mother, Penny Holbrook, to my sister, Cassandra Reid, and to my husband, Djamel Hamdad. I could not have finished this book without them.

Introduction

Devotional Piety and Islamic Law

Aḥmad Ibn Taymiyya, the famous fourteenth-century jurist known today as the watchdog of Islamic orthodoxy, had a brother named ʿAbd Allāh, who appears in medieval biographical dictionaries as a jurisconsult (*muftī*), a devotee (*ʿābid*), and an ascetic (*zāhid*), among other things. Although ʿAbd Allāh had an excellent education and even taught Islamic law for a time, he is said to have preferred solitude, and took to remaining in his house during the day so as to avoid people. By night he went to pray in abandoned mosques outside the city of Damascus. Renowned for his devotional piety, he made the Pilgrimage to Mecca many times, performed at least one minor miracle, and when he died in 727/1327 he was buried among the tombs of the Sufis. Only one author mentions that he was blessed with unusual mystical insight, which suggests that his Sufi qualities were not, chiefly, what made him into a pious exemplar, into a man of such perfection that others sought, or were encouraged, to pattern their own lives on his.[1]

[1] Al-Ṣafadī calls ʿAbd Allāh a devotee, a mufti, and an exemplar (*qudwa*); al-Jazarī calls him also an ascetic and a scrupulous man (*wariʿ*), among other things; and Ibn Rajab, adding to the list, mentions his "perceptive abilities" (*ʿirfān*), which suggests an inclination towards Sufi mysticism, and also reports a "well-known incident" (*amr mashhūr*) concerning him. ʿAbd Allāh was known for giving large amounts of charity, even though he himself was poor and kept few possessions. A fellow traveller on the Pilgrimage caravan one year searched his luggage and noticed that he was carrying no wealth. Later, the man saw him dispersing gold "in huge amounts." Ṣalāḥ al-Dīn Khalīl ibn Aybak al-Ṣafadī, *Aʿyān al-ʿaṣr wa-aʿwān al-naṣr*, ed. ʿAlī Abū Zayd et al., 5 vols. (Damascus, 1997–8), II, 692–3; Shams al-Dīn Muḥammad al-Jazarī, *Tārīkh ḥawādith al-zamān wa-anbāʾihi wa-wafayāt al-akābir waʾl-aʿyān min abnāʾihi*, ed. ʿUmar ʿAbd al-Salām Tadmurī, 3 vols. (Sidon, 1998), II, 214–16; ʿAbd al-Raḥmān ibn Aḥmad Ibn Rajab, *Kitāb al-dhayl ʿalā Ṭabaqāt al-Ḥanābila*, 2 vols. (Beirut, [1981]), II, 382–4.

Islam is often distinguished from other religions because of its emphasis on textual learning and a type of religious authority that is based on knowledge of texts. So why, in a society that revered its scholars so highly, was a misanthropic ex-jurisconsult held up as an exemplar? What seems to have fascinated his biographers was his departure from learned society, not his privileged position within it. One biography articulates this especially clearly: ʿAbd Allāh's escapes were frequent, and he would have liked to make them permanent "despite" his having mastered law (*fiqh*), Arabic grammar, history, both ancient and recent, and other fields. In fact, his rejection of society would have made sense quite easily to medieval readers of the biographical dictionaries where his life is recorded, for several disparate reasons. He was best known, then as now, for being the brother of an astounding but notorious legal genius and social activist; no aspect of his life would be read as being isolated from the famous controversies that involved his family. ʿAbd Allāh and a third brother once accompanied Aḥmad when he was sent to prison in Cairo for five months after being hounded by colleagues over theological issues.[2] The other brother, Zayn al-Dīn, accompanied Aḥmad to prison voluntarily on two other occasions. Given this background, ʿAbd Allāh's efforts to display disdain for the world of learning as well as the mundane world and its luxuries might be read as a stylized rejection of specific realities and not merely as misanthropy or as a classic renunciation of society. His actions become infinitely more noteworthy in the context of the learned society to which he belonged, both in fourteenth-century Cairo, where he was imprisoned along with his brothers, and in his home city, Damascus, where he died while Aḥmad was again in prison serving a final period of incarceration.

Law and Piety in Medieval Islam is a study of the intersection of personal piety and the culture of Islamic law in the late medieval period. Using primary sources that range from chronicles and biographical dictionaries to legal manuals, fatwa collections, and hortatory treatises, I examine what it meant to be an exemplary Muslim in the Ayyubid and

[2] Sherman Jackson explains several of these and translates Ibn Taymiyya's eloquent rebuttal in "Ibn Taymiyyah on Trial in Damascus," *Journal of Semitic Studies* 39, 1 (1994): 41–85. See also D. P. Little, "The Historical and Historiographical Significance of the Detention of Ibn Taymiyya," *International Journal of Middle East Studies* 4, 3 (1973): 311–27. On other issues that gave Aḥmad Ibn Taymiyya the modern reputation as a defender of orthodoxy, see Muhammad Umar Memon, *Ibn Taimīya's Struggle with Popular Religion: With an Annotated Translation of his Kitāb iqtiḍā' aṣ-ṣirāṭ al-mustaqīm mukhālafat aṣḥāb al-jaḥīm* (The Hague, 1976).

Mamluk periods. The book focuses in particular on the role of the body in Islamic ritual practice as well as on more personalized kinds of ritual behavior. In terms of the "culture of Islamic law," I mean this in a broad sense. I address the more informal aspects of this culture: first of all, by examining quotidian uses of law by pious Muslims during a period that was crucial to the development of the corpus of Islamic legal texts, many of which are still in use today; and second, by seeking to explain how the scholars of religious law fit into their society. Without understanding broader themes in medieval Islamic religious culture, it is difficult to appreciate how or why legal writings were important to ordinary piety – and, indeed, vice versa.[3]

This study deals with the Ayyubid and the Mamluk periods for reasons that have to do more with developments in religious practice than with political history, although these were not always unrelated. This span of time, from roughly 1170 to 1500 C.E., is what I will refer to as the late medieval period. By examining evidence from the surrounding centuries, the precise character of late medieval religious culture becomes clearer, and for this reason examples from the mid-1100s and the early sixteenth century are presented as well. Ayyubid rule accounts for roughly one-third of the period under consideration here. During it we see what might be described as the adolescence of several institutions that will be discussed in this book, ones that would see even more growth under the Mamluks: the land-grant (*iqṭāʿ*) system of the military administration that gave individuals the right to collect taxes on designated lands; charitable support for the needy and for religious scholarship through the construction of endowed buildings; and an expanding judicial system.[4] The Ayyubids were a large extended family, members of which ruled much of the Middle East from 569/1174 to 658/1260. Within a decade of Saladin's founding the dynasty in Cairo, they controlled the western

[3] As Christopher Taylor points out, without understanding the law and its role in social and religious life, few things about medieval piety make sense: *In the Vicinity of the Righteous: Ziyāra and the Veneration of Muslim Saints in Late Medieval Egypt* (Leiden, 1999), 125–6.

[4] Adam Sabra provides a superb introduction to the topic and terminology of medieval charitable foundations (and also a clear explanation of the land-grant system) in "Public Policy or Private Charity? The Ambivalent Character of Islamic Charitable Endowments," in *Stiftungen in Christentum, Judentum und Islam vor der Moderne: auf der Suche nach ihren Gemeinsamkeiten und Unterschieden in religiösen Grundlagen, praktischen Zwecken und historischen Transformationen*, ed. Michael Borgolte (Berlin, 2005). See also his article "The Rise of a New Class? Land Tenure in Fifteenth-Century Egypt: A Review Article," *Mamluk Studies Review* 8, 2 (2004).

Arabian peninsula (the Hijaz, with its holy cities of Mecca and Medina), Yemen, Syria, and Iraq. The Ayyubid ruler, the sultan, based in Cairo, was the major power; the provinces were ruled by princes from the family, sometimes as a confederation, sometimes as more or less independent petty states. Sultans and princes alike took the title "al-Malik," meaning ruler or king. Across the region sons succeeded fathers, cousins succeeded cousins, nephews succeeded uncles, and in one case an uncle succeeded his nephew.

By contrast, many sultans – and virtually all of the political administration – of the Mamluk empire were former military slaves of Central Asian Turkic origin. While sometimes their sons were installed as sultans, a large number gained power after having served in the personal entourage of a previous ruler. It would be impossible to describe here fully the unique system of slave (*mamlūk*) and owner (a freed *mamlūk*) that characterized the Mamluk period, or the strength of social bonds that tied slaves not only to their masters but to each other in the military "households" in which they grew up, but there is substantial secondary literature on this topic.[5] The elite cadre of *mamlūk*s who rose to the position of commander (amir) were major players in political life and benefactors of religious culture. The sons of *mamlūk*s could not, in theory, inherit rule or their fathers' military positions, but were integrated into the cultural elite of the cities under Mamluk control. Throughout Mamluk rule, from 1260 to 1517, power was firmly consolidated at Cairo; the provinces were administered by amirs who were appointed by and generally loyal to the ruler. The period was characterized by factionalism among groups of *mamlūk*s belonging to various powerful military households. As with Ayyubid rule, there were frequent changes of power, some violent, but this did not necessarily mean instability for the empire as a whole.

In terms of geography, I have attempted to limit myself to the lands under Ayyubid and Mamluk control. Cairo and Damascus provide an obvious focal point for this study because of their importance as centers of learning, the high level of patronage associated with their rulers, the number of prolific authors who made these cities their home, and, most importantly, because they attracted pious travellers from across the

[5] For example, Jo Van Steenbergen, "Mamluk Elite on the Eve of an-Nāṣir Muḥammad's death (1341): A Look behind the Scenes of Mamluk Politics," *Mamluk Studies Review* 9, 2 (2005): 173–99; Nasser Rabbat, "Representing the Mamluks in Mamluk Historical Writing," in *The Historiography of Islamic Egypt, c. 950–1800*, ed. Hugh Kennedy (Leiden, 2000), 59–75; and a number of articles in Thomas Philipp and Ulrich Haarmann, eds., *The Mamluks in Egyptian Politics and Society* (Cambridge, 1998).

Islamic world.[6] Yet it is this last attribute that makes the geographical range of my study also inevitably wider, since I hope to demonstrate how pious practices were easily understood and transmitted across Islamic cultures. Authors such as al-Udfūwī, who wrote a fourteenth-century biographical dictionary for Upper Egypt, provide geographical breadth and confirm that the same types of piety existed elsewhere. Similarly, ʿAbd Allāh Ibn Farḥūn, al-Fāsī, and al-Sakhāwī are good examples of authors whose cities of choice, Medina and Mecca, were, like Cairo and Damascus, crossroads of pious activity. Examples from Iraq, Spain, and India are also relevant in demonstrating the scope of this shared piety. This is not to suggest that there were no local developments or unique manifestations of piety in specific places. The distinctive qualities of Sufi piety that emerged in Anatolia, for example, have been well documented by Ahmet Karamustafa and Cemel Kafadar.[7]

Given that Sufi mysticism may be the most familiar aspect of medieval Islamic piety, its relative unimportance in ʿAbd Allāh Ibn Taymiyya's life story bears further consideration. He lived and was buried in a milieu in which Sufism and other currents of piety intermingled, as a number of studies of medieval Damascus have recently shown.[8] While the topic of Sufism has received a good deal of attention, most of the other elements in his biography have not. Most important of these is the fact that he is described as being "draped in the gown of asceticism."[9] For more than a century the prevalent argument has been that as Sufism rose to dominate Islamic piety, the strict asceticism of early Islam was left behind. Far

[6] Indeed, one scholar has estimated that more than half of the scholars (*ʿulamāʾ*) in twelfth-century Damascus were not native born: J. Gilbert, "Institutionalization of Muslim Scholarship and Professionalization of the ʿUlamāʾ in Medieval Damascus," *Studia Islamica* 52 (1980): 112. The draw of Cairo for Sufis and scholars from other parts of the Islamic world is described by Jonathan Katz in chap. 4 of his monograph on a fifteenth-century autobiography, *Dreams, Sufism and Sainthood: The Visionary Career of Muḥammad al-Zawāwī* (Leiden, 1996).

[7] Ahmet Karamustafa, *God's Unruly Friends: Dervish Groups in the Islamic Later Middle Period, 1200–1500* (Salt Lake City, 1994); Cemal Kafadar, *Between Two Worlds: The Construction of the Ottoman State* (Berkeley, 1995).

[8] The definitive work on Damascus remains Louis Pouzet's *Damas aux VII/XIII siècle: Vie et structures religieuses d'une métropole islamique* (Beirut, 1988); see also the excellent study by Daniella Talmon-Heller, *Islamic Piety in Medieval Syria: Mosques, Cemeteries and Sermons under the Zangids and Ayyūbids (1146–1260)* (Leiden, 2008). Joseph Meri has urged us to consider an even wider interreligious context for some aspects of Muslim piety in *The Cult of Saints among Muslims and Jews in Medieval Syria* (Oxford, 2002).

[9] "wāsiʿ qamīṣ al-zuhd": al-Ṣafadī, *Aʿyān al-ʿaṣr*, II: 693. The phrase seems to evoke the ample garments and elegant fabrics worn by more worldly learned men in this period.

from rejecting it altogether, Sufism – according to this model – absorbed asceticism and its practices, imbued them with new spiritual meaning, and made them standard parts of the Sufi Path. By implication, asceticism for its own sake was no longer an ideal that had much currency after the ninth or tenth century.[10]

If ʿAbd Allāh Ibn Taymiyya were simply an exception, a leftover ascetic type from the early Islamic centuries, he might merit no more than a footnote, but references to similar figures abound in the late medieval sources. These figures are remarkable for the extreme devotion manifested in their vows of solitude or fasting, their love of prayer, voluntary poverty, meager diets, itinerancy, or other forms of bodily mortification. They could be the sons of amirs, shopkeepers, widows, slaves, or, like ʿAbd Allāh, jurists. Some are described as Sufis and others are not. But they all bear a strong resemblance to the ascetics of early Islam – whom, I will argue, they very consciously sought to emulate. Their numbers suggest that a distinct ascetic tradition continued to exist and thrive, one that owed no necessary allegiance to Sufism even if these two types of piety often overlapped. For the Ayyubid period, Anne-Marie Eddé and Daniella Talmon-Heller have both shown that asceticism, sainthood, voluntary poverty (becoming a *faqīr*), and minor miracles were common among holy men generally, and were not just the purview of the Sufis. Eddé argues that ascetic saints and Sufis in Aleppo were two separate categories of holy people, and she urges historians to take note of the distinctions between them.[11]

[10] Somewhere between the tenth and fourteenth centuries, this model postulates, Sufism "reached maturity as a social movement," when organized brotherhoods (or "orders") supplanted the individualism and asceticism of the earliest Sufis, according to Ira Lapidus, *A History of Islamic Societies*, 2nd ed. (Cambridge, 2002), 137, 90–4; Roy Mottahedeh has argued that the rise of Sufi brotherhoods beginning in the Buyid period displaced ascetic piety: see *Loyalty and Leadership in an Early Islamic Society* (Princeton, 1980), 148. According to Annemarie Schimmel, "the orders have contributed to converting Sufism into a mass movement – a movement in which the high ambitions of the classical Sufis were considerably watered down": Annemarie Schimmel, *Mystical Dimensions of Islam* (Chapel Hill, 1975), 239. See also Tawfīq Ṭawīl, *al-Taṣawwuf fī Miṣr ibbāna al-ʿaṣr al-ʿUthmānī* (Cairo, 1988); in his preface and chapter 1 Ṭawīl presents a similar model of the stages between solitary Sufism and the communal Sufism of the Mamluk period. Of these authors, only Schimmel and Ṭawīl wrote directly on Sufism; the others illustrate how these arguments about Sufism have permeated overviews of socio-religious developments in Islam. Christopher Melchert traces the argument back to Louis Massignon's *Essai sur les origines du lexique technique de la mystique musulmane*, published in 1922 (Christopher Melchert, "The Ḥanābila and the Early Sufis," *Arabica* 48, 3 [2001]: 353). The first part of Massignon's book had been submitted to a press that was bombed in 1914, the same year in which Reynold A. Nicholson published *The Mystics of Islam*, where we find the same argument in his introduction.

[11] Anne-Marie Eddé, *La principauté ayyoubide d'Alep (579/1183–658/1260)* (Stuttgart, 1999), 419–22. In the texts she studied Talmon-Heller finds no reference to the spiritual

This is an important point, for asceticism may have been crucial to the Sufi Path, but it was also crucial to the culture of Islamic law; ascetical attitudes and practices were seen as appropriate for the keepers of divine law. I would stress also the fact that common supererogatory practices such as nighttime prayer and voluntary fasting have a long history in Islamic piety, and were not seen in late medieval Islam as being predominantly Sufi ones. Sufis will make frequent appearances in the following chapters as jurists, hermits, and scholars, alongside other pious men and women, but this is not a book about Sufism.[12] What Sufism actually was in the Ayyubid and Mamluk periods still has not been clearly defined, in fact.[13] My comments in this introduction are intended to render problematic the category of the Sufi, which too often remains a catch-all category for pious persons.

The Meaning of Devotional Piety

Sources from the thirteenth, fourteenth, and fifteenth centuries catalog a broad spectrum of religious behavior, from the ordinary to the stellar to the transgressive. Making sense of that spectrum requires a vocabulary that allows us to describe common patterns in piety. Yet we still lack the descriptive language with which to discuss piety in broad terms. One may be able to discern various strands or styles present in late medieval Islam: juridical piety, Sufi piety, Ḥanbalī piety, learned piety, antinomian

quest, no evidence of Sufi doctrine, and no presence of brotherhood affiliation, though she still affirms Sufism's role in popular Ḥanbalī piety and sees asceticism as a sign of latent Sufism: see Daniella Talmon-Heller, "The Shaykh and the Community: Popular Ḥanbalite Islam in 12th–13th Century Jabal Nablus and Jabal Qasyūn," *Studia Islamica* 79 (1994): 117–20; Daniella Talmon-Heller, "*The Cited Tales of the Wondrous Doings of the Shaykhs of the Holy Land* by Ḍiyā' al-Dīn Abū ʿAbd Allāh Muḥammad b. ʿAbd al-Wāḥid al-Maqdisī (569/1173–643/1245): Text, Translation and Commentary," *Crusades* 1 (2002): 113.

12 On the nature of late medieval Sufism, one is best served by studies focusing on its contexts, such as Richard McGregor's study of a father and son who founded a Sufi order in the southern cemetery in Cairo. He provides valuable insight into the theology and daily spiritual life of Sufism in the Mamluk era. See Richard J. A. McGregor, *Sanctity and Mysticism in Medieval Egypt: The Wafā' Sufi Order and the Legacy of Ibn ʿArabi* (Albany, 2004); and also, among other excellent articles in a recently edited volume, Adam A. Sabra, "Illiterate Sufis and Learned Artisans: The Circle of ʿAbd al-Wahhab al-Shaʿrani," in *Le développement du soufisme en Égypte à l'époque mamelouke*, ed. Richard J. McGregor and Adam Sabra (Cairo, 2006).

13 Although I hope that by describing the wider context of piety, a definition may be within closer reach, McGregor has recently pointed out that currently what is needed is not "new and better definitions" of Mamluk Sufism but ways around the "methodological bottlenecks that obstruct sound historical treatment of the subject." See Richard McGregor, "The Problem of Sufism," *Mamluk Studies Review* 13, 2 (2009): 83.

piety, the piety of the hadith folk (people engaged in the study and transmission of reports of the Prophet's words and deeds and also those of his Companions), and so on. ʿAbd Allāh Ibn Taymiyya exhibited all of these, yet no single one describes him well. I will argue that Shaykh ʿAbd Allāh represents a category of piety that was widely valorized by medieval Islamic society. His asceticism was not an aberration, but rather is evidence of a powerful continuity in Islam which lent to medieval piety a deeply ingrained and richly contoured sense of the importance of individual actions. What draws together the variety of ascetics, jurists, hermits, and other religious figures in medieval Islamic society is something I will call devotional piety. I take this phrase from the Arabic word *taʿabbud* (bodily devotion; supererogatory worship), which so frequently appears in descriptions of holy people, rather than from *taqwā*, another word also translated as piety but which may be more precisely defined as piousness or a god-fearing attitude. Devotional piety is in a sense an umbrella term for a diffuse set of attitudes in medieval Islamic culture, attitudes that are expressed through personal religious practice and that I believe lie at the heart of both individual asceticism and certain forms of Sufism.

Devotional piety was distinguished by the pursuit of God's favor through practices that were superadditional to the required rituals of Islam, by an emphasis on the body as an instrument of worship, and by the rejection of worldly pleasures – or even society itself. This form of piety was accessible to all Muslims, not only because of the role its exemplars often played in their communities as the beneficiaries of charity, as the destinations of pious travel, or as sources of advice and blessing, but also because these exemplars were emulated by large numbers of Muslims. Excess in a particular action, such as making the Pilgrimage many times on foot or staying awake all night in prayer, could make an individual man or woman famous. It was often a solitary path, not only because of the importance of removing oneself from society but also because inherent in the very nature of this piety was a degree of nonconformity, or at least individual choice. In other words, the element of uniqueness was proof of a person's holiness. Although in most cases devotional activities were based on the required rituals of Islam or the practices of Muḥammad and his Companions, there was considerable latitude in the way individuals chose to develop them.

Concentric Circles of Piety

To some degree, devotional piety appears to be distinct from learned piety, the locale of which might be the madrasa, the mosque, or the state-supported judicial hierarchy.[14] Medieval authors perceived this difference: Ibn al-Jawzī, introducing his famous biographical dictionary of godly men and women, the *Ṣifat al-ṣafwa*, says that he will include in it all types of pious people "*except* those who became famous for knowledge alone and did not become famous through asceticism and bodily devotion."[15] The criterion Ibn al-Jawzī used is precisely the topic of my study. Asceticism (*zuhd*) and bodily devotion (*taʿabbud*) are the foundation of medieval religious culture; it was excellence in these areas, and not learning alone, that made someone – even a scholar – worthy of emulation as well as praise. Chapter 1 deals with the longevity of asceticism in Islamic piety and its meaning in late medieval culture. Chapter 2 explains bodily devotion in depth, using the example of voluntary fasting.

Ibn al-Jawzī's decision about whom to include in his book is puzzling, however, considering the great heights to which the pursuit of religious knowledge had risen in his lifetime. As for the centuries after his death, Jonathan Berkey describes the cultural importance of an extensive and vibrant educational network in Mamluk Cairo, one that was bound together by patterns of teaching and study more durable than the institutional structures that often served as places of instruction. This network drew into its midst both traditional families of scholars and new recruits from less significant backgrounds, among them the sons of slaves and immigrants to the city from the provinces and farther abroad. Michael Chamberlain writes of the way in which prominent families made use of a similar network in Damascus to gain social status and political authority.[16] Within these networks, scholarly achievement and the accumulation of knowledge would appear to be the main criteria of pious fame, not least of all because the transmission of knowledge itself was "first and foremost an act of piety."[17]

Although Sufi scholars figure prominently in the networks of both cities, solitary ascetics and local holy men (Sufis among them) do not. The learned were revered, but learned piety was not necessarily the most

[14] See Leonor Fernandes, *The Evolution of a Sufi Institution in Mamluk Egypt: The Khanqah* (Berlin, 1988). Jonathan Berkey, however, emphasizes in *The Transmission of Knowledge in Medieval Cairo* (Princeton, 1992) how the pursuit of knowledge was not necessarily tied to institutions, for instruction in the religious sciences took place in private homes as well as mosques, madrasas, and *zāwiyas*.

[15] My emphasis: "dūna man ishtahara bi mujarrad al-ʿilm wa lam yashtahir bi'l-zuhd wa'l-taʿabbud": Abū'l Faraj ʿAbd al-Raḥmān Ibn al-Jawzī, *Ṣifat al-ṣafwa*, ed. Maḥmūd Fākhūrī, 4 vols. (Aleppo, 1969–73), I, 13.

[16] Michael Chamberlain, *Knowledge and Social Practice in Medieval Damascus, 1190–1350* (Cambridge, 1994).

[17] Berkey, *Transmission of Knowledge*, 55.

representative of medieval Islamic practice. While Ibn al-Jawzī could hardly be described as averse to scholarship, being himself a prodigious legal scholar and historian, his emphasis sets up a dichotomy between the book and the body that – however artificial it may be – is well worth pursuing. In a religion so often described as being tied to scripture, religious authority in Islam would seem to be most efficiently gained through learning and secured with words, either verbal or written. But the ways in which it could be achieved through the body and bodily practice has received far less attention than it deserves, despite the existence of texts such as Ibn al-Jawzī's *Ṣifat al-ṣafwa*, which focuses almost entirely on the bodily practices of holy men and women.

The problem is not that modern scholars have failed to identify bodily piety as an important theme in medieval Islam. On the contrary, Chamberlain stresses that it was by means of the cultural practices *associated* with knowledge (*ʿilm*) that scholars achieved their social distinction. To the young aspirant who sought to emulate him, a teacher "was as much a model of bodily norms as he was a carrier of truths." A scholar's credentials did not consist solely in the textual knowledge he had acquired but in "the whole complex of manners, moral conduct, deportment, and scripted forms of self-presentation that in sum made up the notion of *adab*."[18] And indeed it was Berkey who first described in such rich detail how the transmission of religious knowledge in medieval Islam was a cultural practice that continually exceeds modern notions of scholarship in the academy; at times, he notes, the study session was a devotional occasion rather than a purely scholastic endeavor.[19] I rely on the work of these two historians and others who have worked on the culture of religious scholarship as the framework for my approach.

Still, the piety of the body has never been treated extensively as a topic of its own, perhaps because it is not characteristic of any one group in society in particular. Berkey and Chamberlain both focused, in a sense, on the human infrastructure of elite religious life in Cairo and Damascus, and if my analysis is cast in terms of a broader human geography, this approach is only possible because of their scholarship on some of society's most visible groups: the scholars (*ʿulamāʾ*) and notables (*aʿyān*). I proceed from the premise that the antinomian ascetic, the professor of

[18] Chamberlain, *Knowledge and Social Practice*, 123, 107. In chapter 4, he discusses ritualized behavior in the personal relations between shaykhs and their students. His observations hold true for men and women outside the network he describes, and this is where I hope to add something to his superlative commentary on those practices.

[19] Berkey, *Transmission of Knowledge*, 212–13.

law, and the devoted housewife were all people who interacted with cultural notions of piety, if less often with each other. For these reasons, my study is organized around features of their piety rather than the social classes or groups who adopted it.

What Ibn al-Jawzī probably meant to suggest by his decision to omit famous learned men was merely that without the piety of bodily devotion (*taʿabbud*) and asceticism (*zuhd*), knowledge alone was an insufficient criterion for fame. Indeed, knowledge as a strategy for acquiring fame and social capital might have been precisely what Ibn al-Jawzī was proscribing in his decisions about whose lives he would record for posterity in the *Ṣifat al-ṣafwa*. In the Arabic sources from the two centuries after Ibn al-Jawzī, one can find with relative ease perfect examples of both devotional piety and learned piety: a woman so devoted to the hajj that she left her husband behind and travelled to Mecca without him on her second Pilgrimage;[20] a scholar such as Taqī al-Dīn al-Subkī, whose family had a long history of judgeships and professorships. Yet these two types of piety were not mutually exclusive choices, given the fact that so many figures appearing in our texts were drawn to both. The lives of scholars and other sorts of pious people, whether mendicants, wandering Sufis, or solitary ascetics, often intersected in the cities where temporary and permanent lodging was provided for them and on the roads crossing the Middle East where men and women travelled in search of knowledge or on pilgrimage.[21] Scholarly and solitary pursuits were often concentrated in the same person. Reclusive ascetics might still be teachers of hadith or law no matter how far from town they lived, and a great many scholars who achieved fame for their knowledge also demonstrated an equal fervor for bodily devotion.

But these pursuits do, however, say different things about the ideals of Islamic piety in this period. There was a rather beautiful tension between the value placed on expertise in Islamic learning and the common practice of proving one's faith with the body and not the mind; between the path of piety that could lead towards a position of great renown in the mosques or madrasas of Cairo, Baghdad or Damascus, and the one that led not just towards solitude but towards a true disregard for the pedestal

[20] This was Uns bint ʿAbd al-Karīm al-Karīmī, who made the Pilgrimage "in the company of her husband and then by herself during his lifetime": Shams al-Dīn Muḥammad ibn ʿAbd al-Raḥmān al-Sakhāwī, *al-Ḍawʾ al-lāmiʿ li-ahl al-qarn al-tāsiʿ*, 12 vols. in 6 (Beirut, 1966), XII, 11.

[21] On the different occasions for travel see Carl Petry, "Travel Patterns of Medieval Notables in the Near East," *Studia Islamica* 62 (1985).

many others sought. That tension remains unresolved throughout this period. Chapter 3 will demonstrate how the constant pull of those two poles of isolation and social responsibility, an essential element in Islamic piety, was revivified by new problems in late medieval society.

ʿAbd Allāh Ibn Taymiyya was above all an exemplar of these concentric circles of piety. Two aspects of his piety provide clues that will be followed throughout this study: his abandoning society for the solitude of deserted mosques; and the activities he performed inside them. Al-Ṣafadī described the shaykh's sojourns, which sometimes lasted for days, not as the Sufi spiritual retreat known as *khalwa*, but as periods in hiding, a self-imposed exile.[22] Evoking an analogy with the Prophet's emigration from Mecca to the safety of Medina, this sharp statement of antisocial unhappiness gained its sting because of ʿAbd Allāh's background as a jurist and his inevitable association with other jurists, some of whom were instrumental in the indictments against his brother. What led him to those isolated places is just as important. It was his devotion to supererogatory worship (*taʿabbud*) that on these occasions prevailed over his communal responsibilities and scholarly pursuits; in fact, he deliberately left his house whenever he expected to be visited or consulted.[23] As if in response to Ibn al-Jawzī's dictum about what made someone an exemplar, his biographers – esteemed scholars to a man – called particular attention to the fact that ʿAbd Allāh authored no books at all. All of this was designed to show that ʿAbd Allāh did not wear the label of the scholar or mufti comfortably, despite substantial evidence of his legal expertise.[24] This perpetual discomfort was part of what made him a holy man. And certainly it bolstered the reputation of his family as one of singularly high standards both in piety and as actors in contemporary legal and political debates.

One expects to find holiness in the figure of a solitary shaykh: torn from the context of teaching and learning in the cities, the piety exhibited through his personal behavior is obviously what one is meant to find interesting. But increasingly, and over the course of the thirteenth century in particular, it was the jurists who were depicted as holy men, and

[22] al-Ṣafadī, *Aʿyān al-ʿaṣr*, II, 693. The author makes a clever word play here, using first the word *mahjūra* (abandoned) for the mosques and then the verb *hajara* for ʿAbd Allāh's staying there.

[23] Ibn Rajab, *Dhaylʿalā Ṭabaqāt al-Ḥanābila*, II, 383.

[24] al-Ṣafadī reports also that many among the learned elite considered ʿAbd Allāh to be "closer to the path (*ṭarīqa*) of the scholars (*ʿulamāʾ*) than was his brother.": *Aʿyān al-ʿaṣr*, II, 693.

it was they who best served as exemplars of the world-renouncing piety that focused so heavily on the body of the worshipper. At first glance it would appear that this was so simply because scholarly skills and bodily devotion converged in the person of the religious jurist. This is only partially true. ʿAbd Allāh's ascetic departure from the city brought him into close proximity, spatially if not literally, with the more antinomian ascetic characters of Islamic society, for there were many other holy men who frequented similarly desolate places. They sometimes refused to conform to Islamic standards of dress and cleanliness, or even neglected ritual duties altogether. Several modern scholars have emphasized that these unusual figures were not entirely on the margins of society, since some were deeply revered by the residents of Damascus and Cairo.[25] But where others have attempted to show how their actions were reversals of normative Islamic behavior (albeit ones that served to reinforce what *should* be normative), I have sought in the concluding chapter to detect the logic of their actions in light of the central themes in medieval Islamic piety. I argue that a person who appeared to reject social conventions or religious duties did so in response to and in conversation with the dominant discourse, which was that of Islamic law. The statements antinomian ascetics made with their bodies were sometimes meant to explain Islamic law rather than to overturn it. It was in fact interaction with the law – knowing it, following it faithfully, or even breaking it – that dominated their personal decisions about how to worship God.

Biography and the Challenges of Hagiography

Modern scholars of medieval Islamic history are accustomed to approaching biographical sources with a certain amount of skepticism, especially when it comes to stories of famous holy men and women of the distant past. The difference between biography and hagiography in these sources is difficult to discern, for the historical gap between subject and author was often filled with embellishments and marvelous details. Lost in that gap were some of the more unsavory episodes of a person's career when they no longer fit the agenda of a later author who compiled the biographical portrait; at times miracles were granted to the pious not by God but by human authors who had a point to prove.[26] Islamic biographical

[25] For examples see Pouzet, *Damas*, 223–4; Boaz Shoshan, *Popular Culture in Medieval Cairo* (Cambridge, 1993), 10–11; Chamberlain, *Knowledge and Social Practice*, 130–3.

[26] For example, Michael Cooperson's excavation of early accounts of two prominent ninth-century figures, Aḥmad Ibn Ḥanbal and Bishr al-Ḥāfī, shows how their stories

compendia, one must conclude, cannot be used as a treasury of accurate detail about the subjects' lives.

Yet at the same time no phrase could better describe the biographical genre in late medieval Islam than "a treasury of detail." By this time, the authors were voracious collectors of information, both biographical and historical. Chase Robinson has described an "explosion" of contemporary history writing in the twelfth and thirteenth centuries, where the vogue among historians was not to rewrite the story of Islam and its famous men and women from the beginning, though many did, but rather to turn to recent decades for their subject matter.[27] Authors frequently chose to provide supplements for existing works of chronography and prosopography, adding only a few years to the works of their predecessors, or in several cases expanding on their own; some biographical dictionaries even contained reports of people still living.[28] It is obvious from the way authors in the fourteenth and fifteenth centuries such as Ibn Rajab, Ibn Ḥajar, al-Sakhāwī, and Ibn al-ʿIrāqī mined the works of their immediate predecessors that thoroughness and breadth were much prized. They were quick to point out the mistakes and biases not only of their competitors (who often wrote works nearly identical to their own) but also

were rewritten in light of both political situations and popular notions of piety: Michael Cooperson, *Classical Arabic Biography: The Heirs of the Prophet in the Age of al-Maʾmūn* (Cambridge, 2000), chaps. 4 and 5; Nimrod Hurvitz has made similar arguments about the agenda of the custodians of Aḥmad Ibn Ḥanbal's biography in "Biographies and Mild Asceticism: A Study of Islamic Moral Imagination," *Studia Islamica* 85 (1997). Jawid Mojaddedi has shown how a single early text in the Sufi biographical tradition, al-Sulamī's *Ṭabaqāt al-ṣūfiyya*, was reworked and rewritten by at least five later authors (including Ibn al-Jawzī, whom he does not discuss) to serve contemporary purposes. As such, the Sufi *ṭabaqāt* literature cannot serve as a stable – or indeed reliable – source of historical information. Jawid A. Mojaddedi, *The Biographical Tradition in Sufism: The Ṭabaqāt Genre from al-Sulamī to Jāmī* (Richmond, 2001), 180, and for similar comments on al-Qushayrī see 107, 178.

27 Chase Robinson, *Islamic Historiography* (Cambridge, 2003), 101.

28 al-Dhahabī's *Tadhkirat al-ḥuffāẓ* contains some biographies of hadith experts who were still alive when the work was written: Shams al-Dīn Muḥammad ibn Aḥmad al-Dhahabī, *Kitāb tadhkirat al-ḥuffāẓ*, ed. Zakarīyā ʿUmayrāt, 5 vols. in 3 (Beirut, 1998). Several authors, including Zayn al-Dīn al-ʿIrāqī, his son Ibn al-ʿIrāqī and Ibn Ḥajar, wrote supplements to al-Dhahabī's *ʿIbar* (which commences with the Prophet's *hijra* to Medina in 622 C.E.) within a century of his death but in total added only a few years to the original text. Li Guo has published an excellent study of this new model: Li Guo, *Early Mamluk Syrian Historiography: al-Yūnīnī's Dhayl Mirʾāt al-zamān*, 2 vols. (Leiden, 1998) vol. I; Sami Massoud uses a micro appoach to explain the "complex of borrowings" in three texts that are characteristic of fourteenth-century history writing: Sami Massoud, *The Chronicles and Annalistic Sources of the Early Mamluk Circassian Period* (Leiden and Boston, 2007), 7.

of their informants.[29] In addition, their works represent an astonishing amount of new research from disparate sources. Al-Fāsī, for example, gathered information from inscriptions on buildings and gravestones in Mecca.[30] In the end, historians and biographers may have written more for each other and for later generations of scholar-researchers than for a popular audience.[31]

The authors' personal contacts and trusted informants were trumpeted as the bedrock of medieval biography. Much like modern journalists, al-Ṣafadī kept pre-written obituaries of prominent persons on file before they died, and his informants too seem to have been ready with appropriate quotations.[32] This suggests that, while they lived their lives, both scholars and their informants were aware that biographical detail collecting was ongoing, particularly in the milieu of religious scholarship. One suspects that not a few of them acted accordingly. We are no more able to prove the veracity of their reports than we are of earlier sources, but the biographical genre was by now full of personal observations, and these observations could be framed in ways that are alternately fresh and extremely formalized. The medieval authors all spoke a common language when it came to discussing piety. That is, informants and authors responded in conventional ways when called upon to provide accounts of religious figures. But in the details one can see what was considered truly new or out of the ordinary, or truly holy, along with plentiful confirmation of what the dominant motifs in Ayyubid and Mamluk piety were.

29 For example, al-Yāfiʿī quibbles with al-Dhahabī's rendition of a biography they both cited from an earlier source, and he addresses the problem of condensing various accounts: ʿAbd Allāh ibn Asʿad al-Yāfiʿī, *Mirʾāt al-jinān wa-ʿibrat al-yaqẓān*, 4 vols. (Hyderabad-Deccan, 1918–20), IV, 203.

30 He specifies these sources, for example, in two entries on women who died before his lifetime: Taqī al-Dīn Muḥammad ibn Aḥmad al-Fāsī, *al-ʿIqd al-thamīn fī tārīkh al-balad al-amīn*, ed. Muḥammad ʿAbd al-Qādir Aḥmad ʿAṭā, 7 vols. (Beirut, 1998), VI, 370–1; his research practices are discussed by Richard Mortel, "Madrasas in Mecca During the Medieval Period: A Descriptive Study Based on Literary Sources," *Bulletin of the School of Oriental and African Studies* 60, 2 (1997): 237.

31 See Robinson's insightful comments on readership of historical works, *Islamic Historiography*, 105–14.

32 D. P. Little, "al-Ṣafadī as Biographer of his Contemporaries," in *Essays on Islamic Civilization Presented to Niyazi Berkes*, ed. D. P. Little (Leiden, 1976), 198. Modern authors describe al-Ṣafadī as a key figure who both broadened and narrowed the biographical genre: Humphreys sees the *Wāfī bi'l-wafāyāt* as the culmination of a universal approach to biography that replaced more specialized works on people of particular locales or professions: R. Stephen Humphreys, *Islamic History: A Framework for Inquiry*, rev. ed. (Princeton, 1991), 189; Robinson notes that the *Aʿyān al-ʿaṣr* was the first work of prosopography devoted solely to an author's contemporaries: Robinson, *Islamic Historiography*, 101.

Certain authors such as Ibn Ḥajar and Ibn Rajab (d. 795/1392) can be useful for much earlier periods because they were particularly scrupulous about citing their sources, some of which are no longer extant. In many cases these historians offered a more thorough and thoroughly researched perspective on the subjects of their obituaries or biographies than that of the original authors. The issue of revisionism does arise with all these sources, and in the revisions some of the most vivid expressions of shifts in piety can be found. Chapter 4 deals with precisely this issue. Using the theme of scrupulosity in the performance of the rituals of purification, it demonstrates how rewritten biographies follow developments in Islamic law as well as Islamic piety. In this case it becomes clear that, over the course of several centuries, attitudes about fulfilling perfectly the requirements of ritual law and the intended purpose of the rituals themselves were sometimes incompatible.

As for the question of miracles and hagiography, Éric Geoffroy has surveyed the individual biases of authors from the fourteenth to sixteenth centuries who either favored or disparaged extreme forms of piety.[33] Similar biases can be traced in earlier authors as well. For instance, al-Yāfiʿī considered al-Dhahabī to be overly terse in praising miracle workers and gnostics.[34] On a case-by-case basis, however, one finds that the biases have little consistency. If Ibn Kathīr, for example, was often intolerant of flamboyant holy men, he nevertheless wrote a glowing report of a follower of the most antinomian figure of the early thirteenth century, ʿAlī al-Ḥarīrī.[35] Contemporary conflicts about the recently deceased are what make the medieval sources so fascinating and useful, and by the thirteenth century, if not earlier, patterns of notoriety were just as well honed as those of praise.

In any case, what is more important than the individual outlook of each author is the overwhelming consistency with which medieval biographers point out the same main features of what made people holy. They do so through an infinite variety of specific examples, and it is these examples

[33] Éric Geoffroy, *Le soufisme en Égypte et en Syrie sous les derniers Mamelouks et les premiers Ottomans: Orientations spirituelles et enjeux culturels* (Damascus, 1995), 19–32. This is a comprehensive study of late medieval Sufism, the only we have, and as such is very useful. A major drawback of his survey, however, is that he tends to consider all holy men to be Sufis.

[34] al-Yāfiʿī, *Mirʾāt al-jinān*, IV, 169, on ʿAbd Allāh al-Yūnīnī (d. 617/1221). Compare with the biography in Shams al-Dīn Muḥammad ibn Aḥmad al-Dhahabī, *al-ʿIbar fī khabar man ghabar*, ed. Ṣalāḥ al-Dīn Munajjid and Fuʾād Sayyid, 5 vols. (Kuwait, 1960), V, 67–8.

[35] See Ismāʿīl ibn ʿUmar Ibn Kathīr, *al-Bidāya wa'l-nihāya*, ed. Aḥmad Abū Mulḥim et al., 14 vols. in 8 (Beirut, 1987), XIV, 113 on Shaykh Aḥmad al-Aʿqaf.

that are my focus. I use biographies both as a reflection of how the authors, almost invariably pious men, viewed other pious people and as a credible source of information about exemplary action. While I believe that the *genre* of obituary writing by the thirteenth century is fundamentally different from that of hagiography, in terms of its general purpose and its audience, an overlap between the two genres is surely a valuable way of discerning the major themes in what constituted holiness.[36]

The difference between biography and hagiography in medieval Islamic literature is a topic that has not been exhausted. But I would argue simply that we need not read praise, even the hyperbolic praise of the medieval Muslim biographical tradition, as being aimed only at the creation of saints. Nor should we dismiss reports of miracles in biographical texts as attempts at hagiography.[37] Furnishing a miracle story that was already in circulation was, it would seem, considered a duty by some authors and not others. Holy men who were credited with miracle working do raise an interesting challenge in a study of piety. Several of the figures I study appear in Richard Gramlich's typology of Islamic miracles, but I have used the same source material for different kinds of information.[38] Where he traces patterns in extraordinary phenomena, it is precisely the patterns of the other attributes of these men (for miracle workers were apparently only men) that is my focus: their asceticism and daily devotional habits, their nonmiraculous interactions with ordinary Muslims, and the effect such interactions had in shaping conceptions of pious comportment. As Catherine Mayeur-Jaouen has pointed out, Gramlich's approach, in failing to take into account the historical context of medieval miracles, reduces the impact of the message they were intended to convey. Her analysis of miraculous interventions in missions involving the liberating of captives (by the saint Aḥmad al-Badawī, for example) shows how skepticism about these miracles confirms that larger social issues were being discussed; miracle stories are neither "timeless" nor do they serve solely hagiographical purposes.[39]

[36] al-Yāfiʿī is a good example of an author who combines both styles. He includes many more stories of miracles performed by Sufis and holy men whom he admired than most authors do, while simultaneously writing straightforward biographies of other figures.

[37] I have used hagiographical works such as al-Shaṭṭanūfī's *Bahjat al-asrār* and al-Shaʿrānī's *Ṭabaqāt al-kubrā* sparingly, but sometimes they provide an interesting complement to historical narratives.

[38] Richard Gramlich, *Die Wunder der Freunde Gottes: Theologien und Erscheinungsformen des islamischen Heiligenwunders* (Wiesbaden, 1987).

[39] Catherine Mayeur-Jaouen, *al-Sayyid Aḥmad al-Badawī: Un grand saint de l'Islam égyptien* (Cairo, 1994), 305–34.

Other genres of literature prove equally fruitful, particularly those that relate to positive law (*fiqh*). Treatises on deviation from or innovations in religious practice (*bidʿa* treatises) are one of these. Such texts were typically addressed to a popular audience and are valuable in charting the changing moods of piety; several recent studies have analyzed this literature in depth.[40] Collections of substantive law (*furūʿ al-fiqh*) written between the late twelfth and the fifteenth centuries have formed a significant portion of my research as well. These collections are generally legal manuals comprising the authoritative opinions and actual rules of a specific legal "school" or *madhhab*. A legal scholar would present anew material from a previous manual, updating where necessary. Even though the changes in actual rulings are most often incremental from one text to the next, they can still shed valuable light on contemporary issues.[41] In the longer manuals there is a great deal of commentary. Debates that took place among previous generations of jurists are preserved in full; new material, such as decisions recorded in fatwas, finds its way into these texts of *furūʿ al-fiqh* as well.[42] I focus in particular on works by Ibn Qudāma al-Maqdisī (d. 620/1223) and al-Nawawī (d. 676/1277) because of their personal involvement in devotional piety. Al-Nawawī himself was an exemplar of incomparable importance in the thirteenth century, as were Ibn Qudāma and especially his older brother in the twelfth. Comparing biographical material with popular texts written by jurists and with their formal legal writings is yet

40 Maribel Fierro, "The Treatises against Innovation (*kutub al-bidaʿ*)," *Der Islam* 69 (1992); and the extensive study by Raquel Margolit Ukeles, "Innovation or Deviation: Exploring the Boundaries of Islamic Devotional Law," Ph.D. thesis, Harvard University, 2006. Discussed in the treatises are the legitimacy or illegitimacy of various religious practices. One example is the custom of celebrating the birthday of the Prophet, and the specific devotional practices and/or public behavior associated with such an occasion. If a practice or custom had not been initiated by the Prophet Muḥammad (or lacked textual support indicating his approval from the hadith), it was an innovation. While innovations could be either positive or negative, and Ukeles describes vigorous debates that went on among jurists in the medieval period, the treatises tend to look at the negative in the interest of protecting religion and society. For this reason I think the word *deviation* is often a more useful translation of *bidʿa*. On the Prophet's birthday and related popular observances see, in addition to Ukeles, Marion Katz's excellent study, *The Birth of the Prophet Muhammad: Devotional Piety in Sunni Islam* (London and New York, 2007).

41 See also two case studies on legal change: Abraham L. Udovitch's pioneering study of developments in commercial law during the Fatimid period, *Partnership and Profit in Medieval Islam* (Princeton, 1970), and, more recently, Marion Katz's fascinating work on early ritual law, *Body of Text: The Emergence of the Sunnī Law of Ritual Purity* (Albany, 2002).

42 On this process, see Wael B. Hallaq, *Authority, Continuity and Change in Islamic Law* (Cambridge, 2001), esp. 180–294.

another way of tracing trends in contemporary piety; this is the strategy I employ in Chapters 2 and 4.

There are a number of other genres of legal literature that I have used, but a word must be said about the use of hadith. Because the accounts of Muḥammad's words and deeds (and those of his family and Companions) are of paramount importance in Islamic law – legal debates were often won with arguments referring to (or offering interpretations of) particular hadiths – the late medieval commentaries on collections of hadith can certainly be classified within the field of jurisprudential literature. Finally, it is significant that, in many cases, the authors of biographical dictionaries and chronicles were jurists. As observers of events, of both praiseworthy trends and disturbing innovations in contemporary practice, these author-jurists sometimes registered their own legal opinions in the historical texts they wrote; we can at times detect the impact of events on their formal legal writings.[43]

As the chapters progress, the book focuses more closely on the relationship between the law as a set of texts and the social position of the men who wrote and enacted it. The jurists' role in guiding medieval society went beyond the classic texts they wrote and the legal opinions they rendered. Legal experts were public figures whose actions – and devotional piety – were more carefully observed and copied than were those of any other group in society. My emphasis on legal writers as participants in piety – indeed, as the single most influential group of exemplary men – is what I hope will distinguish this study from other works on the same period. The most revered among them, figures such as al-Nawawī, were fully involved in the social issues of their day. Sometimes these men set standards through their own public actions. At times they were also influenced by others – a colleague or a member of their family, for example. In either case, these standards find their way into Islamic substantive law in subtle ways, a process that suggests that works on *furūʿ al-fiqh* can serve as a repository of Islamic ethics. Discussions of ritual law (laws pertaining to ablutions, prayer, and fasting, for example) in these texts are places we can expect to find evidence of changes in piety. Yet I also show how other topics in Islamic law, from charitable endowments to farming practices, can similarly reflect or reveal changes in religious ideals and ethical standards.

[43] One of these author-jurists I will discuss is the historian Abu Shāma, murdered in 665/1268; Konrad Hirschler brings him to life and discusses some of his controversial legal opinions in a lively study: *Medieval Arabic Historiography: Authors as Actors* (London and New York, 2006).

By the middle of the tenth century the four "schools" (*madhāhib*, sing. *madhhab*) of Sunnī jurisprudence that developed around the legal methods and opinions of four distinctive legal scholars from the eighth and ninth centuries C.E. are considered to have reached maturity. Much work has been done on this formative period of Islamic law, which spans the years from 750–950.

The later medieval period is the time when what I will call the culture of Islamic law came into being. For one thing the judiciary grew substantially in size and administrative sophistication. By the year 1200 knowledge of the law was no longer limited to a few legal experts. Some men acquired this knowledge informally by studying with one legal scholar at a time. Others learned about Islamic law as part of the training offered at the various institutions of higher education that were being founded in increasing numbers throughout this period. There was nothing to prevent women from studying it too, and some of them did, although they were not able to use their knowledge in a professional capacity by serving as judges. Certainly, a large number of women studied the two major sources of Islamic law: the Qurʾān and the collections of hadith. Being knowledgeable about the law was so much a part of medieval piety that even illiterate holy men made a point of showing that they were familiar with its precepts. Finally, by including law in a cultural history of medieval models of piety, I intend the book to dispel common misconceptions about the "dry legalism" of medieval Islam, an old Orientalist phrase still used today by some cultural historians of the Islamic Middle East. On the contrary, the law proves to be one of the richest sources for the creative impulses of individuals throughout this period. This era produced great legal scholars whose commentaries are still widely used today. What was it about this culture that gave us a legacy of such lasting significance? How did this concept of piety have such depth and vibrance throughout all levels of society?

1

The Persistence of Asceticism

Considering the number of hours that pious men and women spent awake at night in prayer, reciting the Qurʾān in spare moments during the day, weeping, walking endlessly, or suffering from a hunger caused by daily fasts or meager meals, surprisingly little has been written about the devotional life of medieval Muslims. One tends to think of these pursuits as solitary and quiescent, taking place beyond the notice of ordinary people. Yet in biographical notices, evidence of these activities is easy to spot because medieval Islamic piety itself was in fact more active than contemplative, full of personalized rituals and idiosyncratic bodily habits, which caught the attention of relatives, neighbors, colleagues, and eventually the medieval authors who recorded what they heard or saw. For instance, the scholar Naṣīḥ al-Dīn Ibn al-Ḥanbalī recalled in some detail the daily routine of a jurist named Ismāʿīl Ibn Nubāta, who had studied with his grandfather and uncle:

> He used to study the Qurʾān a great deal, and he would undertake that from midnight onwards. Then at dawn he would pray by the Baradā river in front of the Citadel and perform the afternoon prayer at the spring of Baalbek, and vice versa. And often he read along the way either the Qurʾān or the Hidāya, I'm not sure which.[1]

Many minor holy figures were commemorated in the biographical and historical sources with merely a concise label of merit or identification: a

[1] Ibn Rajab, *Dhayl ʿalā Ṭabaqāt al-Ḥanābila*, I, 351. The *Hidāya* is a well-known manual of substantive law (*furūʿ al-fiqh*) particular to the Ḥanbalī *madhhab* (one of the four Sunnī legal schools), written by Abū'l-Khaṭṭāb al-Kalwadhānī (d. 510/1117).

person might be called an ascetic (*zāhid*), a devotee (*ʿābid*, *mutaʿabbid*) or a Sufi; a chaste man or woman, a selfless one or a scrupulous one. More often than not several of these applied. When no further details were offered, medieval readers could fill in the blanks in a way that modern readers cannot without first understanding what each term meant. Yet pursuing the meaning of every label for a holy person is a frustrating task since several of them bleed into one another, even in the hands of the lexicographers. To take one example, the term *nāsik*, sometimes translated as "hermit," has the following definition in a late twelfth-century dictionary, the *Nihāya fī gharīb al-ḥadīth*:

> A devotee (*mutaʿabbid*) is called a *nāsik* when he has purged from his soul the blemish of sin, just as dross is from a refined ingot. Thaʿlab was asked about what a *nāsik* is, and he said, "He is what is extracted from a nugget. That is, he is an ingot of unadulterated silver, as though he had purified his soul and made it exclusively ready for God Most High."[2]

The metaphor plays upon the fact that a related word, *nasīk*, means gold or silver, and a *nasīka* is a rough chunk of gold or silver. Nothing in the definition, however, suggests a solitary lifestyle. The relationship between purification of the soul and a hermit's life becomes only slightly clearer in the hands of the lexicographer Ibn Manẓūr (d. 711/1311–12), who writes of another word from the same root:

> The noun *al-nusk*, [also pronounced] *al-nusuk*, means worship and obedience and all that by which one is brought nearer to God. Thaʿlab was asked, "Is fasting designated '*nusuk*'?" He replied, "Every duty to God Most High is called '*nusuk*.'"[3]

This explains why Ayyubid and Mamluk chroniclers applied the term *nāsik* not to hermits in particular but to anyone especially given to

[2] Majd al-Dīn al-Mubārak Ibn al-Athīr, *al-Nihāya fī gharīb al-ḥadīth wa'l-athar*, ed. Maḥmūd Muḥammad Ṭanāḥī and Ṭāhir Aḥmad al-Zāwī, 5 vols. (Qum, 1364/1985), V, 48. The author died in Mosul in 606/1210. His *Nihāya* is a study of difficult and unusual words that appear in the hadith. Above, he quotes from the ninth-century philological work of Thaʿlab. For an example of the translation of "hermit" for a *nāsik* who lived on nuts and herbs see Michael Dols, *Majnūn: The Madman in Medieval Islamic Society*, ed. Diana E. Immisch (New York, 1992), 378.

[3] Muḥammad ibn Mukarram Ibn Manẓūr, *Lisān al-ʿArab*, 7 vols. (Beirut, 1987), VI, 179; he includes the quotation about the ingot as well. Sufism is not discussed in these definitions. Sufi authors tended to discuss the notion of purification in terms of spiritual progress and the attainment of gnosis (*maʿrifa*) rather than in discussions of acts of servitude or worship.

worship.[4] Acts of worship are crucial to the process of transformation described in the first definition; in other words, *nāsik* is a synonym for *ʿābid* and means simply "a devotee." A third lexicographer who died fifty years after Ibn Manẓūr, however, added an element of asceticism to the mix. The verb *nasaka*, al-Fayyūmī says, means

> He became an ascetic (*tazahhada*), he devoted himself to worship (*taʿabbada*), and thus he is [called] a *nāsik*, the plural of which is *nussāk*, just as the plural of *ʿābid* is *ʿubbād*.[5]

It is immediately clear that it would be impossible to understand what a *nāsik* is without understanding a set of words relating to asceticism and bodily devotion, which are not at all the same thing. But if one were to look up the word for bodily devotion in the famously comprehensive *Lisān al-ʿArab*, one would wind up back at the start: "al-taʿabbud: al-tanassuk."[6]

These definitions were far from being timeless, despite their use of much older sources, since each author was active in the pious milieu of his day.[7] Thus, one wants to know the degree to which these lexicographers' definitions are reflected in other kinds of contemporary sources, ones that describe real people. Unfortunately, there too we find the same knot of terms, and, most persistently, that pairing of asceticism (*zuhd*) and bodily devotion (*taʿabbud*). Neither one, nor their presence in late medieval piety, has been studied in any depth. Although *zuhd* is seldom

[4] Consider these two examples: Ibn Hudaymī (d. 741/1340), a companion of Ibn Taymiyya, was described as an *ʿābid*, a virtuous man (*ṣāliḥ*), and a *nāsik*, who resided in a mosque where "amirs and important people" would visit him: Abū Bakr ibn Aḥmad Ibn Qāḍī Shuhba, *Tārīkh Ibn Qāḍī Shuhba*, ed. Adnan Darwich, 4 vols. (Damascus, 1994–7), II, 157; and a freed slave (*mamlūk*) cum hadith scholar who travelled extensively and was still described as a *nāsik* in al-Dhahabī, *ʿIbar*, V, 42.

[5] Aḥmad ibn Muḥammad al-Fayyūmī, *Miṣbāḥ al-munīr fī gharīb al-Sharḥ al-kabīr li'l-Rāfiʿī*, 2 vols. in 1 (Beirut, 1978), II, 230. Al-Fayyūmī died in 770/1368.

[6] Ibn Manẓūr, *Lisān al-ʿArab*, IV, 240. Likewise under the entry n-s-k: "the verbs *nasaka* and *tanassaka* both mean *taʿabbada*" (ibid., VI, 179).

[7] Ibn al-Athīr's research on hadith and its vocabulary was itself the most pious of scholarly pursuits. The jurist Ibn Manẓūr served for a time as the Shāfiʿī qadi of Tripoli in North Africa. (One scholar has suggested that it was the Syrian Tripoli.) Then he moved to Cairo, where he held a post in the chancery until he died in 711/1311–12; at some point he also travelled to Damascus, seeking to learn from scholars there. See Aḥmad Mukhtār ʿUmar, "Ibn Manẓūr al-Lughawī: al-ʿĀlim al-Ḥā'ir bayn Miṣr wa-Lībyā wa-Tūnis," *Revista del Instituto Egipcio de Estudios Islámicos en Madrid* 18 (1974–5). Al-Fayyūmī was renowned as a jurist, teacher, and poet in Upper Egypt; his biographer reports several of his "undisputed" minor miracles: Kamāl al-Dīn Jaʿfar al-Udfūwī, *al-Ṭāliʿ al-saʿīd al-jāmiʿ asmāʾ nujabāʾ al-Ṣaʿīd*, ed. Saʿd Muḥammad Ḥasan (Cairo, 1966), 145–9.

recognized as a significant and independent trend in the thirteenth or fourteenth century, at least asceticism is familiar as a building-block of piety in many religions. By contrast, bodily devotion or *taʿabbud* is so obviously central to Islamic piety in all ages that it has hardly been noticed in any of them.[8]

Taʿabbud is the elaboration of familiar gestures of submission to God, and as a style of piety it has two essential components: commitment to the required devotional acts (*ʿibādāt*) of Islam such as prayer and fasting; and an even greater enthusiasm for supererogatory worship, where a person might choose to perform extensive fasting and extra prayers well beyond what Islam requires.[9] At the beginning of our period, the late twelfth century, *zuhd* at first appears to consist of a set of attitudes inherited from early Islam. Even a century later Ibn Manẓūr, for example, would define it as "the opposite of desirousness and greed," and Ibn Taymiyya would explain that having asceticism (*zuhd*) with regard to a thing means having a lack of desire for that thing.[10] But in nearly every historical case, these

[8] Variations in cultural formation across the Islamic empire in many ways prevent attempts at synthesis, but local studies such as Richard Bulliet's *Patricians of Nishapur* are highly useful. He provides a sketch of when and where the terms *zāhid*, *ʿābid* (which he translates as "pietist") and *ṣūfī* became prominent from the ninth to eleventh centuries C.E. However, his work is not a study of the terms themselves or the actions that defined them: Richard Bulliet, *The Patricians of Nishapur: A Study in Medieval Islamic Social History* (Cambridge, Mass., 1972), 41–2. Bulliet's study can be compared with Michael Bonner, *Aristocratic Violence and Holy War: Studies in the Jihad and the Arab-Byzantine Frontier* (New Haven, 1996), esp. chap. 4 and the Appendix. Manuela Marín has studied female piety in al-Andalus (tenth to fourteenth centuries C.E.) and suggests that while *ʿābid*, *zāhid*, and *ṣāliḥ* were labels shared by both sexes, *ṣūfī* and *nāsik* were reserved for males: Manuela Marín, "Retiro y ayuno: Algunas prácticas religiosas de las mujeras andalusías," *al-Qanṭara: Revista de Estudios Árabes* 21, 2 (2000): 472–3. I am grateful to Maribel Fierro for this reference.

[9] The meaning of *taʿabbud* depends on the context. In biographies I read it, in most cases, as a slightly stronger version of the word *ʿibāda*: that is, as a word meaning "worship." Although the two terms are often used synonymously, I would like to call attention to the possibility of extra energy or dedication associated with *taʿabbud*, a quality conveyed by many words derived from fifth-form Arabic verbs connoting emphatic actions or actions in which someone does something to or with one's self. My reading of *taʿabbud*, in subsequent chapters, highlights also the two prominent meanings of the term found in legal texts. The first is *taʿabbud* referring to a discrete act of worship as an act of faith – a performance that God requires or is pleased by, but which "has no rational meaning" beyond this. The second is *taʿabbud* as a synonym for an act of supererogatory worship, or *nāfila*. The jurist Ibn Qudāma, for example, typically uses *taʿabbud* in this sense instead of *nāfila*. The contradiction between the two legal meanings can only be resolved by seeing *taʿabbud* as referring to the way in which obligatory worship and voluntary worship are performed *as acts of bodily devotion*.

[10] Ibn Manẓūr, *Lisān al-ʿArab*, III, 207; Taqī al-Dīn Aḥmad Ibn Taymiyya, *Majmūʿ fatāwā Shaykh al-Islām Aḥmad ibn Taymiyya*, ed. ʿAbd al-Raḥmān ibn Muḥammad ibn Qāsim

attitudes are only made manifest through bodily performances. Medieval ascetic performances were not ritual ones, at least not in the strict sense of worship (*ʿibāda*), and this is what makes *zuhd* fundamentally different from *taʿabbud*. Ascetics often followed their own rules of behavior, which sometimes took on a ritualistic element (such as eating the food at meals in a certain order), but none of these were *ritual duties* or properly forms of supererogatory worship. Rather, much as in early Islam, later medieval ascetic practices that have to do with diet, with austere types of dress and other elements of "harsh living" – such as sleeping on the floor – all emphasize bodily discomfort.

Al-Fayyūmī's fourteenth-century definition of a *nāsik* as an ascetic who also devotes himself to worship may have aimed to show how committing oneself to the pious life could be achieved in these two separate ways: by abstaining from worldly pleasures (*zuhd*) or by devoting oneself to acts of worship (*taʿabbud*). Accordingly, one could easily be a devotee but not an ascetic. To be sure, not every pious man dressed in the coarse clothing commonly worn by ascetics; some ate well, owned slaves, and accumulated great fortunes.[11] It is harder to imagine that most ascetics were not also devotees. But al-Fayyūmī might have meant instead that these two strands of piety were inseparable (though not indistinguishable) from one another at the time he was writing. They were closely related above all through the use of the body.

Using the specific case of voluntary fasting, Chapter 2 will discuss in greater depth how in the thirteenth and fourteenth centuries *taʿabbud* became central to piety in a new way, as increasingly heavy practices of worship became normative among exemplary Muslims. Yet that trend cannot be studied separately from developments in contemporary asceticism, for if Islamic ritual established the body as the central site of pious expression, it was the ascetics who amplified the possibilities of what this meant. As sister styles of piety, *zuhd* and *taʿabbud* helped to define each other, but a difference is discernible in the role the body plays in each of them. In Islamic asceticism the body is consistently used as the object of a

al-ʿĀsimī, 35 vols. (Riyadh, 1381–6/1961–6), X, 616. The best overview of concepts in early asceticism is Leah Kinberg, "What is Meant by *Zuhd*," *Studia Islamica* 61 (1985). She surveys definitions of *zuhd* attributed to famous ascetics from the eighth to tenth centuries C.E.

11 For example, the exegete and philosopher Fakhr al-Dīn al-Rāzī (d. 609/1209) is described as a pious exemplar who wept while preaching. He is simultaneously described as a chubby man who possessed great wealth, owned slaves, and wore handsome apparel (al-Dhahabī, *ʿIbar*, V, 18).

sacrificial gesture; the results tend to be experiences of physical sensation (the scratching of coarse fabric, for example). In the practices of *ta'abbud* the human figure becomes ideographic of worship itself.

Medieval chroniclers tended to make reference to large categories that made up Islamic society: the amirs (the military elite), the *'ulamā'* (the scholars), the *a'yān* (the notables), or the Sufis; modern historians have tended to ask questions about the relations between these groups. If the ascetics and devotees of the Ayyubid and Mamluk periods have been almost entirely overlooked by the latter, it is only partly because these social types have frequently been consigned to the realm of Sufism.[12] It is also because, though the devotees and ascetics numbered in the thousands in any given century of Islamic history, they did not necessarily constitute groups capable of social action. That is, medieval authors do not describe them playing a role in events as a group, but rather as individuals, unlike the Sufis or the amirs.[13] Instead of attempting to create new (or resurrect old) categories of "the devotee" and "the ascetic" to add to the medieval mix of social identities, this chapter will show how individuals from all of these groups could take part in piety, represent piety or borrow from it – sometimes shamelessly. A good example of the latter can be found in Ibn Taghrībirdī's account of the rapid rise of the amir Tankiz al-Ḥusāmī, a high-ranking commander and former military slave whose daughter married the Mamluk sultan al-Nāṣir Muḥammad.

Tankiz was already the governor of Damascus when he spent several months in 714/1314 in Cairo enjoying the hospitality of the sultan, who lavished upon him gifts of horses and loads of fabric worth 120,000 dinars. This was just the beginning point of Tankiz's influence in politics (which would last for thirty years), but by the end of the visit he had incurred the resentment of his fellow amirs, for good reason:

> When he bade farewell to the sultan he asked him, among other things, to dismiss the Amir Kujkun from office. The sultan granted his every request and made over to him a charter for the mandate of rule in all the Syrian provinces together. He then [required] that all of its regional governors correspond with [Tankiz] about the state of their affairs, and that the form of salutation for him should be: "May God strengthen the defenders of His Noble Personage," after it had been: "May God

[12] This is a point made by Kinberg in "What Is Meant by *zuhd*," 27.

[13] On groups referred to in the sources as "the Sufis" committing acts of violence see Tamer el-Leithy, "Sufis, Copts and the Politics of Piety: Moral Regulation in Fourteenth-Century Upper Egypt," in *Le développement du soufisme en Égypte à l'époque mamelouke*, ed. Richard McGregor and Adam Sabra (Cairo, 2006).

> strengthen the defenders of His Honor," and that to his honorific titles should be added: "al-Zāhidī, al-ʿĀbidī, al-ʿĀlimī, Ḳāfil al-Islām, Atābak al-juyūsh."[14]

In the blink of an eye, these titles made Tankiz not only viceroy of Syria and commander-in-chief of the Syrian army, but an ascetic, a devotee, and a scholar to boot. He would later sponsor the construction of a mosque, a *dār al-ḥadīth*, and several bathhouses, along with the refurbishing of other religious buildings, but thus far in his career there seems to be no evidence of unusual devotional piety, asceticism, or learning.[15] In fact, these "titles" of piety held by governmental representatives were simply forms of address used in correspondence to show respect and honor, according to Aḥmad ibn ʿAlī al-Qalqashandī (d. 821/1418). Al-Qalqashandī was a chancery clerk in Mamluk Cairo, where he wrote a voluminous secretarial manual cataloguing the proper usage of these titles, among hundreds of others. He complained that they had proliferated by his day to the point where they had been trivialized.[16]

But though they could be bestowed without substantive proof of pious action, they had not lost their potency. When the sultan conferred these titles upon Tankiz and forced men of inferior position to address him this way in correspondence, he effectively secured the amir's position as

[14] Jamāl al-Dīn Yūsuf Ibn Taghrībirdī, *al-Nujūm al-zāhira fī mulūk Miṣr wa'l-Qāhira*, 16 vols. (Cairo, 1963–72), IX, 130. In this proclamation, the change from *anṣār al-janāb* to the loftier *anṣār al-maqarr al-sharīf* corresponded to his promotion to a closer position (literally and figuratively) to the sultan. On the significance of changes of title see C. E. Bosworth, "Laḳab," *EI²*. Anne Broadbridge describes how these forms of address were used by the Mamluks in their diplomatic relations with regional allies and rivals in a fascinating study: Anne F. Broadbridge, *Kingship and Ideology in the Islamic and Mongol Worlds* (Cambridge, 2008), 139 ff.

[15] Although at some point Tankiz had studied hadith, nothing else suggests that these titles were merited by pious acts. Ḥayāt Nāṣir al-Ḥajjī sees the promotion as a reward for good service; he notes also that Tankiz had been the *mamlūk* of the sultan's brother, al-Ashraf Khalīl, and suggests this as an additional factor in Tankiz's success (*Dirāsāt fī tārīkh salṭanat al-Mamālīk fī Miṣr wa'l-Shām* [Kuwait, 1985], 202, 209–16). See also Stephan Conermann's intriguing study of his character: "Tankiz ibn ʿAbd Allāh al-Ḥusamī al-Nāṣirī (d. 740/1340) as Seen by his Contemporary al-Ṣafadī (d. 764/1363)," *Mamluk Studies Review* 12, 2 (2008). For background on Tankiz's political career see Amalia Levanoni, *A Turning Point in Mamluk History: The Third Reign of al-Nāṣir Muḥammad Ibn Qalāwūn* (Leiden, 1995), 68–72.

[16] Aḥmad ibn ʿAlī al-Qalqashandī, *Ṣubḥ al-aʿshā fī ṣināʿat al-inshāʾ*, 14 vols. (Cairo, 1964), V, 491–3. In his discussion of "al-ʿābid" as an honorific title, he specifies that it is sometimes used by "men of the sword and the pen" (meaning those in government service) and one example of this is its use by the governors of Syria (ibid., VI, 19). See also his discussion of "al-zāhidī, al-ʿābidī" for the governors of Damascus and Aleppo (ibid., VI, 131–2).

well as his reputation. What sort of prestige did these terms confer? Why at this point in Islamic history were these social identities desirable for a military man? Roy Mottahedeh has suggested that as the Sufi brotherhoods became important in the social structure of Islam beginning in the Buyid period (mid-tenth to mid-eleventh century C.E.), the more loosely defined concept of *taqwā* (piety) "associated with asceticism and supererogatory acts of worship, survived as an ideal in Islamic society, with its 'leading men' of limited influence."[17] If so, it might be tempting to see Tankiz's titles of *zāhidī* and *ʿābidī* as the imposition of classic or classical Islamic traits onto a Mamluk commander of Turkish origin and dubious faith.[18] But if asceticism and supererogatory acts of worship were typical kinds of piety in this period instead of a faded ideal, the story of Tankiz becomes relevant in a new way: it is significant that individuals who held power in this period wished to adorn themselves with "titles" of common piety when they had not done so in earlier centuries. The answer to why they did lies in the status achieved by the figures these titles were meant to evoke.

The Meaning of Medieval Asceticism

Sultan al-Nāṣir Muḥammad did not have to search far back in Islamic history to find examples of great ascetics and devotees. The two centuries before Tankiz lived were in fact heavily populated with ascetics, so much so that it is indeed difficult to tell whether their numbers signal a resurgence of asceticism or are evidence of its health and survival through many centuries of Islamic history.[19] In the late twelfth century,

[17] Mottahedeh, *Loyalty and Leadership*, 148.

[18] The theory that foreign-born Mamluks, who were sometimes seen by medieval Egyptian and Syrian historians as being alien to local Islamic culture, needed to secure their authority through patronage of Islamic culture is no longer accepted uncritically. See Ulrich Haarmann, "Arabic in Speech, Turkish in Lineage: Mamluks and their Sons in the Intellectual Life of Fourteenth-Century Egypt and Syria," *Journal of Semitic Studies* 33 (1988). The religious upbringing of Mamluks in the barracks is one alternative explanation of their motivation for becoming patrons; Jonathan Berkey, surveying these theories, points out further that as adults individual Mamluks not only contributed to local Islamic culture but also participated in its formation ("The Mamluks as Muslims: The Military Elite and the Construction of Islam in Medieval Egypt," in *The Mamluks in Egyptian Politics and Society*, ed. Thomas Philipp and Ulrich Haarmann [Cambridge, 1998], 163–73).

[19] Although a survey of asceticism from the tenth to twelfth centuries is beyond the scope of this discussion, there is no reason to believe it died out. Lev's study of late Fatimid piety certainly suggests a continuity rather than a revival: Yaacov Lev, "Piety and Political

the beginning of the period under consideration, there was probably no better example of contemporary asceticism than Shaykh Ibn al-Mannī, the beloved teacher of a great many Ḥanbalī scholars of law and hadith. His reputation drew students from all across the Middle East, a claim confirmed by a report that the *ribāṭ* (convent or small lodge) of one of his colleagues, itself a place frequented by mendicants and jurists alike, was besieged by an overflow of travellers who came to Baghdad to see the shaykh.[20] Ibn al-Mannī was a man who, like many others in his day, had consciously chosen a life of piety. "I received an inheritance from my father of 20 dinars and bought something with it, then sold that and made a profit," he recalled. "I feared that trade was becoming agreeable to me and that I would become preoccupied with it. So I resolved to make the Pilgrimage, which I did, and devoted myself exclusively to knowledge." He went on to become a legal scholar of such fame before he died in 583/1187 that Ibn al-Jawzī proclaimed, "All the Ḥanbalī jurists of today in all cities can be traced back to him and to his circle."[21]

As in many accounts of pious men and women, the architecture of this biography steers the reader's attention towards the physical details of the subject's life. In the primary descriptive paragraph where one of Ibn al-Mannī's students meticulously recounted his shaykh's personal characteristics, one learns that Ibn al-Mannī went on to develop the ability to live a singularly bare existence:

> He gave fatwas and taught for about seventy years. He neither married nor took a concubine. He never rode a mule or horse; he owned no slaves and never wore sumptuous garments, only the clothes of piety. Most of his sustenance he would drink from a cup of meatless broth. When some bit of good fortune was bestowed on him, he distributed it among his students.[22]

The points of continuity with earlier Islamic asceticism are readily apparent in this passage. Above all the shaykh is represented as a figure of humility. The lack of ostentation, evinced by his wearing pious garb and

Activism in Twelfth Century Egypt," *Jerusalem Studies in Arabic and Islam* 31 (2006): 289–324.

[20] Ibn Rajab, *Dhayl ʿalā Ṭabaqāt al-Ḥanābila*, II, 63–4. Modern editors have vocalized his name in several ways, most often al-Mannā or al-Mannī.

[21] Ibid., I, 360. Nearly two centuries later, Ibn Rajab, who furnished this quotation from Ibn al-Jawzī, concurred: "Until now, this is as he says," and protested that contemporary Ḥanbalīs mistakenly believe that the two greatest influences were Muwaffaq al-Dīn Ibn Qudāma al-Maqdisī, himself a student of Ibn al-Mannī, and Ibn Taymiyya.

[22] Ibid.

his walking instead of riding, is consonant with a pious ethic that had currency in Muslim society long before and well after Ibn al-Mannī's day, among ascetics and non-ascetics alike.[23] Self-sacrifice and stylized humility were, by the twelfth century, ancient cultural ideals that still held sway in the contemporary conception of *adab*, or civility. Ibn al-Mannī's behavior is thus the reflection in a single man of widespread social values.

Lifelong celibacy and a severely curtailed diet, on the other hand, are ascetic strategies that have no intrinsic connection to the gentlemanly quality of humility. The shaykh's abstention from sexual relations and from all but the most rudimentary of meals suggests a daily struggle with the carnal body. Such behavior raises questions about the nature of Islamic asceticism in this era and how, if at all, it differed from its roots in the eighth century. Was medieval asceticism concerned with avoiding sin, or was it a means of liberating the soul? Was it a rejection of worldly pleasures or an abhorrence of the flesh? Was it disciplinary, perhaps even penitential? Or did that satisfaction with bare necessities constitute its own pleasure?

There are, in fact, few things that are new about ascetic piety in the Ayyubid and Mamluk eras. The common practices of eating little, having few possessions, dressing in simple or rough clothing, and even celibacy, all had clear antecedents in earlier periods. The sentiments that accompanied them had prevailed among ninth-century ascetics, who spoke in vivid terms about their disdain for the world and its physical pleasures. Their acts of renunciation made them a distinctive category in society – again, not a formal one, but a familiar one nonetheless. One significant shift can be seen in the sheer scope of asceticism at the close of the twelfth century: ascetics were not just recluses, jurists, or hadith scholars but administrators of the army, viziers, and traders.[24] The easy categorization of religious figures into specific groups was no longer possible, for

[23] For example, Ādīna al-Ṭaṭarī (d. 709/1309), the chief of police in Ilkhanid Baghdad, was remarkable for walking to the mosque every Friday for prayers: Shihāb al-Dīn Aḥmad Ibn Ḥajar al-ʿAsqalānī, *al-Durar al-kāmina fī aʿyān al-mīʾa al-thāmina*, ed. ʿAbd al-Wārith Muḥammad ʿAlī, 4 vols. in 2 (Beirut, 1418/1997), 2: 202. In the early ninth century al-Muḥāsibī had devoted an entire book, entitled *al-Riʿāya li-ḥuqūq Allāh*, to the topic of avoiding hypocrisy and ostentation; it was a common subject for other authors thereafter. See Ira Lapidus, "Knowledge, Virtue and Action: The Classical Muslim Conception of *Adab* and the Nature of Religious Fulfillment in Islam," in *Moral Conduct and Authority: The Place of* Adab *in South Asian Islam*, ed. Barbara Daly Metcalf (Berkeley and Los Angeles, 1984), 38–61.

[24] Examples of amirs being described as *zuhhād* are relatively rare, but see al-Yūnīnī's description of one *amīr-zāhid* (Guo, *Early Mamluk Syrian Historiography*, II, 78).

previously distinct social boundaries had dissolved in the face of what had become a common, broadly shared type of piety. The tenacity with which Muslims from the Ayyubid period onward cleaved to old patterns indicates how appropriate asceticism was perceived to be in contemporary contexts.

Two other differences in late medieval asceticism suggest a change in outlook. First, the preoccupying fear of God is largely gone from the accounts of late medieval ascetics. One presumes that the fear still existed, yet the sources vocalize it less consistently than they had in the tenth or eleventh century.[25] More surprisingly, the frequent references to "hope for a short duration" on earth – a characteristic feature of early *zuhd* – have simply disappeared from the later medieval sources. Nimrod Hurvitz and others have argued that a shift in asceticism occurred during the ninth century, where the severe asceticism of the first two centuries of Islam was gradually replaced either by mysticism or by a milder sort of *zuhd* that de-emphasized bodily practices.[26] If one accepts this premise, it would explain the fewer references to fear of God, and it would also mean that there must have been a revival of a severe kind of asceticism several centuries later. I will suggest, however, that these changes in outlook can be explained by a growing preoccupation with the body and the belief in God's love of acts of devotion rather than a waning interest in severe asceticism. Again and again, the stories in late medieval historical narratives indicate the expansion of a severe ascetic tradition that was widely practiced. In looking at whether stringent asceticism experienced

[25] Fear of God – what Melchert calls "the deliberate cultivation of anxious fear" – is mentioned in passing in some biographies of thirteenth-century ascetics and Sufis, as in al-Yāfiʿī's biography of Quṭb al-Dīn Ibn al-Qasṭallānī (*Mir'āt al-jinān*, IV, 202–3). The trait is mentioned also in Ibn Rajab's account of the ascetic ʿAbd Allāh ibn Taymiyya (discussed in the introduction). But it was much more common earlier: al-Sulamī's Sufi and ascetic women wept not out of love for God but out of personal fear or out of pity for their fellow Muslims: Abū ʿAbd al-Raḥmān al-Sulamī, *Early Sufi Women: Dhikr an-niswa al-mutaʿabbidāt aṣ-ṣūfiyyāt*, ed. and trans. Rkia Cornell (Louisville, 1999). Melchert provides many other examples: Christopher Melchert, "Exaggerated Fear in the Early Islamic Renunciant Tradition," *Journal of the Royal Asiatic Society* 21, 3 (2011): 299–300.

[26] Nimrod Hurvitz describes mild asceticism as an ethical outlook and code of conduct in "Biographies and Mild Asceticism"; Kinberg says that *zuhd* was no longer equated with neglect of the body: Kinberg, "What is Meant by *Zuhd*," 30–1. In Lev's definition, neither a reclusive lifestyle nor poverty are requisite features of mild asceticism; it is not "socially disruptive": Lev, "Piety and Political Activism," 311–13. Melchert describes a piety that encouraged "deliberate austerity but disapproved of extremes": Christopher Melchert, "The Piety of the Hadith Folk," *International Journal of Middle East Studies* 34, 3 (2002): 430.

continuity or revival one would want corroborating evidence from chronicles and biographies prior to the Ayyubid period showing that ascetics actually began to treat their bodies more gently.

Ibn al-Mannī, for one, did not. Though blind and deaf from the age of forty, "he used to be his own servant, not burdening any of his companions nor imposing on them for anything, except when he might lean on someone's arm for support along the road." In spite of his frail condition, one student recalled:

> His nourishment every day was two loaves of flatbread, but sometimes he didn't even eat them. Another of his companions told me that some days he left aside a portion of the two loaves as payment to the water-carrier. The furthest he went in eating condiments with the bread was that he would use one loaf of bread to buy some meatless broth to go with the other. I never once saw him put any oil on it, even though he could have afforded it, content with just that.[27]

All this passage says, albeit in several different ways, is that he ate almost nothing in addition to avoiding fancy condiments. If Ibn al-Mannī's actions seem scripted to conform to the pattern of earlier ascetics, they probably were. Much of the anecdotal information about him comes from one of his students, al-Buzūrī, a famous storyteller in Baghdad who wove together fragments of other people's recollections into a unified whole. It is almost impossible that al-Buzūrī would have been ignorant of descriptions of Aḥmad Ibn Ḥanbal, the ninth-century "founder" of the legal school to which he and Ibn al-Mannī belonged, such as the following:

> He often seasoned (*ya'tadimu*) [bread] with vinegar; at times I saw him eat a slice of bread, shaking the dust off it, placing [it] in a plate and sprinkling some water on it until it softened, after which he would eat it with salt. I never saw him buy pomegranates or quince or any other fruit except (that he bought) watermelons which he ate with bread or grapes or dates.[28]

Hurvitz cites this passage as an example of the "mild asceticism" espoused first by Ibn Ḥanbal and actively promoted by biographers after his death. But a comparison of the two passages about meals yields a substantial clue about how later medieval *zuhd* is different from its antecedents. A mild ascetic, Hurvitz points out, would choose a diet stripped of all luxury,

[27] Ibn Rajab, *Dhayl 'alā Ṭabaqāt al-Ḥanābila*, I, 361.

[28] Hurvitz, "Biographies and Mild Asceticism," 51–2.

symbolizing rejection of social status and the food of the upper classes, yet would eat enough to satisfy himself. Indeed, Ibn Ḥanbal's meal was mean but not necessarily meager, and elsewhere he is described as having enjoyed modest food in decent quantities. An extreme ascetic would pay attention to quantity as well as quality: by reducing the amount he ate, he added the physical experience of hunger to his diet.[29]

Ibn al-Mannī seems to have done just this, even while he conformed almost perfectly (at least in al-Buzūrī's telling) to the original pattern of Ibn Ḥanbal. The difference between the eating habits of Aḥmad Ibn Ḥanbal and Ibn al-Mannī is subtle, but the reappearance of an interest in hunger signals what would become a distinguishing feature of late medieval piety. The *zāhid*s of the next two centuries after Ibn al-Mannī were so conscious of the high standards set by Ibn Ḥanbal and others that in trying to live up to them they produced a new ethos of their own. In seeking to reenact earlier patterns of piety or asceticism, some late medieval ascetics went even further in making explicit statements of social criticism and unyielding moralism or in demonstrating a concern with personal salvation through worship and austerity. As they did so, the separation between proper comportment and bodily practice was erased, and the body again became the focus of severe forms of sacrifice. What is nascent in Ibn al-Mannī's practice becomes ever more clear in the next two centuries, particularly in biographical texts: moderation recedes from the picture.

The copious detail collected on this single aspect of Ibn al-Mannī's piety – his diet – and the expectation that it would have been read with enthusiasm are typical of both earlier and later biographies. But the attention given to Ibn al-Mannī's physical condition suggests that it was what he did with or to his body as a blind, elderly man that was of real interest. In pious biographies from the late medieval period, the body of the abstemious worshipper is consistently presented as the focal point of information, and this is precisely where *zuhd* and *taʿabbud* begin to blur. Besides the determination to persist in ritual activities and to abide a perpetual hunger, Ibn al-Mannī's willingness to suffer because of those choices and his ability to sustain such a harsh lifestyle made him not so much a saint as a champion.

The contradictory athleticism of old and weakened men was a standard theme in late medieval biographies of the pious exemplars, and there was a limitless supply of unique twists and embellishments which kept

[29] Ibid., 56–7.

the theme alive. Two centuries later, for example, the famous Damascene hadith scholar Yūsuf al-Mizzī (d. 742/1341), a Shāfiʿī who taught at the Dār al-Hadīth al-Ashrafiyya, was said to have been "content without the refinements of fine clothing and food, steeds or shoes." He also bathed in cold water into his nineties and continued to travel all the way across town, from the Citadel to the district of al-Ṣāliḥiyya, on foot.[30] These fragments, any of which might sound innocuous in isolation, gain a different significance when presented in a structured list. Walking instead of riding was a typical sign of humility; for him it was a typical physical ordeal. So too bathing in cold water was unnecessarily humble for a man of his stature and thus clearly intended as an act of self-deprivation; for an elderly man it was downright dangerous and therefore also a sign of extreme physical rigor. According to Abū Ṭālib al-Makkī, an influential jurist and mystic who died in 386/996, the pious forebears (*al-salaf*) had condemned even minor ablutions in cold water as being "tantamount to the [style of] ritual worship among monks (*bi-ʿidl ʿibādat al-ruhbān*)."[31]

Al-Mizzī's lack of ostentation, twinned with an appetite for hardship that old age did not lessen, was an attitude frequently affirmed by the actions of his colleagues. Pious men who retired from teaching or public life sought not repose and ease but the opportunity to devote themselves more fully to worship and ascetic practice.[32] Maintaining or increasing severely ascetic traits in old age was so common that religious scholars who preferred leisure late in life were almost an oddity.[33]

In fact, this personal commitment to hardship may account for why many less influential figures were commemorated in the medieval sources

[30] Ṣalāḥ al-Dīn Khalīl ibn Aybak al-Ṣafadī, *Kitāb al-wāfī bi'l-wafayāt*, ed. H. Ritter et al., 29 vols., Bibliotheca Islamica Series 6 (Wiesbaden and Istanbul, 1962–97), XXIX, 245. Chamberlain uses the apt phrase "ascetic athleticism" in reference to transgressive holy men who lived in Damascus around this same time (*Knowledge and Social Practice*, 133). The Dār al-Ḥadīth al-Ashrafiyya where al-Mizzī taught until his death was located near the Citadel; among his many famous students were Ibn Daqīq al-ʿĪd, al-Nawawī, Ibn Taymiyya, and the historian al-Yūnīnī.

[31] Abū Ṭālib Muḥammad ibn ʿAlī al-Makkī, *Qūt al-qulūb fī muʿāmalat al-maḥbūb wa-waṣf ṭarīq al-murīd ilā maqām al-tawḥīd*, ed. Saʿīd Nasīb Makārim, 2 vols. (Beirut, 1995), II, 2:177.

[32] We may assume that sometimes this was specifically in preparation for death. For example, the chief qadi (*qāḍī al-quḍāt*) ʿIzz al-Dīn Ibrāhīm Ibn Jamāʿa (d. 767/1366) in the last year of his life left his high position "for the sake of *ʿibāda*" at the holy mosques of Mecca and Medina: Ibn Kathīr, *Bidāya*, XIV, 334.

[33] See for example Walī al-Dīn Aḥmad ibn ʿAbd al-Raḥīm Ibn al-ʿIrāqī, *Dhayl ʿalā'l-ʿIbar fī khabar man ʿabar*, ed. Ṣāliḥ Mahdī ʿAbbās, 3 vols. (Beirut, 1409/1989), II, 543, on the scholar Sirāj al-Dīn al-Qūṣī in Cairo, who was inclined towards relaxation and holding gatherings in his house.

along with the great figures of the age. The details provided allowed the reader to assemble a portrait of the holy person's gestures or habits and to marvel at the unusual combinations these created. A sense of awe surrounded those who endured physical afflictions, and were "patient in misfortune."[34]

The Case of Celibacy

The emphasis on bodily hardship was also pervasive among the healthy, and those who did not receive their burdens from God went about discovering ways of creating their own. While more of these will be discussed in the next chapters, perhaps the most illuminating form of self-imposed hardship is celibacy. Like Ibn al-Mannī, other pious men and women took up a lifelong challenge against their bodily desires from an early age, and despite the strong tradition condemning celibacy in both the Qurʾān and the hadith, a surprising number of medieval devotees and ascetics never married. That this was a purposeful decision rather than a missed opportunity is clear from the way al-Dhahabī called attention to a thirteenth-century hadith transmitter who had "neither wife nor dependants – and likewise lived his brother, the jurist Ibrāhīm."[35] Permanent bachelorhood had, in fact, often been specified as an option for those inclined towards a life of devotion, and medieval jurists conceded that a man need not marry if he was disinclined to do so – an option that in theory did not exist for women.[36] Al-Ghazzālī (d. 505/1111) had presented this choice vividly in

[34] For examples see Shihāb al-Dīn ʿAbd al-Raḥmān ibn Ismāʿīl Abū Shāma, *Tarājim rijāl al-qarnayn al-sādis wa-al-sābiʿ, al-maʿrūf bi'l-dhayl ʿalā'l-rawḍatayn*, ed. Muḥammad Zāhid ibn al-Ḥasan al-Kawtharī, and ʿIzzat al-ʿAṭṭār al-Ḥusaynī (Cairo, 1366/1947), 198; Guo, *Early Mamluk Syrian Historiography*, II, 76; and ʿAbd al-Razzāq ibn Aḥmad Ibn al-Fuwaṭī (attrib.), *Kitāb al-ḥawādith: wa-huwa al-kitāb al-musammā bi'l-Ḥawādith al-jāmiʿa wa'l tajārib al-nāfiʿa wa'l-mansūb li-Ibn al-Fuwaṭī*, ed. Bashār ʿAwwād Maʿrūf and ʿImād ʿAbd al-Salām Ra'ūf (Beirut, 1997), 207–8. Christian attitudes towards bodily suffering and disability provide obvious points of contrast; some of these become especially clear in Robert A. Orsi, "'Mildred, Is it Fun to be a Cripple?': The Culture of Suffering in Mid-Twentieth-Century American Catholicism," in *Catholic Lives, Contemporary America*, ed. Thomas J. Ferraro (Durham, N.C., 1997), 19–64. I am grateful to Stephen Johnson for this reference.

[35] Shams al-Dīn Muḥammad ibn Aḥmad al-Dhahabī, *Muʿjam muḥaddithī al-Dhahabī*, ed. Rawḥiyya ʿAbd al-Raḥmān al-Suyūfī (Beirut, 1993), 111–12; for another example see Ibn Kathīr, *Bidāya*, XIV, 320, on Shams al-Dīn Ibn al-ʿAṭṭār (d. 765/1363). The prohibition on celibacy derives from a Qurʾānic verse stating that God did not prescribe monasticism and that Christian monks, though well intentioned, erred when they believed that it would please him (Qurʾān 57:27).

[36] Muḥyī al-Dīn Yaḥyā ibn Sharaf al-Nawawī, *Rawḍat al-ṭālibīn*, ed. ʿĀdil Aḥmad ʿAbd al-Mawjūd and ʿAlī Muḥammad Muʿawwaḍ, 8 vols. (Beirut, 1412/1992), 363. Al-Dhahabī

his popular treatise the *Iḥyāʾ ʿulūm al-dīn*, which was widely read in the centuries after his death: while he defined marriage as part of the natural, Qurʾānic order of things, he simultaneously depicted bachelorhood as a preferable status for men who sought God. Those who were already free from selfish desires indeed need *not* undertake what some described as the "punishment" of matrimony nor assume the "burden" of providing for spouses and children.[37] In the end he recommended married life, and worship within its confines, but only after having issued some unforgettable warnings about its ills. Pious attitudes towards marriage had been conflicted from the beginning, if al-Ghazzālī's ample supply of quotations from early Sufis, ascetics, and even Companions of the Prophet may be taken as indicators of sentiments circulating in earlier centuries. Clearly it was marriage, not celibacy, in these classic statements that was a form of struggle; celibacy was a special privilege.

However, approbation of lifelong bachelorhood was seldom articulated by religious scholars after al-Ghazzālī, and the discourse against marriage was tempered by an equally strong exhortation to avoiding anything resembling monasticism. In the thirteenth century the jurist Ibn Daqīq al-ʿĪd, for example, condemned the celibate lifestyle of severe ascetics (*al-mutazahhidūn*) as being injurious to their souls.[38] The idea that marriage and devotion to God were incompatible persisted, but within limits. Badr al-Dīn Ibn Jamāʿa (d. 733/1333) warned students about the precariousness of family life in no uncertain terms: "He who marries is sailing on a sea, and when he has a child he is sunk." Yet this scholar, who had family ambitions and children of his own, only recommended postponing marriage until after one had concluded one's studies.[39] Ibn Qayyim al-Jawziyya (d. 751/1350) objected strongly even to Ibn Jamāʿa's stance, particularly when bachelorhood was made a condition for enrollment or residence at a pious institution such as a madrasa or *ribāṭ*.

notes that two of his female teachers never married, and although one cannot assume that this was their choice, the fact that he mentions their marital status makes it sound as if these were pious decisions. Shams al-Dīn Muḥammad al-Dhahabī, *Muʿjam shuyūkh al-Dhahabī*, ed. Rawḥiyya ʿAbd al-Raḥmān al-Suyūfī (Beirut, 1410/1990), 199, 202.

37 Abū Ḥāmid Muḥammad ibn Muḥammad al-Ghazzālī, *Iḥyāʾ ʿulūm al-dīn*, 4 vols. (Beirut, n.d. [1888]), II, 32 ff. His text is full of contradictory views on wives: they are pleasant companions for men, but also a financial drain and source of annoyance. This section of the *Iḥyāʾ* has been published by Madelain Farah as *Marriage and Sexuality in Islam: A Translation of al-Ghazali's Book on the Etiquette of Marriage from the Ihya* (Salt Lake City, 1984); see esp. p. 70 for the arguments discussed above.

38 Taqī al-Dīn Muḥammad ibn ʿAlī Ibn Daqīq al-ʿĪd, *Iḥkām al-aḥkām: sharḥ ʿUmdat al-aḥkām*, ed. Ṭāhā Saʿd and Muṣṭafā al-Hawārī, 2 vols. (Cairo, 1976), II, 187.

39 Chamberlain, *Knowledge and Social Practice*, 110.

Though it was generally accepted that a beneficiary must comply with the stipulations set by the building's endower, how, Ibn Qayyim asked, could someone be required to do something contrary to the customs of Islam, "such as bachelorhood, for example, or abandoning marriage?" And how could a requirement of monkery (*tarahhub*) be deemed sound when a well-known Prophetic saying – "There is no monasticism in Islam" – renders it invalid? "Clearly," he retorts, "were this stipulated for the wealthy instead of the poor, most of the jurists would recognize it as a baseless stipulation."[40]

To be sure, old-fashioned stories in which the desire to live chastely triumphs over the institution of marriage continued to be told anecdotally, but the morals they imparted now have a formulaic ring. Ibn Farḥūn describes a shaykh in fourteenth-century Medina who, after long resisting wedlock, was pressured into accepting a marriage arranged by his friends in the city. The man's instincts were proven right when the pretty bride stripped off her clothing to reveal a body covered in tattoos. As tattooing was one of the signs of the denizens of hell, he divorced her without having once touched her, and never married again.[41] The anecdote

[40] Shams al-Dīn Muḥammad Ibn Qayyim al-Jawziyya, *I'lām al-muwaqqi'īn 'an Rabb al-'Ālimīn*, ed. Muḥammad 'Abd al-Salām Ibrāhīm, 4 vols. (Beirut, 1414/1993), I, 236–7. His comments echo the opinion that his teacher, Ibn Taymiyya, expressed in a fatwa. For a discussion see Yahya Michot, "Un célibataire endurci et sa maman: Ibn Taymiyya (m. 728/1328) et les femmes," in *La femme dans les civilisations orientales*, ed. C. Cannuyer, Acta Orientalia Belgica 15 (Brussels, 2001), 183. This remained a controversial issue for several centuries. In a fatwa from the fifteenth century, al-Wansharīsī responded to a question about married men at madrasas holding down rooms while enjoying married life elsewhere: should they be replaced with bachelor students without houses or wives? He answered that indeed they should, for students were required to take part in the madrasa's activities of worship and learning: Aḥmad ibn Yaḥyā al-Wansharīsī, *al-Mi'yār al-mu'rib wa'l-jāmi' al-mughrib 'an fatāwā ahl Ifrīqiyya wa'l-Andalus wa'l-Maghrib*, 13 vols. (Rabat, 1981), XI, 262–3. At Sultan al-Nāṣir Muḥammad's *khānqāh* in Cairo, his Sufis were not allowed to live outside the complex, and contact with the outside world was forbidden (Fernandes, *The Khanqah*, 31, 58). Richard T. Mortel gives two examples of institutions in Mecca where bachelorhood was required, one for Sufis founded at the end of the twelfth century, a second for needy unmarried Muslims from North Africa ("*Ribāṭ*s in Mecca During the Medieval Period: A Descriptive Study Based on Literary Sources," *Bulletin of the School of Oriental and African Studies* 61, 1 [1998]: 38–40). On *ribāṭ*s for women and on women who remained single, see the invaluable study by Yossef Rapoport, *Marriage, Money and Divorce in Medieval Islamic Society* (Cambridge, 2005), esp. chap. 2.

[41] 'Abd Allāh ibn Muḥammad Ibn Farḥūn, *Tārīkh al-Madīna al-munawwara (al-musammā Naṣīyat al-mushāwir wa-ta'ziyat al-mujāwir)*, ed. Ḥusayn Muḥammad 'Alī Shukrī (Beirut, 2001), 115. Tattooing, and especially tattooers, were condemned because of the Qur'ānic prohibition of altering God's creation (e.g., Qur'ān 3:119). In his critique of tattooing and

suggests that those who managed to live chastely avoided certain misery, and the tattooed woman appears to represent all that was unholy in contemporary women. Around this same time, we even find a case of a qadi, the chronicler al-Maqrīzī's great-uncle, who never married "on the advice of his father."[42]

But this odd piece of fatherly wisdom was altogether rare, for bachelorhood was not widely condoned – least of all by parents. By the Ayyubid period, choosing not to marry ran contrary to the structure of scholarly life as well as the Prophet's practice. The family trees of many scholars were impossibly large; through multiple marriages men and women solidified political or social connections and populated the elite spheres of the cities of the Middle East.[43] In addition, men also availed themselves of the pleasures their female slaves could provide, pleasures to which they were entitled by law. In the Mamluk period household slaves were a requisite sign of high social standing, even among the pious.[44] As distinguished and scrupulous a man as Ibn Daqīq al-ʿĪd, the Shāfiʿī chief judge in Cairo, "took many concubines and had many children, [all of] whom he named after the ten Companions of the Prophet," who had been assured of reaching paradise.[45] The nephew of the jurist Taqī al-Dīn al-Subkī was also "much given to taking concubines, and was said to have bedded more

branding for pious reasons Ibn Baydakīn cites a hadith condemning female tattooers, referring to a Bedouin custom that had not died out by the medieval period (Idrīs Ibn Baydakīn al-Turkumānī, *Kitāb al-lumaʿ fīʾl-ḥawādith waʾl-bidaʿ*, ed. Subhi Labib, 2 vols. [Cairo and Wiesbaden, 1986], I, 45).

42 al-Sakhāwī, *al-Ḍawʾ al-lāmiʿ*, II, 290. The uncle's name was Ismāʿīl ibn Aḥmad ibn ʿAbd al-Wahhāb al-Makhzūmī. Contributing to Ismāʿīl's decision, perhaps, was a bad experience in his youth: he had been deeply afflicted by desire for a man, and one night he dreamt of someone reciting a poem about desire. He woke up remembering the words, and a short while later the object of his affection died suddenly. Sakhāwī reports having heard the story from al-Maqrīzī, but I have not found it in the *Sulūk* or *Durar al-ʿuqūd*.

43 See Rapoport, *Marriage, Money and Divorce*.

44 Being pious and keeping concubines had never been incompatible. Indeed, even Aḥmad Ibn Ḥanbal bought a slave to keep as a concubine. On the rights of the owner over his female slaves and the place of concubines in medieval households, see Shaun Marmon, "Domestic Slavery in the Mamluk Empire: A Preliminary Sketch," in *Slavery in the Islamic Middle East*, ed. Shaun Marmon (Princeton, 1999), 1–24; Marmon also discusses attitudes towards owning slaves among high-ranking officials and scholars, such as Ibn Taghrībirdī. See also Yossef Rapoport, "Women and Gender in Mamluk Society: An Overview," *Mamluk Studies Review* 11, 2 (2007): 8–16; and Baber Johansen, "The Valorization of the Body in Muslim Sunni Law," *Princeton Papers: Interdisciplinary Journal of Middle Eastern Studies* 4 (Spring 1996).

45 al-Ṣafadī, *Aʿyān al-ʿaṣr*, IV, 582.

than a thousand slave girls."[46] A healthy libido was not incompatible with an exemplary lifestyle, at least among the scholarly elite.[47]

The issue of concubines reveals an important pattern in medieval asceticism. On the one hand, a failure to marry was not necessarily tantamount to a vow of celibacy in a society where female slaves were owned by pious men. On the other, some exemplary ascetics made a point of rejecting them. Concubinage was not universally condoned, despite its being ubiquitous in certain social classes; the thirteenth-century jurist al-Nawawī was careful to point out in rebutting the opinions of his colleagues that although a man was not obliged to marry, marriage had been preferred over concubinage by his predecessor, the great Shāfiʿī scholar al-Juwaynī.[48] In *fiqh* texts, marriage was consistently presented as the solution to the problem of human sexuality, and it was urged upon ordinary people as the most effective way of controlling the natural lust felt by both sexes. Those who could not afford to marry were told to fast, and those who were incapable of fasting were urged to wed.[49]

By extension, those who chose not to marry – and al-Nawawī himself was one such man – were capable of something profoundly challenging, and those who also specifically declined to take concubines even more so. A man capable of going without female companionship must possess, yet again, an almost unnatural sort of strength. Thus if we return to the meaning of Ibn al-Mannī's celibacy it is clear that in the late twelfth century reports of his decision to forgo all female companionship conveyed

[46] Ibn Ḥajar, *Inbāʾ al-ghumr bi-abnāʾ al-ʿumr*, ed. Muḥammad ʿAbd al-Muʿīd Khān, 7 vols. in 4 (Beirut, 1406/1987), II, 237. This was Quṭb al-Dīn ʿAbd al-Laṭīf ibn ʿAbd al-Muḥsin al-Subkī (d. 788/1386).

[47] Although Ibn Daqīq al-ʿĪd was described as "exceedingly scrupulous" and "thoroughly pious" most authors downplay his asceticism if they mention it at all. In the account given by his student al-Ṣafadī, his predilection for taking concubines is paired with another uncontrollable habit, his *waswasa fī'l-ṭahāra* (which will be addressed in Chapter 4), rather than in the list of his fine qualities. See also Muḥammad ibn Shākir al-Kutubī, *Fawāt al-wafayāt wa'l-dhayl ʿalayha*, ed. Iḥsān ʿAbbās, 5 vols. (Beirut, n.d.), III, 443, where he is not called an ascetic; Tāj al-Dīn ʿAbd al-Wahhāb al-Subkī, *Ṭabaqāt al-Shāfiʿiyya al-kubrā*, ed. Maḥmūd Muḥammad al-Ṭanāḥī and ʿAbd al-Fattāḥ Muḥammad al-Ḥilw, 10 vols. (Cairo, 1964–76), IX, 207–35; Ibn Ḥajar, *Durar*, IV, 58–60.

[48] al-Nawawī, *Rawḍat al-ṭālibīn*, V, 364.

[49] Several of the legal schools urged marriage on those whose desires could not be curbed by fasting; the Mālikīs say that a man incapable of fasting to avoid unlawful intercourse in fact *must* marry. See ʿAbd al-Raḥmān al-Jazīrī, *al-Fiqh ʿalā'l-madhāhib al-arbaʿa*, 5 vols. (Beirut, n.d.), IV, 12–17. These opinions reflect a hadith that counsels those who cannot afford to marry to fast instead in order to curb their desire: Muḥammad ibn Ismāʿīl al-Bukhārī, *Ṣaḥīḥ al-Bukhārī* (Beirut, 1422/2001), 934, hadith nos. 5065 and 5066.

a message quite distinct from those of early Muslim celibates. Just as his diet established a pattern where humble tastes combined with an appetite for physical experiences of deprivation, his conjugal status affirmed a lack of appetite in other matters. Wives and concubines were presented at the beginning of a list of luxuries he eschewed. Horses, slaves, fine clothing, and pleasant food followed on the women's heels. His ability to endure without these things should be read as proof of voluntary ascetic sacrifice rather than as demonstrations of humility or as evidence of misogyny.[50]

Strangely, though, while medieval biographers might draw attention to a person's failure to marry (and in one case a woman in the late thirteenth century even had the word "virgin" engraved on her tombstone), the texts also register a sense of ambivalence that had not been present earlier.[51] Many of al-Nawawī's biographers, for example, neglect to mention his marital status altogether.[52] Whereas the early ascetics, when refusing to marry, often made bold statements defending their choice, the later medieval ones seldom did so. The early rejection of marriage could signify worries about physical purity, fear of distraction from God, or apprehension about sexuality, but most of all it was emblematic of a person's departure from worldly society and all of its concerns.[53] By the thirteenth century most unmarried exemplars were active in the life of the cities. Those who chose celibacy were hardly recluses or holy men who lived on society's margins, but were instead some of its towering figures of scholarly achievement.

Following Ibn al-Mannī's pattern, al-Nawawī appears to have remained not just single but celibate throughout his life. One can be fairly certain that he did not console himself with concubines, for quite apart from his negative legal opinion of them cited above and the lack of references to any children, ascetic impulses dominated every aspect of his life. The fame al-Nawawī gained from his legal scholarship was dwarfed by the personal virtues he exhibited: his fearlessness in challenging the sultan's authority; his daily fasts and dislike of fancy foods; his preference for threadbare clothing; his having no servants; his scrupulosity in rejecting

[50] Among less pious men, not marrying could be a sign of stinginess or antisocial disdain. For two examples see Ibn Kathīr, *Bidāya*, XIV, 194, on Ibn al-Katānī; and Ibn Rajab, *Dhayl ʿalā Ṭabaqāt al-Ḥanābila*, I, 320, on Ibn al-Khashshāb.

[51] For the account of the virgin see Taylor, *In the Vicinity of the Righteous*, 95.

[52] Even al-Nawawī's student ʿAlī ibn Ibrāhīm Ibn al-ʿAṭṭār avoids discussing it in the hagiography he produced, the *Tuḥfat al-ṭālibīn fī tarjamat al-Imām Muḥyī al-Dīn*, ed. Abū ʿUbayda Mashhūr ibn Ḥasan al-Salmān (Riyadh, 1414/1994).

[53] Bonner suggests that among the early exemplars celibacy had to do with fear of pollution: *Aristocratic Violence*, 127.

gifts and bribes.[54] To certain authors celibacy was clearly one of these virtues, and in Ibn Qāḍī Shuhba's account al-Nawawī's never having married was twinned with the ability to forgo food for hours on end. He started his day with a sip of liquid, and ate nothing until after the evening prayer.[55] What Ibn Qāḍī Shuhba's description suggests is that al-Nawawī remained single not because he had mastered his desires, or disdained women, or sought to deprive his body of pleasure, but because he was free from longings, as though it were a trait with which he was endowed at birth. It is in the profusion of detail about a scholar who departed from the normal, even dynastic, impulses of his colleagues that a distinctive but unspoken alternative discourse emerges in which celibacy is part of model behavior precisely because it was so abnormal. And perhaps some of al-Nawawī's other biographers were silent on this subject for fear that readers would misconstrue his failure to marry as a rejection of marriage instead of as proof of his unique abilities.

Ibn Taymiyya, also unmarried, was said to have been "devoid of longings for food, clothing and sex," according to al-Dhahabī. In what seems intended as a pious pun, al-Dhahabī continues: "He took no pleasure in anything other than knowledge: its diffusion, its documentation and acts which were in accordance with it."[56] This confirms again how "natural" continence rather than a vow of celibacy could be cause for admiration. In a more stark example of this absence of sexuality, another man, Sulaymān ibn Ḥamza (d. 715/1316), was praised for never having had a wet dream.[57] Being blessed with an innate mechanism of self-control was a profound measure of his uprightness, and unblemished sleep was his reward. So pervasive had the discourse of ascetic strength become by the Mamluk period that these signs of abnormality in men who strove for

[54] See for example, Shams al-Dīn Muḥammad ibn Aḥmad al-Dhahabī, *Tārīkh al-Islām wa-wafayāt al-mashāhīr wa'l-a'lām*, ed. 'Umar 'Abd al-Salām Tadmurī, 53 vols. (Beirut,1987–2000), L, 248 ff.

[55] Abū Bakr ibn Aḥmad Ibn Qāḍī Shuhba, *Ṭabaqāt al-Shāf'iyya*, ed. 'Abd al-'Alīm Khān, 4 vols. (Hyderabad-Deccan, 1978–80), II, 198.

[56] al-Dhahabī, *Mu'jam muḥaddithī*, 26. Al-Dhahabī, who studied with Ibn Taymiyya, did not intend this as a compliment, however. According to Caterina Bori, who has examined a more detailed biography (often quoted by medieval authors), al-Dhahabī lists his teacher's flaws – celibacy being one of them. Caterina Bori, "A New Source for the Biography of Ibn Taymiyya," *Bulletin of the School of Oriental and African Studies* 67 (2004). Yahya Michot has considered the fascinating paradox of Ibn Taymiyya's celibacy and his disapprobation of it in more depth in "Un célibataire endurci." In any case, it seems that the shaykh's lifelong bachelorhood was not for the sake of piety.

[57] Ibn Ḥajar, *Durar*, II, 87.

piety, while hardly commonplace, show up not in the lives of saints but in those of well-known jurists and qadis.[58]

In late medieval asceticism, celibacy cannot be easily distilled to a single meaning, partly because there was no contemporary discourse extolling its virtues.[59] To one author it could epitomize the repression of sexual appetites; to another, the absence of desire altogether. On the one hand, celibacy was seen as a kind of ascetical sacrifice, but on the other, it could merely be a symptom of devotion to another love. Ibn Taymiyya and al-Nawawī were both described as being preoccupied with the pursuit of knowledge to the exclusion of physical pleasure. Others filled their days and nights with acts of bodily devotion (*taʿabbud*), leaving them no time for family, and perhaps this demonstrates even more clearly the affirmative aspects of celibacy; rather than an extreme dissociation from worldly concerns, it could signify an extreme attachment to other things: to ritual worship, or to knowledge, or to the law. All were plausible reasons for remaining celibate, and the sources sometimes state these reasons explicitly: Shaykh ʿĪsā ibn Aḥmad al-Yūnīnī in Baalbek, an ascetic, devotee, and mystic who died in 654/1256, "never married during his lifetime because his hours were saturated with worship – except once when he made a [marriage] contract with an elderly woman called Umm Yūsuf, who was his servant, out of fear that when he took food from her his hand might touch hers."[60]

That notion of saturation is crucial to late medieval piety. Ibn Baṭṭūṭa remembered that a woman in Mecca had divorced her Sufi husband because of his nighttime vigils and his obsession with circumambulating the Kaʿba. Presumably on grounds of nonperformance of marital duties, a divorce was approved by the local qadi, who happened to be the wife's father.[61] By the thirteenth century the elaborate ways in which exemplars

58 Not surprisingly, Sulaymān was a distinguished judge and jurist who served as chief qadi of Damascus; he was also the great-great grandson of a very famous *zāhid* of the generation after Ibn al-Mannī, Shaykh Abū ʿUmar Ibn Qudāma (d. 607/1210). His genealogy is a useful measure of the generational force propelling ascetic behavior in the fourteenth century.

59 That is, although misogyny may be seen in any number of anecdotes, and the theme of marriage as a corrupting distraction had not died out, celibacy was *not* promoted as a solution.

60 Quṭb al-Dīn Mūsā ibn Aḥmad al-Yūnīnī, *Dhayl Mirʾāt al-zamān*, 4 vols. (Hyderabad-Deccan, 1374/1954), I, 25. The point is that the shaykh erred on the side of caution even with a woman who would not have incited desire in him; and it is only the Shāfiʿīs who insist that desire necessitates the performance of ablutions. The author, who met him as a young man, draws particular attention to this shaykh's scrupulosity in matters of ritual purity, which will be discussed in Chapter 4.

61 Shams al-Dīn Muḥammad Ibn Baṭṭūṭa, *The Travels of Ibn Baṭṭūṭa A.D. 1325–1354*, trans. H. A. R. Gibb, 5 vols. (Cambridge, 1958–71), I, 221.

proved their commitment to God were dramatic, time-consuming, and, apparently in some cases, unbearable for others.

Yet it is the prominent status and citywide respect attained by an ascetic scholar such as al-Nawawī (or Ibn al-Mannī for that matter) that explains what made medieval Islamic asceticism quite different from its eighth-century origins. Even by the Ayyubid period, ostentatious displays of wealth were by no means only the purview of the merchants, amirs, and sultans. Fine clothes were donned by scholars and jurists who could offer as justification the fact that the Prophet himself had appreciated handsome garments, and they wore them as a mark of power and distinction from ordinary folk. As Michael Chamberlain has pointed out:

> Some among the civilian elite adopted a style not very different from that of wealthy and powerful amīrs. They wore luxurious clothing, rode about on caparisoned donkeys, kept slaves, and traveled about in state accompanied by large retinues. Men at the top of scholarly and military networks had similar styles of self-glorification. The chief qāḍī had slaves (*ghilmān*) as one of the perquisites of office, traveled in state, and rode riding animals in the city like a high-ranking amīr.[62]

From the end of the twelfth century prominent religious men who were scholars no longer provided a point of contrast with worldly society, but instead formed a stratum of its elite. They had considerable power in the cities of Damascus and Cairo, and in smaller towns as well, deriving that power from appointments to prestigious positions at madrasas or in the judiciary. But Chamberlain also emphasizes that deliberate statements of asceticism by men in high positions were widely praised and encouraged.[63] If scholarly training and high position earned them respect, self-sacrifice could win them a different sort of esteem, precisely because it meant that they had willingly given up what many of their peers longed for. In urban contexts, asceticism no longer entailed a rupture with the world: al-Nawawī's celibacy, his plain diet and shabby clothing must have been at least in part unspoken statements of criticism of his colleagues as well as proof of his piety.

In making such statements no half measures would do, and this explains why moderation is so consistently missing from the examples discussed above. Moderation survived as a positive trait, of course.[64] Ibn

[62] Chamberlain, *Knowledge and Social Practice*, 100.

[63] Ibid., 101–7.

[64] While the Qur'ān encourages voluntary acts of worship, several verses specify moderation and kindness to oneself in these acts, such as 73: 20 on reading the Qur'ān by night: "recite as much of it as is easy [for you]" (mā tayassara minhu).

Taymiyya, unusually, was said to have had moderate tastes in all worldly things, from clothing to food. However, this moderation is consonant with his consistent censure of excessive forms of worship and unnecessary exuberance in adhering to the rules of law. Much more often, moderation appears in biographies of men who participated in political life, such as the qadi Shihāb al-Dīn al-Qaysarānī, who "took a position in the chancery and discharged his duties with the utmost restraint in matters of dress, slaves (*mamlūks*), riding beasts, steeds and other things." When authors drew attention to a high-ranking official's moderate appetite, it was usually furnished as proof of his social conscience, as a counterbalance to his position of authority, and as a sign of his refusal to abuse the power his office gave him.[65] Especially in such cases, it is clear that modest tastes were a form of sacrifice appropriate for specific settings. But they were not appropriate for ascetics: moderation alone was not enough to make someone famous as a pious exemplar. On the contrary, it was through an unequivocal departure from moderation and normal conduct that medieval devotees and ascetics were able to distinguish themselves from the rest of society. The style of piety consistently portrayed in their biographies is imbued with a sense of intensiveness and even reflexiveness. "He left the army and *taʿabbada*," meaning he gave himself over to religious practices or he worshipped extensively or intensively; "He studied for a while in his youth, then he became an ascetic (*tazahhada*), gave himself over to God (*taʾallaha*) and his name became renowned."[66] There was nothing abstract about their dedication to God, for devotional piety has little to do with the strength of faith except where it is proven by bodily actions.[67] It is the force of commitment to either ritual worship or ascetic practices, or both, that provides the key to understanding the religious culture to which they belonged.

The language of excess yields important clues about how one might enter the circle of the pious elite, for it is endemic in stories of conversion to the holy life. Once a person left his profession, position in society, or

[65] al-Ṣafadī, *Aʿyān al-ʿaṣr*, V, 553. Al-Kutubī described the vizier Ibn Ḥināʾ in a similar manner: he restrained himself in matters of food and clothing, and likewise "his donations were many and his modesty ample" (*Fawāt al-wafayāt*, III, 255).

[66] An example of this language is found in al-Dhahabī, *Muʿjam shuyūkh*, 303, on ʿAbd al-Raḥmān al-Qarāmazī.

[67] Significantly, most of the verbs relating to devotional piety have no secondary meaning; there is no other context in which they are used except for excessive religious devotion. The exception is *taʿabbada*, which can also indicate the act of subjugation, where God as well as a human master can "take someone as a slave" (Ibn Manẓūr, *Lisān al-ʿArab*, IV, 240).

even his family, it remained only for him to demonstrate a bodily commitment to the holy life, whether it was characterized by ritual devotion, asceticism, or Sufism. While one would expect that joining the ranks of the Sufis was a more formal affair, because the *murīd* might go through specific steps in order to become the student of a Sufi master, there are in fact few differences in the way all such pious conversions were portrayed.[68] They merely required a reversal of priorities, and in most cases a bit of dramatic action as well.

The attraction of converting to a life stripped of worldly concerns seized people at random, and in one case rather violently. In 637/1239 the amir Sulaymān Ibn Niẓām al-Mulk, who was in charge of the Niẓāmiyya Madrasa in Baghdad, attended one of Sibṭ Ibn al-Jawzī's sessions. He was so taken with what he heard in the sermon "that he became impassioned, rent his gown and uncovered his head. Then he stood up, and the preacher and the group witnessed that he set free all the slaves he possessed, put all his property into pious endowments and freed himself from all his possessions." The moment was so impressive that a poet composed verses about it.[69] At other times it was merely the contrast between the old livelihood and the new life that conveyed that moment of rupture. Several authors mention a poet and soldier (*jundī*) in the service of al-Nāṣir Ibn al-ʿAzīz who abandoned his position in the army to become a Sufi *faqīr*, dying at the age of sixty-eight in the Fayyūm district of Egypt in the year 670/1271–2.[70]

[68] Compare, for example al-Ṣafadī, *al-Wāfī*, XV, 388 and al-Kutubī, *Fawāt al-wafayāt*, II, 65, on the amir Asad al-Dīn Ibn Mūsak, who became an ascetic with al-Kutubī's similar account of a conversion to Sufism: *Fawāt al-wafayāt*, III, 39. For other examples see Ibn Ḥajar, *Durar*, II, 260 and I, 57.

[69] Ibn al-Fuwaṭī, *Kitāb al-ḥawādith*, 124. It is interesting that the man who inspired this exuberance was raised by his grandfather Ibn al-Jawzī, who was critical of these overt displays of religious fervor. He writes in his *Kitāb al-quṣṣāṣ wa'l-mudhakkirīn* that when a preacher sees someone in the audience "claiming to have an ecstatic experience and crying out, he should warn that person." Then he illustrates this point using the precedent of Ḥasan al-Baṣrī: "Whenever he saw someone pretending to have an ecstatic experience of this sort who had torn his clothes, he informed him that such action was inspired by the devil, for the truth does not corrupt." Cited in Merlin Swartz, *Ibn al-Jawzī's Kitāb al-Quṣṣāṣ wa'l-Mudhakkirīn* (Beirut, 1986), 225. On his preaching career and immense popularity see Talmon-Heller, *Islamic Piety In Medieval Syria*, 128–39. For a similar episode where members of an audience "abandoned their worldly occupations" in response to a sermon given in 1093 C.E., see Jonathan Berkey, *Popular Preaching and Religious Authority in the Medieval Islamic Near East* (Seattle, 2001), 53.

[70] Taqī al-Dīn Aḥmad al-Maqrīzī, *Kitāb al-sulūk li-maʿrifa duwal al-mulūk*, ed. Muḥammad ʿAbd al-Qādir ʿAṭā, 8 vols. (Beirut, 1418/1997), II, 80; al-Kutubī, *Fawāt al-wafayāt*, III, 39. This was ʿAlī ibn ʿUthmān al-Sulaymānī al-Irbilī. Al-Kutubī says he devoted himself to Sufism and became a *faqīr* (*taṣawwafa wa-ṣāra faqīran*), so his voluntary poverty was clearly connected to his conversion.

For a man like Shaykh Abū ʿUmar Ibn Qudāma, however, the process was a gradual one. Well trained in *fiqh* and grammar, he seemed poised to become a great scholar, but "worship (*ʿibāda*) distracted him from the transmission of texts."[71] This is an evocative description of how uncompromising the desire for worship could become. What men like Abū ʿUmar converted to and how they spent the remainder of their lives is not always described in any detail, but in a few cases authors described the new routines they established. Ibn Kathīr reports that in 679/1280–1 the controller of the sultan's finances in Damascus, Abū al-Ghanāʾim Muḥammad ibn Muslim, abandoned his government position and committed himself to "ritual devotions, copying texts and hadith." Of the three, his forte seems to have been excessive writing: "He used to write three quires in a single day."[72] But the intensity of his scholarly activity parallels that of his bodily devotions.

At other times a change in costume evokes differences between the new company these converts kept and the old circles they rejected. The amir Asad al-Dīn Sulaymān Ibn Mūsak, whose father and grandfather had distinguished themselves in the service of Ayyubid sultans, suddenly "left [government] service and became an ascetic (*tazahhada*); he began wearing coarse clothing, took up the company of scholars, eliminated the majority of his wealth and contented himself [with the remainder]."[73] Likewise Shuhda bint ʿUmar al-ʿUqaylī, a wealthy woman of Damascus, became an ascetic upon the death of her brother and abandoned the splendid clothing to which she was accustomed.[74] In a less complete conversion, Ibn Baṭṭūṭa once traded clothes with a poor man in preparation for a period of devotional practice with a holy man in Delhi. When he was finished, he donned his fine garments again and returned to the service of Delhi's sultan. It was not merely a matter of dressing the part so that others would recognize whose company one had joined or left: moments of disrobing were crucial to the process of transition. Ibn Baṭṭūṭa recognized the anagogical importance of the clothing he left behind when he

[71] Abū Shāma, *Tarājim*, 71. Medieval biographers focused specifically on what preoccupied their subjects on a daily basis. Thus we find men and women who were, like Abū ʿUmar, *kathīr al-ṣalāt* (full of prayer), *kathīr al-tilāwa* (given to Qurʾān recitation), or *kathīr al-ṣawm* (fasting a lot).

[72] Ibn Kathīr, *Bidāya*, XIII, 316; Abū al-Ghanāʾim died in 680/1281–2.

[73] al-Ṣafadī, *al-Wāfī*, XV, 388; al-Kutubī, *Fawāt al-wafayāt*, V, 25. He was the son of the amir ʿImād al-Dīn who served al-Malik al-Ashraf, and grandson of the *amīr al-kabīr* ʿIzz al-Dīn al-Hadhbānī.

[74] al-Ṣafadī, *Aʿyān*, II, 529; the reference to *al-libās al-fākhir* could perhaps also be read metaphorically as the trappings of pride.

remembered much later: "I had [on] a quilted tunic of blue cotton ... and as I put it off and dressed in the Sultan's robes, I upbraided myself."[75]

Contradictions

Earlier scholars had debated the merits of excessive devotion and moderation, but after 1200 there were remarkably few voices calling for the latter, and even fewer critics of contemporary asceticism. One of the last of them was Ibn al-Jawzī, who wrote of the dire consequences of some of these conversions:

> The common man learns about the censure of this world in the Holy Qurʾān and in the hadith and thinks that redemption lies in abandoning it; but he fails to understand what the blameworthy world is, so Satan deceives him by whispering: "You cannot be redeemed in the hereafter except by abandoning this world." Then the man goes his own way into the hills and keeps away from fellowship, the community and knowledge, and he becomes like a wild animal, while Satan makes him believe that this is true asceticism. And why shouldn't it be so, since he heard it said of so-and-so that he wandered about and of so-and-so that he devoted himself to worship [*taʿabbada*] in the hills. Sometimes that person had a family and consequently it perished, or a mother and she wept at his absence.[76]

That these pious decisions had consequences for families is not often attested in the sources.[77] What Ibn al-Jawzī was reacting to was the dangers of rejecting society and its blessings, one of which was the supervision learned men could provide. However, Ibn al-Jawzī's critique of asceticism remains a crucial point in the history of devotional piety, for his stern gaze also extended to nearly every one of the traits for which Ibn al-Mannī and many other exemplars gained renown. Abhorrence of food, for example, was an old sentiment of renunciation, but the severity

[75] Ibn Baṭṭūṭa, *Travels of Ibn Baṭṭūṭa*, III, 766–7.

[76] Abū'l Faraj ʿAbd al-Raḥmān Ibn al-Jawzī, *Talbīs Iblīs* (Beirut, n.d. [1966]), 145–6.

[77] One exception was a mid-thirteenth-century Jewish woman who appealed to the head of the Jewish community in Egypt to intervene with her husband who had taken to frequenting a Sufi shaykh. The letter she sent evokes exactly what Ibn al-Jawzī described: she complains of being left alone with three children to raise while "her husband has become completely infatuated with [life on] the mountain with al-Kūrānī." The text with commentary is in S. D. Goitein, *A Mediterranean Society: The Jewish Communities of the Arab World as Portrayed in the Documents of the Cairo Geniza*, 5 vols. (Berkeley and Los Angeles, 1967–88), V, 472–4.

with which medieval ascetics embraced it was a trend that alarmed Ibn al-Jawzī:

> One of Satan's deceits is that he makes them believe that *zuhd* is the forsaking of lawful things, so we find among them one who won't eat more than barley bread, and someone else who will not taste fruit. Another diminishes his food until he makes his body wither and punishes himself by wearing wool and depriving it of cold water.[78]

This is not the way of the Prophet and his Companions, Ibn al-Jawzī points out. Rather, he says, they felt hunger when they had nothing to eat, and when they found food they ate it. Moreover, the Prophet took pleasure in eating meat and chicken; he also liked sweets, and found cold water pleasant.

But in fact, barley bread was exactly the kind of food that was being touted as a noble choice two centuries later by a scholar who was a great admirer of Ibn al-Jawzī, Taqī al-Dīn al-Ḥiṣnī (d. 829/1426). Addressing his female readers in the preface to a biographical dictionary of early holy women, al-Ḥiṣnī emphasized that the Prophet Muḥammad often had no more than plain barley for a meal. He could have had anything from the land that he desired, yet instead he pleaded, "O God, let the sustenance of the family of Muḥammad be bare subsistence."[79] Al-Ḥiṣnī explains: "He sought from his Lord Most High only nourishment (*al-qūt*), not something to satisfy the appetite. Most people do just the opposite, seeking plenty and rejoicing in what is temptation: and that is property and children." He then cites the Qur'ānic verse where these words are found.[80] The Prophet's example and the legacy of early Islam could be, and was, invoked by both sides of the debate.

Ibn al-Jawzī's harsh comments about contemporary ascetics depriving themselves of good food are puzzling in light of the fact that he was a great admirer of Ibn al-Mannī, who sustained himself on bread and occasional servings of meatless broth. More perplexing still is the fact that the

[78] Ibn al-Jawzī, *Talbīs Iblīs*, 146.

[79] Taqī al-Dīn Abū Bakr ibn Muḥammad al-Ḥiṣnī, *al-Mu'mināt wa-siyar al-sālikāt*, ed. Aḥmad Farīd Mizyadī (Beirut, 2010), 16. A biography of al-Ḥiṣnī is found in al-Sakhāwī, *al-Ḍaw' al-lāmi'*, XI, 76–7.

[80] Qur'ān 8:28 reads: "And know that your property and your children are a temptation (*fitna*)." The last part of his comment and the Qur'ānic verse are not present in the print edition of al-Ḥiṣnī's text, but they are in both the Cairo and Paris manuscripts: Kitāb al-mu'mināt wa'l-ṣāliḥāt wa'l-ayqāẓ min al-mahlūkāt, Dār al-Kutub al-Miṣriyya MS Taṣawwuf, 4241, 5r; also Kitāb sayr al-sālikāt al-mu'mināt al-khayrāt, Paris, Bibliothèque Nationale, MS Arabe 686, 4r.

early women al-Ḥiṣnī wrote about were culled from Ibn al-Jawzī's own biographical dictionary of male and female devotees, the *Ṣifat al-ṣafwa*. There one finds early holy women who embodied the most extreme forms of asceticism and *taʿabbud*: they starved themselves and wept furiously; they dressed not only in woolen garments but in hairshirts and veils made of haircloth; one wore iron cuffs and kept a chain from which she suspended herself at night, presumably to keep herself awake for prayer.[81]

In fact, Ibn al-Jawzī's two most famous books on religious practice, the *Ṣifat al-ṣafwa* and the *Talbīs Iblīs*, contradict each other in the most fundamental of ways. The *Talbīs* continually castigates devotees, ascetics, and Sufis for their exaggerated practices, yet its author dedicated the *Ṣifat al-ṣafwa* to men and women from those same groups who became famous for many of the same practices.[82] The only evident strategy he occasionally employed for distinguishing the good devotees and ascetics from the bad was a simple one: he merely switched the vocabulary, replacing the words "ascetics" (*zuhhād*) and "devotees" (*ʿubbād*) with the more emphatic forms *mutazahhidūn* and *mutaʿabbidūn*.[83] Among the latter, excessive behavior was either all for show or severely misguided – but it was the same behavior praised by Ibn al-Jawzī in the *Ṣifat al-ṣafwa* nonetheless.

Reading the *Talbīs Iblīs*, one sees the limitations of using texts of critique as a source for cultural history.[84] Medieval Islamic hortatory literature is always somewhat artificial in its style of argument: it consistently depicts the contemporary situation as dire, the loss of past forms of piety as lamentable. Castigating the common people for their ignorance and misguided behavior was one of its conventions.[85] The simplest way of

[81] See for example two anonymous "female devotees," one *ʿābida* from Jerusalem, the other from Raqqa, in Ibn al-Jawzī, *Ṣifat al-ṣafwa*, IV, 252 and 198. These two are repeated in al-Ḥiṣnī, *al-Muʾmināt*, 85; for other examples see Ibn Baydakīn al-Turkumānī, *Kitāb al-lumaʿ*, I, 405.

[82] The contradiction is present in his other works as well, such as the obituaries he wrote in the *Muntaẓam*, a source frequently cited by later authors such as Ibn Rajab.

[83] For example, compare his report of Shaykh Ibrāhīm ibn Dīnār in Ibn Rajab, *Dhayl ʿalā Ṭabaqāt al-Ḥanābila*, I, 239 with a passage in the *Talbīs Iblīs*, 140 on fasting.

[84] That is, the authors and their arguments need to be contextualized; Jonathan Berkey's *Popular Preaching*, which focuses on the similar genre of sermons and the role of preachers in medieval Islam, shows precisely how this can be done.

[85] See, for instance, an argument about the decline of the Sufi shaykh–*murīd* relationship in Muḥammad Ibn al-Ḥājj al-ʿAbdarī, *al-Madkhal*, ed. Tawfīq Ḥamdān, 4 vols in 2 (Beirut, 1415/1995), III, 174–6. See also Muhsin Mahdi, "The Book and the Master as Poles of Cultural Change in Islam," in *Islam and Cultural Change in the Middle Ages (Fourth Giorgio Levi Della Vida Conference)*, ed. Speros Vryonis (Wiesbaden, 1975).

reconciling Ibn al-Jawzī's two works is to suggest that the author was an elitist who looked uncritically upon colleagues of whose sincerity he was certain. He forgave them their excesses, but argued in favor of moderation and supervision for the anonymous masses. The latter was a typically medieval sort of argument, but it does not get at the heart of the problem. For one thing, the characters in the *Talbīs Iblīs* are not always anonymous. For example, he writes: "I once saw a shaykh, one of the devotees (*mutaʿabbidūn*), called Ḥusayn al-Qazwīnī who walked a great deal during the daytime in the Mosque of al-Manṣūr. I asked the reason for his walking and was told, 'In order not to sleep.' And that is ignorance, according to holy law and to reason."[86] Perhaps, confronted by the beginning of an apparent surge in piety happening somewhere in the period before his death, he had qualms about asceticism and other trends becoming faddish: the fine examples offered by elite men and women of the past were lost in the enthusiasm of the masses.[87] But if so, why write the *Ṣifat al-ṣafwa* at all if he did not intend to fan those flames?

Reading the *Ṣifat al-ṣafwa* one recognizes the limitations of using this type of source as well. Hagiographies of past exemplars are not unlike hortatory treatises. Where the treatises are purposely despondent about contemporary society in the hopes of stirring readers to act better, the hagiographies do something similar by emphasizing exaggerated forms of "correct" behavior. Were these merely tales of heroes and heroines, or were they meant to be copied? Of the large number of thirteenth-century male exemplars who "lived harshly" and wore rough clothing in the style of the ascetics of old, only a few dressed in hair shirts.[88] This particular trait was not, in other words, successfully resurrected by the authors of hagiographical texts. No women in the Ayyubid period appear to have been wearing hair-cloth veils or chains, nor does one imagine that male authors wanted them to. But on the other hand, the ascetic climate of the medieval Near East was certainly nourished by stories told by Ibn al-Jawzī and others. The best way to judge the scholarship of Ibn al-Jawzī is to assume that the truth about what most people were actually doing

[86] Ibn al-Jawzī, *Talbīs Iblīs*, 137.

[87] Christopher Taylor describes "an ascendant paradigm of exemplary piety" happening somewhere in the period after 1200. Among its characteristic qualities are: mastery of personal desire, poverty, absence of material need, generosity, honesty, graciousness, eccentricity and special awareness, repentance, resistance to unbelief and hypocrisy, and commitment to the pious life. That list, replete with signs of "classical" Islamic asceticism, resonates in the medieval biographical dictionaries: Taylor, *In the Vicinity of the Righteous*, 89.

[88] For one example, see Ibn Farḥūn, *Tārīkh al-Madīna*, 107, on Asad al-Rūmī.

is visible in neither of his works. Nor was he torn in two different directions. Rather, it was important for a scholar to write works tailored to several different kinds of Muslims: the lazy, misinformed, or deviant on the one hand, and the overenthusiastic, misguided, or arrogant on the other. In the fifteenth century al-Ḥiṣnī solved the problem posed by the two texts and put Ibn al-Jawzī's hagiographies to new use by combining the biographical genre with the hortatory. A severe bodily asceticism that abhorred hypocrisy and ignorance was the result.

Was Women's Piety Distinct from That of Men?

Although al-Ḥiṣnī was not the only author to write a book about women, the decision to address commentary directly to a female readership was rarer. His project raises the central question of whether women's bodily piety differed significantly from that of men: given the ease of conversion to the pious life described above, how welcome were women in the ranks of the pious elite? Recent scholarship has begun to catalog the contributions made by medieval women to the transmission of Islamic knowledge, as both patrons and participants.[89] These studies suggest that, more than in any other area, they freely participated in the transmission of hadith. It is therefore not surprising that many medieval women shared the ascetic frame of mind that was fashionable in their day, since many of the basic arguments for living the ascetic life were based upon the Prophet's example as preserved in the collections of hadith.[90] Ritual practices were,

[89] On these topics see for example Jonathan Berkey, "Women and Islamic Education in the Mamluk Period," in *Women in Middle Eastern History: Shifting Boundaries in Sex and Gender*, ed. Nikki R. Keddie and Beth Baron (New Haven, 1991); Asma Sayeed, "Women and Hadith Transmission: Two Case Studies from Mamluk Damascus," *Studia Islamica* 95 (2002); Omaima Abou-Bakr, "Teaching the Words of the Prophet: Women Instructors of the Hadith (Fourteenth and Fifteenth Centuries)," *Hawwa* 1, 3 (2003); Howyda al-Harithy, "Female Patronage of Mamluk Architecture in Cairo," *Harvard Middle Eastern and Islamic Review* 1, 2 (1994). Rapoport provides additional analyses of these themes and also an excellent survey of the literature in"Women and Gender in Mamluk Society."

[90] Other disciplines were less open to women, but evidence does show that some women authored books and others excelled in religious law (*fiqh*) to an extent that rivaled their male colleagues (see for example al-Ṣafadī's comments on the famous Fāṭima al-Baghdādiyya: *A'yān al-'aṣr*, IV, 28–9). They transmitted not only collections of hadith but also books on asceticism, theology, Sufism, and law. For example, a fifteenth-century scholar named Bayram bint Aḥmad al-Dīrūṭiyya was brought up in the circles of jurists and Qur'ān reciters frequented by her father, and she herself is described as a Mālikī; she memorized the *Riyāḍ al-ṣāliḥīn* of al-Nawawī, the *Burda* of al-Būṣīrī, al-Ghazzālī's

of course, even more accessible to women than scholarly activity was, although considerably less research has focused on this topic. There were no inherent impediments faced by female worshippers when it came to supererogatory fasting and prayer, for example, and many women were noted for their devotion to these forms of worship.[91]

In the eyes of most medieval authors women were no less deserving than men of fame for their good actions or their impressive knowledge, and Ibn al-Jawzī, for instance, reproached Abū Nuʿaym for having left out famous female devotees who, "despite their femaleness," could serve as guides for men.[92] But if most of the medieval biographical collections include entries on women, the entries typically lack the detail found in stories devoted to men. This may partly reflect the fact that women's lives were more private; the informants, who were always male, must have known them from a distance – through formal study sessions, for example – or by reputation only.

Nevertheless, several areas of pious expression were either peculiar to women or forbidden to them. For example, shocking behavior with a pious purpose, such as going unwashed or making a point of neglecting religious duties, is never a trait associated with women.[93] Antinomian holy women seem not to have existed at all in medieval Islam. But perhaps the issue of equal "access" to extreme behavior is a fruitful area of inquiry nonetheless, one that can best be addressed by considering specifically female behavior. In this case, the topic of modesty is a particularly instructive one. Women were prevented by social custom and Islamic law from wearing scanty clothing – which among men was among the

ʿAqīda, and a famous treatise on Mālikī law written by Ibn Abī Zayd al-Qayrawānī (d. 386/996) who was also a critic of Sufism (al-Sakhāwī, *al-Ḍawʾ al-lāmiʿ*, XII, 15).

91 There are not many instances in which jurists undertook to legislate women's voluntary practices, but one specific instance is discussed by authors such as al-Nawawī, *Rawḍat al-ṭālibīn*, II, 253: if a woman wants to undertake a vow to fast every day, her husband's permission is required. The implication is that such a vow might not leave her the strength to fulfill conjugal and household duties.

92 Ibn al-Jawzī, *Ṣifat al-ṣafwa*, I, 29–30. Later texts, such as Ibn Rajab's famous biographical collection, included no women; al-Suyūṭī's entries on Ḥanbalī women (as well as other Ḥanbalī men left out by Ibn Rajab) are published at the end of the print edition, *Dhayl ʿalā Ṭabaqāt al-Ḥanābila*, II, 455–73.

93 I would argue that comparing men's and women's practice on the basis of transgressive behavior sets up an artificial span of activity in settings that are difficult to compare. The lives of women were not solitary, but between the household or the *ribāṭ* where women resided and the cemeteries and garbage heaps where the more antinomian male devotees and Sufis strayed, women found little opportunity to create their own environments. One important exception of a woman who lived alone at a sanctuary is discussed in Chapter 3.

most obvious markers of asceticism. Men who wore short garments or a single garment as a sign of contentment with poverty and hardship were not considered immodest. Shaykh Abū ʿUmar Ibn Qudāma, for example, often went out in winter wearing only a tunic on his body, with no robe over it and without the traditional leggings (*sarāwīl*) that served as undergarments beneath it. Leaving the body vulnerable to cruel weather, even if it meant exposing sections of the body that were customarily covered, was a specific kind of bodily statement unavailable to women.[94]

Female modesty, on the other hand, found its most fervent champion in a woman from a prominent Meccan family who had received a large number of teaching licenses for texts she had studied. Information about her comes from the qadi Najm al-Dīn Muḥammad Ibn Ẓuhayra, who told the historian al-Fāsī about his grandmother, Umm Kulthūm (d. 777/1375–6):

> She spent a whole year married to her husband, the Qadi Shihāb al-Dīn Aḥmad Ibn Ẓuhayra, without letting him seeing her face. And he lived with her until the day she died having never seen her brow or glimpsed her hair. Nor did he ever see her eat. If she saw one of her daughters go out without their heads covered, she would beat them for it. She was good and intelligent, possessed of chasteness and virtue (*ṣiyāna*).[95]

If her husband never saw her eating, it was probably because she would have to lift her face veil to do so. (Though less likely, the statement could also be a way of affirming her daily fasting or her ascetic appetite.) Umm Kulthūm was a woman who relented only after a year of marriage in according her husband the status of a family member; even after that she continued to wear at least a headscarf to bed. As the account focuses so narrowly on veiling – and not unveiling – within the home as well as without, it would seem at first that Umm Kulthūm was a unique exemplar of a piety appropriate for women, one that lacked the element of physical rigor so common for men.

And yet this account is structured in a way that parallels those involving ascetic holy men such as Ibn al-Mannī. The same language of negation pervades the text and serves to point out her "superhuman" qualities:

[94] The rules of modest dress were lifted in the case of elderly women: see Qurʾān 24:60. Such a loosening of restrictions is present in Ibn al-ʿArabī's account of a female saint in Seville: "Although she was so old and ate so little, I was almost ashamed to look at her face when I sat with her, it was so rosy and soft" (Muḥyī al-Dīn Ibn al-ʿArabī, *Sufis of Andalusia: The Rūḥ al-Quds and al-Durrat al-Fākhira of Ibn ʿArabī*, trans. R. W. J. Austin [Berkeley, 1971], 143).

[95] al-Fāsī, *al-ʿIqd al-thamīn*, VI, 461–2.

Umm Kulthūm kept hidden from her husband as much bodily activity as possible, and furthermore it was she who regulated and restricted desire in the household. Enforcing her own code of modesty, one clearly not followed by all women in Mecca, was unnecessary in much the same way that Ibn al-Mannī's celibacy had been. So too her standards of modesty for girls of an unspecified age were evidently much higher than most, and, by describing it, her grandson intends to affirm her scrupulous conformity to Islamic law. She ruled her domain, not only in meting out punishment to her female children and in rearranging the intimacy of that domain, but also as the "author" of statements made outside the household.

Since veiling of some sort was standard dress for women, it was overdoing it in contexts where veils were unnecessary – in the home and the marriage bed, as well as for children – that indicates why her modesty became a quality of distinction. It was the excessiveness of Umm Kulthūm's practice as well as the trait of modesty itself that were remembered two generations later. She does not transcend her gender in this story, but there was no sense in which she needed to: women were praised, and apparently sought to be praised, for making extraordinary statements about the body. Another theme in women's piety illustrates the same problem in a different way. One expects that wives who were praised for staying in their homes did so as a sign of their chasteness and obedience to both their husbands and the laws regarding the segregation of the sexes. Al-Fāsī, for example, mentions a woman who only left her house in Mecca to perform the hajj – that is, for just a few days every year.[96] When al-Ṣafadī claims that his wife Fāṭima only left her house to go the public bath, he was able to affirm in the same breath both her chastity and her devotion to upholding the laws of ritual purity, which for women means performing the major ablution at the conclusion of menstruation.[97] But retreat from the world in one's home was common among pious men as well. Minimizing social intercourse with people, or even avoiding them altogether, was an attribute ascribed to many pious men in the thirteenth and fourteenth centuries, such as the ascetic devotee Shaykh Isrāʾīl al-Khālidī (d. 695/1296), who did not leave his house except to go to the communal prayers on Fridays, and the jurist Shaykh

[96] Ibid., VI, 410.

[97] al-Ṣafadī, *Aʿyān al-ʿaṣr*, IV, 30. On the dangers of the one place she would visit, the bathhouse, see Mounira Chapoutot-Remadi, "Femmes dans la ville mamlūke," *Journal of the Social and Economic History of the Orient* 38, 2 (1995), 153.

Muḥammad al-Akhmīmī Ibn al-Qāṣiḥ in Cairo who "stayed in his house except in emergencies."[98]

Medieval readers, especially the ascetics among them, must have considered al-Ṣafadī's statements about his wife with such examples in mind. At the very least, one cannot presume that their readings of Fāṭima's exemplary behavior were limited to the themes of obedience or female chasteness. The sources consistently bear out the fact that women were deeply involved in acts of supererogation and asceticism and were as heartily praised for them as were their male peers. While the paucity of detailed stories about women's actions and the lack of verbal statements attributed to female devotees and ascetics – let alone books authored by them – makes any study of medieval piety somewhat lopsided in its treatment of the two sexes, there is no reason to suspect that a survey of female piety is impossible. And yet without comparing the traits of men and women together, some of the complex and intersecting messages about asceticism – so characteristic of medieval piety in general – are less apparent. The topic of women's piety and how it differs from men's deserves to be treated in greater depth, but to the extent that devotional piety and asceticism were accessible to both sexes, though not necessarily genderless, women's involvement in piety can and indeed should contribute to our understanding of how piety as a whole was constructed in the medieval period.

[98] Ibn Kathīr, *Bidāya*, XIII, 322; Muḥammad ibn Rāfiʿ al-Sallāmī, *al-Wafayāt*, ed. ʿAbd al-Jabbār Zakkār, 2 vols. (Damascus, 1985), I, 53. One could curtail social intercourse even having left the house: al-Sallāmī mentions another man who was "godly and good, not mixing with anyone and not speaking about things which did not concern him" (ibid., I, 33; also in al-Ṣafadī, *al-Wāfī*, V, 371).

2

"Devote Yourselves to Deeds You Can Bear"

Voluntary Fasting and Bodily Piety

> While the Prophet was delivering a sermon, he saw a man standing, so he asked who he was. They said, "It is Abū Isrāʾīl who has vowed that he will stand and never sit down, and he will never come in the shade, nor speak to anybody, and will fast." The Prophet said, "Order him to speak, and have him come into the shade, and make him sit down, but let him complete his fast."[1]

Of the diverse practices that characterize devotional piety in the medieval period, none was more popular or more expressive of the contemporary concern with the body than voluntary fasting. During the month of Ramaḍān the community as a whole would participate in an obligatory fast each day, commencing after a meal at the end of night and punctuated by another at sunset. Supererogatory fasts, by contrast, were not corporate, except on certain days of the year and in times of crisis. Voluntary fasting was seldom a purely private undertaking, however, for despite the exhortations of pedants who begged the faithful to fast without calling attention to themselves, some people clearly made great displays of their piety. We have, for example, an account of the impressive fasting schedule of one of the Mamluk sultans, al-Ashraf Barsbāy (r. 825/1422–841/1438):

> He was much given to fasting, summer and winter alike, for he would generally fast on the thirteenth, fourteenth and fifteenth of every month. He also fasted the first and last days of the month while diligently keeping up days of fasting on Mondays and Thursdays, to the point where he would go out hunting on his fast days and sit on the picnic blanket,

[1] al-Bukhārī, *Ṣaḥīḥ*, 1187, hadith no. 6704.

> fasting while he personally served food to the amirs and his troop of bodyguards. After the blanket had been lifted up, he would wash his [own] hands, as if on an equal level with ordinary people.[2]

Medieval Muslims seem to have had an appreciation for stories that revealed the details of those who mastered the ability to fast regularly, for the authors of our texts frequently knew the specific foods and fasts preferred by the humblest of devotees as well as those of sultans.

A person might undertake a voluntary fast for any number of reasons, and although the types of fasts were limited in number, the variations upon them conceived by devotees and ascetics were limitless. Ascetic uses of food account for a large part of this variety in the medieval period, so much so that it appears impossible to disentangle pious attitudes towards fasting from those of asceticism in general. Therefore, the meaning of fasting and its role in medieval devotional piety must first be sought in the personal styles and habits of individuals. As distinct motives come to the surface, it becomes clear that attitudes about fasting were undergoing subtle changes from the end of the twelfth century onward, and not only as a result of trends in asceticism. These changes are visible also in thirteenth-century legal explanations of the voluntary fasts that are condoned in Islamic ritual law. In fact, juridical discourse provides us with one of the most compelling types of commentary on shifting notions of the use of the body.

This chapter begins with an examination of the voluntary fasts that were favored in this period. I then consider a series of questions that help to explain their prevalence. Why were some types of fasts chosen over others? What was the purpose of these voluntary practices? Were there any limits on how much one should fast? The second part of the chapter considers the historical development of an especially difficult fast, known as the "perpetual" fast, which was controversial – in terms of Islamic law – and yet often favored by jurists in their own personal practice.

Features of the Islamic Fast

Supererogatory fasting is a topic of extraordinary richness, and it is surprising that it has been almost entirely neglected in scholarly studies on Islam. Even the obligatory fast of Ramaḍān, required of Muslims every year, has not received the attention it deserves.[3] As a point of departure,

[2] Ibn Taghrībirdī, *al-Nujūm al-zāhira*, XV, 108.

[3] A fascinating exception which covers some aspects of voluntary fasts is Marjo Buitelaar, *On Fasting and Feasting: An Ethnographic Study of Ramadan in Morocco* (Oxford and

fasting in the medieval Christian world provides a source of comparison within easy reach, not least because it has been amply described by modern historians. It is readily apparent that medieval Christians and Muslims alike might consider difficult fasts to be an effective means of controlling the self as well as a sign of utter personal dedication to the divine. However, the relative absence in the Islamic tradition of other themes – such as prolonged self-humiliation, a preoccupation with bodily fluids such as blood and breast milk, and an almost florid passion for God (or Christ) – suggest that the nuances of Islamic fasting need to be more fully explored.[4]

One of the themes that shows through most plainly in Islamic texts from the Ayyubid and Mamluk periods, whether biographies or legal treatises, is how the expert fasters felt neither hatred nor disgust towards the body. If anything, many of their statements suggest that they simply, or deliberately, ignored it and all of its complaints. Nor is the conception of the human form as a hindrance to spiritual enlightenment (found in some Sufi theoretical literature as well as in early and medieval Christian sources) often expressed. For most medieval devotees the body was merely a plastic instrument to be exploited in daily use. The hunger it experienced as a result of long fasts or ascetic meals may have fascinated observers, but the devotees themselves seldom dwelt on its sensations. This is puzzling, of course, because the body is so obviously central to the practices of devotional piety in general, and fasting in particular. But their actions were not primarily about suffering, nor even truly about the soul, but about worship. This was what one was supposed to do with one's person, and how much one did could make someone a revered figure or simply a decent Muslim. To this end, the faster's body did have to

Providence, 1993); also André Möller, *Ramadan in Java: The Joy and Jihad of Ritual Fasting*, Lund Studies in History of Religions 20 (Lund, 2005). The best discussion of the basic principles of fasting remains C. C. Berg, "Ṣawm," *EI*. On Ramaḍān and comparisons with fasting in other religious traditions see S. D. Goitein, *Studies in Islamic History and Institutions* (Leiden, 1968), 90–110, and also K. Wagtendonk's interesting but problematic study, *Fasting in the Koran* (Leiden, 1968).

[4] In particular, see Carolyn Walker Bynum's pathbreaking study, *Holy Feast and Holy Fast: The Religious Significance of Food to Medieval Women* (Berkeley, 1987), which provides substantial information on Christian practices and attitudes, male as well as female, toward fasting and the body. For further discussion of the themes listed above see Donald F. Duclow, "The Hungers of Hadewijch and Eckhart," *The Journal of Religion* 80, 3 (2000): 421–41. Jewish traditions of ascetic fasting may provide a closer parallel, though considerably less has been written on the topic. See, however, Eliezer Diamond, *Holy Men and Hunger Artists: Fasting and Asceticism in Rabbinic Culture* (Oxford and New York, 2004).

be tended to, but only for the purpose of continuing to fast: overusing the body was not about the pathos of suffering for God.

The role of food in medieval Islamic piety, a related issue, is subtler – or at least less predetermined than in the Christian tradition, where particular foods have such significance.[5] A number of Muslim ascetics ate barley bread in imitation of the Prophet, and even in imitation of his poverty, but not as symbolic of his body. Nor was there any possibility of a divine presence in food.[6] Instead, pious food practices in medieval Islam can be read as strong expressions of how the devotees managed and utilized their own bodies for the purpose of worship. It was in these uses rather than in particular kinds of food that others recognized religious significance. In accounts of fasting, and in the dialectic between the body and food, some of the clearest messages about medieval Islamic piety can be found.

As for the structure of the fast, there are many consonances among the fasting practices of the religious traditions of the Middle East. Most notably, the fast from sunrise to sunset is found in all three Abrahamic faiths. In addition to a shared theme of atonement as a motivation for undertaking certain fasts, Mondays and Thursdays are associated with fasting in both Judaism and Islam. An even more direct connection may be posited for the Islamic festival of ʿĀshūrāʾ that began, according to some early Muslim traditions, when the Prophet and his community in Medina observed a fast along with their Jewish neighbors.[7] Calendrical fasts, common in the Coptic Church, are also found in the Muslim devotional year, although the accompanying proscription of particular foods, such as milk, meat, or fish, is unknown in Islam. This is a major point of difference: where some Christian fasts are defined by regulations about

[5] To take an example from Bynum, Henry Suso apportioned a symbolic meaning to every bite he took during a meal: one for each member of the Trinity, and one for Mary; he chewed each bite five times for the wounds of Christ; the apple that called out to him, "Eat me!" needed no exegesis in order for his readers to grasp the Edenic reference: Bynum, *Holy Feast and Holy Fast*, 104–5.

[6] That is, the divine could not be made substantial in any way. The possibility of blessings (*baraka*) being transmitted through food was widely acknowledged in the medieval period, but this relates to the human quality of holiness, not divinity.

[7] Although, as Maribel Fierro notes, this was not the only explanation offered for the origins of ʿĀshūrāʾ, it indicates that early Muslim scholars recognized connections with the Jewish model of fasting. A further historical correspondence she mentions is the fact the day of ʿĀshūrāʾ in Sunnī Islam and Yom Kippūr in Judaism have at times been celebrated as joyful occasions, though for different reasons: Maribel Fierro, "The Celebration of ʿĀšūrāʾ in Sunnī Islam," *The Arabist: Budapest Studies in Arabic* 13–14 (1995). See also Megan Reid, "ʿĀshūrāʾ (Sunnism)," *EI*[3].

what types of food can be eaten at normal mealtimes, the Islamic fast (*ṣawm*), whether voluntary or obligatory, can only mean abstinence from food altogether during daylight hours.

In the medieval period, we can be certain that the different religious communities were aware of the fasting practices of their neighbors.[8] The existence of structural similarities would not have surprised a chronicler such as al-Jazarī in Damascus, who noted that on October 2, 1330:

> The fasting day of the Assembly fell on Sunday, and the Great Feast was on Monday. And that day was the Fast of the Jews – which is on the 10th of Tishrī, and Tishrī is the beginning of the Jewish year – and they disappeared into their houses. Thus the holidays of the two religious communities, Islāmiyya and Isrā'īliyya, fell on the very same day. Truly God directs the right course![9]

However, shared attitudes about fasting among the three faiths were probably less discernible to medieval Muslims, who understood their own tradition of voluntary fasting as being faithful to the model of the required fast during Ramaḍān. The general "truths" about fasting (for example, it pleases God) and its physical and moral etiquette are derived from the Qur'ān and the stories of Muḥammad and his Companions. This etiquette, these meanings, continued to develop over many centuries through the exemplary practices of men and women as well as in writings on asceticism, Sufism, and the pious life. They were still developing in the thirteenth and fourteenth centuries, a period when many important legal commentaries and works on substantive law, including ritual law, were being written.

Part I: Difficulty and Duration

Although selecting a fast was a matter of individual choice, a number of fasting patterns were common in the medieval period. To start with, a great many devotees fasted every day beginning at dawn, putting no

[8] In a colorful later example, al-Sha'rānī mentions an early sixteenth-century Muslim eccentric named Ibrāhīm ibn 'Usayfīr who slept in churches and proclaimed, "No one fasts a true fast unless he abstains from mutton on fast days as the Christians do. As for the Muslims who eat mutton and chicken on fast days, their fasting is invalid in my eyes": 'Abd al-Wahhāb ibn Aḥmad al-Sha'rānī, *al-Ṭabaqāt al-kubrā*, 2 vols. in 1 (Beirut, 1408/1988), II, 140.

[9] al-Jazarī, *Tārīkh*, II, 401. He is speaking here of the day of the hajj month when the pilgrims stop at Mount 'Arafa; on this day the rest of the Muslim community is encouraged to observe a fast.

food or liquid into their mouths until sunset. For example, in his memoirs Usāma Ibn Munqidh praised the virtues of his family's nursemaid and slave, Lu'lu'a, who raised three generations of children in northern Syria while fasting by day and praying by night.[10] When practiced year-round and for years at a time, this was known as the *ṣawm al-dahr*, or "perpetual fast."[11] Spending the nighttime hours in prayer frequently complemented this fast, and in fact almost all who undertook it sought to make things more difficult for themselves. Shaykh Abū 'Umar Ibn Qudāma's body, we are told, was left visibly gaunt from the amount he fasted and stayed awake at night. Not only did this holy man keep up the routine of not eating during the day: when he did eat, his meal was barley bread and when he slept, his bed was a mat.[12] Shaykh Abū'l-Thanā' (d. 609/1212), known in Baghdad for his kindness and friendly demeanor, fasted constantly, recited the Qur'ān in full every day and "barely ate beyond nibbling the threads of his turban."[13] The perpetual fast, examined in detail in the second part of this chapter, became the mark of the true exemplar, for none was deemed harder and none could be longer.

According to one's personal desire other voluntary fasts might be undertaken instead, following the Prophet's example, for the better part of a certain month or months, or on certain days of the year, the month, or the week; or in repeating patterns of days of fasting and not fasting. A faster would ordinarily choose one of these as something like a *regula*. But in the medieval period some devotees arranged several at once in a distinctive calendar of observances. Taqī al-Dīn al-Jazarī was one such person; his brother, the Damascene chronicler, recalled that he fasted "on Mondays and Thursdays, most of Rajab and Sha'bān, the month of

10 Usāma Ibn Munqidh, *The Book of Contemplation: Islam and the Crusades*, trans. Paul M. Cobb (London, 2008), 199. The phrase Ibn Munqidh (d. 584/1188) uses to describe Lu'lu'a – "ṣawwāma, qawwāma" (fasting, praying) – is formulaic, an abbreviation for fasting by day and staying awake at night in prayer.

11 The fast is sometimes synonymously called *al-ṣawm al-dā'im*.

12 Abū Shāma, *Tarājim*, 71. A figure who will be referred to often in this chapter, Shaykh Abū 'Umar was the elder brother of the legal scholar Muwaffaq al-Dīn Ibn Qudāma al-Maqdisī (d. 620/1223), author of the *Mughnī*. He died in 607/1210. See Daniella Talmon-Heller, "The Shaykh and the Community"; see also Pouzet, *Damas*, 209–10.

13 Yūsuf ibn Qizughlī Sibṭ Ibn al-Jawzī, *Mir'āt al-zamān fī tārīkh al-a'yān*, VIII, part 2 (Hyderabad-Deccan, 1952), 526. The author recalled this detail from a visit he had made to the shaykh's *ribāṭ* in Bāb al-Azaj; his grandfather had great affection and respect for this shaykh. Also in Abū Shāma, *Tarājim*, 82. Ibn Rajab (*Dhayl 'alā Ṭabaqāt al-Ḥanābila*, II, 63–4) adds that Shaykh Abū'l-Thanā al-Na''āl was a preacher (*wā'iẓ*) whose *ribāṭ*, though dishevelled on the outside, was filled with both mendicants and jurists, many of whom had travelled to see Ibn al-Mannī.

Ramaḍān, six days in Shawwāl, the 9th of Dhū'l-Ḥijja, and Muḥarram."[14] When one adds up the days, it is easy to see how a pious person might fast much of the year without attempting to fast perpetually.

All of these fasts and several more, such as Sultan al-Ashraf Barsbāy's fast on the three middle days of each month, are recommended in late medieval juridical texts.[15] Adhering to the Islamic rubric of fasting during Ramaḍān, from which all manner of supererogatory fasts during the year were derived, the fast during daylight hours was the most common type. However, in some cases nothing was eaten for days at a time, though this was more unusual and seldom condoned by the jurists.[16] Ibn Baṭṭūṭa's shaykh in Delhi, Kamāl al-Dīn al-Ghārī, could fast for ten and sometimes twenty days straight without food. After witnessing this, Ibn Baṭṭūṭa spent months conditioning himself to fasting for five days at a time, at the end of which he would eat a meal of plain rice.[17] The word he uses here is *wāṣala* (to continue), rather than *ṣāma* (to fast).

This "continuous fast" was based on the Prophet Muḥammad's *ṣawm al-wiṣāl*, a practice he tried to prevent his Companions from undertaking because of its severity, according to several hadiths.[18] Because the Prophet

[14] al-Jazarī, *Tārīkh*, III, 637.

[15] This is a remarkably complete, though still not exhaustive, list of fasts that are condoned in Islamic law. To complicate matters, the four Sunnī legal schools differ about several of them. For example, the Ḥanafīs disapprove of fasting the six days in Shawwāl consecutively; the Mālikīs dislike specifically choosing the thirteenth, fourteenth, and fifteenth for fasting. A comparison of the areas of congruence and difference regarding particular supererogatory fasts can be found in al-Jazīrī, *al-Fiqh ʿalā'l-madhāhib al-arbaʿa*, I, 485–8. For a thorough examination of the voluntary fasts according to the Ḥanbalī *madhhab* see Muwaffaq al-Dīn ʿAbd Allāh Ibn Qudāma, *al-Mughnī*, 14 vols. (Beirut, n.d. [1928]), II, 97–117; for the Shāfiʿīs see al-Nawawī, *Rawḍat al-ṭālibīn*, II, 251–4; Muḥyī al-Dīn Yaḥyā ibn Sharaf al-Nawawī, *al-Majmūʿ: sharḥ al-Muhadhdhab*, ed. Zakarīyā ʿAlī Yūsuf, 19 vols. (Cairo, 1966–9), VI, 436–56.

[16] Most jurists say that this kind of fasting is either disliked (*makrūh*) or outright forbidden (*ḥarām*). An important exception is Ibn Qudāma, *Mughnī*, II, 102, who explains that the Prophet forbade it only out of concern for his Companions. Proof of its being acceptable, the author says, is the fact that they went on doing it after he died. For an earlier opinion see al-Ghazzālī, *Iḥyā'*, I, 238.

[17] Shams al-Dīn Muḥammad Ibn Baṭṭūṭa, *Riḥlat Ibn Baṭṭūṭa*, 2 vols. in 1 (Beirut, n.d.), II: 329–30, 410; Ibn Baṭṭūṭa, *Travels of Ibn Baṭṭūṭa*, III, 627, 766.

[18] The Prophet would sometimes pass several days without eating or drinking – some authorities say it was during Ramaḍān, others say at the end of a month. When people began to copy him and found it very difficult, he forbade it, saying, "You are not like me in this matter, for [while] I spend my night, my Lord feeds me and provides me drink. Devote yourselves to deeds you can bear": Muslim ibn al-Ḥajjāj, *Ṣaḥīḥ Muslim* (Beirut, 1420/2000), 466, hadith no. 8; al-Bukhārī, *Ṣaḥīḥ*, 337, hadith no. 1922. For a brief discussion of when and why an action of the Prophet might not be recommended for emulation see Mohamed Hashim Kamālī, *The Principles of Islamic Jurisprudence*

had discouraged it, legal literature did not dwell on the correct way to carry out this fast: as a result, it was unusually mutable. It could last for a few days, or much longer, as was the practice among the Sufi followers of Abū Madyan (d. 594/1197 in Tlemçen) who undertook a continuous fast for forty days as a rite of initiation. Sometimes water was drunk at sunset throughout the fast, a physical necessity after a few days.[19] The continuous fast highlights the interest in bodily exertion so common among exemplary fasters, but, significantly, it was seldom one they chose.

The *ṣawm al-wiṣāl* was also problematic for a reason that has to do with an essential principle of the Islamic fast.[20] As the verb *wāṣala* indicates, the continuous fast emphasized connecting one day to the next without breaking for a meal, and this definition points to the centrality of the meal of *ifṭār* at sunset in regular fasting. Eating and not eating are equally vital to the Islamic conception of the fast.The hours of daylight are governed by a strict set of bodily rules relating to abstention from food, drink, and sexual activity. At dusk the restrictions are lifted. The two physical states of deprivation and gratification are not equivalent, since fasting is done solely for God, and outside the month of Ramaḍān it is not a "normal" state of being. But the contrast between them is sacrosanct, and eliding one day into the next would be contrary to the very structure of the fast. What the sunset meal marked was not merely

(Cambridge, 1991), 52. For a condemnation of the *ṣawm al-wiṣāl* as an innovation that people mistakenly believe is a good act see Shihāb al-Dīn ʿAbd al-Raḥmān ibn Ismāʿīl Abū Shāma, *Kitāb al-Bāʿith ʿala inkār al-bidaʿ wa'l-ḥawādith*, ed. Mashhūr Ḥasan Salmān (Riyadh, 1410/1990), 106–15.

[19] Vincent Cornell, *Realm of the Saint: Power and Authority in Moroccan Sufism* (Austin, 1998), 137. For a precedent see Schimmel, *Mystical Dimensions*, 115. For a vivid account of what happens to the body during successive stages of not eating, see Padraig O'Malley, *Biting at the Grave: The Irish Hunger Strikes and the Politics of Despair* (Boston, 1990), 114–15.

[20] Some scholars have translated *ṣawm al-wiṣāl* in ways that suggest a mystical meaning and reflect its usage among Sufis, such as "the fast of intimate union" (e.g., Cornell, *Realm of the Saint*). Sufis employed the word *wiṣāl* to mean "arriving" at a spiritual state or "union" with God. There is no mystical meaning in the phrase as it appears in the hadith or in juridical discussions. In his fourteenth-century dictionary, the *Lisān al-ʿArab*, Ibn Manẓūr specifies one meaning of *wāṣala* as having to do with connecting two things or continuing something, as in "continuity in fasting." Subsequently he explains that the Prophet forbade *al-wiṣāl fī'l-ṣawm*,"and that is [when someone] does not break his fast for two days or a few days." The Prophet also, he says, forbade *al-wiṣāl fī'l-ṣalāt*, or continuity in prayer: Ibn Manẓūr, *Lisān al-ʿArab*, VI, 450. On *wiṣāl fī'l-ṣalāt* see Abū Shāma, *Kitāb al-Bāʿith*, 112. Muḥyī al-Dīn Ibn al-ʿArabī, a jurist as well as a Sufi scholar and poet of great renown, engaged with juridical discourse and also offered mystical explanations of why these practices were valid. See his commentary in *al-Futūḥāt al-Makkiyya*, 4 vols. (Beirut, 1988 [1876]), I, 637–8.

the changeover from day to night, but the separation between those two states.

Two fatwas, written by scholars who died half a century apart in the early Mamluk period, reveal this particularly clearly. In both cases, a man who wished to have intercourse with his wife during the day in the month of Ramaḍān wanted to know whether he could break his fast early by eating and then have intercourse without an expiatory act being required. In the first fatwa, al-Nawawī pointed out that what broke the fast – intentionally eating – required only repentance and an additional "make-up" day of fasting. In the second, Ibn Taymiyya addressed the core issue of whether it was solely the act of eating or the sexual act as well that broke the state of fasting and necessitated expiation; since the acts were linked by the man's intention, he ruled that an act of atonement was required.[21] Most likely the husband simply hoped to avoid the heavier penalty associated with intercourse, yet on another level his question is an example of how the meal of *ifṭār* was widely understood to be the symbolic release from the bonds of fasting. In practice, the meal took on a sanctity of its own. Nowadays, during the month of Ramaḍān the meal is typically eaten in a festive mood, which mirrors the lavish preparation of food. Among the medieval ascetics who fasted voluntarily and usually alone, the meal of *ifṭār* could be a somber occasion and frugal indeed.[22] In both cases it is understood to be unlike regular meals.

[21] Muḥyī al-Dīn Yaḥyā ibn Sharaf al-Nawawī, *Fatāwā al-Imām al-Nawawī*, ed. Maḥmūd al-Arnā'ūṭ (Damascus, 1419/1999) 57–8; Ibn Taymiyya, *Majmū' fatāwā*, XXV, 260–3. Briefly, most jurists say that breaking an obligatory fast by intercourse is a sin requiring an act of expiation (*kaffāra*) at least on the part of the husband, such as two months of fasting, freeing a slave, or feeding the poor. Intentional eating requires only that the day be "replaced" by fasting later. The issue in these two fatwas is whether propitiation for the act of intercourse, which was the intention for breaking the fast, was necessary once the fast had already been broken by eating. Ibn Taymiyya gives a useful review of the opinions of the four Sunnī legal schools in his response. The question put to al-Nawawī also included a query about whether multiple acts of intercourse each required an act of *kaffāra*; he answered that it was required only once. On atonement for light sins, see Christian Lange, "Expiation," *EI³*.

[22] Interestingly, while authors often described what pious people ate to break their fasts, the historical sources never mention the food eaten at the meal of *saḥūr* before daybreak. The Prophet did not say either meal was obligatory, but since not eating between two days of fasting is "forbidden" or "disliked," one of the meals is thus required. *Ifṭār* and *saḥūr* are both designated "strongly recommended" (*mustaḥabb*) in legal texts, and each has its merits: it is said that *saḥūr* has *baraka* (blessings) and that it distinguishes the Muslim fast from that of the Jews and Christians (*ahl al-kitāb*): Ibn Qudāma, *Mughnī*, III, 100–1.

Ascetic Diets, Legal Fasts

Just as there is a formal distinction between regular fasting (*ṣawm*) and going without food (*ṣawm al-wiṣāl*), an even more important distinction must be drawn between fasting and ascetic practices relating to diet. A man might be described as thin or as eating extremely little, but not as "full of fasting."[23] Some ascetics ate only a single type of food or trained their bodies to accept a level of nutrition just shy of starvation. The Mālikī jurist Abū Bakr al-Ṭuraynī, living in the Nile Delta, refused to eat meat for a number of years, fearing that the local supply came from herds stolen by Bedouin raiders. Even in better times he ate only what he could grow in the earth, and restricted his intake of food so severely that "no one else could have endured it." In the end it was thought possible he had starved to death. But for all this, he was not known as a faster, and in most accounts of his life the word *ṣawm* is never mentioned.[24] This suggests that dieting and fasting were chosen for different reasons, and must be treated as separate practices. Indeed, as we will see, there is no formal connection between them as far as Islamic law is concerned.[25]

Yet the boundaries between the disparate types of diets and fasts were blurred not only by the fact that many people were drawn to both but also by the common desire to make an individual course more arduous. The supererogatory practice of fasting extra days could be made more severe by breaking the fast with a single piece of fruit or with water alone. Eating only bread was more difficult when one ate just a small amount of it, no matter the time of day. An ascetic might combine a distinctive diet with formal fasting in a life that revolved largely around food or carefully chosen ingredients, on the one hand, and lack of food, on the other. The jurist al-Nawawī, for example, was a perpetual faster who refused to eat fruit; a fourteenth-century jurist in Medina, Mūsā al-Marrākushī, only permitted himself pepper as a seasoning for his evening meals.[26] There

[23] For example, al-Kutubī's description of Burhān al-Dīn al-Fazārī (discussed below) says that he was "qalīl al-ghidhā' jiddan": al-Kutubī, *Fawāt al-wafayāt*, I, 33.

[24] Al-Ṭuraynī died in 827/1424. His contemporary biographers call him "the ascetic of the age" yet seem hesitant to state his cause of death too plainly, saying "perhaps he died from too little food": al-Maqrīzī, *Sulūk*, VII, 106; Ibn Taghrībirdī, *al-Nujūm al-zāhira*, XV, 124–5. Interestingly, a later scholar, al-Sakhāwī, changed the passage found in al-Maqrīzī so that it says that al-Ṭuraynī "fasted a lot": al-Sakhāwī, *al-Ḍaw' al-lāmi'*, XI, 65.

[25] I am using the word dieting in the sense of a dietary regime: the regular restriction of food intake according to its amount, or its type, or both.

[26] al-Dhahabī, *Tārīkh al-Islām*, L, 252; Ibn Farḥūn, *Tārīkh al-Madīna*, 117. There were specific reasons behind al-Nawawī's avoidance of fruit, which will be discussed at length in

were, in other words, hundreds of possible diets in cascading degrees of severity that the devotees combined with fasts to carve out short-term or lifelong routines for themselves. Some of these were too mild to be noted by historians, and it is worth contemplating how very little we know about the lives of those men and women, particularly the latter, who like Taqī al-Dīn al-Fāsī's grandmother Juwayriyya received only a brief obituary: he described her as "virtuous and good in the manner of the pious forebears," and says that she died fasting in Medina at the end of the month of Muḥarram, 795/1392.[27]

If the difficulty of cataloguing all these combinations of fasting, eating, and abstaining is at once apparent, Islamic law makes a much clearer classification of legitimate types of *ṣawm*, which has nothing to do with the level of rigor involved or what was eaten. A legitimate fast as a form of worship is either obligatory (*wājib*) or supererogatory (*taṭawwuʿ*). Explanations of *ṣawm* found in the hadith, in medieval compendia of substantive law, and in popular religious texts routinely stressed how fasting is not meant to be grueling, as it is abstinence rather than hunger that is the intended obligation. Dispensations are granted for any conditions that make it unbearable, such as travel or sickness, and the medieval jurists were careful to say that a person who felt hunger too keenly could stop fasting.[28] Furthermore, a voluntary fast could be abandoned for any reason without the penalty of making up for it later, according to some jurists, but they agreed that it was better to finish it.[29]

Yet in practice, these exits were rarely taken. For example, Abū Muḥammad al-Warghamī, the head of the Sufis in Tunis and a respected Mālikī jurist, was so devoted to the perpetual fast that Ibrāhīm Ibn Farḥūn, who met him in Medina in 792/1390, noticed that he kept it up even on long journeys.[30] The kind of interplay here between knowledge of ritual

the following chapter. Al-Marrākushī's choice of pepper, on the other hand, appears to have been a purely renunciatory statement.

[27] al-Fāsī, *al-ʿIqd al-thamīn*, VI, 375.

[28] al-Jazīrī, *al-Fiqh ʿalā'l-madhāhib al-arbaʿa*, I, 502.

[29] al-Nawawī, *Rawḍat al-ṭālibīn*, II, 251. Nawawī says that if someone fasts voluntarily he is not required to finish it, but it is preferable to do so. Likewise, he does not have to make up for a broken fast by fasting later, but that too would be preferable. Finally, if he has a reason for breaking it there is no disapproval, meaning he is neither urged to persist nor required to complete it later.

[30] Ibrāhīm ibn ʿAlī Ibn Farḥūn, *al-Dībāj al-mudhahhab fī maʿrifat aʿyān ʿulamāʾ al-madhhab*, ed. Muḥammad al-Aḥmadī Abū al-Nūr, 2 vols. (Cairo, 1975), II, 331–3. The verb used here is *sarada*, which means to continue without interruption. For a fascinating discussion of what Mālikī law says about the obligation that ensues when one does not break the fast on a journey, see Ibn Rushd, *The Distinguished Jurist's Primer:*

law and personal taste features in many fasting projects in this period. Both al-Warghamī and Ibn Farḥūn recognized that maintaining a fast while travelling made a certain kind of statement about piety. Self-imposed hardship in carrying out a particular devotional activity (fasting while travelling) and the activity itself (the *ṣawm al-dahr*) were, technically, two separate acts of devotion. For devotees such as al-Warghamī the rules of substantive law could provide not merely guidelines for legally sanctioned forms of worship but the baseline from which to develop further types of devotional acts. This interplay may be counted as another style or method of personalizing fasts, one that is wholly different from those involving the design of a diet in which there is a restriction of the amount of food eaten, abstention from certain foods, or reliance on only a single kind of food.

It is worth considering an earlier case where the interplay between substantive law and individual choice – about food as well as fasting – made for a more complex result. Usāma Ibn Munqidh recalled in some detail the habits of a "learned ascetic" he came across in eastern Anatolia named Abū ʿAbd Allāh Muḥammad al-Bustī (d. 570/1174–5), a perpetual faster who also had settled on a diet where he would "drink no water, eat no bread and no kind of cereals. His fast he would break with two pomegranates or a bunch of grapes or two apples. Once or twice a month he would eat a few mouthfuls of fried meat."[31] The food of *ifṭār* receives an unusual degree of attention from medieval authors and observers. The choices of food, however – Shaykh Abū ʿUmar eating only barley bread and Shaykh al-Bustī eating none, for example, or al-Nawawī eating no fruit and al-Bustī eating only fruit – are explained only occasionally. In some cases the source of inspiration is clear, as with barley bread being a meal the Prophet would eat during lean times in Medina. The meaning of avoiding bread, on the other hand, is harder to discern. Interestingly enough, the historian Ibn al-Mustawfī had, while still a child, also visited Shaykh al-Bustī in Irbil, and he similarly recorded with precision the shaykh's diet: he avers that al-Bustī "never in his life ate bread, [rather he drank] just a little bit of milk."[32] Allowing perhaps for a seasonal change

Bidāyat al-Mujtahid wa Nihāyat al-Muqtaṣid, trans. Imran Ahsan Khan Nyazee, 2 vols. (Reading, 1994–6), I, 344–8.

[31] Ibn Munqidh, *An Arab-Syrian Gentleman and Warrior in the Period of the Crusades: Memoirs of Usāmah ibn-Munqidh*, trans. Philip K. Hitti (Princeton, 1987), 204.

[32] We do not know of course whether Ibn al-Mustawfī remembered the man's diet or heard of it later while writing his history of Irbil. He describes al-Bustī as a Sufi, not a learned ascetic, and says that his *zāwiya* in Irbil, which the historian had visited with his father, was

of diet, the parallel observations suggest that what the shaykh avoided eating was just as important as what he chose to eat; indeed, this configuration of "never ate" and "ate only" is standard: sometimes whole food groups were counted out, and sometimes a single one chosen. In addition to the quantity eaten, forgoing the pleasure of eating a range of foods was a sign of an abstemious and unrelenting ascetic.

What interested Usāma was not the choice of fruit as sustenance but how al-Bustī had reached the point of being able to sustain that diet of no bread or water, and, moreover, sustain it while fasting. Al-Bustī explained:

> I first fasted and suffered from hunger. But I found that I could stand the suffering. I then suffered from hunger for three days, saying to myself, "I will let food be [like] dead animals, which are allowed only in case of necessity after three days." I found myself able to stand that. Then I gave up regular eating and drinking. Now my system [*nafs*] is accustomed to it and does not resist its practice. Since then I have continued to do it.[33]

The word *nafs* is one of those peculiar words that can mean several contradictory things. The *nafs* appears as a term in Islamic philosophy, Sufism, and general usage meaning the soul or spirit, but in some cases specifically the "lower self" where physical appetites are located. Equally important for the case of al-Bustī is the more mundane meaning of *nafs* as a synonym for body (*jasad*).[34] All of these meanings may come into play here, and thus Hitti's translation of *nafs* as "system" perfectly captures the ambiguity of corporeal and abstract nuances in the word.

Though his brief continuous fast was only preparation for a more regular one, the way al-Bustī portrays that phase of bodily mortification is curiously morbid. The image that preoccupied him in his hunger, dead animals, was derived from the Qur'ānic prohibition of eating improperly slaughtered meat or carcasses that are found already dead.[35] He did not,

still known by the name of al-Bustī: Sharaf al-Dīn Abū'l-Barakāt Aḥmad Ibn al-Mustawfī, *Tārīkh Irbil: al-musammā Nabāhat al-balad al-khāmil bi-man waradahu min al-amāthil*, ed. Sāmī ibn al-Sayyid Khammās al-Ṣaqqār, 2 vols. (Baghdad, 1980), I, 112.

33 Ibn Munqidh, *An Arab-Syrian Gentleman*, 204; Ibn Munqidh, *Kitāb al-iʿtibār*, 171–2.

34 Ibn Manẓūr, *Lisān al-ʿarab*, VII, 231. The connection between all these meanings is, of course, the ability to refer to one's self or oneself, meaning the whole person, some aspects of which are purely physical, others conceptual.

35 See Qur'ān 16:116, 2:168, and 6:147, cited in J. Schacht, "Mayta," *EI*². I have found no evidence of jurists specifying that a state of necessity ensues after three days without sustenance. Two centuries later, Ibn Baṭṭūṭa gave an account of Shaykh Kuhrānī in Delhi who, in addition to perpetually fasting, often went without food until carrion became licit: *Riḥlat Ibn Baṭṭūṭa*, II, 329.

of course, actually eat carrion flesh. Instead, he chose to forgo permissible food until starvation became a real possibility, at which point, according to Islamic law, such meat is no longer forbidden. The inversion of the permissible (*ḥalāl*) and the prohibited (*ḥarām*) is part of al-Bustī's logic here. During the fast he considered all food as carrion, which by the end of the three days he was theoretically free to eat. The whole point of this exercise, which again takes a point in substantive law as its inspiration, was to force his body to withstand the difficulty of the perpetual fast while eating almost nothing.

His negative view of food, as something at least temporarily forbidden and repulsive, is rarely articulated so powerfully in the Islamic sources.[36] It may not have been shared by many pious Muslims, or even by many ascetics, but his words are proof of how wide the margins of behavior could be when fasting and severe dietary regimes were combined. In contrast to the state of fasting, there were no rules or laws governing the restriction of food since the latter is not a formal category of worship (*ʿibāda*). This afforded the ascetics great latitude in expressing devotion through their hunger or their seemingly capricious choice of diet. The amount of detail offered underscores how food played a role, both concrete and symbolic, as the currency of pious transactions between God and the devotee. In their careful selection of foods, or the amount of food, to be consumed, many fasters not only abstained for God during the day, they also ate for God at night. Throughout this period, these approaches to food were constantly entwined as devotees and ascetics sought to create specific messages about how they used their bodies.

A Lacuna: How Much Fasting Is Too Much Fasting?

The impulse towards difficulty was at work even among those who were only fasters and not ascetics, such as Sultan Barsbāy, the ruler who was famous for his hunting parties. It is clear in his case why trends in fasting demand to be analyzed separately, for ascetic attitudes towards food do not account for the pattern he established. His stacking of fast days – in summer and winter, twice a week, at the beginning and ends of months and so on – raises an important question: was this too much? Although each of the sultan's fasts was ascribed to the Prophet, there are no hadiths

[36] *Mayta* technically refers to meats prohibited for a variety of reasons, but to the jurists and among Muslims generally the term is emotionally charged, evoking something viscerally repellent in the way that rotting carcasses – rather than merely dead animals – are, according to Mohammad H. Benkheira ("Chairs illicites en Islam: essai d'interprétation anthropologique de la notion de *mayta*," *Studia Islamica* 84, 2 [1996]: 26–7).

stating that the Prophet did them all at once, or even consistently. One often-cited hadith portrays Muḥammad as sometimes fasting so much that his Companions thought he would never cease and sometimes not fasting for so long that they thought he would never fast again.[37] Thus in observing several different fasts simultaneously, Sultan Barsbāy was not following a single custom of the Prophet, but rather several of them.

As we saw above, one place someone could turn to for answers about both when and how to fast were the contemporary texts of substantive law (*furūʿ al-fiqh*). The jurists' task in these *furūʿ* texts was to decide whether a particular fast had or had not been condoned by the Prophet. If he had condoned a fast, then it would be a valid and recommendable practice (*masnūn*). The continuous fast, for example, was designated *makrūh* (disliked, disapproved of) or *ḥarām* (prohibited) not because the jurists deemed it to be excessive but because Muḥammad had said not to do it. The sultan's schedule, on the other hand, highlights what appears at first to be a lacuna in Sunnī substantive law, for the medieval texts of *furūʿ* that explain the various types of supererogatory fasts do not tell people how much or how little of it to do. That is to say, when it came to matters of voluntary worship, Islamic substantive law was not prescriptive. The jurists discussed what counted as legitimate practice but did not dictate what *should* be done. There was little room, at least in this type of legal literature, for considerations of excessive fasting.[38]

Legal questions over which fasts to undertake did arise, and they are sometimes addressed in fatwas. Ibn Taymiyya, for example, was asked to give a fatwa on the following problem:

> A man had vowed to fast on Mondays and Thursdays and then began to think it was better to fast for two days and break the fast for two days. But that couldn't be arranged without it ending up that either he fasted on four days of the week, and broke it on three, or broke it for four days and fasted for three. Which is better?

Ibn Taymiyya answered that if he shifted from fasting on Monday and Thursday to fasting for a day and then eating for a day, it would be a shift

[37] For thirteenth-century discussions of this hadith see Abū Shāma, *Kitāb al-Bāʿith*, 166–7; and ʿIzz al-Dīn ʿAbd al-ʿAzīz ibn ʿAbd al-Salām al-Sulamī, *al-Fatāwā al-Mawṣiliyya*, ed. Īyād Khālid al-Ṭabbāʿ (Damascus and Beirut, 1999), 107–8.

[38] A fascinating exception is Ibn Qudāma's commentary on the perpetual fast, which will be discussed below. There are a few instances when the jurists do prescribe what should be done, such as when an action was clearly, as part of the *sunna*, a voluntary practice so well established and laudable that it should be observed by all – fasting on the day of ʿĀshūrāʾ, for instance.

for the better.[39] At issue, for Ibn Taymiyya, were the legal consequences of not accomplishing what one vows to do. This is permitted, he says, if the task one has promised to do is exchanged for an even more positive one. He gives the example of someone who vowed to pray at the al-Aqṣā mosque in Jerusalem and then ends up praying at one of the mosques in Mecca or Medina instead.

Ibn Taymiyya did not need to address the fact that the weekly-alternating-two-day fast was not among those listed by the jurists, for there would have been nothing wrong with it so long as the man complied with the rules of fasting.[40] Someone could remain true to the spirit and the form of Islamic voluntary fasting while performing a fast not discussed by the jurists. But what really seems to have troubled this particular faster, who seems not to have realized that daily alternation would solve his even/odd problem, was whether to favor with his extra day the state of the fast or the state of the feast as he arranged his week. The real question was: Should he define himself as a faster or an eater? Ibn Taymiyya offered no guidance on this point.

If Islamic law, as a body of literature, does not condemn excessive fasting, and all valid voluntary fasts are sanctioned, then the logical conclusion seems to be that there is no such thing as too much fasting. In fact, from a legal standpoint, this is true. And it seems probable, given the broad interest in substantive law among the pious, that it also translated into a sentiment that lies behind cultural practices of fasting in late medieval Islam. If there was a social conception of excess being a good thing when it relates to worshipping God, the term "excessive" ceases to apply in this context. Or, rather, the term can be applied only in a positive sense: the men and women who fasted much of their lives were exceptional – that is, exceptionally pious – but were fully within the bounds of acceptable Islamic practice.[41] Their frequent fasting caused no anxiety among the

39 The fast that Ibn Taymiyya suggests is known as David's Fast: Ibn Taymiyya, *Majmūʿ fatāwā*, XXV, 289–90.

40 In other words, people were not told to limit themselves to the "canonical" fasts listed by jurists. The jurists merely list as many fasts as they think have merit by virtue of their being mentioned in the hadith. In the *Iḥyāʾ* al-Ghazzālī adds several to the usual list, including a three-day program: one day of fasting and two of eating. But in this text he is not concerned with specifying which practices had been vetted by previous jurists as much as with presenting a wide range of religious exercises that might benefit a worshipper: al-Ghazzālī, *Iḥyāʾ*, I, 237–8. In his commentary on Shāfiʿī law, however, he sticks to the basic list set forth by his legal school (al-Ghazzālī, *al-Wajīz fī fiqh al-Imām al-Shāfiʿī*, ed. ʿAlī Muʿawwaḍ and ʿĀdil ʿAbd al-Mawjūd, 2 vols. [Beirut, 1997], I, 241).

41 In pursuing this question, I benefited from a discussion with Professor Hossein Modarressi; he bears no responsibility for shortcomings in the conclusions I have drawn.

jurists. On the contrary, far from showing signs of disapproval, the jurists themselves often embraced heavy fasting schedules. Increasing the *difficulty* of a practice was a different matter and a somewhat grayer area. As will be discussed later, one jurist did voice concerns about the potential dangers of fasting, particularly when combined with severe eating habits, but he addressed them in a different genre of religious commentary.

Motives and Benefits

Well before the fifteenth century the impulse behind Sultan Barsbāy's "excessive" fasting was readily understood. Apart from any personal motives that could lead devotees to select a particular kind of supererogatory fast, there is one important reason why they all would want to fast voluntarily and often – a reason so basic that it is easily obscured by the creative patterns exhibited by individuals. Their fasts fall into the general category of supererogatory pious acts, or *nawāfil* (the singular of which is *nāfila*). Extra prayers at night are the best-known example of *nawāfil* because the Qur'ān mentions them specifically, but one also finds people who "fasted as *nāfila* most of the time."[42] Heavenly reward for these acts is at once implicit, because they please God, and explicit, since the specific rewards are described in abundant detail in the hadith. In the broader conception of the term, just about anything that was lawful and intended as a gesture of devotion to God was deemed a *nāfila*, even if it was not a formal practice of worship. Walking to a mosque instead of riding is an excellent example. These voluntary acts were always good, and it is important to note that they did not have to be difficult in order to gain merit. This most fundamental building-block of Islamic piety explains, in large part, the popularity of frequent fasting. It also partially explains the appeal of strenuous fasting in the late medieval period. Yet there were other motivations for voluntary fasts that medieval Muslims would have understood.

Ibn Taghrībirdī's pleasant depiction of Barsbāy fasting at his private picnics suggests that this was the sultan's chief area of expertise

[42] Nighttime prayer is referred to in the Qur'ān, e.g., 17:81. When one scholar was described as being distinguished by "self-control, piety, godliness and observance of both the sunna and the *nawāfil*," it refered to discrete acts of voluntary worship that could include both fasting and prayer: Ibn Rajab, *Dhayl ʿalā Ṭabaqāt al-Ḥanābila*, I, 226. In the example of the man who "fasted as *nāfila* most of the time," the emphasis is on the voluntary nature of an ongoing practice. This was Qadi Ṣadr al-Dīn of Baalbek, who will be discussed further in Chapter 3. In his case the term may have distinguished not only the voluntary from the obligatory but also what was truly "surplus" from what was commonly recommended as supererogatory practice: al-Yūnīnī, *Dhayl Mir'āt al-zamān*, I, 244.

in godliness, and simultaneously, of course, the setting underscored his conviviality with his comrades. But news of his acts of voluntary worship was bound to reach the public domain, and one wonders if he intended to cleanse not just his soul but also his public image. Fasts were a common way of atoning for misdeeds, even among sultans.[43] In order to answer the question of why a strenuous approach to fasting was so prevalent from the thirteenth century onward, however, it is necessary to consider the available meanings of the Islamic fast current at the time.

For many who lived in this period, the meaning of supererogatory fasting would have been influenced by earlier Sufi authors who discussed fasting as a means of freeing the heart from desire and from the concerns of the mortal world. For some of them, fasting could also be a technique, a stage in training the soul along the path towards knowledge of God.[44] Many pious men who engaged in long or difficult fasts in the Ayyubid and Mamluk periods were indeed Sufis, and food and hunger frequently appear as motifs in connection with them, as was the case with Shaykh al-Bustī's continuous fast. In a typical anecdote, a travelling Sufi preacher named Muẓaffar Ibn Shāshīr (d. 607/1210), known for his wit, was once sought out by someone who complained to him in private, "I am sick and hungry." His response was: "Praise your Lord, for you have been restored to health!"[45] Yet there are several reasons for being cautious in ascribing Sufi tendencies to all fasters, or equating difficult or "extreme" fasting with the practices of Sufism.

For one thing, although Ibn Shāshīr's rejoinder is characteristically Sufi (that is, edifying retorts like this one are common in stories of Sufis), the valorization of hunger is a much older theme, and it had appeal for many types of Muslims.[46] In addition, the programs of fasting that

[43] See Maribel Fierro, "Caliphal Authority and Expiation in al-Andalus," in *Islamic Legal Interpretation: Muftis and their Fatwas*, ed. Muhammad Khalid Masud, Brinkley Messick, and David S. Powers (Cambridge, Mass., 1996), 55–62.

[44] Freeing the heart and the suppression of bodily desires, for instance, appear in Abū Ṭālib al-Makkī's discussion of fasting, from which al-Ghazzālī quotes long passages almost verbatim: Abū Ṭālib al-Makkī, *Qūt al-qulūb*, I, 156, 159–61; al-Ghazzālī, *Iḥyā'*, I, 234–6. However, there is little discussion in either text of the possibility of achieving intimate knowledge of God through fasting. For an informative overview see Valerie J. Hoffman, "Eating and Fasting for God in Sufi Tradition," *Journal of the American Academy of Religion* 63, 3 (1995); for other examples of mystical interpretions, see Schimmel, *Mystical Dimensions*, e.g., 316; 376.

[45] Abū Shāma, *Tarājim*, 77; Ibn Kathīr has his name as Ibn Sāsīr: *Bidāya*, XIII, 67.

[46] See Bonner, *Aristocratic Violence*, 155–84 on ascetic attitudes toward restriction of food in early Islam. Although some of these were embraced by Sufis, Schimmel asserts that

individual pious men and women designed for themselves go far beyond a stage on the Sufi Path. The Sufi fasters mentioned in the historical texts are not usually *murīdūn* (novices) but rather senior shaykhs who fasted into old age. Medieval Muslims trusted that devotional practices brought them closer to God but did not necessarily understand this in a mystical sense.[47] Nor did they articulate a link between bodily practices and knowledge of God. The impulse towards extreme fasting in this period comes from broader Islamic notions of what voluntary devotional acts (*nawāfil*) mean, and perhaps more plainly from the precise ways the body can be used in Islamic worship. If the sources are not explicit about why excessive fasting became so common in the late medieval period, the answer can only be found by asking questions about the themes associated with voluntary fasting during these centuries.

There was an apparently widespread conviction in the medieval period that making fasting arduous had a beneficial effect. This may have been the case because so many beloved and saintly contemporary figures had distinguished themselves by undertaking strenuous fasts; their ability to excel in this way was evidence of their saintliness. (On the other hand, it may be that these figures were drawn to fasting because people found it so impressive.) To begin with, even regular fasting was seen as a difficult undertaking when not performed communally. Ibn al-Ḥājj, writing in the fourteenth century, alerted readers to the laxity of women's fasting practices in a text devoted to religious deviation (*bidʿa*). During Ramaḍān, according to Islamic law, a woman who is menstruating must not fast on those days but instead make up for them by fasting after the month is over. In his day, Ibn al-Ḥājj claimed, some women were fasting while menstruating and then, when Ramaḍān ended, would not make up for the days during which they had been menstruating.

> Some of them justify that by saying that fasting is harder for them while everyone else is breaking their fasts. There is no dispute here: she who

"the great [Sufi] masters have always acknowledged that hunger is only a means to spiritual progress, not a goal in itself": *Mystical Dimensions*, 116.

47 That is, the aim of reaching "nearness" to God was not generally construed as a mystical pursuit, but rather as something achieved through adhering to the rules and rituals of Islam or through other pious acts. Al-Ḥiṣnī, discussing the meaning of *ikhlāṣ* (sincerity and constancy in one's religious actions), says: "Ikhlāṣ means that he desires through his obedience to achieve nearness (*al-taqarrub*) to God": al-Ḥiṣnī, *al-Muʾmināt*, 14. Ibn Taghrībirdī explains that the amir Sayf al-Dīn Sūdūn (d. 850/1446) had this in mind when he provided a new roof for the Sanctuary in Mecca: "In doing so, he desired nearness (*al-taqarrub*) to God Most High for this deed": Ibn Taghrībirdī, *al-Nujūm al-zāhira*, XV, 517.

does this is sinning (*āthima*). She is still required to make up for those days, and furthermore repentance is also obligatory for her.[48]

The women's complaint related to the difficulty of fasting at mealtimes or when preparing food for a meal one could not eat.[49] Their justification perhaps sheds light on the motives of Sultan Barsbāy, who made his voluntary fasting harder not only by doing it frequently but also by participating in meals without eating. How widespread the practice discussed by Ibn al-Ḥājj may have been is debatable, since women who were at all educated were not likely to have misunderstood the basic requirements of *ṣawm*.[50] Indeed, the historian al-Ṣafadī noted with pride that his wife Fāṭima "rushed to make up for her days of menstruation during the month of Ramaḍān" by fasting on the days immediately following the month's end.[51]

Short voluntary fasts often had strong currents of repentance or hopes for salvation, and in such contexts the decision to increase the level of difficulty is not surprising. The first *ṣawm al-wiṣāl* that Ibn Baṭṭūṭa performed was a spontaneous response to being put under guard by the sultan of Delhi for frequenting the cave of a popular local shaykh who had fallen from favor. Sure that he was going to die, Ibn Baṭṭūṭa was suddenly inspired by God to begin reciting a verse from the Qurʾān. He said it thirty-three thousand times and then began nine days of fasting, breaking his fast with nothing but water at sunset. He ate one meal on the fifth day and every day read the Qurʾān in its entirety. This demonstration of

[48] Ibn al-Ḥājj, *al-Madkhal*, I, 272. Huda Lutfi discusses this passage as an example of Ibn al-Ḥājj's views on women's practices in "Manners and Customs of Fourteenth Century Cairene Women: Female Anarchy versus Male Sharʿi Order in Muslim Prescriptive Treatises," in *Women in Middle Eastern History: Shifting Boundaries in Sex and Gender*, ed. Nikki R. Keddie and Beth Baron (New Haven, 1991), 99–121.

[49] I believe it is possible to see the Prophet's call for voluntary fasting during the first six days of the following month, Shawwāl, as a way of perpetuating the community's preparedness for fasting, thus accommodating women and those who had missed days because of sickness or travel. For example, "Whoever fasts the month of Ramaḍān as well as six days of Shawwāl has achieved the *ṣawm al-dahr*": Muslim, *Ṣaḥīḥ*, 494, hadith no. 204. Ibn Qudāma cites the dissenting opinion of the Mālikīs: people who fast the first six days in Shawwāl "add something to Ramaḍān which is not part of it": *Mughnī*, III, 102–3.

[50] The law prohibiting fasting during menstruation would have been widely known, but, judging from Ibn al-Ḥājj's comments, the details of how one makes good the lost days may have been less clear. They are spelled out in legal discussions of *qaḍāʾ*, an act done to compensate for a dispensation granted – e.g., for temporary sickness or menstruation during Ramaḍān.

[51] al-Ṣafadī, *Aʿyān al-ʿaṣr*, IV, 31.

piety earned him his freedom, which, he noted, was an extremely unexpected outcome considering the capricious and bloodthirsty habits of the sultan.[52] Not only is this a vivid example of why someone might increase the difficulty of a fast, it also shows how effective that increase could be. Ibn Baṭṭūṭa thanked God profusely for his deliverance; his captor meanwhile must have read the performance as a protest. Fasting as a hunger strike was unusual but not unprecedented, and when combined with Qurʾānic recitation and supplications to God, Ibn Baṭūṭṭa's ordeal would have been hard to ignore.[53]

While the true fasters – those who were described as "full of fasting" (*kathīr al-ṣawm*) – had chosen to make this form of devotional piety a regular part of their lives, supererogatory fasts often were not expressions of piety per se. It would be hard to overestimate how strong the belief in the efficacy of fasts tended to be in this period and, at the risk of stating the obvious, how widely available fasting was, or rather the body was, as a means of achieving a specific goal: to obtain God's forgiveness, to thank him for a bounty bestowed, to atone for a misdeed, to prepare oneself for death.[54] The same impulse to increase the level of difficulty arises in these contexts too, so that even a common supererogatory practice, one recommended by the jurists, such as a three-day fast during the middle days of a month, could be made challenging in ways not discussed in legal texts. When Ibn al-Zamlakānī, the Shāfiʿī qadi of Aleppo, fell mortally ill in the year 727/1327, he was travelling with his son, Taqī al-Dīn, to Cairo where he expected to receive from the sultan a new appointment as the chief qadi of Damascus. It was during the month of Shaʿbān, a time thought to be especially beneficial for propitiatory acts. He told his son he was dying, and then, Taqī al-Dīn recalled, "he ordered me to fast for a while. After that he ordered me to fast for three days, breaking my fast at the end of the day with water mixed with frankincense." Changing the type of fasts performed sounds like a technique of training the *nafs*, as it had been with al-Bustī. Indeed, in another version, which emphasizes the father's Sufi leanings, the son says, "Because he was my shaykh, he

[52] Ibn Baṭṭūṭa, *Riḥlat Ibn Baṭṭūṭa*, 409–10; Ibn Baṭṭūṭa, *Travels of Ibn Baṭṭūṭa*, III, 765–6.

[53] In a parallel story, Mufarraj al-Damāmīnī (d. 648/1250–1), an Ethiopian slave who later became greatly renowned as a saint, used fasting as a means of protest: "After he was purchased, he spent six months without eating or drinking. His master beat him, but he remained unmoved": ʿUmar ibn ʿAlī Ibn al-Mulaqqin, *Ṭabaqāt al-awliyāʾ*, ed. Nūr al-Dīn Shurayba (Cairo, 1393/1973), 472.

[54] For a compelling discussion of how the issue of ritual efficacy has been dealt with in contemporary scholarship see Marion Katz, "The Ḥajj and the Study of Islamic Ritual," *Studia Islamica* 98/99 (2004).

ordered me into solitude (*khalwa*) and ordered me to fast for three days, breaking my fast each day with water and frankincense."[55]

His father sent him to the mosque on the third night of the fast, which coincided with the holy night of Niṣf Shaʿbān, and there, while praying, the son received a vision:

> A great shrine appeared to me [poised] between heaven and earth. Outside it were ladders and stairs, on which people were climbing from earth towards heaven. So I climbed with them and started seeing inscriptions on every step: "Deputyship of the Royal Treasury," and on the following step: "Office of the Exchequer," and on the next: "Clerkship of Official Correspondence," and on the following steps: "Madrasa of so-and-so," and "Judgeship of Aleppo." When I got to this step, I felt anxious and then returned to my senses.[56]

These were the positions and appointments his father had held over the course of his life, and the judgeship of Aleppo was indeed the last post Ibn al-Zamlakānī would hold.[57] He died not long after, knowing his ascent towards heaven had been confirmed.

The story is a strange one. The vision belonged to the father, and the fast to the son. Could Ibn al-Zamlakānī have designed the water-only fast to ready his son for a visionary experience, perhaps in advance of his own death? It was, after all, timed to coincide with Niṣf Shaʿbān, the fifteenth of the month, which was popularly thought to be the night when life or death was decreed for all creatures; the night is spent in prayer because it is said that "God would descend to the lowest heaven, grant his forgiveness to those seeking it, food to those begging for it, and health to the sick." And, another hadith says, for the three days leading up to it, the Prophet beseeches God for mercy for his people.[58] Was the

[55] Ibn Ḥajar, *Durar*, IV, 48. Ibn al-Zamlakānī was famous for his animosity toward Ibn Taymiyya and for having written a refutation of Ibn Taymiyya's positions on divorce and visiting graves. See Ibn Kathīr, *Bidāya*, XIV, 136–7.

[56] al-Kutubī, *Fawāt al-wafayāt*, IV, 8–9.

[57] Ibid., IV, 7. Despite his prestigious positions and having the respect of his colleagues, Ibn al-Zamlakānī was hated by the people of Aleppo, who rejoiced when he was recalled to Cairo. He struggled with visions and delusions, which affected how he acted and caused such animosity that al-Kutubī suggests he may have been poisoned. On the position of clerk, Carl F. Petry comments: "The identification of clerks with Sufism, with its connotations of popularly acknowledged piety, that is implied by this pattern contrasts markedly with the image of all bureaucratic agents as arms of the state. In fact, the clerks enjoyed a special position in the bureaucracy, as indicated by their relative immunity from Mamluk harassment": *The Civilian Elite of Cairo in the Later Middle Ages* (Princeton, 1981), 213.

[58] For these and other hadiths see M. J. Kister, "'Shaʿbān Is My Month': A Study of an Early Tradition," in *Studia Orientalia: Memoriae D. H. Baneth Dedicata* (Jerusalem, 1979), 24–6.

water-only fast meant to increase the chance of Ibn al-Zamlakānī obtaining God's forgiveness? In that case, the fast as well as the vision belong to the father. Though the jurists agree that it is not possible to undertake a fast for someone else, even if that person is sick and incapable of fasting, the vision seems to suggest that this is precisely what happened.[59]

Such stories are useful in establishing the contours of how the body was reduced to a useful object in worship: borrowing someone else's person as the site of a religious performance is a particularly apt example of how medieval bodies could be put to use. If a medicinal additive such as frankincense mitigated the effects of not eating, it also betrays the fact that the fast prescribed was deliberately difficult.[60] Completing a difficult fast demonstrated mastery over the body and its physical sensations by virtue of having willingly surrendered it to strenuous tasks that please God – in Taqī al-Dīn's case, for the sake of a father. More typical stories of fasters emphasize in a less obvious manner the same theme of distance from physical sensations such as hunger and exhaustion, as we will see.

Part II: The Case of the Perpetual Fast

Regardless of the ways in which medieval devotees and ascetics could make a fast more difficult, Islamic fasting itself is challenging for reasons beyond the hunger it provokes. It has its own etiquette, shared by those who fast during Ramaḍān and those who fast voluntarily: one should be joyful both when fasting and when breaking the fast; one should be generous and virtuous, avoiding quarrels even when provoked by slander.[61] Thus fasting for long periods requires, in addition to maintaining control over hunger and sexual desire, a more or less permanent commitment to an ethic of kindness and cheerfulness. The medieval sources note that many exemplary fasters – and the perpetual fasters in particular – were able to do this. In one description of Shaykh Abū ʿUmar Ibn Qudāma, the

[59] It is legitimate, however, to fast on behalf of a person who dies with a fast unfinished or owed as expiation, according to some jurists: Ibn Rushd, *The Distinguished Jurist's Primer*, I, 349–51.

[60] The frankincense would have been burned and pulverized before being added to water. Some risk was involved: "It increases the reasoning power and eliminates loss of memory. It checks diarrhoea and vomiting, calms palpitation of the heart but can also lead to mental disturbances": A. Dietrich, "Lubān," *EI*²; also [ʿAbd Allāh ibn Aḥmad Ibn al-Bayṭār], *Traité des simples par Ibn el-Beïthar*, trans. Lucien Leclerc, 3 vols. (Paris, n.d. [1877–83]), III, 200–4.

[61] On the quality of happiness see Qurʾān 2:183; on the other virtues see for example Muslim, *Ṣaḥīḥ*, 485, bāb 29 and 30; Ibn Qudāma, *Mughnī*, III, 111.

ubiquitous pairing of "fasting by day and praying at night" was replaced by the phrase "he fasted perpetually and never stopped smiling."[62] In contrast to the somber demeanor associated with her profession, the famous hadith transmitter Zaynab Bint al-Wāsiṭī (d. 795/1392) was described by her student al-Dhahabī as "a devotee, fasting by day and praying by night, humble and charming."[63] The frequent references to charming and smiling perpetual fasters suggest that this attitude was not just a quality much prized in late medieval Islamic culture (though one suspects that it was), but rather an impressive feat like any other that the exemplars strove to accomplish.

Difficult enough in its own right, the *ṣawm al-dahr* was seldom an isolated practice. For many it was only the threshold of piety. Shaykh Abū ʿUmar's schedule of pious activities in Damascus, for example, was busy indeed: since his youth, reports Abū Shāma, he had prayed through the night and always kept up all the daily prayers; for the last third of each night he would go out to the mosque in the darkness and pray until dawn; in the mornings he taught lessons on the Qurʾān; in the afternoons he read it alone; on Fridays after prayer he would visit the cemetery; on Tuesdays and Thursdays he would climb Mount Qāsyūn and pray at Abel's tomb for the afternoon; on his way down, he collected firewood, tied it in bundles and carried it to the residences for widows and orphans.[64] It was a long climb in both directions for a faster who could not avail himself of water. Shaykh Abū ʿUmar seemed determined to prove that neither fasting nor any other acts of devotion could diminish his physical abilities. The only sign of strain that betrayed him was a body made thin by eating barley bread.

[62] Ibn Kathīr says, "He was full of devotion, asceticism and nighttime prayer; he fasted perpetually and he never stopped smiling" ("Kāna kathīr al-ʿibāda wa'l-zahhāda wa'l-tahajjud wa yaṣūmu al-dahr wa kāna lā yazūlu mutabassiman"): *Bidāya*, XIII, 64. Abū Shāma quotes someone as saying that "the light of devotion (*ʿibāda*) was upon him, and he never stopped smiling": *Tarājim*, 71. Likewise, Shaykh Abū'l-Thanāʾ al-Naʿʿāl, mentioned earlier, was also portrayed as friendly and smiling: "kāna shaykhan muhīban, laṭīfan, kayyisan, bāshan, mutabassiman, yaṣūmu al-dahr ...": Abū Shāma, *Tarājim*, 82.

[63] The last two adjectives are *khāshiya* and *fātina*: al-Dhahabī, *Muʿjam shuyūkh*, 203. On seriousness as a quality promoted by the hadith transmitters of the ninth and tenth centuries C.E. see Melchert, "The Piety of the Hadith Folk," 427–8. Refraining from laughter (as opposed to not smiling) was a typical ascetic trait in the period Melchert discusses, and was based on the depiction of Muḥammad's self-control as reported in the hadith. But the medieval ascetics and devotees, even non-fasters, were so frequently described as smiling that there is clearly a different theme at work.

[64] Abū Shāma, *Tarājim*, 71. He prayed at the Cave of Blood (Maghārat al-damm), a hallowed spot on Mount Qāsyūn, so named because the murder of Abel was supposed to have occurred there.

Yet the perpetual fast is a curious choice for a devotee such as Shaykh Abū ʿUmar since it is the one with the most complicated history. An often-cited hadith suggests that fasting as a semi-permanent bodily state was something the Prophet had sought to eradicate.

> ʿAbd Allāh ibn ʿAmr reported: The Prophet came to me and said, "Haven't I been informed that you stay awake at night in prayer and fast during the day?" I replied, "Yes." He said, "Do not do that. Pray at night but also sleep; fast and then eat, because you have a duty to your body, and a duty to your eyes, a duty to your guest and a duty to your wife.[65] May you live a long life! It is sufficient for you to fast for three days each month, since every good deed receives a ten-fold reward, and thus it is [like fasting] the whole year." But I insisted and so was I burdened: I said, "I can fast more than that!" And the Prophet said, "Then fast three days every week." Still I insisted and again was I burdened: I said, "I can fast more than that!" So the Prophet said, "Fast as the Prophet David used to fast." I asked, "And what was David's fast?" He replied, "Half the time."[66]

Strangely, the Prophet's solution of "David's Fast" – fasting and eating on alternate days – is scarcely mentioned in historical texts from the late medieval period, even though writers such as al-Ghazzālī had promoted it over the perpetual fast, and Ibn Taymiyya preferred it to fasting on Mondays and Thursdays.[67] And in another version of this hadith, cited by Ibn al-Jawzī, when ʿAbd Allāh asks to do better than David's Fast, the Prophet replies, "There is nothing better than that."[68]

Some medieval scholars, at least those who were not themselves undertaking a perpetual fast, may have been alarmed by the popularity of the practice among their contemporaries, yet few criticized it in genres of social commentary. If these hadiths and the many others like them suggest that the *ṣawm al-dahr* should have been categorized as *makrūh* ("disliked") in Islamic law, by the medieval period this was by no means the case. Shaykh Abū ʿUmar's brother Muwaffaq al-Dīn Ibn Qudāma (d. 620/1223), the renowned Ḥanbalī jurist, and the equally famous Shāfiʿī scholar al-Nawawī (d. 676/1277) both note that there had been differences of opinion among earlier jurists regarding this fast, yet in the end they side with those who assert that it is "not disliked" on two conditions. In the *Rawḍat al-ṭālibīn*, al-Nawawī reports:

[65] Or possibly "your body has a right to you," etc.

[66] Bukhārī, *Ṣaḥīḥ*, 346, hadith no. 1975. There are several versions of this hadith in the canonical collections.

[67] al-Ghazzālī, *Iḥyāʾ*, I, 238.

[68] Ibn al-Jawzī, *Talbīs Iblīs*, 139–40.

> The author of the *Tahdhīb*, among others, designated the perpetual fast *makrūh*. Al-Ghazzālī said it is *masnūn* (permissible). And most say: If someone fears injury from it or neglects his duties because of it, then it is disliked. If not, then it is not disliked. And in that case it is desirable that he break his fast on the days of the Feasts and the days of *tashrīq*.[69]

Fasting is prohibited on the few days of the year when the Islamic community feasts together, namely on the two holy days of ʿĪd al-Fiṭr and ʿĪd al-Aḍḥā and during the three days of *tashrīq*, when pilgrims in Mina are celebrating the conclusion of the hajj. So, for healthy people, if the year-round fast is broken on those occasions, there is no other legal objection.[70] The implication is that only the days of feasting would have made the Prophet forbid ʿAbd Allāh ibn ʿAmr from perpetual fasting.

The discourse on the *ṣawm al-dahr* was still evolving well into the thirteenth century, as al-Nawawī's presentation shows. In this passage al-Nawawī has condensed the statements of his predecessor al-Rāfiʿī (d. 623/1226) who had written a commentary on al-Ghazzālī's *Wajīz*. However, he omits a section where al-Rāfiʿī spells out why the perpetual fast was disliked and proceeds directly to the favorable opinion of al-Ghazzālī. Following this gap, the third or majority opinion ("and most say ...") serves to qualify and ultimately remove the objection. The positive and negative opinions are no longer distinct, but rather dependent on each other. Yet al-Rāfiʿī had said specifically that the Prophet was not a perpetual faster, and had cited both a second hadith involving ʿAbd Allāh ibn ʿAmr and one stating even more plainly that Muḥammad had prohibited the perpetual fast.

Commenting rather negatively upon al-Ghazzālī's claim that the *ṣawm al-dahr* is recommendable, al-Rāfiʿī says that a practice can be *masnūn* in two ways.

> The first is that the Prophet did it regularly, so the *ṣawm al-dahr* is not *masnūn* according to this meaning. The second is that it is [something he] recommended, and as for the *ṣawm al-dahr* having this quality, there is also discussion. The author of the *Tahdhīb*, may God have mercy on him, among others, expressed the opinion that in its nature the fast is *makrūh*. They offer in support of this view two things: the fact that the Prophet told ʿAbd Allāh ibn ʿAmr, "He who fasts perpetually has not fasted. A fast for three days each month is a perpetual fast,"

[69] al-Nawawī, *Rawḍat al-ṭālibīn*, II, 253.The *Tahdhīb* was written by al-Baghawī (d. 516/1122), a famous Shāfiʿī jurist and hadith expert.

[70] Al-Shāfiʿī is the authority most scholars cite as having identified the problem of the feast days, e.g., Ibn Qudāma, *Mughnī*, III, 97–8.

> and the fact that it is reported [about the Prophet] that, "He forbade the perpetual fast."[71]

He goes on to explain, or perhaps concede, that "most" jurists agree that if people fear for their health it is *makrūh*, and otherwise it is acceptable. They attribute the Prophet's having forbidden the fast either to the possibility of bodily harm or to not breaking the fast on the feast days. Nevertheless, the fact that al-Rāfiʿī felt the need to remind people, let alone jurists, of what is required for something to be designated *masnūn* in Islamic law – "recommendable" being one of the more familiar terms in the legal lexicon – would seem to make his views on the matter rather plain.

Going back a step further, al-Ghazzālī himself had expressed doubt as well, not in the *Wajīz* but in the *Iḥyāʾ*, where he noted that some previous jurists disliked the perpetual fast. In his opinion this was on account of two things, the first being the prohibition of fasting on feast days.

> The other is that the faster develops a distaste for the custom (*sunna*) of the sunset meal, and he makes fasting an encumbrance (*ḥijr*) on himself, even though God likes you to take advantage of His easing of requirements as much as He likes you to follow His prescriptions to the fullest extent. If none of this is involved, and the person foresees the improvement of his soul through the *ṣawm al-dahr*, let him do it. A number of the Companions and Successors did so.[72]

The loss of appetite or taste for food combined with a misguided enthusiasm for difficult rituals were serious risks that he felt compelled to address in a work aimed at guiding ordinary worshippers rather than jurists. Yet he concludes with a laudatory hadith describing how the perpetual faster will escape the fires of hell. One cannot call al-Ghazzālī's attitude merely ambivalent, for his approbation and his warning are both strong.[73]

[71] ʿAbd al-Karīm ibn Muḥammad al-Rāfiʿī, *al-ʿAzīz sharḥ al-Wajīz al-maʿrūf bi'l-Sharḥ al-kabīr*, ed. ʿAlī Muḥammad Muʿawwaḍ and ʿĀdil Aḥmad ʿAbd al-Mawjūd, 14 vols. (Beirut, 1997), III, 247–8.

[72] al-Ghazzālī, *Iḥyāʾ*, I, 238. I have translated the term *al-ifṭār* as sunset meal rather than breaking the fast, but either might be meant here. When he discusses the perpetual fast in the *Wajīz* he says merely, "In general, the *ṣawm al-dahr* is *masnūn*, with the stipulation of breaking the fast on the two festival days and the days of *tashrīq*": al-Ghazzālī, *al-Wajīz*, I, 241.

[73] Though he does little more than clarify the points raised by Abū Ṭālib al-Makkī in the tenth century, his clarification may be an attempt to make the warning stronger. The neglect of the *sunna* is mentioned by al-Makkī; for al-Ghazzālī this neglect relates specifically to loss of interest in the meal of *ifṭār*: *Iḥyāʾ*, I, 238. His praise of the fast is slightly cooler than al-Makkī's in the *Qūt al-qulūb* where the author speaks of the positive effect

In the section that follows, he proceeds to explain at length the high regard the Prophet had for David's Fast, stressing that it is even more difficult than the *ṣawm al-dahr*.[74] Since he alluded to the risk of the perpetual fast becoming an obsession, perhaps the only way he could convince people not to undertake it was to offer them something even more challenging. Judging from the historical sources of the Ayyubid and Mamluk periods, which so rarely mention David's Fast, he did not succeed.

The failure to settle the issue once and for all before the twelfth century meant that it resurfaced as a contemporary issue thereafter, and the continuing discourse is one of the best places to track the evolving meanings of fasting. A hint of danger continued to dog nearly all formal discussions of the *ṣawm al-dahr* in the thirteenth century. Neglecting to follow the behavior of the Prophet was rarely the basis of the critique: whereas to al-Ghazzālī the danger had been largely linked to neglect of the *sunna*, at the close of the twelfth century the issue of physical harm became more central to the critique.

"The Devil has deceived people and made perpetual fasting seem good to them," writes Ibn al-Jawzī in the *Talbīs Iblīs*. While permitted if the person breaks the fast on the holy days of feasting, it nevertheless remains dangerous:

> It can deplete a person's strength so much that he becomes incapable of supporting his family and prevents him, due to chastity, from [marital relations with] his wife. In both *Ṣaḥīḥ* we find that the Prophet said: "You have a duty to your spouse." How many obligations will such a person neglect because of this supererogatory performance?[75]

Although the *ṣawm al-dahr* was not a vow of celibacy, the exigencies of daytime fasting, nighttime recitation, and a few hours of sleep left little time for bodily desires of any kind. One can see why David's Fast might be preferable and therefore, to some of the devotees, perhaps less attractive. In the end, Ibn al-Jawzī had to concede that some of the earliest Muslims had fasted perpetually. But he is quick to add that they were still able to uphold their duties to their families, or that, more commonly, they had no family at all.

of the fast on the heart and its role in breaking the *nafs*, or lower self (*inkisār nafsihi*). Once the faster recognizes that being in that state is good for his spiritual well-being, it is nearly obligatory that he fast: al-Makkī, *Qūt al-qulūb*, I, 158.

74 Ghazzālī also mentions, for those who find David's Fast too strenuous, the option of fasting for one day and breaking the fast for two: *Iḥyā'*, I, 238.

75 Ibn al-Jawzī, *Talbīs Iblīs*, 139. Like al-Ghazzālī, a second problem he mentions is that the person has neglected to take the "better" option that is available, namely David's Fast.

On one level his comments reflect the tension, noted also by al-Ghazzālī, between two ideals of behavior: doing what God asks; and doing a great deal more than required by God for His sake. To Ibn al-Jawzī, the latter threatened the social order – a recurring complaint in the *Talbīs Iblīs*. As his argument progresses, however, his anxiety focuses more narrowly on the body of the faster:

> A number of people in previous generations fasted perpetually, eating coarse food and only a little of that. Some went blind; others had their brains dry up. This is neglect of the obligatory duty to the body, urging it beyond what it can bear, and so is not permitted.[76]

The popular practice of mixing ascetical pursuits into already difficult ritual acts is, for this author, the source of the problem with the *ṣawm al-dahr*. The passage brings to mind the account of his contemporary, al-Bustī, who settled on a diet of pomegranates and grapes after having sought out the limits of what his body could bear while fasting. What was for al-Bustī a kind of calculated curiosity here appears to be either curiosity unchecked or self-mortification gone awry. This attention to bodily limits struck Ibn al-Jawzī as characteristic of ascetics who undertook the perpetual fast; and as we have seen, many if not most perpetual fasters in his day adopted ascetic diets. It was a trend he found disturbing.

Almost immediately, Ibn al-Jawzī's claims were rebutted by Ibn Qudāma, who wrote in the *Mughnī* that if someone were to suggest that the Prophet Muḥammad had objected to the *ṣawm al-dahr*, his reply would be:

> [The Prophet] only disliked the perpetual fast because of its weakening effect and its resemblance to celibacy (*tabattul*). Aside from that it is great indeed because of how it saturates time with worship and obedience.... There is no disagreement about its being recommendable.[77]

The possible dangers of the fast were admittedly severe ones, and given the negative opinion of celibacy in Islamic discourse, it is surprising that the devotees, and particularly the jurists, did not steer clear of the perpetual fast.[78] Why then did such a great number of them in the Ayyubid and Mamluk periods continue to choose the *ṣawm al-dahr* when it seems the

[76] Ibid., 140.
[77] The phrase about saturation is "istighrāqihi al-zamān bi'l-'ibāda": Ibn Qudāma, *al-Mughnī*, III, 103.
[78] For a fourteenth-century definition of *tabattul* as "cutting oneself off for the sake of worship" see Ibn Baydakīn al-Turkumānī, *Kitāb al-luma'*, I, 149–58.

most dubious, legally, and when there were ongoing concerns about its effects on the bodies and lives of its practitioners? One answer appears to be that the especially pious were inclined to walk that line precisely because they could. They could master the fast without falling prey to physical weakness or monkery. What appealed to them about that challenge is the key to understanding voluntary fasting in the medieval period.

Health and Excess

The discrepancy between the views of Ibn al-Jawzī and Ibn Qudāma, both Ḥanbalī jurists, relates to the issue of how the body is used in supererogatory worship in general, and specifically to the question of whether hardship in supererogatory performances is good or bad. The inherent excess of the perpetual fast received a nod of acknowledgment from Ibn Qudāma, and simultaneously bothered Ibn al-Jawzī because it violated his conception of the health of the body. Ibn Qudāma, for his part, was strongly committed to the overuse of the body. For one thing, his older brother Shaykh Abū ʿUmar, so revered in Damascus, was perhaps the city's finest example of the style of worship preferred by ascetic devotees – and a perpetual faster. But his concluding statement is more telling, and amusing, than any argument considered thus far. To lend a final piece of support to his argument in favor of the perpetual fast, Ibn Qudāma points out that the Prophet in another hadith had also forbidden ʿAbd Allāh ibn ʿAmr to read the Qurʾān excessively, telling him that saying "Lā ilāha ..." (there is no god [but God]) three times was like reading a third of the Qurʾān. So, Ibn Qudāma concludes, "this refers to the goodness of doing it even a little, and not to a dislike of doing it a lot."[79]

Nothing could better summarize the prevailing attitudes of these times towards supererogatory practices in general. After Ibn al-Jazwī, and over the course of the thirteenth century, the tension surrounding the perpetual fast arose not so much over whether the Prophet had sanctioned the fast or prohibited it, nor even over the issue of moderation in worship. The center of piety, in legal discourse, had shifted: excess in devotional practice was by now a given.[80] And thus the locus of tension was in the grayer area between enthusiasm and bodily harm.

[79] Ibn Qudāma, *Mughnī*, III, 103. Participants in popular devotional practices considered by some jurists to be dangerous innovations shared his point of view, according to Ukeles: "If congregational prayer is a virtuous activity, would not an extra congregational prayer be additionally virtuous?" (Ukeles, "Innovation or Deviation," 18).

[80] Currents in medieval European Christian piety provide an interesting parallel, although there the debate over excessive enthusiasm and bodily harm in the end – by the eleventh

A century later that tension is no longer perceptible, and its disappearance was precipitated by the rising popularity of a discourse about the body, which increasingly focused on its upkeep. Dietary advice fell within the responsibilities of scholars such as Ibn Jamāʿa, who counselled young people to enhance their memory for learning texts by avoiding sour apples, baklava, and vinegar, which would make them "senseless and stupid."[81] Medical treatments and diagnoses, the latter often dispensed rather freely by biographers, begin to intertwine with discussions of worship. When Ibn Kathīr noted the death in 734/1333 of the imam Zayn al-Dīn ʿAbd al-Raḥmān Ibn ʿUbaydān, a Ḥanbalī scholar and ascetic in Baalbek, he emphasized that the man had been greatly esteemed for his command of hadith, jurisprudence, and Sufi theory. Sometime before his death, Ibn ʿUbaydān began to exhibit strange behavior, according to the author, who explains: "Either his mind became afflicted or else he exerted himself too strenuously in his religious exercises and his insides burned up from hunger. He saw apparitions that weren't there."[82] Ibn al-Jawzī, who like Ibn Kathīr was not a physician, had used similar language in his theory of what happens to the brains of perpetual fasters who do not eat enough.[83]

Their comments evoke remarkably clearly tenth-century medical hypotheses, such as those of al-Majūsī. Trained in the medical theories of Galen and Rufus, al-Majūsī claimed that the brain could be affected by the "burnt-up humours" of the body. A build-up of black bile causes melancholy, and then "patients are given over to cares, broodings, anxieties and evil imaginings."[84] In borrowing this kind of terminology to describe Ibn ʿUbaydān, Ibn Kathīr was not issuing a critique of the man or his behavior. On the contrary, he provided a seemingly unemotional statement of possible diagnoses; at most, one discerns perhaps a note of regret over the loss of a respected and saintly figure. In other words, as a result of devotion Ibn ʿUbaydān's strange behavior was entirely comprehensible; for the risks of devotional excess were well known by this point in time. That the result of the shaykh's activities could possibly be read as

and twelfth centuries – had swung towards moderation, according to Giles Constable, "Attitudes Toward Self-inflicted Suffering in the Middle Ages," in *Culture and Spirituality in Medieval Europe*, Variorum Collected Studies Series 541 (Aldershot, 1986), 23.

81 Chamberlain, *Knowledge and Social Practice*, 146.

82 Ibn Kathīr, *Bidāya*, XIV, 176. This shaykh (possibly Ibn ʿAbīdān instead of ʿUbaydān) died around the age of sixty in 734/1333.

83 Ibn al-Jawzī, *Talbīs Iblīs*, 146.

84 Manfred Ullmann, *Islamic Medicine*, trans. Jean Watt (Edinburgh, 1974), 77.

a mishap rather than a dire warning is telling. After all, people were never praised in the medieval period for moderation in worship.

For some five centuries, Muslim doctors had studied Galenic pathology and other Hellenistic writings on medicine. The circulation of medical knowledge into non-medical circles was not new; indeed, it was a subject in the curricula of madrasas and a topic studied by rulers as well as students.[85] What is new is how historians, biographers, and social critics from the late twelfth century onward borrowed medical terminology to explain the results of pious activities. Earlier authors had not done this because they had not conceived of either the body or piety in quite the same way.[86] A general interest in the pathology of worship is suggested by discussions in which the focus is not on the cures available to ailing worshippers but on how they managed to persist in their devotions. If flawed, a body was likely to break down, and it required special care and maintenance. Al-Ṣafadī's assessment of the revered Shāfiʿī scholar Burhān al-Dīn al-Fazārī, a man given to fasting who died in 729/1328, is revealing in this regard: "He had a weakly constitution and his body was thin. His face was pretty and white, his skin was soft and he was straight of stature. He ate extremely little and was always snacking on the fruit of drumstick trees to repel the extreme dryness in his constitution."[87]

Again, illness commands attention. The drumstick tree is a species of the carob "resembling a large peach tree, abounding in Alexandria and having an admirable yellow flower," whose characteristics, according to several Muslim physicians, are coldness and wetness.[88] Whether Burhān

[85] Maimonides, for example, wrote a guide to health for the Ayyubid ruler al-Mālik al-Afḍal. See Max Meyerhof, "Sultan Saladin's Physician on the Transmission of Greek Medicine to the Arabs," in *Studies in Medieval Arabic Medicine: Theory and Practice* (London, 1984), 169–78. On medicine and the Hellenistic sciences taught in thirteenth-century madrasas see Chamberlain, *Knowledge and Social Practice*, 85. Background on views of medicine may be found in Franz Rosenthal, "The Defense of Medicine in the Medieval Muslim World," *Bulletin of the History of Medicine* 43 (1969). Rosenthal shows how in the tenth century medicine was defended as being no stranger than folk remedies; by the thirteenth century it was argued that medicine was natural and created by God (ibid., 525).

[86] Even in cases where disease was not related to piety, extensive medical conclusions were now part and parcel of biographical information. For example al-Kutubī wrote of a hadith transmitter, Ṣafī al-Dīn al-Qarāfī (d. 723/1323), that "when he grew older, he was beset by dryness and black bile [which produces melancholy] and then he became troubled and inclined towards solitude and was always talking to himself": al-Kutubī, *Fawāt al-wafayāt*, IV, 98.

[87] al-Ṣafadī, *al-Wāfī*, VI, 43–4; al-Kutubī, *Fawāt al-wafayāt*, I, 32–3.

[88] Edward William Lane, *An Arabic–English Lexicon*, 2 vols. (London, 1984 [1877]), I, 830–1. According to Ibn al-Bayṭār, this was the opinion of al-Maṣīḥī, who died in the

al-Dīn was already thin and made weaker by fasting or whether fasting had made him thin, this description shows how medieval authors – and others – had more than a passing interest in the physical health of their contemporaries. Burhān al-Dīn himself recounted how he had once met a shaykh on his travels who warned him to turn towards Aleppo and away from Cairo, which "is a hot place and will not agree with your constitution."[89] Did a more widespread awareness of medical knowledge propel this interest? It may have. But it is much more likely that medical terminology now fit with the authors' views on bodily piety. A few decades later, in the mid-fourteenth century, the Ḥanbalī jurist Ibn Qayyim al-Jawziyya was promoting a popularized form of medical science, one that combined the Prophet's practices with various prescriptions of the Greek physicians and their Muslim heirs. Seeking physical health and spiritual well-being were complementary aims to Ibn Qayyim, and he counselled his readers to be mindful of both. But the medieval conception of the worshipper's body was not necessarily a holistic one, for in Ibn Qayyim's view the purpose of good health is to enable the worshipper to carry out his duties to God.[90]

Even if one assumes that Burhān al-Dīn al-Fazārī and Ibn ʿUbaydān had been diagnosed by physicians and not by the authors themselves, the fact that those diagnoses were worthy of inclusion in an obituary along with dates of birth, teachers, and special habits in piety is significant. The "scientific" approach of al-Ṣafadī and Ibn Kathīr is but one small sign of the increasing objectification of the body of the devotee. As noted in Chapter 1, holy men were routinely praised for performing difficult rituals when infirm or suffering from disease; withstanding constant bodily complaints of any kind was a common feature of devotional piety. Not surprisingly, fasting and ascetic food practices in the fourteenth and fifteenth centuries continue to express a concern with the physical limits of endurance.

early eleventh century, and also of al-Rāzī, but there was little consistency on the attributes of this plant; another authority said the *khiyār shanbar* was hot and humid: *Traité des simples*, II, 64–7.

[89] Quoted by Ibn Ḥajar, *Durar*, II, 43. People speculated about the source of this shaykh's "secret powers," some believing he had knowledge of alchemy, others that he was trained in medicine.

[90] Ibn Qayyim al-Jawziyya, *The Medicine of the Prophet*, trans. Penelope Johnstone (Cambridge, 1998), 16, 150–1. His treatise aims to show how Greek medicine and the Prophet's *sunna* are compatible, but also to establish the superiority of the medicine of the Prophet.

Ibn al-Jawzī stands as one of the rare critics of what he saw as patterns of obsession and self-abuse. In one passage he is at pains to explain that he is not, in principle, against asceticism's aim of curbing bodily desires:

> It behooves a man to know that his person (*nafs*) is his mount. One must [treat it] with kindness in order to arrive at one's destination still on its back. So let him consume what is beneficial to it and forgo the things which injure it: satiety, and excess in satisfying cravings. Truly those things injure both body (*badan*) and faith (*dīn*). Moreover, humans vary in their constitutions. When the [desert] Arabs wear wool and confine themselves to drinking milk, we do not censure them because the "mounts" of their bodies (*abdānihim*) can bear that. Likewise when the people of the Sawād wear wool and eat vinegar pickles, we do not blame them. Nor would we say of one of them, "He burdened his body," because this is the custom of that people. On the other hand, when the body is leading a life of ease, having grown up in comfort, we do indeed forbid its owner to burden it with something that injures it.[91]

Whether these practices were good or bad had nothing to do with what the Prophet had done, and Ibn al-Jawzī's departure in this passage from his usual form of critique is striking. The danger described is purely physiological, and although he might have resented the inference, Ibn al-Jawzī's language exemplifies current attitudes even while he criticizes them.[92] As much as Ibn al-Jawzī might have disliked the overuse of the body in worship, he shared his era's conception of the body as a mute but useful object. He merely saw it as more fragile than did many devotees and ascetics. Almost two centuries later, Ibn Baṭṭūṭa's shaykh in Delhi used the same imagery in cautioning him not to attempt longer fasts than he could bear – but with the goal of helping him to ultimately succeed at long fasts. The shaykh quoted the words of the Prophet that Ibn al-Jawzī

[91] Ibn al-Jawzī, *Talbīs Iblīs*, 146. This is a perfect example of how *nafs* can clearly mean the body of a person rather than the self; he uses the terms *badan* and *nafs* interchangeably throughout this passage. D. S. Margoliouth notes a preference for this bodily meaning of *nafs* in a note to his translation of the passage in "The Devil's Delusion of Ibn al-Jauzi," *Islamic Culture* 10, 3 (July 1936): 340. Ibn Qayyim also used the desert Arabs as an example: "Bedouin and desert dwellers suffer from simple illnesses, so for their medication simple drugs suffice" (*Medicine of the Prophet*, 8).

[92] He introduces the topic of ascetic diets by stating that the Prophet had not deprived himself of good food. The passage relies increasingly on Galenic theory as it progresses: "People think that dry bread is sufficient as sustenance for the body (*badan*). Even though it could suffice, such a restriction is still harmful from a certain point of view: the humours of the body will lack the sour and the sweet, the hot and the cold, the solidifying and the purgative" (Ibn al-Jawzī, *Talbīs Iblīs*, 146).

had alluded to: "He who breaks down from exhaustion has neither covered ground nor spared a mount."[93]

The existence of such attitudes towards the body in medieval Islamic culture helps to explain why so many devotees chose severe programs of fasting, ones that tested a person's stamina. But the question remains: why the *ṣawm al-dahr* in particular? The perpetual fasters of the medieval period were not under the mistaken impression that they were emulating the Prophet. Of the many fasts they could choose, they selected one that he had not practiced himself, and had perhaps even forbidden. Like Ibn Qudāma, they may have focused on the implication that the *desire* to fast excessively was something the Prophet had in fact accommodated. Perhaps some had heard that al-Ghazzālī had designated it *masnūn*. At the end of the thirteenth century, a person who read al-Nawawī's short and very popular compendium of Shāfiʿī law, the *Minhaj al-ṭālibīn*, would have found it listed alongside other supererogatory fasts and stamped with a synonymous label of *mustaḥabb* (strongly recommended).[94]

Towards the middle of the fourteenth century the arguments against the *ṣawm al-dahr* had been all but effaced, the protests about physical harm quelled. In a vade mecum on ritual practice written by a Shāfiʿī scholar in Mecca, Aḥmad al-Kazarūnī (d. 764/1362), entitled "The Book of What Suffices for a Worshipper," the author states simply that a fast "is said to be disliked if continued for a whole year."[95] No mention is made of the feast days. The restriction of not fasting every day of the year appears to have become a major component of the fast itself, where it had

93 Ibn Baṭṭūṭa, *Travels of Ibn Baṭṭūṭa*, III, 766.

94 Al-Nawawī says it is *sunna* to fast: on Mondays and Thursdays; the day of ʿArafa; the day of ʿĀshūrāʾ and the day preceding it; on the "white" days (that is, the thirteenth, fourteenth, and fifteenth of every month when the moon is full); and six days in the month of Shawwāl, preferably consecutively. "It is *makrūh*: to single out Saturdays for fasting; and for someone who fears injury or being unable to fulfill his duties to fast perpetually (the days of the feast and *tashrīq* excepted). Otherwise it is *mustaḥabb*": Muḥyī al-Dīn Yaḥyā ibn Sharaf al-Nawawī, *Minhāj al-ṭālibīn*, ed. Aḥmad ibn ʿAbd al-ʿAzīz al-Ḥaddād, 3 vols. (Beirut, 1421/2000), I, 439–41.

95 His list is as follows: "Fasting for six days in Shawwāl in a row, on the Day of ʿArafa for someone not on the ḥajj; on ʿĀshūrāʾ and the ninth; on the "white" days; on Mondays and Thursdays; and at the beginning and end of a month. And the best kind of fasting is the fast on alternating days; and [as for] continuing [to fast] perpetually for a year, it is said to be disliked (*makrūh*); and singling out Fridays and Saturdays is disliked for it is not consistent with custom, whereas one fasts on Nis̄ f Shaʿbān only because it is an agreed-upon custom." Note that yet again the *ṣawm al-dahr* and the preferable Fast of David are discussed together: Abū'l-Abbās Aḥmad ibn Muḥammad al-Kazarūnī al-Zubayrī al-Shāfiʿī al-Madanī, Kitāb kifāyat al-ʿābid, Dār al-Kutub wa'l-Wathāʾiq al-Qawmiyya, MS Fiqh Shāfʿī Ṭalaʿat no. 137, 11 r.

not been so before, or at least authors call attention to it in descriptions when it would seem unnecessary to do so: in the later fourteenth century, for instance, another Shāfiʿī scholar was careful to eat for a month of every year "so as not to fall into the perpetual fast."[96] He was obviously acquainted with the restrictions regarding the *ṣawm al-dahr*, and as a scholar he would have been aware of the original issues surrounding it. But since he was only prohibited from fasting on five days of the year, why take an entire month off? He seems to have thought carefully about the restriction and, in complying with it, decided to honor it by rigorously not fasting. That is, his personal fast focused at least partially on the idea of following the rule of the restriction "excessively."

Another layer in explaining the popularity of the fast, and the presumption that it was permissible, might be that medieval perpetual fasters found support for their undertaking from the exemplary practices of earlier generations. In favor of the *ṣawm al-dahr*, these fasters could cite precedents set by some of the Prophet's Companions, among whom, according to some traditions, were the caliph ʿUthmān and ʿĀʾisha.[97] Many early ascetic men and women were perpetual fasters as well. Their stories, continuously recycled from earlier collections throughout the centuries, were widely available in medieval biographical texts such as those written by the skeptic Ibn al-Jawzī, along with al-Dhahabī, Ibn Ḥajar al-ʿAsqalānī, and others who promoted these models of pious behavior. The principal characters of those stories, whether Companions of the Prophet or ninth-century ascetics, were as much available for emulation as was Muḥammad's own example. As time went on and the tradition of the perpetual fast continued, pious men and women of more recent memory – and even contemporary holy figures – provided further inspiration.[98] From the point of view of a fourteenth-century devotee who was not a jurist, the approbation may have appeared seamless.

Bound and Collared

Yet the deeper meaning of the perpetual fast and its place in medieval Islamic worship is better explained in terms of the reasons why people

[96] al-Sakhāwī, *al-Ḍawʾ al-lāmiʿ*, IV, 135–6. This was the sayyid ʿAbd al-Raḥmān ibn Muḥammad Ṣafī al-Dīn al-Ḥusaynī, who died in 864/1460.

[97] Aron Zysow has drawn my attention to al-Nawawī's defense of the *ṣawm al-dahr* in the *Majmūʿ*. Explaining the hadith about ʿAbd Allāh ibn ʿAmr, al-Nawawī suggests that this Companion was old and weak when the Prophet forbade him to fast perpetually; ʿUmar and ʿĀʾisha are also mentioned here as perpetual fasters: al-Nawawī, *Majmūʿ*, VI, 451–2.

[98] See Taylor, *In the Vicinity of the Righteous*, esp. chap. 3.

chose it over more highly recommended ones, such as David's Fast, and the way they used the fast in their lives. To this end, it may be helpful to compare two perpetual fasters in dramatically different circumstances. The first is Shaykh Qāsim al-Takrūrī, one of many men and women who took up residence in Medina in order to be near the tomb of the Prophet.[99] He lived for a time at the Ribāṭ al-Marāgha, a building endowed for benefit of the "destitute Sufi faqirs," which means he had chosen complete poverty. Shaykh Qāsim became known for his constant wandering in the mountains and open desert around Medina, where he sustained himself on wild plants and on the fish he caught in pools and swamps.[100] When he came into town on Fridays, he would give some of these to his loved ones. As a sign of his strength of faith, "he hung a thick iron collar around his neck to remind him of the conditions of the afterlife." For this he was censured by critics, who told him, "You are departing from the *sunna* and perpetrating *bid'a* (deviation)." Collars of iron, trappings of the damned in hell, were emphatically not proper forms of pious adornment. The Prophet himself had specifically condemned wearing them.[101]

As a result, Shaykh Qāsim gave up the practice – only to be criticized for another; for it turned out that he would habitually continue his perpetual fast even on the days of the two Feasts. When someone spoke to him about it, he protested in a vivid statement of medieval self-diagnosis: "If I eat anything I will get sick!" Having adjusted to the pattern of not eating except at nightfall, this injunction threatened both his system and the life of precautionary behavior to which he had devoted himself. Nevertheless he was told: "Eat! even if only a single grain of food. If you don't, you are sinning, according to juridical consensus."[102] Though twice

[99] His name indicates that his family origins were in the African kingdom of Takrūr in Mali. If he had grown up there he might have been brought from his homeland as a slave, or left it voluntarily to go on the Pilgrimage. The famous hajj journey of Mansa Mūsā and 15,000 of his Takrūrī subjects took place twenty years previously, in 724/1324 according to Mamluk authors such as al-Maqrīzī and Ibn Khaldūn. See Abdullah 'Ankawī, "The Pilgrimage to Mecca in Mamlūk Times," in *Arabian Studies*, ed. R. B. Serjeant and R. L. Bidwell (London, 1974).

[100] Ibn Farḥūn, *Tārīkh al-Madīna*, 122–3. Shaykh Qāsim also gets a brief mention in Ibn Ḥajar, *Durar*, II, 144: he was "one of the virtuous ascetics who resided in Medina and wandered in the mountains and did not come in [to town] except on Fridays. He died in Dhū'l-Ḥijja, 747 [1347]."

[101] For commentary on the hadiths regarding iron collars, and an argument against wearing them, see Ibn Baydakīn al-Turkumānī, *Kitāb al-luma'*, I, 146.

[102] Ibn Farḥūn, *Tārīkh al-Madīna*, 123. His story is reminiscent of Ibn al-Jawzī's description of worshippers who isolate themselves in the mountains and stray from the path of the *sunna*: *Talbīs Iblīs*, 145.

corrected, there is no reason to assume that the shaykh was unlearned. On the contrary, he may have known the relevant juridical opinions and still decided upon a path more certain to save his soul. Indeed, according to Ibn Farḥūn, he was revered for his detachment from worldly affairs, and this detachment was exemplified as much by his daily fast as by his escape to the wilderness. He clung to the practice presumably in the hopes of accruing heavenly rewards while on earth. Where his iron collar reminded him constantly of hellfire, the fast appears to have been insurance against its flames.[103]

And yet someone fully immersed in the affairs of the world with high status in society might use the fast in a strikingly similar manner. The vizier Bahā' al-Dīn 'Alī ibn Muḥammad, known as Ibn Ḥinā', was born in Egypt and lived so long that he was "the grandfather of a grandfather" when he died in 677/1279. At the beginning of his life, he worked in a store selling tents. After his luck changed, he took up a position in the sultan's fiscal administration, acquired great wealth, and eventually rose to the position of *wazīr*. Along the way he gained a reputation for piety, always maintaining his scruples and showing great zeal for his work, being generous to the mendicants and Sufi shaykhs, and endowing a madrasa in Cairo. Ibn Ḥinā''s pious impulses extended to his person as well as to his community, for "he imposed on himself the perpetual fast for the duration of his tenure as *wazīr*."[104] The earliest judges in Islam often accepted public office only under duress, so fearful were they of the taint of power, and there are numerous examples of this attitude from the medieval period as well.[105] Men who became viziers, by contrast,

[103] Jonathan Berkey writes, "The truism that the Islamic tradition is more world embracing than is the Christian misleads us if we allow it to obscure the approbation of the renunciation of worldly pleasure and the fixation on death and judgment which undergird many expressions of Muslim piety": *Popular Preaching*, 47–8.

[104] The verb al-Nuwayrī used to describe Ibn Ḥinā''s self-imposed task is not *nadhara* but *iltazama* (*iltazama ṣawm al-dahr fi wizāratihi*), which has no relation to formal vowing: Shihāb al-Dīn Aḥmad ibn 'Abd Allāh al-Nuwayrī, *Nihāyat al-'arab fī funūn al-adab*, 33 vols. (Cairo, 1923–98), XXX, 288–9. This information is not found in al-Dhahabī's account: *'Ibar*, V, 315–16.

[105] Other examples will be discussed in Chapter 3, but for earlier examples see Michael Cook, *Commanding Right and Forbidding Wrong in Islamic Thought* (Cambridge, 2000), esp. 123–8 on Ḥanbalī jurists, among whom the tradition of hesitance was so old that it had become a topos by the eleventh century when they were accepting office on a regular basis; see also Irit Bligh-Abramski, "The Judiciary (*Qāḍīs*) as a Governmental-Administrative Tool in Early Islam," *Journal of the Social and Economic History of the Orient* 35 (1997); Daphna Ephrat, *A Learned Society in a Period of Transition: The Sunni 'Ulama' of Eleventh-Century Baghdad* (Albany, 2000), 132–5;

generally had few qualms about assuming the second most powerful office in the state. But Ibn al-Ḥināʾ was not a typical vizier, as his biographers are quick to point out. His temporary use of the *ṣawm al-dahr* was a creative response to an old dilemma. It suggests that being in a state of fasting – or in the state of being bound by a vow to fast – could safeguard someone from corruption or immorality in the way that armor protects the body from harm.

Indeed, the Prophet is remembered as saying, "Fasting is a shield."[106] These words are more than just a metaphor, for the status of the faster is not a normal one. Performing acts of abstinence or rituals of devotion effectively changes the physical state of the worshipper. During the Pilgrimage this is visually apparent, where donning the clothing of *iḥrām* signals that one is bound to uphold the rules of the hajj. It is also characteristic of prayer, where ablutions make *ṣalāt* legitimate and one remains in a state of purity for its duration. Successive days of fasting are therefore marked by a prolonged change of status, both physical and moral, to which one recommits each morning. The state of hunger is broken instantly not only with a bite of food or sip of water but even, according to some hadith, by a malicious word or an impure thought. It was in this altered state that Ibn Ḥināʾ, having reluctantly taken up a position of power, might have sought protection. Whether his reluctance was symbolic or heartfelt is not important. Holding a daily job that would be repugnant to a holy person required a daily ritual that helped to maintain his moral integrity, a protection afforded by the very structure of the perpetual fast.

Although the word for a formal vow, *nadhr*, does not appear in Ibn Ḥināʾ's biography, the temporary nature of his fast is strongly suggestive of one. Had he vowed to fast, there would have been an even more formal change in his status: as noted above, voluntary fasts can be abandoned without penalty unless they are entered into in fulfillment of a vow that is, effectively, a contract with God.[107] Other officials, during

and on similar traditions in late antiquity, see A. J. Wensinck's "The Refused Dignity" in *A Volume of Oriental Studies Presented to Edward G. Browne … on his 60th birthday (7 February 1922)*, ed. T. W. Arnold and Reynold A. Nicholson (Cambridge, 1922), 491–9.

106 Muslim, *Ṣaḥīḥ*, 485, hadith nos. 132 and 133.

107 The chapters on vows in *furūʿ* texts usually give detailed explanations of how a person goes about making up for having broken one. But the issue of breaking a vow of supererogatory fasting comes at the end of the section on *ṣawm al-taṭawwuʿ*, and here the rules regarding vows of fasting, the *ṣawm al-dahr* included, were discussed in connection with particular fasts of expiation (*kaffāra*). See for example al-Nawawī's *Rawḍat*

their rise to power, might have vowed to fast or to free slaves if God allowed them to succeed to the position of *wazīr*. Deeply repentant men and women might vow to atone for their sins, and, given Ibn Ḥinā''s penchant for piety, he may have fasted in constant expiation for having been too involved in worldly matters as well as to protect himself from corrupting influences.[108] Long discussions in contemporary legal texts indicate that these practices were not uncommon in the Ayyubid and Mamluk periods, yet chronicles and biographical sources rarely mention the vocabulary of vowing in connection with pious fasting. That is, the exemplary devotees do not seem to have undertaken long-term activities in fulfillment of a vow formally uttered. Vowing does provide an important clue for understanding the *ṣawm al-dahr* in its medieval context, however. In Shaykh Abū 'Umar Ibn Qudāma's case, the text says specifically, "he fasted perpetually for no reason," apparently to distinguish him from more ordinary people who had cause to undertake the fast as a vow.[109] The clarification also let readers know that his fast was an act of *nāfila*, a purely supererogatory performance he renewed daily by choice. What was impressive about Shaykh Abū 'Umar was his willingness to be bound by the rules of fasting throughout the year.

The *ṣawm al-dahr* was no ordinary form of devotion and here, as with bodily achievements attained by exemplary devotees, one begins to see that by the crucial period of the early thirteenth century, the true meaning of an act that was *nāfila* was evolving into something not merely pleasing to God but a surfeit of worship, the fulfillment of a difficult "vow" of self-denial for no reason. The individual's personal motivation for such an action is almost always elusive. For some perhaps it was indicative of a permanent sense of penitence, where for others it was clearly a feat of worship.

It is hard to calculate the impact of hours spent in hunger and wakefulness except to note that they must have produced, in many people, an

al-ṭālibīn, II, 253, and the historical case possibly represented by Ibn Taymiyya's fatwa, cited earlier.

108 There were many types of vows. As a purely supererogatory act, for example, rulers sometimes vowed to provide the covering for the Ka'ba. Such a vow was binding, and when the Timurid ruler Shāh Rukh made such a vow in 838/1435, it presented a problem for the man who would normally have provided the *kiswa*, the Mamluk sultan al-Ashraf Barsbāy: Ibn Taghrībirdī, *al-Nujūm al-zāhira*, XV, 49–50. For more on vows see Norman Calder, "Ḥinth, birr, tabarrur, taḥannuth: An Inquiry into the Arabic Vocabulary of Vows," *Bulletin of the School of Oriental and African Studies* 51, 2 (1988).

109 Abū Shāma, *Tarājim*, 71.

abnormal set of physical sensations during normal activities. What was attractive about the perpetual fast may provide a clue to other long-term practices of *taʿabbud* among the exemplars of devotional piety. Most of the fasters carried on with their daily business while simultaneously suspending the ordinary patterns of human life. They passed days, months, or even years in an altered, almost consecrated, state like that of the pilgrim during the hajj. The determination to live in a state of bodily alteration lies at the heart of these perpetual devotions. For some, the aim was not only to shift to a different physical state but to reverse the body's needs altogether. After forty days of accustoming himself to difficult fasts and nighttime vigils, Ibn Baṭṭūṭa says, "I found that if I ate, I felt sick, and if I abstained from food, I felt peace."[110] A strange silence follows that sentence. He says nothing more, nothing about a spiritual state achieved, nor about progress towards God. For months he had tried to become a faster, and this was his statement of triumph.

[110] Ibn Baṭṭūṭa, *Riḥlat Ibn Baṭṭūṭa*, II, 410. He had recently spent five months with Shaykh al-Ghārī training himself in fasting. On this second retreat alone in a *zāwiya* he attempted to perfect the *ṣawm al-wiṣāl*. The difference between this and his protest fast (for which he also used the term *wāṣala*) is important: this time he repeated the fast until he was accustomed to it.

3

Charity, Food, and the Right of Refusal

In the medieval Islamic world, just as in other medieval societies, good food was made precious by the exigencies of weather and transport. Though the fertile lands of the region yielded a wider range of fruits and vegetables throughout the year than did most parts of Europe, variety itself was still cause for comment. Thus, Ibn Baṭṭūṭa recorded in compulsive detail what was available in the markets of cities he visited on his travels in India and Africa, and the popular tales of the Arabian Nights tantalized readers with lists of exotic dishes and ingredients.[1] In the Middle East proper, a thirteenth-century chronicler described how one year the staff of the Pilgrimage caravan returning to Baghdad was rewarded with camel-loads of pomegranates, limes and eggplants, rosewater, lemonade, and more.[2] Diets of barley bread were common enough around the Middle East for reasons that had nothing to do with piety, and an act of purposeful abstinence and self-discipline stood out as particularly heroic when something good was on offer, or when it meant forgoing things that were rare.

The feast itself was important in the Muslim cultural imagination through Qurʾānic depictions of the bountiful meals promised in paradise, and it retained those rich connotations of blessing in many more mundane settings as well.[3] Over seven centuries, the famed tradition of

[1] See Ibn Baṭṭūṭa's descriptions of Isfahan (*Travels of Ibn Baṭṭūṭa*, II, 295) and the dishes he ate in Mogadishu (ibid., II, 375–6).

[2] Ibn al-Fuwaṭī, *Kitāb al-ḥawādith*, 219–21. This was the hajj of the year 641/1244.

[3] See Maxime Rodinson's brief but very rich article "Ghidhāʾ," *EI*², and, on the sources, "Recherche sur les documents arabes relatifs à la cuisine," *Revue des études islamiques*

hospitality in Middle Eastern cultures was infused with added layers of meaning as it responded to the repeated emphases in the Qurʾān on charity and generosity. In the medieval period these twin virtues helped to determine common conceptions of dining etiquette and allowed the pious to turn ordinary communal meals into memorable occasions. Lacking the means to throw a feast was no obstacle for the philanthropically minded, and the image of the *fuqarāʾ* (the pious poor) being patrons themselves was a familiar one. A man named ʿAbd Allāh al-Buskarī, for example, left North Africa and a wealthy lifestyle to take up residence at the Ribāṭ al-Dukkāla in Medina, but he retained ideals of being a host that were incommensurate with his new means. His cupboards were bare because he never turned away a pilgrim and always refused payment for a room. At mealtimes he took whatever was on hand – wheat, clarified butter, and honey are mentioned – to give to the visitor. On one occasion when he made dinner for a group of mendicants there was no condiment for the food other than a jar of fruit syrup someone had given him for a medical condition; nevertheless, he commanded that it be poured out.[4]

Al-Buskarī's concern about finding a condiment to offer to guests is not a superfluous detail. The typical meals of ascetics, such as barley bread, were nearly inedible without at least a little oil, and not surprisingly condiments were very often what ascetics chose to give up when it came to their own diets.[5] But having something to lend taste or embellishment to food was a requisite gesture of generosity, and as a host al-Buskarī remained magnanimous at moments when what he could offer was so little as to be merely symbolic, and even, or perhaps especially, detrimental to his health.

Yet the image of the feast could also be employed in ways that questioned these social occasions, and tales of the great ascetics sometimes read like reverse descriptions of banquets. Ibn Farḥūn wrote of another *ribāṭ*-dweller: "He ate no fresh dates, nor the fruit of trees, no grapes, no melon, no meat nor oil of any kind until he grew thin and emaciated."[6]

17 (1949); also Geert Jan Van Gelder, *God's Banquet: Food in Classical Arabic Literature* (New York, 2000), 22–38.

4 Ibn Farḥūn, *Tārīkh al-Madīna*, 60. See also the entry in Ibn Ḥajar, *Durar*, IV, 170. Al-Buskarī, presumably a Sufi, died in 713/1313; on the founder of this *ribāṭ* see al-Sakhāwī, *al-Ḍawʾ al-lāmiʿ*, VIII, 88.

5 The popular preacher al-Buzūrī emphasized this in his tale of Ibn al-Mannī (discussed in Chapter 1). See Ibn Rajab, *Dhayl ʿalā Ṭabaqāt al-Ḥanābila*, I, 361.

6 Ibn Farḥūn, *Tārīkh al-Madīna*, 71. This was Shaykh ʿIzz al-Dīn Aḥmad al-Tilimsānī, a companion of the author, who died around 1340 C.E. He was a perpetual faster who kept up prayer vigils at night.

This, in other words, was not a man who had specifically selected bread as his meal, but one who had rejected all those other choices, and in lieu of a menu we see a catalog of self-imposed food prohibitions, which rendered it impossible for him to enjoy a feast. Another ascetic, ʿAlī Ibn al-Munajjā al-Tanūkhī, the Ḥanbalī chief judge in Damascus, was described by Ibn Ḥajar as "ṭayyib al-maṭʿam wa'l-mashrab" (eating and drinking good things). Concerning edible things, the word *ṭayyib* refers to licit substances: the foods God has permitted (*ṭayyibāt*) are by their nature good or pure (*ṭayyib*). Describing the taste of food, *ṭayyib* means good or delicious, and when Ibn Baṭṭūṭa marvelled at the apricots and quinces he tasted in Baṣra, he said they were *ṭayyib al-maṭʿam*.[7] But there was no confusion as to whether the qadi Ibn al-Munajjā was a bon vivant or a Stoic, for the author continues, "He refused to accept food or beverages from anyone, even a friend or a comrade."[8] Ibn al-Munajjā was extra-scrupulous about all he ate and drank even if it meant being suspicious of his companions. It was a different style of self-regulation, but one that also effectively counted out the possibility of accepting invitations to dine.

If good food was blessed because of its mimetic association with paradise, to medieval Muslims it also had the uncanny ability to be morally corrosive, depending on the circumstances in which it was received, eaten, stored, or purchased.[9] Attitudes towards food and dining, whether expressed in a language of avoidance or in gestures of excessive generosity, reveal a ripple of unease among the devotees and ascetics about their place in the social order of late medieval Islam. Stories of giving and receiving food go well beyond merely highlighting the social value of costly commodities or explicating notions of wealth and poverty, though these may often be significant elements within a narrative. Rather, they provide blueprints for the social hierarchy of the pious that explain how holy men and women regulated their relationships with friends and strangers, negotiated their position with respect to different classes, and decided what was acceptable as nourishment for their own bodies.

7 Ibn Baṭṭūṭa, *Riḥlat Ibn Baṭṭūṭa*, I, 152.

8 Ibn Ḥajar, *Durar*, III, 79. As will be shown at the end of this chapter, a confusion between the two meanings of *ṭayyib* sometimes did arise. This qadi, from a family of legal scholars noted for their piety, died in 732/1332.

9 The idea of corrosive foods I have borrowed from Kathryn Kueny's study of wine in early Islamic discourse where she discusses how the hadith, in presenting lists of prohibited foods or ingredients, sought to "identify, define, and contain what is ethically (and therefore cosmologically) corrosive": *The Rhetoric of Sobriety: Wine in Early Islam* (Albany, 2001), 26.

Generosity and abstention, sociability and humility, all were old ideals in Islamic culture. Because they often proved difficult to balance in reality, this chapter focuses in particular on how devotees and ascetics struggled to put old motifs of ideal behavior to new use in ways that highlighted problems particular to contemporary society.

Charity and Table Fellowship

The constant pull of social norms and communal responsibilities enjoined on all Muslims, on the one hand, and the desire to steer clear of worldly concerns, on the other, perplexed many devotees. Holy men in the medieval period often found themselves permanently involved in the supply of food, and the basis of their devotional piety was as purveyors to others. For Sufi shaykhs in particular, providing meals could be a means of solidifying bonds with followers and transferring *baraka*, or God-given blessings. These providers gained renown as paragons of selflessness and service.[10] For example, Muḥammad Ibn al-Sakrān, the "son of the drunkard" from the Ruṣāfa neighborhood of Baghdad, was a virtuous thirteenth-century ascetic who began his life modestly but ended up running a well-staffed center of charitable activity.

> He lived in this district from the beginning of his life and worked his land himself, sharing with travellers whatever it yielded. Then he constructed a place where the poor could seek shelter, and thus it remained for a time. Eventually the place was rebuilt for him as a convent (*ribāṭ*). He cultivated next to this a garden, planting it with date palms and other trees, which he bequeathed as an endowment for the needy. Then a group of virtuous people joined forces with him, each one lending a hand in the tilling, and the productivity [of the place] ceased to be his burden alone.[11]

The decision to serve God by serving food to those in need, which in the Islamic context meant specifically travellers and the poor, was a common enough choice by the mid-thirteenth century. Yet the ideal of the isolated ascetic or the worshipper alone in a cell remained equally available, and Ibn al-Sakrān succumbed to its pull. For after a time, things changed at the garden:

[10] See for example the story of Shaykh ʿAlī al-Bakkāʾ "the Weeper," who died in 670/1271–2, in Ibn Kathīr, *Bidāya*, XIII, 277.

[11] Ibn al-Fuwaṭī, *Kitāb al-ḥawādith*, 397. Ibn al-Sakrān died in 667/1268–9. On the Ruṣāfa neighborhood see Jacob Lassner, *The Topography of Baghdad in the Early Middle Ages: Text and Studies* (Detroit, 1970).

> Then, relying upon his companions, he withdrew, worshipping God and not seeking any food. Whatever they gave him he ate. But if they were occupied elsewhere, he still would not seek it, so that sometimes he would go days without eating. One day he said to his companions, "It seems that you have not been checking on the *fuqarāʾ*, for I have been informed that there is a poor man among you who has not eaten." They made some inquiries and realized that it was the shaykh himself whom they had forgotten. They apologized to him for their work in the service of travellers and begged God for forgiveness.[12]

The convenient reversal of roles here, from caretaker to ward, might indicate that the life of contemplative asceticism and poverty was the more fully endorsed. At first Ibn al-Sakrān's retreat and his refusal to be concerned with food calls to mind the old Sufi practice of *tawakkul*, or reliance on God in all matters and especially for provisions. A few early Sufis were said to have perished when, having departed for the desert, they found nothing to eat.[13] But in the cities and towns of the thirteenth-century Middle East the practice no longer entailed wandering about in search of something edible. Cities were places where the pious could feel secure about relying on the kindness of others. Furthermore, it is the communal aspects of Ibn al-Sakrān's work that are affirmed in his story, where the outlines of a somewhat circular hierarchy begin to emerge. The pious man humbles himself in the menial work of agriculture, growing food to serve to travellers and the poor. Being cared for is a reward for such service. The man who "earns" this type of poverty takes precedence over the traveller. The pious poor man is ultimately the community's most important charge. Refusing to ask for food is a sign of his humility in assuming that role, rather than an act of *tawakkul*. Indeed, the account concludes with a postscript about the famous Shīʿī scholar Naṣīr al-Dīn al-Ṭūsī, who visited Ibn al-Sakrān and asked him, "What is the definition of poverty?" He answered, "This is what I know: the collar of poverty is tight. A big head won't fit through it."

[12] Ibn al-Fuwaṭī, *Kitāb al-ḥawādith*, 397–8. Whether the *fuqarāʾ* mentioned here refer to the voluntary poor, to Sufis, or to the poor in general is unclear. Ibn al-Sakrān is called a virtuous ascetic who lived "in the style of the pious forebears (*al-salaf*)"; however, as there is also a reference in the obituary to his educating the *fuqarāʾ* (*tarbiyyat al-fuqarāʾ*), it is safe to assume that he was also a Sufi.

[13] Schimmel, *Mystical Dimensions*, 116–19. The present evidence, however, does not corroborate Schimmel's observation that "neither strict Hanbalite orthodoxy nor the moderate Sufis accepted the notion of *tawakkul* in an overstressed form. ... In the course of time *tawakkul* came to be stressed more as a spiritual attitude than as an external practice" (ibid., 120).

But particularly in his words of rebuke to his helpers, Ibn al-Sakrān makes it clear that the life of poverty was founded upon – and existed in relationship to – a type of support that he himself by no means rejected. The values governing social relations at Ibn al-Sakrān's compound were mirrored on a massive scale in Ayyubid and Mamluk society. Beginning in the late twelfth century, amirs, sultans, merchants, and wealthy women in growing numbers created pious endowments to provide ongoing support for scholars, Sufis, those generally inclined towards the religious life, and travellers, as well as for the destitute poor.[14] These *waqf*s provided security in the form of housing, clothing, and meals. Ibn al-Sakrān's career must be seen in terms of its broader medieval context: the strong impulse towards voluntary poverty in this period coincided with already durable notions of communal responsibility and systems of patronage. Adam Sabra has described in detail how a trend of public benevolence to the poor continued throughout the Mamluk period. Individual acts of food charity reached epic proportions with the Mamluk sultans, where al-Ẓāhir Baybars fed five thousand people a night in the month of Ramaḍān, and al-Muʾayyad Shaykh during an outbreak of the plague in 822/1419 distributed 28,000 loaves of bread to the residents of Cairo.[15] These grand gestures were not intended to eradicate poverty among the lower classes; rather, they were public displays of largesse and charitable

[14] The most frequent beneficiaries of the pious foundations that provided housing were people who chose the path of God (either as scholars or holy men or both) and the needy. Women typically fell into the latter category, being provided for not as scholars but as unmarried women or widows. On support for scholars see Berkey, *Transmission of Knowledge*; Fernandes, *The Khanqah*. On other kinds of people who were sponsored (the indigent, individual Sufis, and the pious poor) see Mortel, "*Ribāṭs* in Mecca"; for women's housing see Rapoport, *Marriage, Money and Divorce*, ch. 2; on travellers see Olivia Remie Constable, *Housing the Stranger in the Mediterranean World: Lodging, Trade, and Travel in Late Antiquity and the Middle Ages* (Cambridge and New York, 2003). Stefan Heidemann describes the sixth/twelfth century as "a time of renewal and the Islamization of cityscapes": Stefan Heidemann, "Charity and Piety for the Transformation of Cities: The New Direction in Waqf Policy in Mid-Twelfth Century Syria and Northern Mesopotamia," in *Charity and Giving in Monotheistic Religion*, ed. Miriam Frenkel and Yaacov Lev (Berlin and New York, 2009), 154. Much information on cities and buildings in this period can be found in his *Die Renaissance der Städte in Nordsyrien und Nordmesopotamien* (Leiden, Boston, and Cologne, 2002).

[15] Adam Sabra, *Poverty and Charity in Medieval Islam: Mamluk Egypt, 1250–1517* (Cambridge, 2000), 53, 56. While pious endowments for education have been much discussed since Berkey's study was published, Sabra's work on endowments that dispersed food broke new ground. He suggests that the poor could reasonably expect to be fed on major holidays from the benevolence of the amirs, sultans, and wealthy individuals. Other occasions for almsgiving were impending wars, a sultan's bout of sickness, or his restoration to health.

inclinations. This was how a prosperous Muslim might honor the civic obligations described in the Qurʾān and the hadith.[16]

Similar transactions were incorporated into the informal social relations of the community as well, and what concerns us here in particular are the more personal examples of this medieval fervor for food charity, where rich men kept company with the pious poor, treating them to meals in exchange for companionship, knowledge, or blessing, and the pious elite sought to justify their good fortune by sharing it with the destitute. The ensuing clash of lifestyles was a favorite theme of the chroniclers. Ibn al-ʿAdīm tells how the Ayyubid sultan al-Malik al-Muʿaẓẓam once invited an Iraqī hadith transmitter to give a reading in Damascus but the poor man, already badly homesick for Baghdad, suffered such indigestion from the heavy food served by the ruler that he could not perform.[17] Other Ayyubid princes and sultans visited local holy men *in situ*, urging upon them meals or money.[18] Clearly, many holy men of the late medieval period, despite having chosen poverty, were accustomed to receiving support and sustenance from men of the world.

Yet this informal system of charity had its pitfalls, and the pious were advised to be wary of feasts because of the double dangers of gluttony and secular company. In much the same way that some jurists refused public office, many devotees rejected the food of the rich and powerful. Those who did not were chastised by writers such as al-Ḥiṣnī, who had this to say about the Sufi shaykhs of the early fifteenth century:

> They are characterized by ignorance, deviation (*bidʿa*) and a paucity of faith. Haven't you seen one of them, when the tax collector has invited him to a banquet, rushing off to eat it? This is just as bad as highway robbery! If some immoral person, be it a vizier, a corrupt qadi or anyone

[16] By "civic," I mean merely that while the term "neighborly" might be adequate for the time of the Prophet, when the Muslim community was a small one, charitable projects in the late medieval period benefited large numbers of anonymous recipients. Amy Singer's study provides helpful background about the foundation and workings of pious institutions: *Constructing Ottoman Beneficence: An Imperial Soup Kitchen in Jerusalem* (Albany, 2002).

[17] David Morray, *An Ayyubid Notable and his World: Ibn al-ʿAdīm and Aleppo as Portrayed in his Biographical Dictionary of People Associated with the City* (Leiden, 1994), 90.

[18] See for example Dhahabī's account of the lord of Baalbek visiting ʿAbd al-Allāh ibn ʿUthmān al-Yūnīnī, "the master ascetic, the lion of Syria," who died in 617/1221: al-Dhahabī, *ʿIbar*, V, 67–8. Earlier examples include Nūr al-Dīn and Ṣalāḥ al-Dīn, who each had stopped in Ḥarrān to see the city's most famous ascetic, Shaykh Ḥayāt ibn Qays (d. 581/1185–6), seeking counsel and blessings for their impending battles (al-Ṣafadī, *al-Wāfī*, X, 226).

> else, gives him something he accepts it with a smile. That is the very essence of sinfulness.[19]

Brigandage called for the strictest punishment in Islamic law, and the comparison, though hyperbolic, underscores the dangers of how eating with the wrong company could be morally compromising.[20]

Conscientious men who were invited to feasts were in a bind. The Prophet himself never refused an invitation to a wedding banquet; in addition, in later centuries feasts marking circumcisions or holy days were occasions when the presence of a shaykh would be desirable.[21] Long discussions persisted among the jurists about the etiquette of accepting invitations to dine: it is generally obligatory to attend, but some legal experts suggested that a person might do well to check in advance that no wine-drinking or bad behavior would take place. If, upon arriving, the guest finds such wickedness already in progress, he may stay and silently renounce the activity within his heart, "just as though he were striking the perpetrator in his company." All such considerations apply also to women and to their social engagements, as al-Nawawī was careful to point out. And finally, a person who is fasting as a voluntary act of devotion (*nāfila*) should still accept the invitation and break the fast if his abstaining would upset the host.[22] We may therefore take a more lenient view of some of al-Ḥiṣnī's targets, such as the fourteenth-century Sufi jurist ʿAbd Allāh al-Minūfī, who retreated to a tomb in al-Qarāfa, where his sister resided, and "kept up the perpetual fast unless he was invited to a feast, in which case he broke it."[23]

[19] al-Ḥiṣnī, *al-Mu'mināt*, 83. The term for the Sufi shaykhs is "mashāyikh al-zamān min al-mutaṣawwifa."

[20] The punishment for highway robbery (*qaṭʿ al-ṭarīq*) without homicide is amputation of a hand and a foot, according to most jurists.

[21] Al-Ḥiṣnī appears to have used the word *walīma* (banquet) in a general sense, as does al-Nawawī, but a century earlier Ibn Qudāma insisted that only a wedding banquet is a *walīma*: Ibn Qudāma, *Mughnī*, VIII, 104; al-Nawawī, *Rawḍat al-ṭālibīn*, V, 645–6.

[22] al-Nawawī, *Rawḍat al-ṭālibīn*, V, 648–50. The same argument about breaking the fast is made by Ibn al-ʿArabī, a Mālikī jurist as well as a Sufi author, in a section on the legal rules of fasting (*Futūḥāt al-Makkiyya*, I, 651–2). For Islamic discourse on the silent censure of transgressions see Cook, *Commanding Right and Forbidding Wrong*, e.g., 42, 484–90.

[23] Ibn Ḥajar, *Durar*, II, 190. According to Ibn Ḥajar, al-Minūfī did not consider himself a Sufi, though he had both studied with a Shādhilī and was believed by later generations to have been one. Denis Gril offers an intriguing analysis of this renowned figure in "Saint des villes et saint des champs: Étude comparée de deux vies de saints d'époque mamelouke," in Rachica Chih and Denis Gril, eds., *Le Saint et son milieu ou: comment lire les sources hagiographiques*, Cahier des annales islamologiques 19 (Cairo, 2000),

Making moral decisions about dining partners is not unique to Islam, of course, and al-Ḥiṣnī's allusion to the taxman evokes the stance of the Pharisees, who counted tax-collectors and members of several other secular professions as being beyond the pale, particularly at mealtimes.[24] Rules about table fellowship were also erected as barriers between religious communities in the medieval period. Dominican and Franciscan friars, for example, were specially exempted from the Church's general prohibition on dining with Muslims since their mission involved proselytizing Saracens.[25] Within a single religious community, rejection of dining partners signals a different kind of divergence. Eating together implies a covenant between the people present, and refusing to do so breaks it.[26] Though the medieval Muslim devotees who were concerned about table fellowship were not sectarian in their theology with regard to other Muslims, in seeking to limit the company they kept at mealtimes they displayed a set of ethical positions that set them apart.

How this worked is illustrated in the life of Shaykh al-Buskarī, mentioned at the beginning of this chapter. He and his Sufi companions at the Ribāṭ al-Dukkāla lived in such extreme poverty that sometimes they would go days without eating, just as Ibn al-Sakrān had, even though the city of Medina offered ample supplies of food for its pious residents through religious endowments. On one occasion they were rescued by three North African friends returning from work in the gardens of the city who dropped off "some rotten vegetables such as chard, leftover turnips and the like, good only as fodder for mules and horses." The servant at the *ribāṭ* cooked them in a kettle and served the food to the companions when they came in for the evening prayer.[27] Thus far, the account emphasizes both the extreme want and the grateful receipt of food by men who placed their trust in God. But after the companions had eaten

61–82; on his posthumous reputation see Frederick de Jong, *Ṭuruq and Ṭuruq-linked Institutions in Nineteenth Century Egypt* (Leiden, 1978) 15; Mayeur-Jaouen, *al-Sayyid Aḥmad al-Badawī*, 432, 470.

[24] See for example Gillian Feeley-Harnik, *The Lord's Table: The Meaning of Food in Early Judaism and Christianity* (Washington, D.C., and London, 1994), 42, 67–9.

[25] Benjamin Z. Kedar, *Crusade and Mission: European Attitudes towards the Muslims*, (Princeton, 1988), 137; for examples of changing rules about contact with Muslims see Peter Herde, "Christians and Saracens at the Time of the Crusades: Some Comments of Contemporary Medieval Canonists," *Studia Gratiana* 12 (1967): 359–76. See also David Nirenberg's discussion of meat markets in Christian Spain in *Communities of Violence: Persecution of Minorities in the Middle Ages* (Princeton, 1996), 169–72.

[26] Feeley-Harnik, *The Lord's Table*, 86. She continues: "Those who do not eat or drink together are without any obligation to one another, if not actually enemies."

[27] Ibn Farḥūn, *Tārīkh al-Madīna*, 60.

their fill of the supper, the servant took the rest away and threw it outside the city gates where it was eaten by wild animals. The unpleasantness of the food provides a silent contrast with ordinary dining customs: it was a "normal" dinner, except that its fare was fit only for beasts. The companions received bad food from a noble source, and in the process the rotten became edible.

There was nothing impious about good-tasting food, either, so long as good people served it. Shaykh Burhān al-Dīn al-Fazārī (d. 729/1328), the famous but weakly Damascene *faqīh*, used the feast in a paradox of abundance and frugality. He himself ate so little that he was emaciated, yet at least once a month he would prepare a meal for the jurists of the Badhrāʾiyya Madrasa, where he taught. Taking pleasure in serving one's guests with exaggerated humility was a recurring motif in this period, and al-Fazārī made a great display of kissing his guests' feet as he welcomed them. Then he invited them to table, saying, "Keep me company and gratify me!"[28] In other words, it was possible to enjoy food when the circle was closed: inside a madrasa or a *ribāṭ*, in Ibn al-Sakrān's compound in Baghdad perhaps, or at private dinners where food was passed around only by the hands of the pious.

There are, however, uniquely Islamic reasons why the circle of these transactions had to be closed. The succinctness of the Qurʾānic list of forbidden foods and the suggestion in the Qurʾān that God will not burden Muslims in this regard leaves one with the impression of a community that has been given a clear but hardly onerous set of dietary laws.[29] Yet from the perspective of the pious men and women of late medieval Islam, this was far from accurate. For one thing there was a constant possibility of contagion, where normally permissible food was rendered inedible by contact with unclean substances, such as blood or excrement, pork or wine. Such a danger was at least one cause of medieval Muslims refusing to eat with Christians.[30] But the overriding concern had to do

[28] al-Ṣafadī, *al-Wāfī*, VI, 43–4; al-Kutubī, *Fawāt al-wafayāt*, I, 33. While kissing feet was a cultural rather than a religious prescription (and particularly appropriate when meeting someone of high status such as sultans or caliphs), Burhān al-Dīn's words of invitation conform to the host's etiquette prescribed by al-Nawawī, *Rawḍat al-ṭālibīn*, V, 654.

[29] For example Qurʾān 2:173, 16:115. Islamic law, however, produced a longer list of forbidden foods based on other injunctions in the Qurʾān and hadith.

[30] In a famous example, Usāma Ibn Munqidh recorded a report from one of his men who, when he was invited to dine with a Frankish friend, confessed a fear that prohibited food might be served. The Christian host told him his fear was unnecessary: "Eat and be of good cheer! For I don't eat Frankish food: I have Egyptian cooking-women and never eat anything except what they cook. And pork never enters my house." The soldier "ate, though guardedly": Ibn Munqidh, *The Book of Contemplation*, 153.

with an imperceptible source of impurity in food, and one that is often neglected in overviews of Islamic dietary laws, namely the prohibition of eating something acquired through unlawful means or with illegally gained wealth. The specific worries this prohibition caused in the thirteenth, fourteenth, and fifteenth centuries will be discussed extensively in the second part of this chapter, but for the moment it may be cited as the main factor governing attitudes of the pious poor towards the food of wealthy men. Among scrupulous devotees, fear of receiving charity came increasingly to reflect the way in which accepting something offered meant accepting as a consequence the moral status of the donor.

A Critique of Charity: The Glutton

If the pious poor were bound by their ethics to avoid accepting meals from unsavory characters or dubious sources of wealth, it must be remembered that the pious rich had an equally strong urge to supply them with food. These two competing aims sometimes became entangled in actual moments of exchange, and never more so than in the case of Shaykh Muḥammad ibn Khalīl (d. 658/1260), a man affectionately known as al-Akkāl ("the Glutton"). A local celebrity from the town of Qaṣr al-Ḥajjāj outside Damascus, his fame hinged upon the way he tampered with prevailing notions of charity.

> Tales of his taking a fee for what he ate and accepting charity from the amirs and the notables are famous. No one had done that before him, and no one after him followed in his tracks.... Some people disapproved of those who "did business" with him in this manner. A person would fall under his influence and spend whatever amount pleased the Shaykh on food. Each time the person came to him in the dining hall, the Shaykh would increase the requirements for him. Nonetheless he had a handsome appearance, his speech was full of witty expressions, and he had the complete acceptance of all of the people.[31]

His saintly scheme may have worked merely because it was so confusing. By charging someone for charity he turned the traditional relationship of patron and beneficiary into that of client and purveyor, which must have amused many who heard the widely repeated story. The Glutton's price list was conveniently furnished by another author: "His tax on a tray of sweets was five dirhams; five for a beverage; and for cooked food

[31] al-Kutubī, *Fawāt al-wafayāt*, III, 351–2.

anywhere from twenty or thirty dirhams to a hundred, depending on its quantity."[32]

Louis Pouzet identifies Shaykh al-Akkāl as an example of one of the *muwallahūn* or *mystiques excentriques* of medieval Syria, and to a certain extent this reflects the opinion of Ibn Kathīr, who confessed that he found the man's behavior strange.[33] But in none of the sources is the Glutton called a *muwallah*, and the popularity of his story demands a more thorough discussion of its significance. In the first place, growing fat was "simply not done" in saintly society at this time, dominated as it was by ascetic concerns. To this extent al-Akkāl's actions clearly go against cultural conceptions of how a pious person ought to comport himself. Nevertheless, his biographers offer a unanimous chorus of praise for his character.[34]

The Glutton's original aim was only to be a conduit for charity, a person with whom funds or food could be deposited for distribution to the poor, for al-Yūnīnī stresses that "all that came to him he dispersed in the ways of kindness," seeking out deserving people, such as widows and others in need.[35] Contributing to the infrastructure of his region, he erected several mosques and built a minaret for the *masjid* in Qaṣr al-Ḥajjāj. What bothered "some people" about his business practices was neither the gluttony nor the usurious prices he charged his donors: if anyone was at fault in a story so clearly meant as light-hearted, it was these client–patrons. Ibn Kathīr's account says that the people of the town of Qaṣr al-Ḥajjāj besieged the shaykh, competing with one another in trying to get him to eat their charitable offerings.

> And the more he refused, the more delightful people found him. They loved and adored him, and gave him many kinds of sweets, grilled meats and other things. And in exchange he would give them [a demand for] a large fee, no less! This was very odd indeed![36]

The root of the confusion lies less in the transgressive act of overeating than in the nature of the exchange itself. Al-Akkāl's resistance, such as it

[32] al-Yūnīnī, *Dhayl Mir'āt al-zamān*, I, 391. The word for tax here is *ḍarība*.

[33] Pouzet, *Damas*, 225; Ibn Kathīr, *Bidāya*, XIII, 242.

[34] al-Dhahabī, *'Ibār*, V, 249; al-Ṣafadī, *al-Wāfī*, III, 49; Ibn Kathīr, *Bidāya*, XIII, 242. While none of them mention miracles (*karamāt*), Abū Shāma (*Tarājim*, 207) alludes to having discussed tales of al-Akkāl's "rare and wondrous feats" (*nawādir wa-'ajā'ib*) elsewhere, in a book no longer extant. Al-Kutubī found his actions strange and wondrous (*'ājīb*), but says he was marked by "goodness and godliness": al-Kutubī, *Fawāt al-wafayāt*, III, 351–2.

[35] al-Yūnīnī, *Dhayl Mir'āt al-zamān*, I, 391.

[36] Ibn Kathīr, *Bidāya*, XIII, 242.

was, harks back to al-Ḥiṣnī's warning: everyone in Qaṣr al-Ḥajjāj would have known (if only because of al-Akkāl's resistance) how a pious person could be compromised by accepting gifts, and there was something wrong, a whiff of illegality even, about those who were willing to pay in order to override his doubts. In the frenzied atmosphere the Glutton created, and after repeated refusals, his capitulation no doubt satisfied his customers all the more.

Al-Akkāl's reconfiguring an act of benevolence into a privilege laid bare the mechanisms of what was essentially a crude procedure. This becomes clear in the case of the Mamluk amir al-Sayfī, a companion of the future sultan Baybars al-Jashnakīr, who had his own run-in with the Glutton. Al-Sayfī was sitting with his fellow Mamluks being entertained by musicians when he heard about the shaykh for the first time. Intrigued, he stood up and declared, "I will go get him and give him food, regardless of his preferences, and I won't pay him a thing!" But when the Glutton appeared and the amir presented him with a tray of sweets, the shaykh stubbornly refused to eat until he was paid fifty dirhams. Baybars tried in his turn and the shaykh responded again, "By God! For you I will not eat for less than fifty dirhams; for a poor man I'll eat for five." Baybars paid him, and he ate the sweets. By the end of the night, al-Sayfī had paid out three hundred dirhams, Baybars another fifty, and the rest of the Mamluks and musicians a total of five hundred.[37]

While gaining heavenly reward through expenditure presented no problem, legally or otherwise, these patrons were not so much giving charity but instead buying blessings (*baraka*) from a holy man. Ordinarily it was the food distributed *by* a holy man that might contain his *baraka*, and the reversal here only worked because of their greed for it: many people, says al-Yūnīnī, disapproved of those who made these deals (*muʿāmalāt*) out of "rashness."[38] As for the Glutton, his biographers appear to have viewed the fees he levied as a positive kind of usury. This reciprocal arrangement of parting with money and encouraging donations supported the communal good, and it might perhaps be viewed as the medieval Islamic

[37] al-Yūnīnī, *Dhayl Mirʾāt al-zamān*, I, 390. Al-Yūnīnī's source is the historian Ibn al-Jazarī, who says that his father had known the Glutton well. Sabra's chart of charitable obligations expected of men from various military ranks some sixty years later (after Sultan al-Nāṣir Muḥammad's cadastral survey of 715/1315) chimes nicely with the Glutton's fees: Sabra, *Poverty and Charity*, 165.

[38] al-Yūnīnī, *Dhayl Mirʾāt al-zamān*, I, 391. Blessings were usually transmitted through physical contact with a holy person, or with an object he or she has touched, but one could gain *baraka* also through studying with such a person, and even by seeing them in dreams. On this see Meri, *The Cult of Saints*, 101–8.

equivalent of bingo nights at churches, where, for a fee, one has the chance to gain something as well as give. There is a fine logic to his actions: in resisting their advances, he proved that it was the donors who benefited from their acts of charity, at a cost to his own integrity. He was a hustler, to be sure, and certainly no fool, not even a holy one.[39] No one could have missed the fact that his sliding scale of fees highlighted how much more "costly" it was to accept food from the rich or the powerful.

There is a cultural logic to the story as well, one that has important implications for the study of patronage and charity in this period. The technical language of the transaction is central to the meaning of the Glutton's ritual. In many stories where food changes hands, the verb used for both accepting and eating something offered means literally that the person who accepts it will be eating *for* the donor. Thus, al-Dhahabī wrote that the Glutton "rarely ate anything for anyone except for a fee," and Ibn Kathīr says that "the people competed in trying to get him to eat splendid and delicious things for them."[40] The donors' gifts were by no means symbolic. It was not sufficient that al-Akkāl merely receive the food: the ritual was not over until he had consumed it, and perhaps he was justified in being paid for his services, especially on days when his "clients" were spendthrifts.

In medieval stories less focused on the complications of charity, the phrase simply meant that one person had accepted another's offer of food. But if the semantic difference in Arabic between accepting food and eating it for someone else seems a mere nuance, it was widely evocative of the concerns of pious men and women in medieval Islamic culture. Accepting food meant accepting a two-way relationship, and this is why issues of social status were rarely absent during these transactions. The roles could easily be reversed along with the benefits or repercussions for both parties. In contrast to the Glutton, for example, the Sufi shaykh al-Murshidī (d. 737/1337), renowned as a saint in Lower Egypt, was known for miraculously producing food out of season for visitors who included not only the destitute but sultans as well.[41] In such cases, what

39 For a comparison between the *muwallahūn* and Christian holy fools see Dols, *Majnūn*, 403–10.

40 "Lā yakādu ya'kilu li-aḥadin shay'an illā bi-ujra": al-Dhahabī, *'Ibar*, V, 248–9. Ibn Kathīr says of the townspeople: "yatarāmūna 'alayhi li-ya'kala la-hum al-ashyā' al-muftakhira al-ṭayyiba" (*Bidāya*, XIII, 242). The same construction was used in the account of 'Alī ibn Munajjā al-Tanūkhī, the chief qadi of the Ḥanafīs, mentioned at the beginning of this chapter.

41 al-Sallāmī, *Wafayāt*, I, 23; Ibn Kathīr, *Bidāya*, XIV, 190; Ibn Baṭṭūṭa, *Travels of Ibn Baṭṭūṭa*, I, 30–2. A few decades later Ibn al-Mulaqqin described another saint-shaykh in

the wealthy sought and gained was not just a shaykh's *baraka* but the right to table fellowship with him. In a sense, this signalled his approval of their moral status.[42]

If it seems obvious in the story of the Glutton that the point of such transactions is for the supplicant's food to disappear into the body of a pious man, or vice versa in the more typical case of al-Murshidī, things did not always happen this way. In the Ayyubid period, and particularly later under the Mamluks, widened systems of charity ensured that the pious poor and the destitute poor ate at a safely anonymous distance from the donors. And this was entirely proper: anonymity *should* be sought by the pious recipients, according to Abū Naṣr al-Sarrāj (d. 378/988), who discussed the question of whether or not Sufis should accept money from *zakāt* funds. They might, but only on condition that "those who paid the alms tax did not know the sufis, and thus could not have been influenced by their status as pious persons."[43]

The distance sanitized the process for the patrons as well. The historian al-Yāfiʿī remembered the horror he felt on the night of Niṣf Shaʿbān when Shaykh al-Murshidī insisted that they bring a delicious banquet to the rabble living at Kūm Qarḥ, people so marginally Muslim that "they do not observe this holy night."[44] On the previous evening al-Murshidī had treated the author to "a feast which would have sufficed for a huge crowd of guests, composed of all different varieties of food." Al-Yāfiʿī recalled, "Inside me was a longing for things I had never in my life tasted, all there before me at that feast. He bade me eat, and I ate as much as I craved."[45] Having enjoyed the evening so much and feeling that he

the same line of work: Ṣāliḥ ibn Najm al-Qalyūbī, who lived not in Qalyūb but in a town some distance outside Cairo, spent his life "serving the devotees (*ʿubbād*) of all classes of society, giving food to every wayfarer." The author, who once stopped at his *zāwiya*, adds: "I myself have received the good fortune of his bounty." This must have been why the shaykh was given the honorific of *al-ʿabd al-ṣāliḥ*, "the virtuous servant," instead of the much more common epithet for a pious person, *al-ʿābid al-ṣāliḥ*, "the virtuous devotee." When al-Qalyūbī died in 780/1378–9, poor men, judges, scholars, viziers, and amirs alike showed up for his funeral: Ibn al-Mulaqqin, *Ṭabaqāt al-awliyāʾ*, 553.

42 It may be instructive to compare the pious poor who dispersed food *in situ* to all social classes with the type of patrons described by Peter Brown in "Town, Village and Holy Man: The Case of Syria," in *Society and the Holy in Late Antiquity* (Berkeley and Los Angeles, 1982), esp. 161–2.

43 Sabra, *Poverty and Charity*, 35.

44 al-Yāfiʿī, *Mirʿāt al-jinān*, IV, 293–4. I assume that Kūm Qarḥ (possibly Kūm Qiraḥ?) is a neighborhood.

45 When guests were brought to the table afterwards, he found himself in the distinguished company of Sharaf al-Dīn Ibn al-Ṣāḥib and his children. This man was "the scion of the famous vizier known as Ibn Ḥināʾ," who was discussed in Chapter 2.

had been specially honored by the saint, the next night it bothered him greatly to see the same food given to men whose company he admittedly shunned. He warned Shaykh al-Murshidī to stay away from them, but to no avail.

Thus in intimate settings, negotiations over charity were especially fraught with tensions about wealth and status. Al-Yāfiʿī's reservations also reveal how there might also be tension not just about *baraka* but about piety itself as something that could be, through social intercourse with a holy person, absorbed, redistributed, or indeed squandered. These tensions disappeared in the distance created by anonymity. The implicit relationship entailed by a gift of food (or money for food) may inhere to some degree in other instances of charitable donation in Islam as well. When someone bestowed a garment upon someone else as a sign of friendship or patronage, the recipient clearly wore it for the donor, although the Arabic does not express this.[46] Yet the discomfort of clothing is seldom mentioned, and accepting garments was not physically or morally crippling in quite the same way.[47] Nor were pages of legal texts devoted to how a garment might become illegal. Only in the process of receiving charity for one's daily bread could the deeds and morals of other people derail one's own progress so effectively.

As a go-between, the Glutton was especially well positioned to demonstrate how a host of possible complications could disrupt the smooth operation of charity that existed in society on a wider scale. All sorts of reasons can explain why his story was so thrilling that it was repeated in most of the major biographical collections: a pious man who traded want for excess, donors transformed into supplicants, the rejection of luxurious food, and the inversion of social classes. The faint connotations of prostituted morals, extortion, overindulgence, bribery, and saint-worship Shaykh al-Akkāl seems to have deflected with witty remarks, and in any

[46] There is some evidence that medieval Muslims were peculiarly aware of the possibility of magical properties in items of fabric or food and the transferability of those properties. For example, see the early thirteenth-century author Ibn al-Miʿmār on initiation into the fraternal groups known as the *futuwwa*, where the transfer of clothing from an elder to a young initiate was loaded with meaning; Ibn al-Miʿmār states that the *sarāwīl* given to the initiate should have been previously worn by the *futuwwa* leader who performs the ritual undressing and dressing of the initiate. This way, his *baraka* will be transferred to the new wearer: Muḥammad ibn Abī'l-Makārim Ibn al-Miʿmār, *Kitāb al-futuwwa*, ed. Muṣṭafā Jawād et al. (Baghdad, 1958), 237.

[47] For an exception see Ibn al-Fuwaṭī, *Kitāb al-ḥawādith*, 71. There are examples of men being reluctant to wear a particular costume, such as the dress of amirs, but these relate more to the desire to continue being identified with one group and not another.

case they made for good drama. Nevertheless, it should be emphasized in particular that his acceptance of patronage represents a kind of holy self-abasement not unfamiliar among the exemplars of devotional piety. There were many other pious people who would have recognized this message and understood his actions as being neither transgressive nor humorous. These more ordinary holy men would have withstood the pressure to accept gifts of food from secular sources, thereby preserving their moral – and, in a sense, bodily – integrity. The Glutton's capitulation paradoxically emphasizes his extreme, self-sacrificing devotion to charity all the more. This was the price he paid for being a patron of the poor himself.

Scrupulous Asceticism: Seeking the Licit

As with the tradition of refusing public office, the hesitance towards accepting food, or money for food, had strong roots in earlier Islamic piety. The brief Qur'ānic exhortations to "eat good things and do good acts" had been extensively developed in the hadith literature, where the Prophet's injunction to "seek the licit" meant finding sources of food that were not just ritually pure, but financially *ḥalāl*. Seeking the licit also has a long history in juristic piety even before its greatest exemplar, Aḥmad Ibn Ḥanbal (d. 241/855), who refused to eat food served in the caliph's dungeon, and it appears in the other Sunnī legal schools as well.[48] The injunction appears consistently in hortatory literature, from Abū Ṭālib al-Makkī and al-Ghazzālī (who developed the theme with considerable vigor) to an anonymous book of counsel written for a local ruler near the end of the twelfth century.[49] The latter, an excellent example of late Saljuk *adab*, illustrated the theme anew by using one of the more colorful hadiths in its support where a donated sheep cries out to warn the Prophet, "Do

[48] For example, Michael Cook discusses a pious goldsmith in the eighth century who was wary of eating the food offered to him by no less an authority than Abū Ḥanīfa (*Commanding Right and Forbidding Wrong*, 5). On Ibn Ḥanbal's recommendations about how far to go in seeking the licit see Cooperson, *Classical Arabic Biography*, 112–14. See also G. H. A. Juynboll, "Some Notes on the Earliest Fuqaha of Islam Distilled from Hadith Literature," in *Studies on the Origins and Uses of Islamic Hadith* (London, 1996), 301. A typical later application of the ethical meaning of *ḥalāl* can be found in al-Nawawī's legal commentary, *Rawḍat al-ṭālibīn*, V, 570, where he indicates that if someone knows that food being served was purchased with illegal funds, he or she must not eat it.

[49] Al-Ghazzālī's chapter on the permissible and forbidden (*al-ḥalāl wa'l-ḥarām*) commences with the topic of legally acquired food (*Iḥyā'*, II, 88–92).

not eat me, for I was acquired wrongfully!" Heeding this warning, the Prophet dispatches the beast to be fed to prisoners of war in Medina, for "eating carrion in time of necessity is permitted."[50] In a convergence of meanings, meat bearing the stain of crime was marked as the equivalent of a carcass or of an animal that had been improperly slaughtered. It was not merely a metaphorical equivalency, for both types of meat are *ḥarām*. Misdeeds did not make the food merely dirty, which would allow for the possibility of its becoming clean again through an act of charity; they turned it into carrion, which was substantively and irrevocably – rather than temporarily – impure. The prisoners ate bad food that was permissible because they found themselves in dire circumstances, not food that had been "cleansed" by an act of the Prophet's charity.[51]

As Marion Katz has pointed out, the intersection of bodily purity, food purity, and ethical purity caused confusion in the early Umayyad period, when the legal discourse on the meaning of "the licit" was still developing.[52] As the issues were made continually clearer over the centuries, one may assume that not only ascetics, jurists, and Sufis but ordinary Muslims as well were familiar with the idea of ethical purity in food, especially through popular texts such as al-Ghazzālī's *Iḥyā' 'ulūm al-dīn*. By the Ayyubid period edible things had become a particularly common locus of discomfort.[53] The meaning of the word *ḥarām* is almost without exception "ridden with misdeeds" rather than "sullied by impure substances (*najāsāt*)" when it appears in stories where food is rejected as inedible. Building upon such strong roots in early Islamic piety, medieval rejections of food can be seen as a topos of pious behavior, yet it was

[50] *The Sea of Precious Virtues (Baḥr al-Favā'id), a Medieval Islamic Mirror for Princes*, trans. Julie Scott Meisami (Salt Lake City, 1991), 139. The prisoners were probably Meccans captured at the battle of Badr in 624 C.E. This version of the hadith suggests that carrion, broadly defined, was bad for everyone and not just for Muslims.

[51] That the notion of temporary or reversible impurity does not appear to apply to illegally acquired food may say something interesting about Islamic views of crime. By contrast, ordinary foods can be made clean again. For instance, wine, an impure (*najis*) substance, can be rendered licit by turning it into vinegar; liquids and dry foods into which a polluted or polluting object has fallen have the possibility of being made pure again by its removal.

[52] Katz, *Body of Text*, 120–1. In a fascinating discussion of an early and short-lived suspicion that ingesting the wrong kind of food can directly affect both one's bodily and ethical purity, Katz cites an anecdote in which the caliph 'Umar ibn 'Abd al-'Azīz (r. 717–20 C.E.) corrects one of his companions about the meaning of the term *ṭayyibāt* in Qur'ān 5:270: "Eat of the good things (*ṭayyibāt*) We have provided for you." His companion assumes that it refers to the range of permissible foodstuffs. 'Umar responds that the verse refers to "legal earnings (*ṭayyib al-kasb*) not good/licit foods (*ṭayyib al-maṭ'am*)."

[53] See Talmon-Heller, "Cited Tales of the Wondrous Doings," 113.

a theme that would gain new meaning as it was put to use in diverse contemporary settings.

In particular, this theme highlights the difference between two distinct strands of medieval asceticism. The motives behind decisions about what not to eat are wholly different from an ascetic wariness about pleasure that characterized a man such as Ibn Taymiyya, who was said to be devoid of longings for food, clothing, and sex.[54] That kind of asceticism involved a battle against desires within the body, not one waged to protect it against the possible dangers that lay without. Concern with ethically permissible foods – seeking the licit in what one ate – stands as its own brand of bodily piety, an asceticism marked by scrupulosity (*waraʿ*) rather than self-mortification or renunciation (*zuhd*). Personal austerity and moral misgivings were separate concerns, even if they might merge in an individual's program of piety. Abū Bakr al-Ṭuraynī, the famously self-mortifying jurist of the Nile Delta, temporarily refused to eat meat for fear that what was sold in the markets came from stock stolen by Bedouin raiders. This was a pious last resort against crime rather than an act of abstaining from luxurious foods – which he also avoided.[55]

Such worries were endemic among the pious in the Ayyubid and Mamluk periods, and in certain individuals they grew acute. One in particular, a woman named Umm Yūsuf Fakhriyya al-Buṣrawiyya (d. 753/1352), merits consideration for several reasons: first of all, al-Ṣafadī's account of her life is one of the longest ones devoted to a holy woman in the late medieval sources; second, she is paradigmatic of several ascetic themes at once, including bodily hardship, concerns about permissible food, and rejection of charity; and third, we see in her example one of the best expressions of the classic kind of suspicion that carries over from early Islam.

Fakhriyya, the sister of two prominent amirs from the Syrian city of Buṣrā, had left home for the purpose of living in the blessed surroundings of a holy city.

> She deserted the world. Nothing would please her but the loftiest abode. Leaving behind her family and her wealth, she sustained herself on just

[54] al-Dhahabī, *Muʿjam muḥaddithī*, 26.

[55] al-Sakhāwī, *al-Ḍawʾ al-lāmiʿ*, XI, 64–5 (discussed in Chapter 2). For another example see al-Yūnīnī, *Dhayl Mirʾāt al-zamān*, I, 402 on Ibn Qiwām, an ascetic saint in thirteenth-century Aleppo who gave up eating meat for the same reason. Meri mentions an incident in which Ibn Qiwām proves his miraculous powers of perception by refusing a dish containing carrots that turn out to have been earmarked for the poor: *The Cult of Saints*, 77.

> a bit of food that was permissible to her and lived in seclusion at the Sanctuary in Noble Jerusalem. She freed herself from inherited possessions and newly acquired ones alike. From her life of opulence she wanted only a jug of water and a loaf of bread.[56]

Although they have a literary ring to them, bread and water were not merely the ingredients of a typically pared-down ascetic diet. They were also the residue of a process of scrutiny. Fakhriyya's departure from her family and their wealthy lifestyle was explicitly linked to her "seeking the licit" elsewhere, and references to her attempts to escape her inheritance and family position appear throughout al-Ṣafadī's account. Her eldest brother, the amir Ṣafī al-Dīn Abū'l-Qāsim al-Buṣrawī, told the author, "My brother Najm al-Dīn [once] brought her 16,000 dirhams that were allotted to her. She gave it all away as charity in a single session, not leaving aside a single dirham." The rest of the time she would take a small amount from her allowance of two hundred dirhams and distribute the rest to the poor. Her brothers' associate, the famous Amīr Tankiz, took a particular interest in Fakhriyya's welfare and "visited her several times bearing gold. But he always left with it, for she never took anything from him."[57]

Her descent into voluntary poverty can thus be seen as a situation forced upon her by the successive choices she made about how to live. The source of her family's wealth is not disclosed, and since her brothers are said to have been upright and charitable, it may have been wealth in general that she avoided.[58] However reluctant she was to accept her inheritance, using some of it to buy bread and water allowed her to survive while avoiding charity, which she considered even more dangerous. Fakhriyya became a famous figure in Jerusalem, where she remained separated from her family for forty years, "poised at the door of the Sanctuary, praying until it was opened so that she could be the first one inside and the last to leave." She lived a solitary life, even refusing assistance in drawing water for her ablutions. Though she depended upon

[56] al-Ṣafadī, *A'yān al-'aṣr*, IV, 34. The author introduces Umm Yūsuf Fakhriyya as "al-Ḥājja, ṣawwāma, qawwāma, al-'ābida, al-zāhida, zāhidat 'aṣrihā, farīdat dahrihā."

[57] Ibid., IV, 35.

[58] The family was connected on the one hand to Ḥanafī legal circles and on the other to government service. On Ṣafī al-Dīn (d. 759 or 760/1358), who had been given an *iqṭā'* and taught at a madrasa, see ibid., IV, 55–7; Ibn Ḥajar describes him as an *amīr-faqīh* (*Durar*, III, 156); on the elder brother Najm al-Dīn (d. 723/1323), who became an *amīr ṭablkhāna* under al-Malik al-Nāṣir, see Ibn Kathīr, *Bidāya*, XIV, 112; al-Ṣafadī, *A'yān al-'aṣr*, IV, 560–1.

family funds, stationing herself at a sanctuary was an unimpeachable solution: the combination of seeking the licit and the decision to relocate to a shrine was not, of course, coincidental. Each was a way of preserving one's moral and spiritual health.

Stories of exemplars more uncompromising than she were well known; indeed, such figures are coeval with the emergence of Islam. The caliph Abū Bakr, it is said, forced himself to vomit after he ate something purchased with money earned by his slave for having once, before his conversion, pretended to be a soothsayer.[59] Whether the fraud or the fortune-telling was more ethically dangerous to Abū Bakr is arguable, but it should be noted that Fakhriyya's own fear of tainted money places the benevolent Amīr Tankiz on a par with the sinful soothsayer. The classic fear of inadvertently ingesting ill-gotten gains that prevented a scrupulous woman such as Fakhriyya from accepting Tankiz's charity would have made her refuse all offers; she was wary of all money, and in this sense her story is timeless.[60]

Problems of Livelihood

According to other exemplary stories told in the late medieval period, however, pious refusals were becoming more and more warranted as new aspects of food history began to be of concern. A specific phrase describing how human bonds were formed through the traffic in food appears with regularity in stories of the ascetics and devotees of the Ayyubid and Mamluk periods. "Eating from the wealth" of someone was another way of saying that a person took money from a donor or patron and, by extension, sustained him or herself with it. The phrase simply meant that the financial sum offered was accepted. So too a man could "eat from" a piece of property he held, meaning that its yield supported him whether he ate the produce or sold it. But for the person who accepted charity, it was the very opposite of a euphemism; here again, a connection between the food ingested and the body's moral health was frequently made explicit in accounts of the pious. When the money "eaten" came

[59] al-Bukhārī, *Ṣaḥīḥ*, 678–9, hadith no. 3842.

[60] Ibn Taymiyya devoted several fatwas to the issue of excessive worry about licit food and money; one of them discusses the saying, "Eating permissible food is impossible: it cannot be found in [our] day," which he says is incorrectly attributed to the pious forebears: Ibn Taymiyya, *Majmūʿ fatāwā*, XXIV: 311; see Abdul Hakim I. al-Matroudi, *The Ḥanbalī School of Law and Ibn Taymiyya: Conflict or Conciliation* (London and New York, 2006), 103–7.

from ill-gotten gains, both it and the food bought with it, like the sheep the Prophet sent to the prisoners, were in and of themselves capable of transmitting sin. Thus choosing one's livelihood and accepting income, whether it came from charity, a salaried position, or other sources, took on crucial importance for men and women who wished to devote themselves to righteousness as well as worship.

Unlike the Glutton and Fakhriyya, many other devotees fled to places where the means of subsistence were more difficult but less complicated, such as Shaykh Qāsim al-Takrūrī, who wandered in the hills outside Medina catching fish and foraging for food, or Sulṭān ibn Maḥmūd, a thirteenth-century ascetic saint from Baalbek who spent a period likewise "sustaining himself on the permissible things of Mount Lebanon."[61] Others turned to private plots of land to earn a living, as did one of ʿAlī al-Ḥarīrī's followers in Damietta, who lived by selling dates grown in his garden.[62] Their attempts at being invisible routinely failed. Certainly some of them intended to be found, and one suspects that making the way hard was part of their plan, a means of humbling the visitor. Indeed, important men, princes, and sultans often faced rejection once they arrived.

When he fell ill in 1235, the Ayyubid sultan al-Malik al-Ashraf Mūsā chose for his shroud a garment that had once belonged to an Ethiopian saint whose name was less important than was the fact that he had spent time in the mountains near Edessa "cultivating saffron on a patch of land and living from the proceeds."[63] It would have been in the days when al-Ashraf was still prince of the region that he visited the Ethiopian there, pressing money upon him, which was routinely refused. Yet at death's door some years later, the sultan selected the tattered sheet this holy man had used for pilgrim's garb out of a collection of rags, skullcaps, and shawls that had belonged to famous holy men. It struck him as a perfect

[61] The former is discussed in the previous chapter; the latter, a man named Sulṭān ibn Maḥmūd, was a companion of ʿAbd Allāh al-Yūnīnī who died in 641/1243–4, according to al-Ṣafadī, *al-Wāfī*, XV, 297. Purposefully seeking *ḥalāl* food in nature is quite different from the notion of reliance on God for provisions (*tawakkul*).

[62] Ibn al-Mulaqqin, *Ṭabaqāt al-awliyāʾ*, 451. See also the example of Shaykh Ḥasan al-Kurdī, who died in 700/1300–1 (not the Damascene *muwallah* of the same name). He lived on what he grew in his vegetable garden in Shāghūr, where he became the object of pious visits. A Sufi as well as an ascetic, he experienced spiritual states (*ḥāl wa kashf*), spent periods in spiritual isolation (*khalwa*), and practiced bodily devotions (*taʿabbud*): Ibn Kathīr, *Bidāya*, XIV, 18; al-Ṣafadī, *Aʿyān al-aṣr*, II, 257–8.

[63] Abū Bakr ibn ʿAbd Allāh Ibn al-Dawādārī, *Kanz al-durar wa jāmiʿ al-ghurar*, ed. Hans Robert Roemer et al., 9 vols. (Cairo, 1960–72), VII, 323; and for a slightly different version, al-Dhahabī, *Tārīkh al-Islām*, XLVI, 272–3. Both authors take the story from Sibṭ Ibn al-Jawzī.

substitute for what he called – amazingly – the "crime-stained" garments in his own royal wardrobe, most obviously because it had been purified by twenty Pilgrimages.

It was not the excess of the saint's devotion alone that purified the garment. No livelihood could be purer (since presumably the man was making use of fallow land) or more opposite of the life of a sultan, no profit more painstakingly gained than by plucking the stigmas of flowers grown on a hillside.[64] The idea that nature abounded in pure sources of food and income where society did not begs the question of why society was so constrained in the first place. Paeans to nature and encomia on the simplicity of rural life, genres that themselves only seem "natural" in places such as Enlightenment Europe, were antithetical to the Islamic ideal of the city as a community of worshippers.[65] Farmers were not envied the lives they led. Isolation on a mountaintop was, according to a well-known hadith of the Prophet, as laudable an undertaking as holy war, but only because a person might concentrate on worship there without becoming entangled in other people's business.[66]

The Ethiopian saint may well have dreaded al-Ashraf's visits. This certainly was the case with a hermit Ibn Baṭṭūṭa and his shipmates found on an island in the Red Sea, who refused to speak to them or eat with them.[67] Nature was good simply because there was less chance of contact

[64] The scarlet threads of saffron are harvested from the three female pistils or stigmas of the *Crocus sativus*. See Ibn Kathīr, *Bidāya*, XIV, 157 and al-Ṣafadī, *Aʿyān al-aṣr*, I, 80 for another shaykh who made use of a piece of fallow land between the cities of Jerusalem and al-Khalīl (Hebron).

[65] That is, nostalgia for the country life crops up in specific periods, and the authors who expressed it sometimes lived at a considerable social and geographical distance from farms. On the "mythologists of sylvan purity" and how their ideas gain and lose currency over the centuries see Roy Porter, "The Urban and the Rustic in Enlightenment London," in *Nature and Society in Historical Context*, ed. Mikuláš Teich, Roy Porter, and Bo Gustafsson (Cambridge, 1997), 176–94.

[66] Al-Nawawī includes this hadith in *Gardens of the Righteous: Riyāḍ al-ṣāliḥīn*, trans. Muhammad Zafrulla Khan (Brooklyn, 1989), 223; those who left for the hills were, in Ibn al-Jawzī's opinion, bound to go wrong in their acts of worship without the guidance of the community with its mosques and learned men (*Talbīs Iblīs*, 145). A rare text valorizing farming, from the early tenth century (and purporting to be a translation of more ancient wisdom), contrasts slothful ascetics with farmers who provide food for society: Abū Bakr Aḥmad ibn ʿAlī Ibn Waḥshiyya, *Kitāb al-filāḥa al-Nabaṭiyya*, ed. Tawfiq Fahd, 3 vols. (Damascus, 1993–8), I, 258–62.

[67] After the troop joined the hermit in the night prayer he sent them away without ever having addressed them. Departing, Ibn Baṭṭūṭa had a sudden wish to remain on the island with him and so turned back, only to find the man so frightening that he returned to the ship. The hermit was dressed in a costume that seems to have reminded him of a Qalandar: "He wore a patched robe and felt bonnet, but had no skin bag nor jug nor staff nor sandals" (Ibn Baṭṭūṭa, *Travels of Ibn Baṭṭūṭa*, II, 391–2). For a later holy man,

with humanity, its greed, compromises, or misdeeds. This seems to be the point of the long account, narrated by the remorseful Sultan al-Ashraf Mūsā, about choosing a shroud: in remote and "pure" settings, a holy man's stylized message of rejection might be proclaimed to the greatest effect. These were places unfamiliar to most readers, and in the absence of details on social and economic life in the mountains of Edessa, for example, the shaykh and the sultan are reduced to stock characters in an exemplary tale about the blameless and the shameful, those unsullied by power or wealth and those tarnished by them.

The city, by contrast, had become hazardous in this period for reasons that were peculiar to the social milieu of piety from the second half of the twelfth century onwards. An early case of disillusionment with urban religious life comes from Aleppo and concerns a shaykh named Rabīʿ ibn Maḥmūd al-Mārdīnī, who died in the year 602/1205–6. His example is important because it is one of the earliest responses to a set of issues that arose in this period. A figure mentioned several times in Ibn al-ʿAdīm's *Bughyat al-ṭalab fī tārīkh Ḥalab*, this ascetic shaykh "only broke his fast for a day or two every month, put his friends before himself, and would not eat from the wealth of a sultan, a soldier or someone who took a payment from an endowment."[68] There is no generalized fear of eating something or sustaining oneself with something that might come from an illegal, or dubious, or merely unverifiable, source; there is no anxiety about charity in general. The list is targeted so specifically that no one could fail to understand that al-Mārdīnī would take money from any other source but these. Indeed, he lived in a cell (*zāwiya*) next to the mosque built for him by the author's grandfather.

The sultan makes an expected appearance, but otherwise the list represents a departure from the complaints of previous generations of Muslims. When he rejects the money of a soldier, a *jundī*, he is referring not to the rank and file (for the Muslim army itself was a worthy recipient of charity) but to the amirs, officers who collected revenue on land granted by the ruler in return for service.[69] Their fiscal rights to the grant (*iqṭāʿ*)

Shaykh al-Ṣanāfīrī, who threw stones at people who came to see him, see Ibn Taghrībirdī, *al-Nujūm al-zāhira*, XI, 118–19; also discussed by Shoshan in *Popular Culture*, 10–11.

68 Kamāl al-Dīn ʿUmar ibn Aḥmad Ibn al-ʿAdīm, *Bughyat al-ṭalab fī tārīkh Ḥalab*, ed. Suhayl Zakkār, 10 vols. (Damascus, 1988–9), VIII, 3594. The last phrase is "man lahu qaṭīʿa ʿala waqf." *Qaṭīʿa* here has the general sense of a share of something, and is not, I think, a word for tax revenue or the earlier term for *iqṭāʿ*. Ibn al-ʿAdīm does intend the latter meaning in other instances, but referring to much earlier examples.

69 Another Aleppan, Shaykh Ibn Qiwām, accepted the money Sultan al-Malik al-Kāmil gave him but redirected it to the army (*jund al-Muslimīn*): al-Yūnīnī, *Dhayl Mirʾāt al-zamān*, I,

might include taxes, duties levied on any number of goods and payments in kind from tenant farmers.[70] The land was returned to the treasury at the command of the sultan, or upon the death of the landholder. At this time a landholder might have the usufruct of an entire village, or several villages, and could increase the taxes at will. He, the *muqṭaʿ*, was sometimes so independent that he had jurisdiction over secular justice in the area he held.[71] Sato Tsugitaka has argued that the *iqṭāʿ* system fundamentally changed the lives of peasants from Ayyubid times onwards when the grantees "strengthened their rule over the peasantry through their *iqṭāʿ* holdings, and brought about an important change in which the village based peasants (*fallāḥ qarrār*) came to be regarded as 'serfs' (*ʿabd qinn*) subordinate to their *muqṭaʿ*." It was only in the first half of Mamluk rule, after 1250 C.E., that the government asserted firmer control over lands granted to the amirs.[72]

The shaykh's final prohibition suggests that corruption was rife in the administration of *waqf*, or at least perceived to be so. It is highly unlikely that the payment he refers to has to do with stipends or salaries given to the staff of a charitable institution such as a madrasa. Rather, he was drawing attention to the management of these buildings. For one thing, the civilian and military elite could safeguard the money they had by

404. For the use of the term *jundī* referring to a landholder in the Ayyubid-era *iqṭāʿ* system see Hasanein Rabie, "The Size and Value of the *Iqṭāʿ* in Egypt 564–761 A.H./1169–1341 A.D.," in *Studies in the Economic History of the Middle East From the Rise of Islam to the Present Day*, ed. M. A. Cook (Oxford, 1970), 129–30. It may also have been a general term for one of the *ḥalqa* military elite of Ibn al-ʿAdīm's day. For other examples see Sato Tsugitaka, *State and Rural Society in Medieval Islam: Sultans, Muqtaʿs and Fallahun* (Leiden, 1997), 38, 64.

70 On goods collected see Tsugitaka, *State and Rural Society*, 160. On free-born farmers being forced to remain on or return to the lands they worked for the *iqṭāʿ* holders see Yehoshua Frenkel, "Agriculture, Land-Tenure and Peasants in Palestine During the Mamluk Period," in *Egypt and Syria in the Fatimid, Ayyubid, and Mamluk Eras III: Proceedings of the 6th, 7th and 8th International Colloquium Organized at the Katholieke Universiteit Leuven in May 1997, 1998, and 1999*, ed. U. Vermeulen and J. van Steenbergen, Orientalia Lovaniensia Analecta 102 (Leuven, 2001), 203–7.

71 Eddé, *La principauté ayyoubide*, 279. The specifics of the *iqṭāʿ* system are not entirely understood for al-Mārdīnī's lifetime. Some land grants to Ayyubid military men were in fact hereditary, although this did not become the norm. (On this see Claude Cahen, "L'évolution de l'iqṭaʿ du IX au XIII siècle: Contribution à une histoire comparée des sociétés médiévales," *Annales. économies, sociétés, civilisations* 8 [1953].) More typically, the lands granted changed hands often, and though the *muqṭaʿ* had a responsibility to improve the property, he had no incentive to do so if it was already productive. In the thirteenth century a provincial deputy (*nāʾib*) or governor (*walī*) was appointed to oversee the administration of *iqṭāʿ*s, and was "responsible for preventing the *muqṭaʿ*s from behaving unfairly vis-à-vis their villagers" (Tsugitaka, *State and Rural Society*, 56).

72 Tsugitaka, *State and Rural Society*, 236–7.

creating a pious endowment and continuing to have a share in its benefits as administrators.[73] Though not illegal, this was sometimes frowned upon, and al-Mārdīnī may have sided with those who took a more stringent view of the practice. On the other hand, his disapproval of the abuse of *waqf* funds in the second half of the twelfth century may be clarified by a rash of incidents reported from the early thirteenth century onwards. Prominent families of scholars used their accumulated wealth to gain access to powerful positions, and in 632/1234, for instance, a leading jurist from the family of the Banū ʿAjam offered the sultan al-Malik al-ʿAzīz a bribe for the chance to become chief qadi of Aleppo: 60,000 dirhams for the appointment and 50,000 annually from fees levied on both the city's *waqf*s and on those he oversaw elsewhere. The sultan refused.[74] In another case, a man who was both the Mālikī chief qadi and the head of the Sufis pilfered ten dirhams from each *waqf* he oversaw in Syria.[75]

Given the financial theme of al-Mārdīnī's list, even the reference to sultans must not have been meant as a critique of their general bad behavior or cruelty, but of something more precise: brave men occasionally dared to object publicly to extra-canonical taxes levied by rulers, the Zangids (who ruled Aleppo until 1183) and Ayyubids among them. This is certainly one reason he might refuse their funds.[76] What is perhaps most important in al-Mārdīnī's story is the way it employs that familiar language of negation: he did not have a grievance against a particular ruler, some local lord's soldiers, or a corrupt local administrator.[77] He made a

[73] Muḥammad Muḥammad Amīn, *al-Awqāf wa'l-ḥayāt al-ijtimāʿiyya fī Miṣr 648–923/1250–1517* (Cairo, 1980), 93–4. The children received these benefits after the death of the *waqf*'s founder; if he or she died without an heir, it could even be earmarked for a freed slave so that the property would not revert to the public treasury. In this way families were able to accrue wealth over several generations.

[74] Eddé, *La principauté ayyoubide*, 106. The man who offered the bribe was Kamāl al-Dīn ʿUmar Ibn al-ʿAjamī, a rival of Ibn Shaddād who is credited with reporting this information.

[75] al-Ṣafadī, *Aʿyān al-ʿaṣr*, III, 543. It was in his role as head of the Sufis (*shaykh al-shuyūkh*) that he oversaw the *waqf*s of the *khānqāh*s in Syria (or possibly Damascus). This evidence appears in the biography of the man who replaced him, ʿAlī ibn Maḥmūd ibn Ḥumayd al-Qūnawī, a Ḥanafī Sufi of Damascus who died in the plague in 749/1348. On the position of *shaykh al-shuyūkh*, see Tāj al-Dīn ʿAbd al-Wahhāb al-Subkī, *Muʿīd al-niʿam wa-mubīd al-niqam (The Restorer of Favours and the Restrainer of Chastisements)*, ed. David W. Myhrman (London, 1908), 176–7.

[76] For background on this see Eddé, *La principauté ayyoubide*, 215–16.

[77] Indeed, he was held in high esteem by the Ayyubid ruler of Aleppo, al-Malik al-Ẓāhir. See Morray, *An Ayyubid Notable*, 101. Eddé describes another of al-Mārdīnī's virtues, his ability to distinguish licit food from *ḥarām* food by sight, and affirms that it was a common trait among ascetic saints at this time (*La principauté ayyoubide*, 417).

decision to categorically avoid having a spiritual debt to all men in any of these positions. Having singled them out as the worst abusers of power he refused their charity, and in doing so he expressed his distance from them, in a sense, through food. What emerges from this point onwards is a mood of suspicion about the correlation of land to power and power to food.

From the same period, a related kind of self-regulation drew attention to the problems of residing in buildings supported by pious foundations. Madrasas, *khānqāh*s, *zāwiya*s, and *ribāṭ*s, all were buildings of this sort that proliferated in the late twelfth century. In Damascus alone, the Ayyubid period saw sixty-three new madrasas and twenty new buildings of the other three types.[78] One of al-Mārdīnī's contemporaries, Yūsuf Ibn al-Malīḥ, was a Shāfiʿī jurist and Qurʾān expert who taught law at the famed Niẓāmiyya Madrasa in Baghdad. After a change of heart, he fell in with the Sufis and for a time took up residence at a *ribāṭ*, a familiar maneuver for disentangling oneself from the politics of the academy. Another change of heart followed, for "he then grew wary of the food of endowments, so he shut himself away in his house where he ate, accepting no benefaction (*birr*) from sultans whatsoever." In the privacy of his own home he embarked on a new, harmless career as a historian.[79] The reference to the food served in the buildings makes just as pointed a statement as had those of al-Mārdīnī. He could have said, for example, that he believed the administrators of endowments to be corrupt. He could have been worried that the man in charge of provisions was not cautious enough about the vendors he frequented; for someone concerned with seeking the licit, trusting someone else with such weighty matters must have been difficult. He could have said that the *ribāṭ*s of the Sufis were places of iniquity. There was no need, because the reference to food provided the most unequivocal statement of rejection. Again, no metaphor is intended; he was able to eat only in his own house. In the tradition of pious suspicion and complaint, a refusal of food brought scrutiny to a whole category – endowed buildings – and also, by extension, to the original source of charity. In this case the scrutiny would fall upon the founder of the endowed building.

The complaints multiplied as reports of new kinds of corruption spread. Problems in the public treasury, particularly regarding confiscated

[78] R. Stephen Humphreys, "Women as Patrons of Religious Architecture in Ayyubid Damascus," *Muqarnas* 11 (1994): 35.

[79] The key phrase is "tawarraʿa ʿan akl al-awqāf": al-Ṣafadī, *al-Wāfī*, XXIX, 334–5. Oddly enough, Ibn al-Malīḥ chose as his topic a history of the sultans.

property – both the property used for building a madrasa, for example, and the lands endowed for its upkeep – were no secret in the Mamluk period. The funding for salaries and stipends at religious institutions could therefore be carefully scrutinized. Tales circulated widely of *iqṭāʿ* land being returned to the treasury, then bought by high-ranking amirs, merchants, or even jurists, who turned them into *waqf* property benefiting their families.[80] Those who considered this property to be illegally owned were hesitant to take a position at a religious building founded in this way; sometimes they accepted a post but rejected its pay and provisions. Even in the Ayyubid period there had been a general sense, among the pious, that teaching positions at well-funded madrasas were a source of pollution, for these positions could be a means of securing status along with a good salary. As Chamberlain points out, just as an amir might win or lose an *iqṭāʿ* through his political maneuverings, so might a member of the civilian elite strive to gain a well-financed position at a madrasa. These two groups, the military elite and the civilian elite, were not just similar, they were linked to each other in the struggles over power and prestige in the city.[81]

Interestingly enough, precautionary stipulations began to be included in endowment deeds by scrupulous founders. A document of foundation inscribed on the walls of the Mirjāniyya Madrasa in Baghdad, dated 758/1356–7, specified that none of the many properties sustaining this *waqf*, from fields and gardens to shops and caravansaries, should be rented out to "someone who seizes property, to an imperious notable, to a military man or to anyone who might run it to ruin."[82] Although

[80] For examples, see Ulrich Haarmann, "Joseph's Law: The Careers and Activities of Mamluk Descendants Before the Ottoman Conquest of Egypt," in *The Mamluks in Egyptian Politics and Society*, ed. Thomas Philipp and Ulrich Haarmann (Cambridge, 1998), 70–2. It was not only the Mamluk amirs who were involved in such transactions: Ibn al-ʿIrāqī reports a meeting in 780/1379 in which the amirs Barqūq and Baraka sought the help of the chief qadis in abolishing land endowments (*awqāf al-arāḍī*) that had been bought illegally from the public treasury. As some of these properties involved the wealth of respected scholars such as Sirāj al-Dīn al-Bulqīnī, who was present at the meeting, the jurists upheld the probity of these estates and refused to dissolve them: Aḥmad ibn ʿAbd al-Raḥīm Ibn al-ʿAṭṭār, *Dhayl ʿala'l-ʿIbar fī khabar man ʿabar*, ed. Ṣāliḥ Mahdī ʿAbbās, 2 vols. (Beirut, 1989), II, 475.

[81] Chamberlain provides a portrait of the late medieval Damascene madrasa system and its foibles in rich detail: on confiscations and financial intrigue see *Knowledge and Social Practice*, 54–60; on the struggle to gain an appointment at a madrasa, 90 ff.; and on wariness about being polluted by these appointments, 101.

[82] The list is "mutaghallab wa mutaʿaziz wa jundī wa man yakhāfahu ghā'ilatahu": E. Combe, J. Sauvaget, and G. Wiet et al., eds., *Répertoire chronologique d'épigraphie*

this list seems to echo that of al-Mārdīnī in Aleppo – and it does in its identification of men in particular positions of power – it mainly reflects the worries a founder in Ilkhanid Baghdad had about how to protect his *waqf*.[83] As for running a property into ruin, Leonor Fernandes has described how a new legal process (or rather a newly legal one) called *istibdāl* (exchange) transformed the cityscape of fifteenth-century Cairo. In the early Mamluk period much of the city consisted of *waqf* buildings or buildings that provided revenue to support them. As these trusts were unbreakable, there were few opportunities for new building projects.[84]

Considered illegal by jurists in the early Mamluk period, including al-Nawawī, these "exchanges" allowed for a person to buy property from an existing *waqf*, which would then be dissolved. This was allowed only on the condition that the property was in such disrepair that it constituted a public hazard. In court hearings the procedure gradually began to be sanctioned, partly when the qadis hearing the cases were put under pressure; sometimes the qadis themselves stood to benefit from sanctioning *istibdāl*. The Shāfiʿī chief qadi, Jalāl al-Dīn ʿAbd al-Raḥmān al-Bulqīnī (d. 824/1421), reportedly ruled in favor of *istibdāl* seven hundred times.[85] Running a piece of endowed property to ruin was a tactic that, in Cairo as well as in Baghdad, paralleled the more simple, but illegal, strategy of confiscation – which continued to be used as well. While the details of founding and maintaining endowed buildings differed in twelfth-century Aleppo, thirteenth-century Damascus, fourteenth-century Baghdad, or fifteenth-century Cairo, the reasons for suspicion were largely the same.

Being wary of the origins of food, the funding for food, and the systems that produced food, a stance so well established by the scrupulousw ascetics of the Ayyubid period, became even more common in the early Mamluk period, and pious refusals even more explicit. There were few figures better positioned to make a refusal more resoundingly heard than the jurist al-Nawawī. Indeed, aside from his brilliance as a scholar, part

arabe, 18 vols. (Cairo, 1931–91), XVI, 186–90. I am grateful to Tamer el-Leithy for this reference.

83 For an almost identical list of stipulations in a *waqfiyya* document in Yazd, and the inefficacy of such stipulations(!), see Ann Lambton, "*Awqāf* in Persia: 6th–8th/12th–14th Centuries," *Islamic Law and Society*, 4, 3 (1997), 302–3.

84 Leonor Fernandes, "*Istibdal*: The Game of Exchange and its Impact on the Urbanization of Medieval Cairo," in *The Cairo Heritage: Essays in Honor of Layla Ali Ibrahim*, ed. Doris Behrens Abouseif (Cairo, 2000), 207.

85 Ibid.

of al-Nawawī's fame even in his lifetime lay in his ability to use actions to illustrate points of social criticism, and sometimes even the finer points of substantive law. Suspicions, apparently justified, about the *ḥalāl* quality of the original source of funding for the endowment might explain al-Nawawī's reluctance to accept the stipend offered at his madrasa, recently established by a wealthy Damascene merchant.[86] And like Ibn al-Malīḥ, al-Nawawī had ongoing concerns not just about how he was paid but about how he should eat.

When asked why he refused to drink cold water and never ate fruit, two typically ascetic choices, he answered, "Damascus is a city full of *waqf*s and confiscated properties which are entailed to them." The new overseers of these agricultural lands, he said, were running them on a sharecropping scheme even though "the practice is disputed by the jurists."[87] In fact, sharecropping in orchards, which the lands around Damascus had in abundance, was a topic being reevaluated by al-Nawawī himself in his legal writings, although earlier Shāfiʿī jurists had permitted it.[88] He continued, "So how can I justify making myself gay by eating these [pleasant] things?" This last statement makes it clear that he was avoiding fruit because it came from confiscated or mismanaged (or dubiously managed) orchards. That is, it was not specifically the food of his own madrasa he refused to eat – although elsewhere he is said to have refused this as well – but food produced on lands that funded endowed buildings in general.

[86] This is a suggestion raised by Chamberlain, *Knowledge and Social Practice*, 61 and 76; see also Ibn Kathīr, *Bidāya*, XIII, 125. The Ruwāḥiyya had been established by Ibn Ruwāḥa before his death in 623/1226 to protect his fortune from confiscation.

[87] al-Dhahabī, *Tārīkh al-Islām*, L, 252.

[88] Al-Nawawī states: "There are two opinions about fruit-bearing trees such as the fig, walnut, apricot, apple and so forth: the old opinion holds sharecropping to be permissible; the new one prohibits it ... I say: the new opinion is more sound": al-Nawawī, *Rawḍat al-ṭālibīn*, IV, 231. This kind of sharecropping (*musāqāh*) refers to perennial trees, primarily date-palms, and vines. Ibn Rushd, writing in the twelfth century, says the Ḥanafī school alone forbids it altogether; see his extended discussion in *The Distinguished Jurist's Primer*, II, 293–300. Regarding whether fruit trees other than date-palms are permitted in these contracts, al-Nawawī has sided with the "sounder" opinion, which appears as far back as Ibn Surayj (d. 306/918). William J. Donaldson examines al-Nawawī's chapter on *musāqāh* in the *Minhāj al-ṭālibīn* along with the classical legal doctrines on the topic in *Sharecropping in the Yemen: A Study in Islamic Theory, Custom and Pragmatism*, Studies in Islamic Law and Society 13 (Leiden, 2000). See also Rudolph Peters' compelling case study that addresses the legal obstacles involved, "Sharecropping in the Dakhla Oasis: Shariʿa and Customary Law in Ottoman Egypt," in *The Law Applied: Contextualizing the Islamic Shariʿa*, ed. Peri Bearman, Wolfhart Heinrichs, and Bernard G. Weiss (London and New York, 2008).

Furthermore, the avoidance of cold water is a reminder that these were gestures of voluntary abstention: distressed over unfair farming practices "conducted with a smile," he forbade himself cold water as well as fruit in a gesture of sympathy on behalf of those who worked the orchards. It was a doubly ascetic statement, both bodily and ethical.[89] Few could have missed the fact that his critique of religious life in the city implicated the sultan directly, for the ruler was ultimately responsible for the confiscated properties al-Nawawī mentions; the properties were recycled through the state treasury over which he had control. Al-Nawawī's role as critic ultimately got him banished from Damascus when Sultan Baybars took exception to a fatwa al-Nawawī had written regarding extra-canonical taxes. After a successful – and indeed consciously exemplary – career in the capital of Mamluk Syria, the jurist died in his hometown of Nawā an exile, but most likely relieved at being able to eat more freely.

A refusal to eat food that was linked to the systems of *waqf* and *iqṭāʿ* thus sent a number of different messages. It could be a critique of the patrons and their ill-gotten gains, or it could call into doubt the more recent history of food served in endowed institutions. Food played no more metaphorical a role in these cases than it did in the story of the Glutton, since the very definition of eating pure food meant that a person had to take care of his or her stomach.[90] It was an old definition, but one that compelled medieval jurists and others who depended upon charitable funds to protest against injustices they perceived as endemic to their livelihoods. They did so either in silent gestures of avoidance or with daring words. But these problems of purity also explain why, paradoxically, men such as al-Nawawī did not depart immediately for the countryside. As exemplars, and often as exemplary jurists, they were bound to remain in the city fulfilling their roles as teachers, as arbiters of justice, and, to be sure, as social critics.

The ascetics' predilection for making lists of food sources to be rejected (the charity of sultans and princes, *waqf* provisions, the judiciary, *iqṭāʿ* holders, corrupt amirs, and men in power generally) is especially convenient for modern historians. The lists provide succinct evidence of how piety in the Ayyubid and especially the early Mamluk period defined itself in response to gradual changes in the fabric of religious culture, and they

[89] A second informant who mentions al-Nawawī's dislike of fruit explains it as a rejection of luxury (al-Dhahabī, *Tārīkh al-Islām*, L, 255).

[90] See for example Ibn Baydakīn, who quotes ancient exemplars such as Fuḍayl ibn Īyād ("He who knows what enters his stomach is an upright man"), Sarī al-Saqaṭī, Bishr al-Ḥāfī and various Companions of the Prophet: *Kitāb al-lumaʿ*, I, 205.

show how the devotees perceived themselves as facing a different set of ethical and social problems than had their forebears. The desire to eat pure food appears so often in chronicles and biographical dictionaries between 1200 and 1400 C.E. that the theme was obviously conventional. But because of each person's individual understanding of the Prophet's injunction to seek the licit, scrupulous men and women applied this concept to the different circumstances of their lives in a changing society.

If the discourse of critique begins to seem relentless by the middle of the Mamluk period, it is not because the ruling elite was evil to the last man. On the contrary, many amirs who received *iqṭā*ʿs took seriously the responsibility for improving their properties by developing the local infrastructure and sponsoring pious projects, such as the building of mosques.[91] Shams al-Dīn Sunqur al-Qishtimurī (d. 698/1299) was a high-ranking amir and former *mamlūk* of Sultan al-Malik al-Manṣūr Lājīn's deputy Mankūtamur who held fiscal rights over some property, probably outside Damascus. Though Sunqur was not an especially influential amir, the chronicler al-Jazarī described the attributes that made him locally famous:

> He was full of faith and chastity, blameless, trustworthy, and diligent in the responsibilities of his office (*wilāyāt*). He would not eat from what the farmers brought him, nor would he feed his riding beasts from it. Rather he paid in dirhams for whatever he needed by way of food and fodder. He had enormous graciousness and was a perfect gentleman. He never hid his face from those who came asking, even if it was to his detriment. He was one of the best men of his time. May God be merciful to him.[92]

In just a few sentences al-Jazarī elegantly grafted the virtues befitting an amir who discharges his affairs with justice and mercy onto the ethical wariness of a scrupulous ascetic.

The use of the phrase "he would not eat from ..." is surely deliberate here, for of course the proceeds of the crops *did* sustain him (and his horses). What he refused were the expected "extras" proffered by peasants

[91] For example, in the later twelfth century Ṣalāḥ al-Dīn (Saladin) created an endowment to support positions for twenty-four eunuchs serving as guards at the tomb of the Prophet in Medina, the revenue for which came from two villages in Egypt. Some century and a half later, the eunuchs had a waterwheel and a sugar-cane press built in one of the towns in order to augment their income, and, from then on, one of them remained there as overseer. See Shaun E. Marmon, *Eunuchs and Sacred Boundaries in Islamic Society* (New York, 1995), 38–9.

[92] al-Jazarī, *Tārīkh*, I, 446.

when a *muqṭaʿ* occasionally showed up.[93] A childhood recollection of Ibn Taghrībirdī's shows that offering gifts to the landlord was a well-known custom: at the age of five during an audience with Sultan al-Muʾayyad Shaykh, he boldly demanded that the ruler give him an estate "with peasants who would bring him sheep and geese and fowl."[94]

Rural villages and the cities they fed were not so far removed from each other in medieval Syria. In the networks of food connecting them the most visible role was often played by an agent who worked for the *muqṭaʿ* in collecting payments and taxes; landlords did not necessarily live on their *iqṭāʿ* estates, and some never visited their properties at all.[95] Except for the laborers themselves, however, no one could have been more closely linked to the original point in the network than the holder of the *iqṭāʿ*. And it was precisely this link that Sunqur made explicit. He made a point of paying the farmers even for the grain he took for his horse, and, by refusing the gifts offered, he thereby acknowledged a familiar form of misconduct perpetrated by his fellow amirs. Such symbolic gestures would have had great social value especially in the decade before Sunqur's death, when the region was beset by cyclical droughts and famines.[96] He died fifteen years before the *rawk* of Sultan al-Nāṣir Muḥammad got underway in Syria and Egypt. Later chroniclers such as Ibn Taghrībirdī and al-Maqrīzī clearly perceived this cadastral survey as being a response to numerous injustices committed by the amirs.[97] Sunqur's actions, when they pointed out the failings of his more ordinary

[93] The "tribute goods" (*ḍiyāfa*) paid to the *iqṭāʿ* holder on an occasional basis (in addition to regular crops) could include fowl, goats, clover, dough, lentils, and cakes: Tsugitaka, *State and Rural Society*, 149. On amirs and their cavalrymen demanding banquets and fodder for their horses from the inhabitants of the property see Taqī al-Dīn Aḥmad al-Maqrīzī, *al-Mawāʿiẓ wa'l-iʿtibār bi-dhikr al-khiṭaṭ wa'l-āthār (al-maʿrūf bi'l-Khiṭaṭ al-Maqrīziyya)*, 2 vols. (Beirut, n.d. [1877]), II, 312–13, cited also by Tsugitaka, *State and Rural Society*, 125.

[94] William Popper, "Sakhāwī's Criticism of Ibn Taghrī Birdī," in *Studi orientalistici in onore di Giorgio Levi Della Vida*, vol. II, Pubblicazioni dell'Istituto per l'Oriente 52 (Rome, 1956), 380.

[95] On the function of the *wakīl* (agent) who worked for absentee landlords, and issues of how taxes were collected and salaries distributed, see Leonor Fernandes, "On Conducting the Affairs of the State: A Guideline of the Fourteenth Century," *Annales islamologiques* 24 (1988).

[96] William Tucker, "Environmental Hazards, Natural Disasters, Economic Loss, and Mortality in Mamluk Syria," *Mamluk Studies Review* 3 (1999), 115 ff.

[97] al-Maqrīzī, *Sulūk*, II, 150; al-Maqrīzī, *Khiṭaṭ*, I, 88; citing the fact that the amirs and Mamluks also took taxes from brothels and taverns, Ibn Taghrībirdī calls their behavior "injustice (*ẓulm*) beyond description" (*al-Nujūm al-zāhira*, 42–55). On the cadastral surveys of this period see Rabie, "The Size and Value of the *Iqṭāʿ*."

peers, represent a familiar kind of commentary through actions that abound in stories of holy men. In addition to displaying graciousness, he imposed on himself guidelines for being *ṭayyib al-maṭʿam* (eating licit food), which, to him, was defined as not abusing his privileges as an *iqṭāʿ* holder. Sunqur serves as a further example of how the critique of power, here a self-critique, was demonstrated through the rejection of food offered.

If these individual examples of self-imposed food regulations suggest that it was only a few members of society who took seriously the connection between the world and the stomach, a final case demonstrates how the issue of *ḥarām* food could be invoked in a wider form of social protest. The pilgrims who joined the Syrian and Egyptian caravans to Mecca in the year 698/1299 were an unfortunate group of travellers whose ordeal began when they were beset by thirst and hunger on the journey. Then, instead of finding sanctuary in Mecca they were attacked and robbed by Bedouin raiders in the holy city. Al-Yūnīnī heard details of the incident from a man who had arrived with the Syrian caravan and stayed on in Mecca after the pilgrimage rites were concluded.

> He mentioned that a total of 11 people, two women and nine men, were killed, and that the ruler of Mecca, Amīr Najm al-Dīn Numayya, received his share of 300 camels that had been plundered from the Egyptian, Syrian, Bedouin, and other pilgrims. He said that after the departure of the pilgrims, camel meat was on sale in Mecca. Most of the [long-term visitors] in the sanctuary refused to eat meat, protesting the looting.[98]

The Meccan rulers had a responsibility to protect pilgrims and their caravans, although their allegiances with the Bedouins sometimes compelled them to look the other way. Najm al-Dīn's collusion in the incident was especially shocking, given that he profited from plunder and murder, and the pious visitors' response was a boycott.[99] If this sounds altogether

[98] Guo, *Early Mamluk Syrian Historiography*, I, 132–3. Guo translates *mujāwarūn* as "residential students," but I have modified this to "long-term visitors" because some of them would have been adults: scholars who came to pursue further study, pious men and women seeking the *baraka* of a stay in the holy city, and even elderly Muslims who came there to die.

[99] The Meccan ruler mentioned in the episode above was Abu Numayy I, the Sharif of Mecca, who died two years later in 1301. "His son Humaidha used to say of him that he had five good qualities: honour, generosity, patience, courage, and poetry. Piety, it will be remarked, is not mentioned": Gerald de Gaury, *The Rulers of Mecca* (New York, 1991), 91–4. For another example of Mamluk outrage at the murder of pilgrims and the diplomatic tiff that ensued see Clifford Bosworth, "Some Historical Gleanings from the Section on Symbolic Actions in Qalqašandī's *Ṣubḥ al-Aʿšā*," *Arabica* 10 (1963): 152–3.

modern, it nevertheless had sound roots in the Islamic legal tradition, which defined fair practices in the marketplace in great detail. In terms of Islamic law, these sojourners in Mecca were doing the correct thing since stolen food was forbidden and should not be sold. In reality, of course, the murder of pilgrims was what precipitated the boycott, for it made the camel meat not just financially impure but truly inedible.

Two related themes that have been discussed in this chapter can be brought together at this point. First is the issue of questionable charitable endowments, which struck the pious as being a contemporary problem. A large number of temporary and permanent residents of Mecca would have been fed and housed through endowed properties in the city, where, by 1300 C.E., according to Mortel, nearly thirty *ribāṭ*s and ten madrasas had been built.[100] If any of the camel meat found its way into the residents' meals, they would be directly concerned. Second, the incident illustrates the ancient theme of how easily someone becomes implicated in injustice or crime through the act of eating. Scrutiny was always warranted. If the concern with eating pure food was often expressed as a general fear, knowing the path food had taken could only make things worse, as the case of the Meccan boycott makes clear. Once again, food purity was at the center of a moral crisis, and abstinence in the form of rejection was the means of resolution.

Juristic Ethics

Islamic society, ideally, strives to make it easy for people to live cleanly and without hypocrisy. It seeks to protect Muslims as well as to regulate their behavior. As custodians of legal knowledge, the jurists and judges not only served as arbiters of correct action but were also expected to be its exemplars, and to this extent their behavior was always public: there was no difference, for instance, between the personal conduct of the qadi and his public administration of justice, nor were the private lives of legal scholars spared public scrutiny.[101] These men were therefore self-regulators, and in this capacity the pious among them helped to define the patterns of social avoidance that became prevalent in the medieval period, since they were charged with negotiating for others the situations they themselves often feared.

[100] Mortel, "*Ribāṭ*s in Mecca"; "Madrasas in Mecca."

[101] On the moral virtues expected of qadis see A. Kevin Reinhart, "Transcendence and Social Practice: *Muftīs* and *Qāḍīs* as Religious Interpreters," *Annales islamologiques* 27 (1993).

Judges in particular sometimes found this a heavy burden. As a source of guidance in behavior, the law was a refuge and an effective means of resistance in an impious society, as al-Nawawī so adeptly demonstrated, but as a source of employment it was also a trap. In his *Dhayl Mir'āt al-zamān* al-Yūnīnī offered a detailed portrait of one qadi's struggle to remain blameless. The Shāfiʿī judge in Baalbek, Ṣadr al-Dīn ibn Naṣr, had been a lifelong friend of al-Yūnīnī's grandfather. Despite the respected position he held, Ṣadr al-Dīn dressed frugally, "and never in all his life did he acquire a mount except once when he bought a mule, but it died before he could ride it."[102] The author recalled the qadi's extreme generosity to the poor, declaring that no visitor passed through town without being graciously hosted by him. But while generosity came easily to Ṣadr al-Dīn, the official hospitality demanded by his office did not.

> Whenever he entertained a rich man, he would set aside an ample portion of the dinner to give as charity to the poor. If there was not enough left over, he would make a meal all over again for them, as if making atonement that way for money squandered in a cause other than God's.[103]

Despite the fact that table fellowship was required by social custom and religious etiquette, he felt culpable nonetheless. His response was to perform an act of penance, and in doing so he borrowed a surprising pattern from Islamic law. If required acts of ritual worship such as fasting or prayer are interrupted or otherwise invalidated, they must be performed again from the beginning. Ṣadr al-Dīn's application of this completely disparate principle of *isti'nāf* to the ritual of making and serving a meal was an unusual and entirely voluntary form of expiation, but for a jurist such legal analogies were within easy reach.

As if to further explain how he coped with the burdens of his office, al-Yūnīnī then explains that the qadi's spare moments were spent in supererogatory prayer and Qur'ān recitation. He also fasted as an act of

[102] al-Yūnīnī, *Dhayl Mir'āt al-zamān*, I, 244. Al-Yūnīnī describes Ṣadr al-Dīn as a scholar, an ascetic, a devotee, and a man of scruples; he died in 656/1256.

[103] Ibid. The peculiar phrase is: "ista'anafa ṭaʿāman li'l-fuqarā' ka-annahu yukaffira bi-dhalika mā anfaqahu li-ghayr Allāha taʿāla." An act of *isti'nāf* is the repeating, from the beginning, of a required act of worship such as prayer if it has been broken by something causing a state of impurity. Al-Yūnīnī also reports that it was the qadi's wife who made the extra food; in a second story the qadi came home one snowy night and bade her make a tray of *qaṭa'if*, a pastry made of flour and almonds. Despite the inclement weather he then set out with it for a mosque, where he had discovered three poor people hungry and sitting in darkness (ibid., I, 245).

voluntary devotion (*nāfila*) "most of the time." Another symptom of discomfort with his station was a dramatically stylized self-reliance, wherein he would purchase his own goods from the market and carry them back to his house. Along the way people would stop him and offer to relieve him of his load, but he declined these kindnesses as a matter of course. Then he would carry his dough to the communal oven instead of letting an errand boy or slave perform the task.[104] Like al-Nawawī, the chief qadi of Baalbek apparently understood the usefulness of creative and dramatic actions. That this performance of humility took place in the marketplace is important, for it reinforces the idea that public spaces were appropriate settings for a qadi's demonstration of correct behavior.

Old virtues of humbleness or self-abasement had become another protective strategy, which, much like the perpetual fast, mitigated the risks of holding a position of high status. These virtues applied even in cases not involving appointment to public office – or perhaps they merely underscored the reasons for turning down appointments offered, for a half century later another scrupulous Shāfiʿī jurist in Damascus made exactly the same statement as Ṣadr al-Dīn by performing errands himself. For his meals "he would collect the ingredients from the market himself and [then carry] the baking tray of dough to the local ovens. Likewise, everything else he would acquire by his own hand, without pride, hypocrisy or affectation."[105] This man, Ibn ʿAttāf al-Kurdī (d. 689/1289), taught law at several madrasas in Damascus but had twice refused an appointment to the judiciary. Trying to convey a sense of his unparalleled moral strength, al-Jazarī described Ibn ʿAttāf as an ascetic, a devotee and exemplar who was "extra-scrupulous (*mutawarriʿ*) and excessively humble (*mutaqanniʿ*), taking extremely little from the world (*mutaqallilan fīʾl-dunyā*)." By stepping into a social sphere that was not his and by disrupting the normal patterns of something as basic as baking bread, Ibn ʿAttāf effectively drew attention to the incompatibility of ascetic principles and the use of a servant's labor. Public displays of moral purity were necessary for the sake of edifying the Muslim community, and equally important for the jurist himself as a way of living in that community without becoming corrupted by society.

God's Law vs. Substantive Law: Taxonomies of the Licit

If displays of humility signal a conformity with the spirit of God's law (*sharīʿa*), it was knowledge of substantive law (*furūʿ al-fiqh*) that

[104] Ibid., I, 244–5.
[105] al-Jazarī, *Tārīkh*, I, 30.

led many jurists to produce their own sets of food prohibitions. When jurists sought to understand the implications of being *ṭayyib al-maṭʿam*, of "eating purely," on a personal basis, they often made their worries about ingesting *ḥarām* food explicit by departing from the teachings of their own legal schools. Not all of their individual prohibitions, in fact, relate to the common tendency to use scrupulosity as a form of social critique. Some of them came to focus narrowly on particular substances and specific types of food rather than on the person from whom it was received. By considering two of these cases, both from Medina and both involving substantive law, we may examine more closely the important trend towards scrupulosity in late medieval Islamic piety. What were the consequences of eating the wrong thing? And to what degree does Islamic law "solve" problems of diet?

The first exemplar of this legalistic pattern of scrutiny was Shaykh Mūsā ibn ʿAlī al-Marrākushī (d. 789/1387–8), a famous Mālikī jurist who was one of Ibn Farḥūn's teachers. Ibn Farḥūn affirms: "For [those who sought] knowledge of Mālikī law, the laws of the other schools, the principles of law, the laws of inheritance and other subjects, he was truly a destination."[106] Since al-Marrākushī was still alive while the *History of Medina* was being written, Ibn Farḥūn asks God to help the shaykh in the ongoing activities to which he had committed himself:

> Among permissible substances, he sustains himself on only the roughest food, eating no meat or dates or butter in the land of the Hijaz. Most of the time, a meager portion of bread with no condiment is prepared for him, and when on occasion he takes something with it, it is only a boiled turnip.[107]

These are several overlapping spheres of meaning in his food prohibitions. He was first of all concerned with the *ḥalāl* quality of any food he ate. Then, among permissible foods he ate nothing luxurious, and of what remained he further whittled down the things he allowed himself to the point where turnips were a rare treat. And finally, he considered certain foods – meat, butter, and dates – to be proscribed.

106 Ibn Farḥūn, *Tārīkh al-Madīna*, 117.

107 This was only the latest phase of an ever-evolving diet, for the author continues: "Back in the day, though, he was content with just plain gruel made of barley flour, during a long period where he was fasting perpetually and constantly keeping nighttime vigils. This he did no matter whether he was healthy or sick. Eventually he fell ill for a long stretch, at which point he broke the fast": Ibn Farḥūn, *Tārīkh al-Madīna*, 117.

This list appears at first to be somewhat random. A likely source of concern regarding dates is the controversy surrounding the date palms planted (and replanted) in the courtyard of the Prophet's tomb in Medina, which at least some scholars in the thirteenth century considered a reprehensible innovation (*bidʿa*).[108] Abū Shāma, citing the earlier opinion of Ibn al-Ṣalāḥ, was bothered by the trees because people were "currying favor [with God] by eating Ṣīḥānī dates in the Noble Garden between the *minbar* and the tomb."[109] The reference to the dates being an Iraqi variety (Ṣīḥānī) and not of Medinan origin may have been a pointed one. Avoiding innovation could well explain why al-Marrākushī declined to eat dates grown in the Hijaz, but if so, what of the butter and meat?

A different explanation of the avoidance of dates reveals the coherence in his food prohibitions. The animals and plants of the sacred territory of Mecca are *ḥarām* because God has made the place inviolable. Living things of all kinds are sacrosanct inside its boundaries.[110] According to hadiths often cited in juridical discussions, the city has been sanctified since time immemorial, and will be so until the Day of Judgment.[111] During his lifetime Muḥammad declared the city of Medina to be a similar refuge, a sanctuary, and once he had done this nearly all the same rules applied. Among the minor points of difference, for example, is that "it is permissible to take the leaves of trees in the *ḥaram* of Medina to use for pillows and cushions."[112] Eventually not only the two cities but the surrounding land – the Hijaz itself – was recognized as sacred territory. What implications would this have for people who live within the region? What are they permitted to eat?

[108] The controversy also had to do with physical alterations to the Prophet's sanctuary in Medina. On this see Marmon, *Eunuchs and Sacred Boundaries*, 82–5.

[109] Abū Shāma, *Kitāb al-Bāʿith*, 153. Ibn al-Ṣalāḥ al-Shahrazūrī was a renowned Shāfiʿī jurist of Kurdish origin who settled in Damascus and died in 643/1245. His manual on the rites of the hajj (*manāsik al-ḥajj*) is still unpublished.

[110] Thus it is said that pilgrims entering the sacred territory of Mecca are not allowed to hunt animals or to pick the leaves and fruit of plants. Combined with this general prohibition, the pilgrim's consecrated state of *iḥrām* makes taboo what is ordinarily permissible: the spilling of blood or the taking of a life (even that of a plant) is temporarily prohibited. The Prophet made a few notable exceptions for creatures that were dangerous: the scorpion, the snake and the rat, the kite and the crow, and rabid dogs.

[111] Shihāb al-Dīn Aḥmad ibn Idrīs al-Qarāfī, *al-Dhakhīra*, ed. Muḥammad Ḥajjī, 14 vols. (Cairo, 1994), III, 335–6; Ibn Qudāma, *Mughnī*, III, 358. On the topic of Arabian sanctuaries being places of refuge for flora and fauna as well as human beings see R. B. Serjeant, "Ḥaram and Ḥawṭah: The Sacred Enclave in Arabia," in *Studies in Arabian History and Civilization* (London, 1981), 41–58; on the spatial dimensions of the term *ḥaram* see Marmon, *Eunuchs and Sacred Boundaries*.

[112] Ibn Qudāma, *Mughnī*, III, 370.

Meat posed little problem for the jurists. Since the prohibition on killing animals was taken to relate to hunting, domesticated animals were acceptable as food because they belonged to humans and not to the sanctuary or to God. But plants, crops, and trees created a more complex legal puzzle. Generally, an exception was made for plants sown by human hands, and to Abū Ḥanīfa this included fruit-bearing trees such as the walnut, the almond, and the date palm. Al-Shāfiʿī stuck to what he felt was the original prohibition of cutting any branch of any tree in the sanctuary, whether tended by man or growing wild. In agreeing with the former, Ibn Qudāma reveals how the essential core of these taboos has to do with the element of wildness. Planted crops are acceptable, he says, and by analogy animals raised in captivity are permissible, but wild beasts that have been tamed are not.[113] The issue was a point of *ikhtilāf*, an area of disagreement among the four Sunnī *madhhab*s.

Clearly, given Ibn Qudāma's extensive consideration of these differing views, the problem of what to eat in sacred spaces was still cause for discussion in the thirteenth century. The Mālikī opinion, which would have been of particular concern to Shaykh al-Marrākushī, follows the more lenient interpretation of the Ḥanbalīs and Ḥanafīs.[114] Mālik himself, according to al-Marrākushī's biographer Ibn Farḥūn, had also stated that the fruit of trees planted in the courtyards of mosques, cemeteries, and the like are *ḥalāl* (permissible) for Muslims.[115] Nevertheless, al-Marrākushī took a dim view of hunting and gathering, defining these activities rather broadly, and refused dates in case they were cut from a living tree that was inviolable.

His proscription of butter and meat are not mentioned by any of the medieval jurists cited here, such as al-Qarāfī or Ibn Qudāma. The only possible explanation is that the shaykh refused to eat all meats and dairy products not for fear of unknowingly eating a substance coming from a wild animal, or not only for that reason, but because the local livestock might graze upon the wild grasses of Medina. The products coming from livestock that ate *ḥarām* plants were by extension *ḥarām*

113 Ibn Qudāma presents all of the views cited here: ibid., III, 364–5. Wheeler advances the compelling argument that the requirements of the hajj having to do with wildness (not killing animals or plucking plants) and the uncivilized state of the pilgrims (bodies ill-smelling, nails unclipped, and hair uncut, etc.) are linked to the noncivilized conditions in Eden, where cultivated foods were as yet unknown and refinements such as perfume unnecessary: Brannon M. Wheeler, *Mecca and Eden: Ritual, Relics, and Territory in Islam* (Chicago, 2006), 65–6.

114 al-Qarāfī, *al-Dhakhīra*, III, 337.

115 Ibn Farḥūn, *Tārīkh al-Madīna*, 37.

for him.[116] Seeking the licit in a sacred locale governed by its own rules must have caused doubt for some other pious visitors to the Hijaz, and especially the jurists among them. Yet the issue of the food of the Hijaz appears not to have been widely discussed outside the genre of substantive law. Abū Shāma, a Shāfiʿī, makes no mention of plants being sacrosanct in his critique of eating dates in the Medinan sanctuary, and it is not mentioned even in some of the more important *furūʿ* texts.[117] One may also assume that the holy city's residents did not generally follow these extra-scrupulous rules, for even among the pious elite such concerns were uncommon.

But the issue arises once more in Ibn Farḥūn's biographical dictionary, and is clarified, during an account of the dissimilar pious achievements of two men, who were brothers by virtue of having both attended the study-circle of another well-known Mālikī jurist.[118] In their joint obituary we see how two wholly different approaches could emerge even among fellow students from a single *madhhab*, and also how medieval Islamic culture valorized these personalized interpretations of the law. The first of the two friends Ibn Farḥūn discusses is the scholar and Sufi Abū ʿAbd Allāh Muḥammad ibn Ḥarīth al-ʿAbdarī (d. 722/1322), also described as an "engaged" saint – that is, one who did good works in the world rather than in isolation.[119] He was also a man of great personal austerity.

> He had been imam of the mosque in Ceuta and possessed licit wealth by way of inheritance. He used to ask God that his death come with the last dirham of that money, and so it was. From the moment he entered the Hijaz until the day he died, all his food, drink and clothing were either things he had brought with him or things he had purchased with his own funds. He dressed nicely and ate well (*yalbasu ḥasanan wa yaʾkulu ṭayyiban*).[120]

[116] Though also raised as a subject of debate, grazing livestock in the *ḥaram* was permitted by the Mālikī jurist al-Qarāfī (*al-Dhakhīra*, III, 337–8); and also, interestingly, by al-Nawawī (*Rawḍat al-ṭālibīn*, II, 439). Ibn Qudāma does not discuss the issue.

[117] The twelfth-century Mālikī jurist Ibn Rushd, for example, makes no mention of the issue of the inviolability of plants in his comprehensive handbook, the *Bidāyat al-mujtahid*.

[118] Their shaykh, ʿUbayd Allāh ibn Abī'l-Rabīʿ, and Ibn Farḥūn's own father were recognized as equally supreme Mālikī muftis in Medina. The two men were fast friends. When someone asked this shaykh a question, he would reply, "Have you asked Ibn Farḥūn?" (meaning the author's father). If there was a difference of opinion they would meet and work it out, then issue an opinion together: Ibn Farḥūn, *Tārīkh al-Madīna*, 75.

[119] He was one of *al-awliyāʾ al-ʿulamāʾ al-ʿāmilīn*, a Sufi type discussed by Geoffroy, *Le soufisme*, 293–7. The combination of *ʿilm* and *ʿamal* was also a feature of al-Marrākushī, discussed above.

[120] Ibn Farḥūn, *Tārīkh al-Madīna*, 76.

Unlike Fakhriyya in Jerusalem, Ibn Ḥarīth had no misgivings about inherited wealth. To him it was safer than any other sort, presumably because his father's living had been an honest one and he therefore knew the money to be licit.

In this passage there is a charming confusion as to whether *ṭayyib* refers to delicious foods or licit foods, and a similar vagueness about handsome or appropriate clothing. That the phrase was intended as a *double entendre* here is clear from the sentence immediately following it, where Ibn Farḥūn turns to Ibn Ḥarīth's companion:

> And as for Shaykh Abū ʿAbd Allāh al-Qaṣṣarī, he wore rough clothing and ate the bare minimum. His only condiments were a single eggplant or a few chickpeas. He would eat no meat or butter from the Hijaz. Dried meat from Syria was procured for him, which he found acceptable.[121]

Al-Qaṣṣarī, who died sometime after 720/1320, was a Qurʾān reciter and renowned miracle worker in exile from Tunis, where his popularity had alarmed the ruler. Syria, as a source of meat, was simply the nearest place that he deemed safely beyond the borders of the Hijaz. Having established the lengths to which al-Qaṣṣarī was willing to go in pursuit of licit substances, Ibn Farḥūn offers a further point of contrast between the two men.

One day Ibn Ḥarīth cooked a delicious (*ṭayyib*, so here too possibly "licit") meal and invited Shaykh al-Qaṣṣarī to dine with him. When al-Qaṣṣarī refused, Ibn Ḥarīth urged him, saying: "Eat! for truly this is more licit than your food. There is nothing suspicious (*shubha*) in it," apparently anticipating the shaykh's penchant for worrying about the geographical source of what was being offered. But instead al-Qaṣṣarī cried in distress: "How could it be purer than mine? Wasn't yours bought with your salary from Ceuta?" Ibn Ḥarīth replied, "Neither a single dinar nor dirham from my fees as imam have I used. Rather I stockpiled those until the sum was enough to buy a residence for myself which I endowed as a property for the Mosque. So if you want to eat, go ahead, and if not, don't!" Two versions of how to eat blamelessly were working at cross-purposes here. In the process of clarification, Ibn Farḥūn allows us to compare these different strategies of scrupulous eating. In the end

[121] Ibid., 76–7. The same pairing of luxurious tastes appears in a biography of another man who "ate fine foods (*al-ṭayyibāt*) and wore soft clothing" in Ibn Kathīr, *Bidāya*, XIV, 194, with no pun intended.

the friends found common ground by agreeing on one important lesson: using a salary from a religious occupation for food was, if not illegal, at least unseemly.[122] The confusion over two disparate topics in substantive law (licit wealth and the law of sanctuaries) that inspired each man is the core of the story, and the men's piety is proven by the fact that this dialogue had to take place before they could share a meal.

Were the consequences of breaking or misreading dietary laws so devastating? If someone feared hellfire for such an infringement, surely this could be avoided through a simple act of expiation, as was the case with a broken fast. Yet the law books neither describe the types of punishment to be expected in the next world for eating *ḥarām* foods, nor do they specify the terms of expiation in this one. Al-Marrākushī and al-Qaṣṣarī may have been motivated by a deep fear of displeasing God. After all, the Qur'ān itself explicitly links food to moral health. But thoroughness in these matters, and thoroughness for its own sake, dictated that a person understand fully the principles behind the arguments in substantive law that indicate what to eat in various circumstances. Thus, taxonomies, not just of licit substances and licit circumstances, but of exceptional substances and exceptional circumstances, were needed. The further categorization of the licit and forbidden on a personal level – that is, not following the conclusions of one's own legal school – created alternative standards.

Conclusion: The Scope of Ethical Asceticism

If later pious men found ever more dramatic ways of displaying their wariness of food, it was because the bounds of scrupulosity had been stretched so wide in the twelfth and thirteenth centuries. Thus we see both repetition and elaboration in pious practices among the ascetics and devotees of the sixteenth century, for instance, who had to contend with all the messages sent by earlier exemplars. Occasionally elaboration had its limits: there was such a thing as having too many scruples. One example will suffice to show the trajectory of a pattern of behavior made famous in the thirteenth century. Al-Nawawī, who exemplifies the ideal of the ascetic jurist, spelled out his scrupulous concerns with scripted behavior at mealtimes. He fasted perpetually, he never ate two condiments

[122] Remuneration for services in religious professions was seen as being undesirable, though many were forced by necessity to accept it. Perhaps it was the idea that the imam of Ceuta would have accumulated enough to live on later in life that worried his companion.

together (because the Prophet had eaten one date at a time out of politeness), and, in what was the ultimate condemnation of city life, "most of what he ate were things his father brought him from Nawā."[123] While it is likely that al-Nawawī's fear of food related to criminal interference with the funding of his madrasa, he may also have been concerned with the physical purity of his meals. The sanitary condition (moral or physical) of the produce in his hometown was verifiable, whereas that of the city's food was not.

Two centuries later, in the *Ṭabaqāt al-kubrā* of al-Shaʿrānī, one finds a more thorough exegesis of what al-Nawawī's concerns meant. The author's grandfather Nūr al-Dīn ʿAlī ibn Aḥmad al-Shaʿrānī (d. 891/1486), a legal expert and a Sufi, considered the food in Cairo to be downright poisonous. Like al-Nawawī he had his mother bring him food from their village, and in addition only drank water straight from the Nile. After studying in Cairo he returned to settle at a *zāwiya* in Sāqiyat Abū Shaʿra, his hometown in the Delta. Nūr al-Dīn was active as a mufti throughout much of the fifteenth century, and in this role he was able to publicize his view that *ḥarām* materials were endemic in the food supply. His grandson recalled:

> He used to say, "The path to God is *ṭayyib al-maṭʿam*," and when he ground grain at the communal mill, he would lift the millstone to empty out other people's flour left beneath it. This he would roll into dough to give to [stray] dogs. Then he would grind his own wheat and clear it away for the people after him.[124]

There could hardly be a gesture more dramatic or, one would think, more offensive to his neighbors than this public demonstration of mistrust. In a larger town, grinding flour was the task of a miller, whose moral responsibilities for cleanliness Ibn al-Ḥājj had outlined in the *Madkhal*.[125] In a village such as this one, milling grain might also have been the mundane task of a servant or wife. Yet Nūr al-Dīn's actions apparently created no

123 Ibn Kathīr, *Bidāya*, XIII, 294.

124 al-Shaʿrānī, *Ṭabaqāt al-kubra*, II, 109. I am grateful to Tamer el-Leithy for this reference. More information on Nūr al-Dīn and his relations with the Sufis and jurists of his day may be found in Michael Winter, *Society and Religion in Early Ottoman Egypt: Studies in the Writings of ʿAbd al-Wahhāb al-Shaʿrānī* (New Brunswick, 1982), 43–4.

125 Ibn al-Ḥājj, *al-Madkhal*, IV, 352. Bakers too were urged to use clean surfaces to roll out their dough (ibid., IV, 362). On millers and bread production see Rodinson, "Ghidhāʾ," *EI*²; he cites an opinion in Mālikī law stipulating that "a wife could not be obliged to grind corn and that her husband, in this case, was to supply her with flour and not grain."

social discord. On the contrary, he taught his neighbors' children and gave liberally to widows and orphans; his position as an exemplary jurist, a Sufi, and a holy man seems to have been secure. In fact, while calling into question the sanitary habits and ethics of his community, al-Shaʿrānī was doing the correct thing in not wasting the suspicious flour, for the earliest legal authors advised that substances that have become irrevocably contaminated be given as fodder to livestock or, according to the strictest view, to "any animal whose meat will not be eaten."[126] Nūr al-Dīn's distrust of what might be called the intermediate stages of food processing did not end there. They drove him to give up a number of other foods, and this began to cause worry.

> Until the day he died, he refused to eat pigeons from the dovecots of the countryside, even though my father, may God have mercy upon him, brought him fatwas from the scholars allowing this. He used to say, "My son, every person makes decisions according to what he knows of God Most High." Then he would explain [regarding the pigeons]: "They eat seeds during the days of harvest and fly off with what they have plucked, and this is why [peasants] make things to scare them away from the threshing floor."

Similarly, he had watched peasants shooing bees away from the flowers on peach and apricot trees, which led him to give up eating honey. The intervention of the muftis, though it failed, makes the account even more interesting, especially since he himself was a mufti. Nūr al-Dīn's son seems to have been anxious about the increasingly extreme outlook of his father, but the plurality of fatwas issued on his behavior may also indicate that al-Shaʿrānī's doubts and his public displays of piety were disconcerting for the majority of his colleagues, men who were familiar with the issues but not as scrupulous as he. One cannot know, of course, whether the fatwas argued that his excessively suspicious behavior was disruptive to the community or merely that bees and pigeons could not perpetrate crimes.[127] In any case, Nūr al-Dīn privileged a different array of legal criteria and chose not to take the advice offered. Al-Shaʿrānī's grandfather is the final exemplar to be considered here, though he does not necessarily

[126] Ibn Qudāma, *Mughnī*, I, 36. Al-Shāfiʿī and Mālik say to give it to livestock; Aḥmad Ibn Ḥanbal made the point about it being given to an animal that would not be eaten, and Ibn Qudāma adds, "meaning one that will not be eaten soon."

[127] The idea of animals as perpetrators of misdeeds occurs elsewhere. One pious man of the early thirteenth century was proud of his cow "who used to go through a sown field without eating from it anything but weeds": Talmon-Heller, "Cited Tales of the Wondrous Doings," 152–3.

mark the zenith of this medieval trend of scrupulosity. His actions were only possible because so many others before him had believed in the validity of precisely the kinds of extreme precautions he took.

Many of the self-imposed food prohibitions considered in this chapter may be read as gestures of cultural critique and, especially when patronage and charity were refused, of outright social resistance. These prohibitions could take the form of temporary protest or embody long-term convictions. From the specific and in some ways simple injunction not to eat food from illegal sources, scrupulous men and women developed personalized food prohibitions in response to what they saw as an open-ended series of moral dilemmas about food. When they refused to eat out of indignation, abstemiousness, or expiation, these exemplars drew wide social and even geographical boundaries around their own bodies.

Finding a moral path in life, one that was not soul destroying, was intimately connected with food in ways that were anything but abstract. The choice of what to eat was a means of negotiating ethical obstacles that were seen as endemic in society. To a certain extent, this way of looking at things was compounded by the fact that in medieval Islam the ingredients themselves had the ability to physically transfer sin or *baraka* in a literal way. Al-Yāfiʿī felt blessed by having eaten Shaykh al-Murshidī's feast; the people who watched the Glutton consuming their food believed that something extraordinary had been accomplished in the process; the fear of the residual effects of mismanagement made the food of madrasas inedible for al-Nawawī and others like him. It was almost always human intervention that imparted to food its harmful or beneficial qualities.

In an era before product labelling, the scrupulous devotees of the medieval period were far ahead of their time in verifying the quality of the food they consumed. Constantly on the lookout for *ḥarām*-grade materials, they were concerned with the overall social purity of the meals they ate as well as the physical purity of its contents. Eating was political because it represented the end result of work and financial gain, sometimes as far back as a previous generation, or even further in the case of inheritance, and sometimes more recently in the fields and on farms that served the major cities of the region. The idea of one's daily bread being connected – via a hidden network of agricultural production and distribution, sales, and profits – to the social conditions of the community that produced it was unlikely to have been a daily concern for many Muslims in the medieval period. So the moments when that network becomes visible to "ordinary" people are especially important indicators of cultural distress.

While few of the medieval techniques, from avoiding meat to rejecting the charity of rulers, were new in Islam, these actions were directed at familiar structures and groups that were peculiar to the medieval age: at the changeable system of taxation and the holders of *iqṭāʿ* property, at tax dodgers, wealthy patrons, and rulers. By the end of the fourteenth century the trend towards abstemious scrupulosity among jurists in particular was so common that the Persian poet Ḥāfiẓ lampooned one of its main themes in a ghazal, saying:

> Last night the jurist at the madrasa got drunk
> and issued a fatwa
> which said, "Wine is forbidden,
> but it's better than the money of endowments."[128]

But even in Ḥāfiẓ's day, statements of refusal had not lost their purchase. Readers and observers were apparently still curious about new tactics devised by the pious for avoiding compromising situations. In Cairo around the same time, Shaykh ʿAlī al-Bālisī, a man known for his devotional piety and knowledge of the law, was so dismayed when his son Najm al-Dīn entered the service of amirs that he would no longer eat at his house.[129] Refusing to eat someone's food is considered bad behavior in most cultures, and it was particularly bad manners in the medieval Islamic context, where generosity and hospitality were supposed to trump personal piety. Yet the devotees and ascetics refused meals with impunity. As exemplars of piety they had the right of refusal, and in refusing they conveyed their social message of how the body was a point of vulnerability. It was, for instance, al-Akkāl's indiscriminate ingestion of "unknown" food offered by the powerful, as well as the amount of it he ate, that truly made him a glutton. One wonders at a ruler such as al-Malik al-Ashraf Mūsā and the amir Tankiz who bore rejection so well and seemingly so often, but they too must have been aware that the devotees became implicated in the system by accepting endowed positions or other forms of charity, and that in the process their bodily and moral integrity could potentially be compromised. The give-and-take between wealthy patrons and the pious poor had become a defining feature of medieval religious life. Ethical asceticism, which dominated so many pious food practices in this period, was not a retreat from the world but a way of engaging with it.

[128] Ḥāfiẓ, *Dīvān ghazalīyāt-i mawlānā Shams al-Dīn Muḥammad Ḥāfiẓ Shīrāzī*, ed. Khalīl Khaṭīb Rahbar (Tehran, 1364/1985), 43, ghazal no. 44.

[129] Ibn Ḥajar, *Inbāʾ*, III, 116. The shaykh died in 777/1375.

4

The Devil at the Fountain

Problems of Ritual

The preceding chapter described the ways in which statements of "pure living" built upon old traditions of Islamic scrupulosity. Those statements about the precariousness of the human condition highlighted the need for vigilance about the moral integrity of the body. The care of the body is, however, even more evident in another set of exemplary actions. The rituals of purification were, not unexpectedly, another area of devotional enthusiasm; yet, interestingly, the exemplars of bodily purity and those of ethical purity were for the most part wholly different groups of people, even though they shared a common love of scrupulosity (*waraʿ*). While the specialists in ethical purity demonstrated forcefully the link between the body and the social world, the men and women concerned with physical purity gave expression to the relationship of the body to the natural world – and only secondarily, it would seem, to the people who filled it.

As with "seeking the licit," attention to ritual purity inspired a watchfulness that tended to escalate. One man who stands out for being characterized by diligence in both areas was Saʿd ibn ʿUthmān Ibn Marzūq (d. 592/1196), the son of a famous theologian and mystic. He sounds familiar in many ways: born in Cairo, Saʿd moved to Baghdad as an adult where he studied law with Ibn al-Mannī and became known as "the Egyptian Ascetic." In addition to being a perpetual faster, "he would not accept anything from anyone and never came to call at the door of a sultan. Each year, some [money] from his property in Egypt would be dispatched to him and he would live on it all year."[1] A flaw in this otherwise

[1] Ibn Rajab, *Dhayl ʿalā Ṭabaqāt al-Ḥanābila*, I, 386. In Baghdad, his father's hometown, he lived at the madrasa of ʿAbd al-Qādir al-Jīlānī, an early twelfth-century Ḥanbalī scholar

exemplary man was pointed out by the historian Ibn al-Najjār, who says that "he had anxiety beyond measure and excessiveness in [matters of] ritual purity." As an example of this anxiety (*waswasa*), he quotes Saʿd's own explanation:

> I belched once. Then another belch rose in my throat, so I rinsed my mouth three times and then swallowed, [suppressing] it. Then I rinsed my mouth three times and spat.

While vomit filling the mouth necessitates a minor ablution according to the Ḥanbalī *madhhab*, to which Saʿd belonged, merely burping does not. Ibn al-Najjār adds, "May God forgive him – this is an egregious error."[2]

Ṭahāra – the whole system of purification including the major and minor ablutions and also the removal of defiling substances from body and clothing – was very much on the minds of legal authors throughout the late medieval period, for it is the most complicated area of ritual law. Not only did these men study and refine the existing legal discourse about purity, they also observed the behavior of friends and family and debated the actions of their predecessors and colleagues. Since most authors of chronicles and biographical dictionaries in this period doubled as experts in religious law, whether as muftis, judges, market inspectors, or, like Ibn al-Najjār, hadith transmitters, the obituaries they wrote sometimes furnished an occasion to comment upon the law and ritual practice. This chapter examines aspects of ritual purity in light of widely reported cases, especially among jurists such as Saʿd Ibn Marzūq, of an affliction identified by medieval authors as *waswās fī'l-ṭahāra* (or synonymously *waswasa fī'l-ṭahāra*), which may be provisionally translated as "anxiety about ritual purity." Most often this anxiety arose during the performance of the minor ablution (*wuḍūʾ*), but other aspects of purification were involved as well.

The phrase was derived from the Qurʾānic image of Satan who would whisper (*waswasa*) in someone's ear and cause him or her to go astray. In the Qurʾān whispering never has a good outcome, for this is how Satan created doubts in Adam and his wife, setting them on a path that led

and one of the most famous Sufis. Al-Jīlānī's teachings gave rise to the Qadiriyya brotherhood, which still thrives today.

[2] Ibid. The Arabic phrase is *zalla fāḥisha*. Ibn Qudāma has a detailed discussion of what *fāḥisha* means in the context of *wuḍūʾ*: burping does not require ablution and this is not a point disputed by any of the jurists (Ibn Qudāma, *Mughnī*, I, 176–8). On the author of the original report, a Shāfiʿī, who died in 643/1245, see Caesar E. Farah, "Ibn-al-Najjār: A Neglected Historian," *Journal of the American Oriental Society* 84, 3 (July 1964).

out of the Garden.[3] Temptations and doubts result in a perilous state of confusion, error, and even rebellion, and chapter 114 takes the form of an appeal to God for protection from this type of danger. In Mamluk times evil or seditious thoughts (*wasāwis*) were still being attributed to the whispered prompts of Satan: Baybars al-Manṣūrī described a plot hatched by the amirs in 698/1299 to murder the unpopular sultan Manṣūr Lājīn using this terminology.[4] The fourteenth-century author Ibn Baydakīn used it to describe the actions of Sufis who danced all night and fell asleep at the mosque during the day, and here it refers to something like a lapse in good judgment. Dancing, he claimed, was a distraction, a preoccupation with something that is not part of the Prophet's *sunna*. The author tells his reader to "defend his heart against immoral beliefs, and preserve it from blameworthy *wasāwis* and from careless slips. Let him not allow any forbidden substances to enter his belly and guard it from doubtful substances as well."[5] The body, in other words, is polluted by unclean substances and the heart or mind by error.

But the history of *waswās* in the specific context of ritual purity is wholly unpredictable. In the late twelfth century the devilish genealogy of the word *waswās* had not been forgotten, and religious critics used it to identify certain forms of deviation from correct practice, as was the case with Sa'd Ibn Marzūq. Yet over the course of the next 250 years the phrase "anxiety about ritual purity" (*waswās fī'l-ṭahāra*) became increasingly common in descriptions of unimpeachable holy men and women, and it ceased to be employed as a form of criticism. Since the very word *waswās* was historically and semantically devoid of any positive connotations, its appearance as a positive trait in the biographies of the pious – and pious jurists in particular – is puzzling. Such a surprising change in the way that some authors read deviance in the people around them is of great significance. In part, it can be linked to evolving conceptions of pious behavior in general within the same period: expending great effort in ablutions was not unlike fasting strenuously, for example. Over the same period the critique of *waswās* continued as well, but even this discourse, as we shall see, began to conform itself to the pattern

3 See Qur'ān 7:20 and 20:120; elsewhere the word is used in the sense of giving in to temptation or wavering in one's faith, e.g., 50:16, and Sūra 114.

4 Baybars al-Manṣūrī al-Dawādār, *Zubdat al-fikra fī ta'rīkh al-hijra*, ed. D. S. Richards (Berlin and Beirut, 1998), 330. For further discussion of Satan's influence in matters of impurity see Ze'ev Maghen, *Virtues of the Flesh: Passion and Purity in Early Islamic Jurisprudence* (Leiden and Boston, 2005), chap. 2, esp. 48–56.

5 Ibn Baydakīn al-Turkumānī, *Kitāb al-luma'*, I, 205.

of contemporary exemplars who exhibited signs of *waswās fī'l-ṭahāra*. It was a religious affliction, for though anxiety about purity struck at random across medieval communities from Mosul to Cairo, it chose its victims only from among the pious.

Their doubts and qualms, I will argue, sometimes arose from a desire for real cleanliness, even though the two formal rituals of purification, the minor ablution (*wuḍū'*) and the major ablution or lustration (*ghusl*) merely accomplish a symbolic cleanliness for the purpose of prayer and a few other religious activities. That is, in terms of dirt and cleanliness, the amount of washing necessary for either ablution is perfunctory at best. For ritual purposes, however, the resulting purity is total since in the sphere of religious activity symbolic cleanliness and actual purity are identical. Yet this was precisely where things went amiss for the men and women beset by anxiety about purity who became known, collectively, as the *muwaswasīn*.

Recently, the notion of symbolic cleanliness in the Sunnī Islamic purity system has been discussed by several modern scholars who, following Mary Douglas, stress that especially in *wuḍū'* the body parts that are washed are quite obviously not the offending members.[6] The face, hair, hands, and feet are ritually washed even though they are not the source of bodily substances that entail ritual purification; nor are the face and head parts of the body that are most susceptible to contact with externally defiling substances. As Kevin Reinhart states succinctly, "Ritual cleansing is only a cleansing for ritual."[7] He argues that the minor ablutions serve to reassert control over bodily functions, sealing the borders of the body after an uncontrollable event such as sleep or defecation; such events usually, but not always, involve the effusion of a substance produced from within. Water provides a "symbolic envelope" inside which the repurified body exists.[8]

[6] See Kevin Reinhart's classic article on the ontological framework of *ṭahāra*, "Impurity/No Danger," *History of Religions* 30, 1 (1990). "How does washing the beard and toes solve a problem caused by defecation, for example?" he asks (ibid., 13); and also Katz, *Body of Text*, 2. He discusses the limitations of Douglas's interpretation when applied to the case of Islamic purity, an issue taken up more extensively by Marion H. Katz in "The Study of Islamic Ritual and the Meaning of Wuḍū'," *Der Islam* 82, 1 (2005) and Ze'ev Maghen in "First Blood: Purity, Edibility and the Independence of Islamic Jurisprudence," *Der Islam* 81 (2004). A review of these perspectives and a comprehensive bibliography can be found in Richard Gauvain, "Ritual Rewards: A Consideration of the Three Recent Approaches to Sunni Purity Law," *Islamic Law and Society* 12, 3 (2005): 333–93.

[7] Reinhart, "Impurity/No Danger," 21.

[8] Ibid., 10–11, 20. Sand may be used for purification when water is not available; this is known as *tayammum* and it has the same envelope-like effect. I have not found any cases

Just as this type of impure status is easily righted, the major ablution (*ghusl*) reverses the impure status that arises from sexual intercourse, ejaculation, menstruation, and childbirth. Furthermore, a third kind of impurity that relates to the defiling substances a person might encounter – wine, for example – is rectified as soon as those things are washed off or otherwise removed. The distinction Reinhart draws between the states of impurity and the ease with which those states are reversed is important for many reasons, in particular as a contribution to the comparative study of purity systems in world religions. As his title suggests, no "real" danger arises from things that cause impurity. Ze'ev Maghen notes that the impermanent, transitory quality of impurity has fascinating implications for Islamic social interaction. Proceeding from the point at which Reinhart left off, he stresses forcefully Sunnī Islam's reluctance to designate whole categories of humans (such as menstruating women) as defiling, a feature that represents a dramatic departure not only from Judaism but from all other religious systems that possess a schema of bodily purity.[9]

Medieval jurists, however, were rarely able to distill the complexity of ritual purity to such a persuasive and logical core, for they themselves admitted to being confused about the topic of *ṭahāra*.[10] In the survey of juridical literature below, only al-Qarāfī, a Mālikī jurist who died in Cairo in 684/1285, provides clear statements confirming Reinhart's explanation of the symbolic nature of purity rituals. More importantly, the perspective offered by personal examples in medieval Islamic history

of *waswās* involving it. Examples of bodily substances that require the minor ablution are excrement, urine, and blood. But as Reinhart stresses, it is the *event* of emanation that entails ablutions; thus defecating, urinating, passing wind, and touching the genitals all precipitate the minor ablution. Other events such as sleep or fainting also cause a state of impurity (*ḥadath*) and require the minor ablution as a kind of safeguard for what the body might have done during loss of consciousness.

9 Ze'ev Maghen, "Close Encounters: Some Preliminary Observations on the Transmission of Impurity in Early Sunnī Jurisprudence," *Islamic Law and Society* 6, 3 (1999): 348–50. Reinhart questions whether the term "impurity" is even appropriate, whether indeed a body can be said to be itself impure, when the character of impurity is so temporary: Reinhart, "Impurity/No Danger," 15. Katz and Wheeler, on the other hand, both contend that ablutions are reminders of the fallen state of humans that resulted from Adam and Eve's discovery of their genitals and bodily functions. Thus *wuḍū'* is required "for those conditions necessary for and definitive of earthly human existence, in sharp contrast to the state of Adam and Eve in the garden of Eden" (Wheeler, *Mecca and Eden*, 58); see also Katz, *Body of Text*, 186.

10 Maghen, "Close Encounters," 353. The burgeoning length of late medieval commentaries on the rules of purification certainly suggests this.

casts an entirely different light on purification and, while not invalidating the findings of Reinhart and Maghen, calls for a reassessment of the logic of Islamic purity.

There is no better example of why this is necessary than the purely unnecessary solution Saʿd Ibn Marzūq decided upon for burping – an "event" that he must have known was not defiling. Erring on the side of caution, he selected a single piece of the Ḥanbalīs' ritual of minor ablution, rinsing the mouth, to use on an emergency basis. In doing so, he articulated very clearly Reinhart's argument about how ablutions serve to reassert control over the borders of the body: Saʿd's response was to immediately redress at its source the event that had occurred. Water suppressed the impulse in his throat, and water washed away the possible impurity. And yet, far from being symbolic, this was a wholly concrete solution to a problem that did not, legally, exist. Given that Saʿd Ibn Marzūq was trained in Ḥanbalī law, his personal approach to purity is a perfect example of the fretting and doubts (*waswās*) of a learned man. It was not due to ignorance about the rules of the minor ablution that he equated burping with vomiting, and he was not in fact actually performing *wuḍūʾ*. His solution places the disruptive body at the source of at least some forms of *waswās*: otherwise normal processes of the body turned threatening, at least to the state of purity. His afflicted colleagues' fears centered more often on unknown and unseen sources of impurity they might have come into contact with without knowing it. Their preoccupation with purity focused more on dangerous substances than on their own bodily functions.

Confusion over the meaning of purity, the procedural aspects of *ṭahāra* and ultimately the aim of purification itself went far beyond legal debate, and in many instances permeated actual practice. When and how the rituals, particularly those of the minor ablution, must be carried out were issues that plagued many devotees who found themselves preoccupied with the pursuit of cleanliness, ritual or otherwise. It is these devotees who, in their role as exemplars in late medieval Islamic society, demand closer scrutiny of the situations in which they felt purification was required. For them, the processes of becoming pure and the tactics for staying pure were hardly efficient. The world was an insecure and threatening place, if not downright filthy, and it demanded that elaborate precautions be taken. Their misadventures with ritual purity provide an unusually rich and at times moving commentary upon life in the cities of the Ayyubid and Mamluk Middle East.

Part I: *Waswās* and the Body

At the end of the twelfth century the problem of *waswās fī'l-ṭahāra* and competing views of purity can best be seen in the example of ʿImād al-Dīn Muḥammad ibn Yūnus, otherwise known as Shaykh al-ʿImād, who was considered one of the foremost Shāfiʿī scholars of his day. Among his legal writings was the *Muḥīṭ*, a work that aimed at integrating legal material from the *Muhadhdhab* of al-Shīrāzī and the *Wasīṭ* of al-Ghazzālī, thereby demonstrating his mastery of the classic books of the Shāfiʿī legal tradition. He resided in the city of Mosul where he wrote a celebrated creedal statement for the Zangid ruler, Nūr al-Dīn Arslān Shāh, who "sought fatwas from him and consulted him in many affairs."[11] Such was his influence at court, in fact, that he succeeded in persuading this ruler to convert from the Ḥanafī legal school to that of the Shāfiʿīs. Shaykh al-ʿImād was not destined to remain a star figure of the Islamic legal tradition, however. After his death in 608/1211 two accounts of his life circulated: one offered by the historian Ibn Khallikān, and subsequently by al-Dhahabī and al-Ṣafadī; the other by Sibṭ Ibn al-Jawzī and Abū Shāma, later echoed by Ibn Kathīr. All of these authors agreed that he was greatly concerned with ritual purity. But the two groups strongly disagreed about what that concern meant, and as such Shaykh al-ʿImād provides a focal point for examining medieval views of *ṭahāra*. He is a character who will remain a point of reference throughout this chapter, more for the light his story sheds on the attitudes of authors stretching across two centuries than for his own less enduring achievements.

"He was vehemently scrupulous and self-mortifying," wrote Ibn Khallikān as he began listing the man's pious attributes. "He wore no new garment until he had washed it and never picked up a pen to write without first washing his hand."[12] Washing new garments would be identified in the fourteenth century as a clear case of *waswās*, though Ibn Khallikān (who died in 681/1282) does not present it as such. Like the refusal to accept food from an unknown source, a preventative measure

[11] Aḥmad ibn Muḥammad Ibn Khallikān, *Wafayāt al-aʿyān wa anbāʾ abnāʾ al-zamān*, ed. Iḥsān ʿAbbās, 8 vols. (Beirut, 1968–72), IV, 254.

[12] Ibid. He is described as "shadīd al-waraʿ wa'l-taqashshuf." Ibn al-Athīr, a native of Mosul, does not mention these details in his very cursory obituary. Ibn al-Mustawfī, one of Ibn Khallikān's sources, reproduced one of Shaykh al-ʿImād's fatwas but interestingly enough did not devote a biography to him in the section of the *Tārīkh Irbil* where one would expect to find him: the section devoted to men of righteousness, asceticism, justice, and faith. (Irbil was the city in which the shaykh was born.)

of washing to guard against impure substances on clothing of unknown provenance was a gesture that would have been easily understood, even though the practice itself was not typical in his day.[13] Shaykh al-ʿImād's anxiety about clothing was not properly linked to ablutions but to an aspect of *ṭahāra* that has yet to be fully examined, though both Reinhart and Maghen discuss it. The minor ablution prepares a Muslim for worshipful activity such as daily prayers and handling or reciting the Qurʾān. Prior to undertaking this obligatory ritual, however, a certain degree of real cleanliness is required: specifically, the removal of obvious (e.g., visible) impure substances from one's garments and hands.[14]

While the actions involved are not ritually scripted and have no sacred meaning, it is clear that the process of removal by water, wiping, or scratching becomes something of a ritual simply because it is a daily custom for those who routinely inspect their garments, and it can be said to be ritualistic, and even ceremonial, by virtue of the role – albeit a subordinate one – that this basic cleanliness actually plays in prayer.[15] The implication of Ibn Khallikān's statement is that Shaykh al-ʿImād not only washed his new clothes to make certain they were pure enough for prayer, but also, holding himself to a higher standard, insisted upon pure clothing for ordinary activities. In addition, not satisfied by the criterion of perceptible sources of impurity – those identified by sight or smell – as the only obstacles, he washed from his clothing invisible stains that may or may not have existed.

The shaykh's second gesture, washing his hand before touching a tool used in the religious sciences, was a more familiar precautionary measure and an apt example of what Michael Chamberlain has called the "ritualization of knowledge." Citing a range of hortatory instructions to men who taught or copied religious texts, Chamberlain shows how scholarly

[13] That is, the historical sources do not indicate that it was common among the pious. However, Aḥmad Ibn al-ʿImād al-Aqfahsī (d. 808/1409) condemns the practice, citing the earlier legal opinions of al-Juwaynī and al-Nawawī (neither of whom mention the word *waswās*), in his *Dafʿ al-ilbās ʿan wahm al-waswās (wa yalīhi Ikrām man yaʿīshu bi-taḥrīm al-khamr wa'l-ḥashīsh)*, ed. Muḥammad Fāris and Masʿūd ʿAbd al-Ḥamīd al-Saʿdanī (Beirut, 1995), 243.

[14] Examples of substances that are irrevocably impure according to Sunnī law include blood, excrement (of humans and certain animals), vomit, pus, carrion meat, and wine. There are also substances on which the Sunnī legal schools differ. The Shāfiʿīs, for example, deem semen to be pure where the others do not.

[15] Some legal manuals discuss the procedure and requirements for cleaning garments in the section on prayer that follows the section on *ṭahāra*. But logically one performs this procedure prior to ablutions so that one does not redefile oneself in the process of removing defiling substances.

tasks were seen as requiring ritual preparation. One author called for students to be ritually pure when they arrived for classes with a shaykh, just as they would be for prayer or when they handled the Qurʾān. Another urged hadith transmitters and copyists to be in a state of ritual purity when they undertook their work.[16] The principal reason for this cautionary purity, according to Ibn Qudāma (d. 620/1223), is the possibility of encountering words of Qurʾānic text in one's writing or dictation. He tried to defuse the trend towards what might be called supererogatory purity, arguing that it is permissible to handle books of law (*fiqh*) and exegesis (*tafsīr*) that contain Qurʾānic passages even when one is in a state of impurity. "The proof is that the Prophet wrote to Caesar [i.e., the Byzantine Emperor Heraclius] a letter which had a Qurʾānic verse in it." He goes on to say that it is also permissible for children in a state of ritual impurity to practice writing the Qurʾān on slates, because the slate is but a workspace for memorization and not a sacred object. Besides, "if we required ritual purity, this would lead to their hating memorizing it!"[17] Despite the fact that he was not alone in voicing disapproval, notable scholars who had trained in law often maintained ritual purity while they taught.[18] Ritual purity, in short, was a state that many medieval Muslims saw as being appropriate for scholarship as well as worship.

What sets *waswās fī'l-ṭahāra* apart from other precautionary trends in purity, or from mere enthusiasm, is partly the vehemence of the anxiety and partly a matter of opinion. For example, Ibn Daqīq al-ʿĪd's mother in Upper Egypt was said to have worried when she found her young son repeatedly washing a mortar that he intended to fill with ink. Al-Subkī, his biographer, had no trouble identifying this as a case of *waswās*, and indeed the child's doubts went well beyond mere scrupulosity.[19] In this case the story is clearly meant to establish Ibn Daqīq al-ʿĪd's precociousness: he grew up to be a jurist of unsurpassed fame, a destiny foreshadowed by that youthful fussiness about issues in religious law.

[16] Chamberlain, *Knowledge and Social Practice*, 126–7, citing Ibn al-Ḥājj and Ibn al-Jamāʿa.

[17] Ibn Qudāma, *Mughnī*, I, 138. He explains that it is only a complete copy of the Qurʾān, the complete message from God, that requires purification before handling. The missive to the emperor, for example, did not constitute a whole Qurʾān (*muṣḥaf*) and therefore its sanctity (*ḥurma*) was not established.

[18] For example, al-Nawawī concurs with Ibn Qudāma (*Rawḍat al-ṭālibīn*, I, 190–2). But his predecessor al-Baghawī (d. 516/1122), one of the most famous Shāfiʿī authors, taught while in a state of ritual purity; it was not a new trend.

[19] al-Subkī, *Ṭabaqāt al-Shāfiʿiyya*, IX, 210. Ibn Daqīq al-ʿĪd eventually held the post of Shāfiʿī chief qadi in Cairo; he died in 702/1302.

The Context

What it meant to have *waswās fi'l-ṭahāra* makes little sense except in the context of the more general concern with purity that was characteristic of pious men and women in the medieval period. If *ṭahāra* is taken to be solely a preparation of the body for prayer or handling the Qur'ān, Shaykh al-ʿImād's elaborate attention to impure substances appears excessive, if not obsessive. If, on the other hand, its component steps are understood as rituals with wider importance for the body, the occasions requiring them tend to multiply. Indeed it would be hard to overestimate the broad approbation of voluntary performances of rituals of purity in this period. A few of these were very common. The ever-exemplary shaykh Abū ʿUmar Ibn Qudāma, for instance, would only sleep in a state of ritual purity, and so performed an ablution at bedtime. From a legal point of view this was unnecessary. The ablutions performed at night would have to be made again upon waking for morning prayers, since a person has to assume that during sleep breaking wind or touching the genitals might occur.[20] Performing voluntary ablutions before going to bed was a custom that met with the approval of Ibn Qayyim al-Jawziyya, who found the relevant hadiths to be a compelling endorsement. Sleep posed a number of medical risks to the body, which he enumerates at length in his fourteenth-century treatise on popular medicine. As a precaution, he recommended the Prophet's purely voluntary habit of performing *wuḍū'* at bedtime wholeheartedly, saying: "If you should die that night, then you die in the original natural state."[21] On this point of supererogatory practice, both the exemplars of piety and ordinary worshippers were urged to follow the same course of action.

So, too, a concern with the performance of *wuḍū'* could be expressed by erring on the side of caution about deciding when ritual purity was required. To some, this meant hurrying to return to a state of purity after something had interrupted or nullified it. Abū Shāma recorded the death in 631/1234 of an imam at the Umayyad Mosque in Damascus, writing that he was a man who had spent his later years "sequestered in the eastern minaret, busying himself (*mushtaghilan*) with ritual purity and prayer."[22] If the state of purity has been maintained between two

[20] The early debate about whether or not touching the genitals necessitated the minor ablution is discussed by Katz, *Body of Text*, 123–35. For late medieval views see Wheeler, *Mecca and Eden*, 48–69.

[21] Ibn Qayyim al-Jawziyya, *Medicine of the Prophet*, 177. On bodily purity as a reflection of inner purity and the equation of ablutions with repentance see Ibn al-Ḥājj, *al-Madkhal*, I, 28–9.

[22] Abu Shāma, *Tarājim*, 162, on al-Burhān Abū'l-Ḥasan Ismāʿīl al-Qurṭubī, who was attached to the Kallāsa *masjid* within the precincts of the great mosque.

daily prayers, then *wuḍū'* need not be performed again before the second. *Wuḍū'* becomes necessary, however, after naps or visits to the toilet, and is recommended by some jurists after losing one's temper.[23] Anyone who spent long periods in constant prayer or reciting the Qur'ān faced a problem not unlike that of the permanent resident of the holy cities of Mecca or Medina in the Hijaz when confronted with meat: although one did not need to be ritually pure inside a mosque, or between two prayers, would it not be better to stay in a state of purity as much as possible? This is most likely why the *imām* was described as being busy with purification as well as with prayer. To someone who erred on the far side of caution, ritual purity became the normal state and impurity a temporary one.[24] The legal terminology of *wuḍū'* may be instructive here: one performs ablutions in order to "renew" the state of purity, not in order to adopt it temporarily. All these examples amount to ways of thinking about purity as a state that might be "normal" as well as desirable for a devotee. Just as severe fasting practices had become acceptable by the thirteenth century, so had a stringent view of the requirement of purification.

The Controversy: Shaykh al-ʿImād and the Pitchers of Water

Though Shaykh al-ʿImād typified a scholarly concern with purity that was popular in his day, his predilection for ritual cleanliness did not inspire uniform confidence among his biographers. Instead, the issue of purity became a prism through which later authors assessed and contested his status. Some authors saw his precautionary actions as signs of *waswās fī'l-ṭahāra* where others did not. Ibn Khallikān had avoided using the phrase, which suggests that he did not want to cast the man in a harsh light. Indeed, Shaykh al-ʿImād's lofty reputation as a jurist makes it hard to see his behavior as deviant.

23 For example, the Prophet says, "Anger comes from the devil, the devil was created of fire, and fire is extinguished only with water; so when one of you becomes angry, he should perform ablution" (Abū Dā'ūd al-Sijistānī, *Sunan Abī Dāwūd* [Beirut, 1991], IV, hadith no. 4784). Another emotional cause of impurity, according to the Ḥanafīs, is an outburst of laughter during prayer, which invalidates the prayer. The Ḥanafī jurist al-ʿAynī notes why other legal schools differ on this point: according to al-Shāfiʿī, laughter during prayer does not invalidate *wuḍū'* because a *najas* substance does not come out of the person's body. "But we say: let him redo both his *wuḍū'* and his prayer": Badr al-Dīn Maḥmūd al-ʿAynī, *Bināya sharḥ al-Hidāya*, ed. Ayman Ṣāliḥ Shaʿbān, 13 vols. (Beirut, 2000), I, 287.

24 See, for example, al-Nawawī, *Rawḍat al-ṭālibīn*, I, 159, on when it is *mustaḥabb* to renew the ablution. According to Katz (*Body of Text*, 119) the Umayyad caliph ʿUmar ibn ʿAbd al-ʿAzīz and others "favored maintaining a continuous state of ritual purity (as opposed to limiting it to its role as a preparation for prayer)."

The first and much longer recension of Shaykh al-ʿImād's life concentrates on his close connections with the Zangid rulers of Mosul and his expertise in law. Al-Dhahabī avers that he was "like a vizier" to Nūr al-Dīn Arslān Shāh.[25] Ibn Khallikān, al-Dhahabī's main source, calls him "the imam of his age" in the foundations of jurisprudence and the juridical controversies of the Shāfiʿī *madhhab*. Students and fellow jurists from other cities flocked to Mosul to study with him. In addition to a proclivity for purification, "he was mild-mannered, polite in his speech and his gestures."[26] One may read this biography as an almost commonplace description of an extraordinary jurist, of a gracious and cautious leading man of Mosul whose piety and knowledge put him on equal footing with the atabeg Nūr al-Dīn himself.

By contrast, it took only a few sentences for Sibṭ Ibn al-Jawzī to convey what he considered the salient facts of Shaykh al-ʿImād's life. Apart from his date of birth and confirmation of his high status as a jurist in Mosul, the material is entirely different in this account. First, the author notes that the shaykh was sent as an emissary to Baghdad upon the death of Nūr al-Dīn to secure recognition for the ruler's heir. Then he lists in quick succession several remaining details:

> He had qualms (*waswās*) about ritual purity: every day he sent his slave to the bridge to fill pitchers with water from a point midway between the banks. Then he would perform his minor ablutions. And he used to, as they say, "swap things" with people. One day he met the *muwallah* Qaḍīb al-Bān. Shaykh al-ʿImād greeted him: "Peace be upon you, my brother, how are you?" Qaḍīb al-Bān replied, "Me, I'm fine. But I've been told that you wash your limbs with pitchers of water every day yet do not practice mortification in the food you eat." Al-ʿImād understood his words and gave up this routine.[27]

This account of Shaykh al-ʿImād's scrupulous purity begins, like Ibn Khallikān's had, with him being beset by doubts as to whether or not he was sufficiently pure. Presumably, the shaykh either believed the water of the Tigris to be cleaner than sources inside the city, or else he required more of it than did other people, or both. These were different practices than those mentioned by Ibn Khallikān. and in fact were the most common forms of *waswās* cited in the twelfth and thirteenth centuries. As

[25] al-Dhahabī, *ʿIbar*, V, 28–9.

[26] Ibn Khallikān, *Wafayāt*, IV, 253–4.

[27] Sibṭ Ibn al-Jawzī, *Mirʾāt al-zamān*, 558–9. The phrase about swapping things is "yuqābilu al-nās."

with Saʿd Ibn Marzūq, the minor ablution is identified as the locus of the shaykh's *waswās*.

The anecdote ends abruptly and perhaps pointedly. The contrast between the social roles of its two main characters accentuates the problem of *waswās* in this episode and begs the question of what exactly needed correcting. It should, of course, be the jurist who showed the correct path to a man who, as a *muwallah*, was an expert in obscure religious truths rather than the laws of religious obligations. A familiar opposition is embedded in their encounter, not only between these two social roles but between ostentation and humility. The reversal of roles highlights the importance of the lesson all the more clearly: a jurist ought to have ascetic habits and ought not to make a show of his piousness.[28] Two small changes appear in Abū Shāma's version, which otherwise follows Sibṭ Ibn al-Jawzī's exactly. The first clarifies what was meant by the euphemism of "swapping things" with people. According to Abū Shāma, the shaykh "as they say, 'did business' with people by selling merchandise on credit."[29] This practice was acceptable in the Shāfiʿī school of law (to which Abū Shāma belonged) but disliked by others, and the remark surely hints at something dubious. In the second change, Qaḍīb al-Bān's reproof is slightly altered, and thus so is the conclusion of the biography: "'But I am told that you wash your limbs with pitchers of water every day yet do not even clean off a piece of food before you eat it.' Al-ʿImād understood his words and gave up the practice."[30] Abū Shāma's version makes the hypocrisy more obvious to readers by contrasting Shaykh al-ʿImād's preoccupation with *wuḍūʾ* with his neglect of a more important duty: he was overly scrupulous about ritual purity while caring little if he ate dirty food – or, read anagogically, food bought with suspicious wealth.

However, in both versions the critique of the shaykh's scrupulosity hinged on the amount of water he used. Elsewhere, in a legal treatise, Abū Shāma had briefly addressed the topic of washing more than three times during the minor ablutions as a wrongful deviation from the Prophet's

[28] Sibṭ Ibn al-Jawzī might have had other reasons for casting Shaykh al-ʿImād in a less than favorable light. The Zangid ruler had converted from the Ḥanafī *madhhab* to the Shāfiʿī not long before the author himself had converted to the Ḥanafī school from the Ḥanbalī. According to Claude Cahen he did this in order to accommodate himself to the Ayyubid rulers in Damascus, who were now all Ḥanafīs. See Claude Cahen, "Ibn al-Jawzī, Shams al-Din," *EI²*. In addition, his grandfather, Ibn al-Jawzī, had written explicitly on the subject of *waswās* in ablutions. The latter's views are discussed at length in this chapter.

[29] Compare Sibṭ Ibn al-Jawzī: "Wa kāna ʿalā mā qīla yuqābilu al-nās wa iltaqāhu Qaḍīb al-Bān yawman ..." with Abū Shāma: "Wa kāna ʿalā mā qīla yuʿāmilu al-nās bi'l-ʿīna."

[30] Abū Shāma, *Tarājim*, 80.

custom.[31] Therefore a second problem created by Shaykh al-ʿImād's *waswās* was immoderate enthusiasm, and once he realized this, the shaykh restrained himself. Medieval readers would probably have recognized both lessons immediately, for, like unlawful food, wasting water was an old topic. Ibn Qudāma and Ibn al-Jawzī (both contemporaries of Shaykh al-ʿImād) had warned against extravagance (*iṣrāf*) in performing the minor and major ablutions, citing opinions that go back to al-Shāfiʿī and Aḥmad Ibn Ḥanbal. Ibn Qudāma's argument opens with a selection of hadiths.

> It is reported that the Prophet passed by Saʿd who was making his ablutions and said to him: "Do not be extravagant." Saʿd asked: "O Messenger of God, is there such a thing as extravagance in water?" He said, "Yes, even if you were at a running river."[32]

It was Saʿd's mother, in another hadith, who remembered the exact amounts that the Prophet said were sufficient for the purpose of the two ablutions: a *mudd* for *wuḍūʾ* and a *ṣāʿ* for *ghusl*. The Prophet's *mudd* measure is sometimes said to be the amount of water contained by two cupped hands.[33] In a third hadith, a man complained to Jābir, one of Muhammad's Companions, that a *ṣāʿ* was not enough for him to perform the major ablution, in which water must cover the whole body right down to the roots of the hair. Jābir grew red with anger, then calmed himself and retorted: "Well, it was sufficient for a man who was better than you and who had more hair!"[34] Such hadiths laid the foundation for economical use of water in rituals that effected a cleanliness that was symbolic rather than real. But because standards of measurement varied so widely across the Islamic world, the issue of water usage continued to be raised in the centuries after the Prophet's death, right down to the twelfth century, when Ibn al-Jawzī assigned a precise amount by weight, saying,

[31] Abū Shāma, *Kitāb al-Bāʿith*, 205. In the passage (located in a section on *ṣalāt al-raghāʾib*) he quotes ʿAbd Allāh ibn Yūsuf al-Juwaynī (d. 438/1047) on how the third washing is *sunna*, and with the fourth one enters into the realm of *bidʿa*.

[32] Muwaffaq al-Dīn ʿAbd Allāh Ibn Qudāma, *Dhamm al-waswās*, ed. Muḥammad Khālid al-Kharsa (Damascus, 1990), 36.

[33] See A. Bel, "Ṣāʿ," *EI*², who estimates that the *mudd* is equivalent to 1¼ pints and the *ṣāʿ* to 5 pints.

[34] Another Companion conceded that a large man might be justified in using more water for *ghusl*: Ibn Qudāma, *Dhamm al-waswās*, 37–8. According to Ibn Qudāma, who cites examples down to Aḥmad Ibn Ḥanbal (d. 241/855), jurists specified various measures using the utensils available to them, such as metal cups, jugs, or leather pouches since the definition of the *mudd* varied over time and in different locales.

"A *raṭl* of water suffices for performing the minor ablution properly."[35] Even allowing for variations in measurements, the pitchers used by Shaykh al-ʿImād were superfluous and wasteful.

The absence of praise and the desultory way in which the facts of Shaykh al-ʿImād's life are presented, as if cobbled together from other sources, make for an odd biography. It may have been the specter of Qaḍīb al-Bān, a well-known holy man who died around 570/1174, that brought the incident to the attention of Abū Shāma and Sibṭ Ibn al-Jawzī, two authors who were writing several generations later at a time when stories of the holy man's miracles in Mosul were circulating as far away as Cairo.[36] Indeed, one might suspect that much of the biography was lifted from an account of Qaḍīb al-Bān, were it not for the fact that in between the description of the jurist's preparations for ablutions and his encounter with Qaḍīb al-Bān, Abū Shāma chose to insert the brief sentence about how he made his money.[37] Failing to expand on why such a detail is significant only makes it more so; the sentence is clearly the fulcrum on which the two parts of the story turn. When Ibn Kathīr set about rewriting the biography a century later, he opted not to keep this paralipsis. In doing so he confirms that Shaykh al-ʿImād's biography was merely a vehicle for the moral concerns of the author. What begins to change, in his hands, is the outlook on scrupulous purity.

While maintaining the same sequence of facts, Ibn Kathīr clarified several points about Shaykh al-ʿImād's life in a way that imparts coherence to the text.

> He had great anxiety (*waswasa kathīra*) in matters of purity. And he used to do transactions with money by invoking the issue of sale on credit. As the saying goes, "You strain out gnats from your drink, yet you swallow camels whole." Doing the opposite would have been better for him. Qaḍīb al-Bān met him one day and said to him: "O Shaykh, I have been told that you wash each of your limbs with a pitcher of water and do not even wash the morsel that you eat in order to cleanse your

[35] Significantly this information is conveyed in his popular treatise, though it could also be found in legal manuals: Ibn al-Jawzī, *Talbīs Iblīs*, 168.

[36] Though the encounter with Shaykh al-ʿImād is not mentioned, stories with moral teachings abound in ʿAlī ibn Yūsuf al-Shaṭṭanūfī's hagiography of Qaḍīb al-Bān in the *Bahjat al-asrār wa maʿdin al-anwār* (Cairo, 1304/1887), 196–8. Gramlich mentions plants and animals conversing with Qaḍīb al-Bān in *Die Wunder der Freunde Gottes*, 384.

[37] "Wa kāna,ʿalā mā qīla, yuʿāmilu al-nās bi'l-ʿīna." Note below that Ibn Kathīr uses "ka-mā qīla" in a different place.

> heart and your stomach." The Shaykh understood what was intended and forsook doing that.[38]

Along with a rise in water usage, Ibn Kathīr's use of biblical language further dramatized the story. Even if not every reader caught the reference, adding the verse from the Gospel of Matthew to Abū Shāma's account leaves no doubt that this time the biography is directly concerned with hypocrisy.[39] If here, as elsewhere, eating was an action synonymous with consuming capital, and unclean food a stand-in for unlawfully gained wealth, then there is no doubt that it must have been the practice of selling merchandise on credit that Shaykh al-ʿImād gave up once he understood Qaḍīb al-Bān's message: the shaykh's heart was affected by the moral qualities of food he put in his stomach, and these two inner organs needed attention. With only a few changes, the biography has taken on a sharper focus, one that centers wholly on financial transactions.

The problem of financial gain through credit transactions was a topic in legal discourse that brought to life a pivotal difference among the four Sunnī legal schools, namely the permissibility of using of a legal stratagem (*ḥīla*) to achieve a legitimate end that would be illegal through more direct means.[40] For example, in seeking to avoid directly benefiting from interest paid on money lent, a creditor could employ as a legal stratagem the type of sale known as *ʿīna* (or *masʾalat al-ʿīna*), "a transaction that disguises an interest-bearing loan in the form of a sale."[41] Actually two transactions are involved. Al-Nawawī, a Shāfiʿī jurist like Shaykh

[38] Ibn Kathīr, *Bidāya*, XIII, 68. In the above passage I have omitted Ibn Kathīr's title for Qaḍīb al-Bān that reads *al-muwallad* instead of *al-muwallah*. (In an older printed edition Qaḍīb al-Bān is identified as a *muʾakah*.) There are other mistakes here as well: the full saying should read "tuṣaffūna al-baʿūḍ min sharābikum wa tastariṭūna al-jimāl bi-ajmāliha," as in Ibn al-Jawzī's biography of Muḥammad ibn Sabīḥ al-Sammāk, who quotes Jesus as having uttered these words (*Ṣifat al-ṣafwa*, III, 175). Here the second phrase reads "tastaru buṭūn al-jimāl bi-aḥmāliha."

[39] The biblical lesson is apt when applied to a man of law: "Woe to you, scribes and Pharisees, hypocrites! For you tithe mint, dill and cummin, and have neglected the weightier matters of the law: justice and mercy and faith. It is these you ought to have practiced without neglecting the others. You blind guides! You strain out a gnat but swallow a camel!" Matthew 23:23–34 (New Revised Standard Version). The verse is consonant with the Qurʾānic view of the consumption of wealth (e.g., Qurʾān 2:188).

[40] For a fascinating study of legal stratagems see Satoe Horii, "Reconsideration of Legal Devices (*Ḥiyal*) in Islamic Jurisprudence: The Ḥanafīs and their 'Exits' (*Makhārij*)," *Islamic Law and Society* 9, 3 (2002). The article surveys the views of the Shāfiʿīs and Mālikīs as well. Horii disagrees with Schacht's portrayal of these strategies as "bogus transactions" meant to prevent people from breaking the letter of the law.

[41] Ibid., 346.

al-ʿImād, explains how it is permissible for someone who wants to borrow cash to gain it via this double sale: "A person other than he sells [him] a thing for a price to be paid at a later date and delivers it to him, then buys it [back] before payment is due for a sum in ready money that is less than that price."[42] Essentially, Shaykh al-ʿImād was a money-lender. Since the two sales are separate, and since each transaction is legitimate, so is the final result, according to the Shāfiʿī school.

It was a complicated area of the law, one that was still being debated when Ibn Kathīr was writing in the fourteenth century. The double sale was denounced by Ibn Qayyim al-Jawziyya, a student of Ibn Taymiyya – who was opposed to the use of legal stratagems in general.[43] Ibn Kathīr had also studied with Ibn Taymiyya, despite being a Shāfiʿī, and so a convincing Ḥanbalī critique of *ḥiyal* could have been the reason for his stern retelling of Shaykh al-ʿImād's biography.[44] But profiting from a double sale would have been an area of personal doubt for some of his fellow Shāfiʿīs too; in an age where so many jurists were exceedingly cautious about their earnings, it is not surprising that Shaykh al-ʿImād received mixed reviews. A truly exemplary jurist would have had scruples about his money as well as his bodily purity.

In the changes made by Ibn Kathīr a new view of purity begins to emerge, where the central opposition in the biography surfaces not between two wrongs (ostentation and lack of self-mortification; misguided enthusiasm and neglect of other duties) but in the contrast between scrupulous purity and ethical impurity. Abundant ablutions were not expressly a problem for Ibn Kathīr, who omits the anecdote about the servant fetching water for ablutions from the Tigris altogether. Indeed, Ibn Kathīr repeated the

[42] al-Nawawī, *Rawḍat al-ṭālibīn*, III, 81–2. There are several variations on this type of sale, but since this one was sanctioned by the Shāfiʿīs we might assume that a scholar of high standing, such as Shaykh al-ʿImād, followed this formula.

[43] Ibn Qayyim, protesting the contemporary reliance on *ḥiyal*, says that invoking the *mas'alat al-ʿīna* is the gaining of interest (*ribā*) by a legal stratagem. Since holy law condemns "the eater of interest and the food bought with it," and expressly forbids taking interest, "there is no doubt about the prohibition of *mas'alat al-ʿīna*." (*Iʿlām al-muwaqqiʿīn*, IV, 132–3). *Ribā* means, in a general sense, financial gain by unlawful advantage. For Shāfiʿīs the double sale was a permissible way of loaning money and being compensated for it. For a discussion of the prohibition of financial compensation for loans see Nabil A. Saleh, *Unlawful Gain and Legitimate Profit in Islamic Law: Riba, gharar and Islamic Banking*, 2nd ed. (London, 1992), 52–6; on Ibn Taymiyya's general view of *ḥiyal* see al-Matroudi, *The Ḥanbalī School*, 98–103.

[44] He specifically drew attention to the *ḥīla* by amending Abū Shāma's phrase about doing business *bi'l-ʿīna* (through sale by credit transaction) to read *mas'alat al-ʿīna*, making it clear that a legal stratagem was being used.

term *waswasa* in describing one of his older contemporaries, Ibn al-ʿAjamī (d. 734/1334), a Ḥanafī jurist at the Iqbāliyya Madrasa in Damascus, as being "eminent, godly, self-mortifying and really full of doubts about water."[45] By borrowing the language of cleanliness to complicate the lesson learned by Shaykh al-ʿImād and evoking an image of plentiful water, Ibn Kathīr (via Qaḍīb al-Bān) is able to make his point about financial probity: if you need a large amount of water to make sure you are pure, your food should be really doused in order to get it clean; you must be thorough in eliminating any taint of illegality in the way you accrue money. The result is that this time around *waswasa fī'l-ṭahāra* emerges as an acceptable trait that throws light on the hypocrisy of his business transactions, the better half of the hypocritical equation. A reader who had not seen Sibṭ Ibn al-Jawzī's or Abū Shāma's versions would form an altogether different image of its subject. For despite Ibn Kathīr's harsher tone, his use of the theme of excessive purity brings this version closer, ultimately, to that of Ibn Khallikān, who had praised Shaykh al-ʿImād for cleaning his new garments and hands.

Thus did the short portrait of a respected jurist who had lived in an earlier generation and in a city far from Damascus, where most of his biographers resided, become the forum in which these authors aired their disparate concerns. Noticeably absent from all three critical accounts of Shaykh al-ʿImād, however discreet the first two might have been, are the standard details about his professional life – his legal training, his teachers, and so on. In these negative portraits the story of the shaykh's *waswās* in ritual purity was nearly all that remained. But the differences evident in the three texts, written over the course of a century, are symptomatic of conflicting attitudes towards the purity of the body between 1200 and the early 1300s. They can be taken as exemplifying once again the larger debate about excess in worship, and Ibn Kathīr's shift in emphasis portends the direction that the debate would take. It was the view of purity *as scrupulosity* that would change. In order to understand why and how that occurred, it is necessary to consider how views of *waswās* had evolved.

Devilish Whisperings

Inaccurate measurements and confusion about how to perform the rituals obviously had little to do with the causes of anxiety, particularly when

[45] The phrase he uses is "kathīr al-waswasa fī'l-maʾ jiddan": Ibn Kathīr, *Bidāya*, XIV, 173; al-Ṣafadī says that Ibn al-ʿAjamī had *waswās fī'l-ṭahāra* (*Aʿyān al-ʿaṣr*, IV, 572); and Ibn Ḥajar later described him as *muwaswasan fī'l-ṭahāra* (*Durar*, IV, 43).

its victims were scholars and jurists. Nor does examining the complicated legal basis of the transgressions of educated *muwaswasīn* – those afflicted by doubts – explain why so many similar patterns of amplified rituals of purity proliferated in the Ayyubid and early Mamluk periods. The causes of *waswās* determined by critics before 1250, if often simplistic, are not insignificant in the trajectory of the affliction. The first two negative portrayals of Shaykh al-ʿImād reflect how indebted his biographers were to the systematically derisive view of *waswās* articulated by Ibn al-Jawzī in the *Talbīs Iblīs*, where two explanations predominate. When he addressed fears about the purity of water used for ablutions, Ibn al-Jawzī specifically criticized those who "wash their garments in the Tigris or, like the Jews do, in a stream" because they worry that a smaller amount of water might not be sufficiently pure. To those worshippers who fret about remote possibilities of pollution in a bowl of ablution water, Ibn al-Jawzī responded: "Holy law holds that it is sufficient that the *source* of the water be pure," as though anxiety about the purity of water was produced largely by a misunderstanding of the basic requirements of *ṭahāra*. The charge of ignorance was perhaps especially intended to sting those who should know better: men such as Shaykh al-ʿImād and Saʿd Ibn Marzūq. For indeed, to Ibn al-Jawzī, doing more than required in order to conform to the letter of the law was an infallible indicator of *waswās*. "Let no one think I am against cleanliness and scrupulosity," he wrote, "but excessiveness which goes beyond the boundary of holy law and is a waste of time – that is what we forbid."[46]

Whether a result of ignorance or ostentation, the problem as it was defined in the late twelfth century was controllable and correctable, as the example of the chastened Shaykh al-ʿImād shows. Earlier, however, the cause of *waswās* in ritual purity had been linked to a failure to digest the symbolic nature of the minor ablution. In the eleventh century al-Ghazzālī had identified what would become the most common form of *waswās* in the next two centuries when he recognized that the enthusiast of ritual purity (*muwaswas*) fears "that the water will not reach all parts of his limbs in just three repetitions because *waswasa* overwhelms him, and so he imposes on himself a fourth."[47] Fear of invalidating a ritual by not performing it perfectly was the main reason behind the fourth washing, and the point of contact between water and skin was where the problem occurred. The common theme over the centuries was this need

[46] Ibn al-Jawzī, *Talbīs Iblīs*, 131–3.
[47] al-Ghazzālī, *Iḥyāʾ*, II, 113.

for extra water and washing; it was a constant in discussions of *waswās*. It is also a sign of how some people tried to achieve a better kind of purity in the course of their minor ablution. For why would a small amount of contact with water be deemed unsatisfactory if some sort of real cleanliness were not sought? A fourth washing is still a long way from bathing in pursuit of cleanliness, but the doubt does appear to have centered on the link between symbolic purity and purification by water.

Not long after Ibn al-Jawzī had voiced his opinions, Ibn Qudāma recognized an element of helplessness in those who were afflicted by anxiety, although he was even more vehement in condemning them. He was the first author to devote a whole treatise to the behavior associated with *waswās*, for previous authors had treated the topic only sporadically, and he also was the first to resurrect the devil so vividly in discussing it. This treatise, *Dhamm al-waswās* (A condemnation of devilish whisperings), was to become the seminal text on the definition and critique of *waswās fī'l-ṭahāra*; it was quoted extensively down to the fifteenth century.[48] Though it deals with a wide range of problem areas, including prayer, most examples of *waswās* cited in the *Dhamm al-waswās* occur during the performance of the minor ablution. The major ablution never produced the same degree of anxiety, for reasons that will be explained below. According to Ibn Qudāma, the *muwaswasīn* are people to whom Satan's whisperings become intelligible. While believing that they are performing ablutions and prayers as the Prophet did, he asserts, they are unwittingly obeying Satan, who uses his subtle skills to lead people – pious people – astray. Judging from one hadith Ibn Qudāma cites, Satan could farm out his chores on occasion. The Prophet said, "Water has its own devil who is called al-Walhān. Beware of the *waswās* of water."[49]

Immediately this hadith focuses attention on the site of ablution, and acknowledges that there is a risk in what might be called the paradox of purity. Al-Walhān, an extra-Qur'ānic devil, was well known to the extent that every author who dealt with the issue of *waswās fī'l-ṭahāra* also mentions this hadith, but he never became a popular figure in Islamic literature. His name, Walhān, means distracted, bewildered, or even out of

[48] Although the title puts it in the praise/blame genre, the terminology he employs throughout is clearly that of a *bid'a* treatise – that is, a text addressing innovations or deviations in religious practice. The devil Iblīs is, of course, omnipresent in Ibn al-Jawzī's *Talbīs Iblīs*, yet the character is mostly a rhetorical device; al-Ghazzālī too mentions hadiths about the devil and *ṭahāra*, but only Ibn Qudāma frames his entire discussion in this way.

[49] Ibn Qudāma, *Dhamm al-waswās*, 36.

one's senses.[50] The existence of a devil specially devoted to water suggests that the kind of *waswās* that surfaced in ritual purity was different from its other forms: while al-Walhān might sow discord among believers by confusing them as to correct practice, he was not the instigator of treacherous plotting and malicious thoughts. Indeed, the nineteenth-century Dutch philologist Reinhart Dozy, who surveyed the usage of the word *waswās* in medieval texts, lists several meanings, from evil thoughts to madness to joy, both of the latter conveyed by the French word *folie*. But Dozy also notes that when *waswās* occurs during the performance of ablutions or prayers, "c'est d'être sujet à des distractions."[51]

Ibn Farḥūn refers to a man thus driven to distraction. Aḥmad al-Qurashī lived in Medina during the latter part of the thirteenth century and was "one of the harsh ascetics (*mutaqashshifīn*) and enthusiasts of purification (*muwaswasīn*) in major ablutions, *ṭahāra* and prayers.... He would arrive at the water source before the muezzin had begun the call to prayer and would not cease performing his ablutions there until people grew annoyed at the abundance of his *waswās*."[52] Although Ibn Farḥūn had introduced Aḥmad al-Qurashī with a glowing endorsement, counting him among "the men of virtue and greatness," he closes with the words: "We ask God to grant us well-being." A note of sympathy conveyed by the prayer acknowledges in a mild way that something was amiss. The notion of mental affliction is articulated more clearly by Ibn Qudāma, who explains that once Iblīs has taken possession of the thoughts of such men, they obey him "in a way that resembles madness (*junūn*) and comes close to the thinking of the Sophists who disbelieve in the realities of things."[53] Philosophers and madmen, both were victims of delusion. Ibn Qudāma's tendency to see *waswās* not merely as a form

50 Fittingly, it is related to the word *muwallah*, the epithet of Qadīb al-Bān. If the devil al-Walhān was the character who sent Shaykh al-ʿImād into an anxious state, the biography turns into a tale of one *muwallah* being corrected by another. This hadith appears in arguments about *waswās* going back at least as far as al-Ghazzālī; the hadith is also cited by Ibn Qayyim al-Jawziyya, *al-Waswasa*, ed. Aḥmad Sālim Bādawīlān (Riyadh, 1415/1994–5), 24; and by later authors down to al-Suyūṭī.

51 R. P. A. Dozy, *Supplément aux dictionnaires arabes* (Beirut, 1981 [1881]), s.v. "waswasa." In other contexts it might retain the sense of evil thoughts or madness, according to Dozy. It can also mean vehement enthusiasm, or having worries or somber thoughts.

52 Ibn Farḥūn, *Tārīkh al-Madīna*, 106. This is an atypical case where the full ablution, *ghusl*, is identified, along with purification in general, as being the focus of anxiety. This incident, though, refers to the minor ablutions performed at the communal basin or fountain (the word used is ʿ*ayn*, for a spring or source).

53 Ibn Qudāma, *Dhamm al-waswās*, 19–20.

of deviance but as insanity is increasingly reflected in the portrayal of contemporary figures.

Indeed, in several historical examples the person beset by *waswās fī'l-ṭahāra* was neither a show-off nor a hypocrite, but someone caught in a loop at the site where ablutions take place. Ibn Baṭṭūṭa evoked the mood of such moments in his account of a holy man he met in Mecca. An exemplar of scrupulosity and asceticism, Muḥammad Ibn al-Burhān was afflicted by *waswās*, or, as H. A. R. Gibb translates it, "tormented by secret vagaries."

> I saw him one day making his ablutions at the tank of the Muẓaffarīya college; he made the ritual washings and then went through them all again, and when he had wiped his head, he wiped it over several times more, but even that did not satisfy him and he plunged his whole head into the tank.[54]

Being tormented by secret vagaries may be too strong a translation of *mubtalan bi-waswās* in light of the fact that so many people are said to have been similarly afflicted. On the other hand, a delusional element of *waswās* is emphasized in the actions Ibn Baṭṭūṭa described. There can be little doubt that Muḥammad Ibn al-Burhān's real concern was performing the ritual perfectly, and that his concern necessitated a more thorough coverage by water than was required. Of all the steps of the ablution, wiping the hair is perhaps the most obviously symbolic: only in the major ablution do the roots of the hair need to be touched by water. This anecdote revisits the question asked earlier: why would more than three washings be desirable if some more thorough cleanliness were not sought at least for those body parts – the hands and feet, face and head – affected by this ablution? In considering this question, one cannot be constrained by theoretical discussions of the logic of purity, for in Ibn al-Burhān's case the logic had broken down. In his abundant use of water, he achieved a kind of cleanliness in seeking to fulfill the ritual. Not being able to achieve the degree of purity he desired through the ordinary steps of *wuḍū'* was what "caused" his *waswās*.

Ibn al-Jawzī and Ibn Qudāma agreed on one compelling reason for people to curb their *waswās* in ablutions. Using an argument typical of Islamic religious critique, they pointed out that a person is likely to miss obligatory duties because of devotion to supererogatory performances. A person performing and reperforming ablutions at the fountain is liable to

[54] Ibn Baṭṭūṭa, *The Travels of Ibn Baṭṭūṭa*, I, 220–1; *Riḥlat Ibn Baṭṭūṭa*, I, 116.

be late for prayers, for example.[55] And indeed, Ibn al-Burhān would miss the beginning of the prayer led by the Shāfiʿī imam because of his ablutions and then repeat over and over, "I meant to, I meant to!" instead of "I intend to, I intend to" – the statement with which prayer commences. His ablutions, and those of Aḥmad al-Qurashī as well, display perfectly the signs of *waswās fī'l-ṭahāra* found in the theoretical literature of the late twelfth and early thirteenth centuries: wasting water and repetitive action. Wasting water is, in a sense, the infraction since the Prophet had said not to do this.[56] But the *waswās*, the *folie*, really lies in repetitive action, and it was not limited to ablutions.

The disastrous consequences of repetitive action, and the devil's hand in it, was brought to light most vividly by Ibn Qayyim al-Jawziyya a few years later. He had been told "by someone he trusted" about a man with a severe case of *waswās* whose habit of excessively repeating the intention to perform prayer spilled over into other aspects of his life.[57] On one occasion, probably in a fit of bad temper, the man swore that he would divorce his wife. He only meant to say the phrase once, for uttering it three times would make the divorce irrevocable according to Islamic law. But the devil would not leave him until he had said the phrase many times, and so the couple separated, leaving the husband overwhelmed with grief.[58] The critics also mention *waswās* in prayer, where the worshipper falls behind because he dwells on the words of prayer while the imam continues on with a prostration.[59] Along similar

[55] Ibn Qudāma, *Dhamm al-waswās*, 21; Ibn al-Jawzi, *Talbīs Iblīs*, 132. The argument is familiar from Ibn al-Jawzī's condemnation of the perpetual fast.

[56] Washing parts of the body more than three times is the most common form of *waswās* cited in the texts before 1300. Wasting water is the second reason not to do this; the first is deviation from the pattern of the Prophet's own performance of the ablution.

[57] Ibn Qayyim al-Jawziyya, *al-Waswasa*, 17. Once the phrase of intention (*niyya*) is uttered (mentally or aloud), prayer can commence; the *muwaswas* becomes trapped at this earliest stage. For other examples see also Ibn al-Jawzī, *Talbīs Iblīs*, 131, 134–5; and Ibn Qudāma, *Dhamm al-waswās*, 27–33. On the role of intention in Islamic rituals see Paul R. Powers, "Interiors, Intentions and the 'Spirituality' of Islamic Ritual Practice," *Journal of the American Academy of Religion* 72, 2 (2004).

[58] During their long separation she married another and had a child with him. After divorcing the second man she returned to her former husband, but "only after he had been nearly destroyed by her departure." This was their only recourse: the wife was obliged to marry someone else, consummate that marriage, and then obtain a divorce. Only in this manner is a couple allowed to remarry after a statement of divorce has been uttered three times (according to some jurists, including Ibn Taymiyya, this had to be on separate occasions), so as to prevent men abusing the ease with which the formula could be pronounced.

[59] Ibn Qudāma, *Dhamm al-waswās*, 34–5. Ibn Qudāma devotes a chapter to discussing people who repeat words from the opening verse of the Qurʾān (al-Fātiḥa) or the profession

lines, Ibn Farḥūn mentions another of the *muwaswasīn* in Medina, Asad al-Rūmī (d. 731/1341–2) who, when reading the Qur'ān aloud, "used to stick to the letters carefully, [frequently stopping] and returning to wherever his soul had left off so that he would not violate a single piece of the recitation."[60] Not being able to get past the initial steps of a ritual performance, whether a gesture or a letter, is where the *waswās* occurred. It was something like a short circuit.

Islamic legal scholars who discussed *waswās* appear to have anticipated modern psychiatric diagnoses of compulsive behavior as the ritual undoing of a compulsive thought. Ibn al-Jawzī says rather bluntly that repeatedly stating the intention to perform prayer was caused by "disorder of the mind and ignorance of the law," a statement other authors attributed to al-Shāfiʿī.[61] However, calling these devotees obsessive-compulsives will not prove to be an enriching path of inquiry for several reasons. For one thing, the causes of modern obsessive-compulsive disorder have been linked, since Freud, to stress and trauma, and more recently to genetics and neurobiology, but the medieval sources are of course silent in every case on personal information of that sort.[62] More importantly, it is not only the victims of *waswās* that are of interest, but their place in society and the way in which their behavior was read by others. Some medieval authors saw *waswās* as an uncontrollable urge to perform a ritual; others saw it as a fulsome type of piety. To all of them, however, the gestures involved were indications of a pious outlook, whether delusional,

of faith (the *shahāda*), laboring over them and purposely stuttering on certain letters so as to elongate them.

60 Ibn Farḥūn introduces him as "one of the *muwaswasīn* in ritual worship among our pious and righteous brethren" and adds at the end, "He was [also] laborious in his major and minor ablutions": Ibn Farḥūn, *Tārīkh al-Madīna*, 152.

61 The phrase is "khabl fī'l-aql wa jahl fī'l-sharʿ": Ibn al-Jawzī, *Talbīs Iblīs*, 134. Al-Ghazzālī said it came from either one or the other: *Iḥyā'*, I, 190. Al-Suyūṭī (who will be discussed below) attributes it to al-Shāfiʿī.

62 An example of a historical approach that applies Freud's theory to ritualized actions is Seymour Byman's "Ritualistic Acts and Compulsive Behavior: The Pattern of Tudor Martyrdom," *American Historical Review* 83, 3 (1978). It should be stressed that the behavior that is repeated is not intrinsically linked to what causes repetitive behavior: washing one's hands repeatedly is not actually caused by a fear of dirt, for example. Yet in the context of the required ablutions, the repeated behavior *was* linked to purity – by medieval observers – and this is what concerns us in this chapter. Finally, the compulsive thoughts of the *muwaswasīn* (which are seldom heard directly from them) might have been undone through ritual action, but also specifically through religious ritual. It may be more fruitful, in the end, to consider *waswās* in ritual purity as a kind of parenthetical ritual, one that took place within the dimensions of a greater one.

misguided, or genuine, for *waswās fī'l-ṭahāra* was always understood to relate to a desire for purity.

Fear of invalidating a ritual obligation is the common link among the various forms *waswās* could take. The repetition dispelled the worry that a ritual had not been correctly performed and thus had been nullified. But the fact that almost every historical example of *waswās* occurring in the thirteenth century had to do with either the minor ablutions specifically or the requirements of purity in general demands to be explained.[63] That people needed to be reminded of the symbolic character of purificatory rituals and also of the distinction between cleanliness and purity in the thirteenth century suggests that Islamic legal discourse was still in the process of confronting a perceived paradox in *ṭahāra*.

Legal Discourse and Symbolic Purity

The Qur'ānic injunction to perform prayer in a state of purity proved from the start to be enormously complicated when it came to procedures for washing, as several scholars of early Islam have shown.[64] By the thirteenth century, legal explanations of the qualities of pure water to be used for ablutions, the sources of impurity, and the correct way to perform each step of the minor ablution took up whole volumes. Al-Qarāfī (d. 684/1285), the author of an influential Mālikī legal commentary, sought to clarify the meaning of purity at the outset before he began explaining the processes of cleaning garments and performing ablutions. The word *ṭahāra*, he says, has many meanings. In ordinary language it means being free from stains. *Ṭāhir*, cleansed, can mean for example the state that is the opposite of menstruation,

> or it can be used figuratively (*majāzan*) to describe a heart that has been cleansed of faults, or a reputation free from blemish. This usage borrows the similitude of an obvious stain to describe a stain that is felt or perceived.

[63] In Ibn Qudāma's treatise, only one chapter does not discuss issues of purity. The others include: *waswās* in stating the intention (*niyya*) for prayer and ablution; wastefulness in the major and minor ablutions; performing the ritual gestures of washing more than three times; overcautiousness in defining what "cancels" the state of purity, such as breaking wind; and various situations where worrying about impurity is not warranted.

[64] John Burton, "The Qur'ān and the Islamic Practice of *Wuḍū'*," *Bulletin of the School of Oriental and African Studies* 51 (1988). Burton studies the connection between the meaning of *wuḍū'*, a word not mentioned in the Qur'ān, and the activities it came to signify. Marion Katz's *Body of Text* describes in more detail the intellectual challenges faced by the early jurists as they sought to establish the contours of the system of Islamic purity.

Abruptly changing tack, he continues, "As for *ṭahāra* in law, it is not a treatment by water or by anything else.... Rather, it is an ancient rule of sacred obligation (*ḥukm sharʿī*) and it means 'making allowable.'" Just as God has made certain foods allowable, He permits His servants to pray in a particular state, that of ritual purity, and thus the word "is applied to the treatment by water or other substances only figuratively."[65] What he means is that in the case of both prayer and food, it happens to be the state of purity that makes them allowable. Only by extension does the word *ṭahāra* mean purification as a procedure. In effect, he first made liberal use of the concept of cleansing (and also stains), but when it came to explaining the rules of law he carefully avoided associating *ṭahāra* with cleanness. In the effort to clarify what purity should mean, al-Qarāfī attempted to wrest the notion of purity away from cleansing or washing so that his readers would remember that the acts of ablution are only performed because God made purity a condition for prayer.

The fifteenth-century Ḥanafī author Badr al-Dīn al-ʿAynī approached the matter from an entirely different perspective. Departing from the strictly Qurʾānic view offered by al-Qarāfī, he acknowledges from the outset that washing only certain parts of the body can appear mysterious and arbitrary to the person undertaking this ritual.

> If you were to ask me, "What is the principle behind the selection of these four limbs for the ritual of *wuḍūʾ*?" I would reply: "Because in the Garden, when Adam (peace be upon him) was forbidden to come near the tree and yet he ate from it, these four limbs were culpable. The legs walked, the hands grabbed, and the face turned towards it. And when Adam knew what he had done, he put his hand on his head as grief struck him, then all his ornaments and clothing fell away from him."[66]

[65] al-Qarāfī, *al-Dhakhīra*, I, 163. He applied the same logic to the word *najāsa*, which in ritual law means the quality of impermissibility rather than physical impurity or uncleanness. In ordinary language, however, the word *najis* (unclean) can indicate a metaphorical stain; he cites a Qurʾānic example of this usage, where the polytheists are "a source of uncleanness." It is *as though* they are ritually impure, not that they actually are substantively impure themselves. On the fascinating legal theory of this jurist, see Sherman Jackson, *Islamic Law and the State: The Constitutional Jurisprudence of Shihāb al-Dīn al-Qarāfī* (Leiden, 1996). Al-Qarāfī's notion of the *ḥukm sharʿī* is discussed on page 116–17.

[66] al-ʿAynī, *Bināya*, I, 142. This passage was cited by an earlier author, the Shāfiʿī jurist al-Aqfahsī, who will be discussed below. See Katz, "The Study of Islamic Ritual," 123. Al-ʿAynī held the positions of *muḥtasib* and Ḥanafī chief qadi in Cairo; he died at the age of ninety-three in 855/1451 (see al-Sakhāwī, *al-Ḍawʾ al-lāmiʿ*, X, 131–2).

The ritual washing of guilty limbs was, in this view, at the root of the actions of *ṭahāra*. Nothing in the Qur'ān links Adam's sin with ablutions or with humanity's obligation to purify themselves.[67] But the concept of sins being washed off figures prominently in several hadiths, and al-ʿAynī chose to make this attitude the basis of his exposition.[68] If his commentary explains yet another facet of why doubts about purity might proliferate, it also demonstrates why substantive law can be so useful in discerning contemporary attitudes. Al-ʿAynī expected his readers to wonder about the logic of purity, and his explanation, we must assume, provided one satisfying answer.

In contrast to these complex explanations, al-Nawawī provided a relatively simple definition in his commentary on a legal text of al-Shīrāzī: *ṭahāra* means cleanliness (*naẓāfa*) in ordinary language. "And in the technical language of the jurists, it means the lifting of the state of ritual impurity (*ḥadath*) and the removal of impurity (*najāsa*)," the latter referring to the impure substances that must be eliminated from clothing and the body prior to ablutions.[69] This definition was widely repeated. Al-ʿAynī, for example, chose to cite it in his *Bināya sharḥ al-Hidāya*.[70] Even Ibn Manẓūr's *Lisān al-ʿArab*, a dictionary known for its thoroughness, which was completed in Cairo shortly after al-Qarāfī's death, proceeds from the notion of actual cleanness rather than from sacred obligation in describing the process a man goes through when he rises for prayer.[71] Most

67 In the Islamic tradition, the sins of Adam are not a burden inherited by humanity. The connection with Adam mentioned here by al-ʿAynī suggests that one washes off one's own sins and in doing so invokes that first moment of human disobedience. Katz notes that the Qur'ānic prophet more directly identified with ablutions is Ayyūb (Job), who was healed by them: *Body of Text*, 122. But the reason why Adam's body was so often the focus of early Islamic speculation about the meaning of purity in humans is that he and Eve, or rather their sins, are associated with the "discovery" of bodily waste and putrefaction (ibid., 186–7); see also Wheeler, *Mecca and Eden*, 83–4, 125.

68 A commonly cited hadith links each step of the minor ablution with the removal of sins from that part of the body. Thus washing the face removes the sins committed by the eyes and so forth (e.g., al-Ghazzālī, *Iḥyā'*, I, 135).

69 That is, substances produced by both the body and external matter. Abū Isḥāq Ibrāhīm Fīrūzābādī al-Shīrāzī, *Kitāb al-Tanbīh fī'l-fiqh al-Shāfiʿī wa-bi-hāmishihi: Taḥrīr alfāẓ al-Tanbīh li'-Imām Yaḥya ibn Sharaf al-Nawāwī*, ed. Ayman Ṣāliḥ Shaʿbān (Beirut, 1995), 13.

70 al-ʿAynī, *Bināya*, I, 137: "*Ṭahāra* in ordinary language means cleanliness (*naẓāfa*). And in technical language it is an expression relating to a quality that transpires from the abatement of ritual impurity (*ḥadath*) and sexual impurity (*janb*), a quality upon which prayer is conditional." Al-ʿAynī had read al-Nawawī's section on purity closely enough to be able to point to specific places where al-Nawawī differs from his legal progenitor al-Shāfiʿī (e.g., I, 141–2).

71 Ibn Manẓūr, *Lisān al-ʿArab*, IV, 200. The author would have been familiar with the legal definitions, as he himself was a Shāfiʿī jurist.

authors, in other words, fail to make such a clear semantic distinction between the ordinary meaning, which relates to bodily cleanliness and the legal and sacred meaning proposed by al-Qarāfī.

In the *Rawḍat al-ṭālibīn* al-Nawawī begins the section on purity, as do many jurists, with the various procedures of cleansing, starting with the real rather than the symbolic: the definition of the phrase "pure water"; the vessels for holding it; identification of impure substances; causes of bodily impurity; and only then the rituals of *wuḍū'*, *ghusl*, and *tayammum*. At the very beginning of the section on pure water he briefly makes the distinction between symbolic and physical *ṭahāra* in a way that is deeply meaningful for our understanding of *waswasa*. Like al-Qarāfī he attempts a linguistic analysis of *ṭahāra* and related terms: one should properly refer to someone who has performed an ablution as being *ṭāhir* (pure), rather than as being *ṭahūr* (clean). But, "after an act of supererogation (*nafl*) in purification such as renewing the *wuḍū'* or making a recommended *ghusl*, or a second or a third washing, saying *ṭahūr* is more sound."[72]

This meant, of course, that in ablutions the degree of achievable purity is fixed; it does not rise or fall according to water usage or thoroughness of ritual washing. One is completely ritually pure after the basic gestures of minor and major ablutions have been completed. If a person is thus pure only once, another term was needed to describe anything beyond that state. But it is interesting that the second term, *ṭahūr*, connotes a stronger sense of physical cleanliness, and as a result the possibility of achieving real cleanliness exists. Thus if someone performed a *nafila* act relating to ablution, he or she might achieve cleanness in addition to the less corporeal state of ritual purity. Al-Nawawī's intentions are not explicit here; it was merely a moment in which an author left the door open for individual motives and actions.

By the thirteenth century the ritual acts themselves were well established, but so were the fundamental disagreements about their meaning. It is tempting to assume that these wide-ranging legal opinions reflect conceptual differences among the four Sunnī schools of law regarding acts of purification, and to some extent they do. However, there is no evidence to suggest that Ḥanafīs have a greater conception of ablutions being a reminder of Adam's sins than do the Mālikīs, for example. Furthermore, significant disagreements continued within each *madhhab*

[72] al-Nawawī, *Rawḍat al-ṭālibīn*, I, 115–16.

as well as among them, especially in the thirteenth century.[73] To a person familiar with some of these explanations the concatenation of guilt, the obligation to pray in a purified state, and the paradox of needing to wash things off by performing gestures that only hint at scrubbing or dousing may indeed have combined to produce anxiety. Legal explanations did not cause *waswās*, but the tales of medieval *waswās fī'l-ṭahāra* and the views of early Mamluk jurists on the meaning of purity should be read as parallel commentaries, especially since so many legal experts were counted among the *muwaswasīn*.

Was Waswās a Ḥanbalī Problem?

In the early thirteenth-century critique of *waswās*, the major theoretical issue had to do with whether or not the rituals of purity could be a form of devotional piety (*ta'abbud*). This was, above all, a concern of the Ḥanbalī school. To Ibn al-Jawzī, for example, there was a simple reason that excessive purity was wrong: "Among the Prophet's Companions, there was no *ta'abbud* in using a lot of water."[74] Ibn Qudāma illustrated his own concerns about excessive purity with a graphic description of the bodily harm that results when a person is influenced by Satan:

> He heeds [Satan's] words about the tormenting of his *nafs* and obeys him in injuring his own body: sometimes by submersion in cold water, and sometimes in the overuse of water and protracted scrubbing. Or he might open his eyes in the water and wash their insides to the point where he damages his sight. Sometimes this [*waswās*] leads to his exposing his private parts to people, and in other cases it gets so bad that children laugh at him and passersby mock him.[75]

[73] An interesting account of an intra-Shāfiʿī dispute over water purity appears in an obituary, where the views of several authors, including al-Nawawī and Taqī al-Dīn al-Subkī, are presented by al-Ṣafadī (*A'yān al-'aṣr*, III, 604–8). For an example in a text on substantive law see al-Nawawī's discussion of wringing out garments (*Rawḍat al-ṭālibīn*, I, 138). Also it is worth noting that the passages from al-Qarāfī and al-ʿAynī cited above are prefatory remarks. As such they contain views that were partly personal, for the introduction to a text was often the place in which the author showed his literary abilities and where he had license to create deeper readings of the topics at hand.

[74] Ibn al-Jawzī, *Talbīs Iblīs*, 132. Here he quoted, without attribution, a letter written in the eleventh century by the Ḥanbalī theologian Ibn ʿAqīl to the vizier Abū Shujāʿ, who was "pious and full of *ta'abbud*, but had *waswasa* in his performance of ritual worship." (Elsewhere Ibn al-Jawzī does quote Ibn ʿAqīl directly on matters of excessive purity, e.g., on p. 168.) The letter makes it clear that ritual ablutions were *not* a form of worship that could be enhanced by supererogatory performance. For the text of the letter see Ibn Rajab, *Dhayl 'alā Ṭabaqāt al-Ḥanābila*, I, 149.

[75] Ibn Qudāma, *Dhamm al-waswās*, 20–1.

The danger of going blind from ablutions calls to mind Ibn al-Jawzī's macabre description of the perpetual fasters' brains drying up. On that topic, Ibn Qudāma had suggested that one could never do too much of a good thing, yet in the *Dhamm al-waswās* he advises worshippers to cleave to the Prophet's *sunna*. (This is, in fact, the only remedy he offers for the affliction of *waswās* in matters of purity.)[76] Coming as it did from a devil-inspired form of madness, the impulse that produced *waswās* was fundamentally different from the desire to perform supererogatory acts of worship (*taʿabbud* or *nāfila*). Ibn Qudāma's view is consistent with a belief that *ṭahāra* is only "the key to prayer" and thus not a form of worship in and of itself.[77]

Understanding the various currents of thought regarding the nature of purity is crucial in deciphering Ibn Qudāma's treatise on *waswās*. His text was more than just an exposition of Ḥanbalī legal views. It was aimed at a popular audience, and his graphic descriptions of the effects of the "illness" were not merely shrill warnings, for around the time that he wrote the *Dhamm al-waswās*, historical examples of men who had *waswās fī'l-ṭahāra* correspond to his descriptions surprisingly closely. In the passage above, Ibn Qudāma could easily have been speaking of a fellow Ḥanbalī immigrant in Damascus, the *faqīh* Shihāb al-Dīn Muḥammad ibn Khalaf al-Maqdisī (d. 618/1221). Abū Shāma recalled that this man was one of the righteous shaykhs living at the former monastery at the foot of Mount Qasyūn.

> I used to see him on Fridays before noon, sitting on the bottom stair of the minbar at the Mosque of the Mount. In his hands would be a book of hadith or collected tales of virtuous men which he would read to people until the muezzin gave the call to prayer. Abī Muẓaffar said: "He was an ascetic, a devotee, scrupulous, and superior in the learned arts ... [to wit] he memorized the *Maqāmāt* of al-Hariri in fifty nights. Then his thoughts became jumbled and his mind deranged. He used to wash the insides of his eyes and went blind because of it."[78]

[76] Ibid., 22–6.

[77] Ibn Qudāma tends to use *taʿabbud* instead of *nāfila* for supererogatory worship because he understands it to mean bodily devotion; thus, it can apply both to obedience to a divine command to worship and to any bodily performance of worship, whether obligatory or supererogatory. Compare with Katz, *Body of Text*, 255, n. 65, on the opinion of al-Shāfiʿī, whose concept of *taʿabbud* has a different meaning: *wuḍūʾ*, *ghusl*, and the removal of *najāsa* are all forms of worship or submission to a divine command (*taʿabbud*).

[78] Abū Shāma, *Tarājim*, 130. The informant he mentions, Abū Muẓaffar, is Sibṭ Ibn al-Jawzī.

Since the phrase *waswās fī'l-ṭahāra* does not appear in this passage, there is nothing to suggest that it caused his debility. Self-induced blindness could have been the result of a progressive mental disorder rather than anxiety about purity. But in a passage quoted by al-Dhahabī, another informant confirms that Muḥammad ibn Khalaf had "excessive anxiety about purity" (*waswasa zā'ida fī'l-ṭahāra*).[79] This time there is no mention of his mind becoming jumbled, unless, of course, *waswasa zā'ida* meant precisely this. The two biographers appear to have been describing the same repetitive behavior in different terms: what led to Ibn Khalaf's damaging his eyes was the plague of doubt.

Further complicating Ibn Khalaf's case is the fact that the hadith contains a precedent for washing the insides of the eyes. Ibn Qudāma himself, in the *Mughnī*, acknowledged that some of his fellow jurists mention washing the inside of the eyes as one custom (*sunan*) of the minor ablution, according to the precedent set by the Prophet's Companion Ibn ʿUmar – who went blind because of it. Another opinion he cites held that washing the eyes was not forbidden, but was more appropriate during the major ablution where other hard-to-reach parts of the body are washed. However, Ibn Qudāma stresses the fact that the practice is not required: "The sounder opinion is that it is not recommended for either *wuḍū'* or *ghusl* because the Prophet did not do it, nor did he order it, and it is harmful. What was related about Ibn ʿUmar is proof of its being disliked because he lost his vision."[80] This is an important clue about the evolution of the affliction, for it demonstrates that what some observers saw as misguided purity or madness to others might seem exemplary. Like the perpetual fast, an ancient tradition of severe practice furnished a precedent, this time by the son of the caliph ʿUmar. Just as Ibn al-Jawzī had tried to dismiss justifications of the perpetual fast that relied on a cast of exemplars from early Islam, Ibn Qudāma had to address a practice in *waswās fī'l-ṭahāra* that could not be reduced to a simple deviation arising after the time of the "pious forebears."

Before moving on to the fourteenth century, when many of these views changed, an answer must be given to the question of whether *waswās* in purity was indeed a Ḥanbalī problem. All the critics of *waswās* from the beginning of our period down to Ibn Qayyim al-Jawziyya in the

[79] al-Dhahabī, *Tārīkh al-Islām*, XLIV, 420. A Ḥanbalī hadith scholar who had studied with Ibn al-Mannī in Baghdad, Ibn Khalaf was well known as a holy man. Al-Dhahabī reports his miraculous intervention during a conflict (*fitna*) in Jamāʿīl, a town in Palestine.

[80] Ibn Qudāma, *al-Mughnī*, I, 88.

fourteenth century were Ḥanbalīs.[81] Two important conclusions may be drawn from their consistent opposition to *waswās*. The first is that they see *ṭahāra* as purely a preparation for prayer, and thus its rituals are not capable of being "borrowed" for supererogatory worship. The second possible conclusion, however, is that these texts of critique do not signal Ḥanbalī self-definition from other Muslim views of purity, but rather the fact that an enthusiasm for diligence in purity was the Achilles' heel of some prominent pious Ḥanbalī men. After all, scrupulosity was especially embedded in their outlook because of Aḥmad Ibn Ḥanbal's prototypical wariness in all matters, and the historical sources show that scrupulousness in ethics and in the performance of ritual very often went together.[82] Therefore, Ḥanbalīs might be more susceptible to *waswās* than others, and if so, the medieval Ḥanbalī authors sought to quell that enthusiasm.

But such an argument could be made for two of the other schools of law. Al-Nawawī's validation of supererogatory purity and, to a certain extent, the hint of a possibility of real cleanness through ablution should lead us to expect that medieval Shāfiʿīs might have had a greater concern with the ritual ablutions. Yet it was al-Shāfiʿī himself who first pinpointed the problem of *waswās* as something caused by madness, and thus knowledge of its existence was coeval with the emergence of this *madhhab*.[83] Furthermore, it would be Shāfiʿī scholars who would continue the critique of *waswās* in the coming centuries, notably al-Aqfahsī (d. 808/1409) and al-Suyūṭī (d. 911/1505). As for the Ḥanafīs, one might in fact expect *wasāwis* about water purity to occur most often among them since Ḥanafīs have more stringent requirements than the other *madhhab*s for the purity of water used in ablutions.[84] And indeed Ibn al-ʿAjamī, discussed above, who was "really full of doubts about water" is a good example of a Ḥanafī jurist plagued by Ḥanafī-style worries. But their strictness relates to the requirement of using running water, whereby any flowing water is purifying, even if simply poured from a vessel. This,

[81] The Shāfiʿī Abū Shāma dealt with the issue of more than three washings in only a sentence, and never employed the term *waswās*.

[82] On this proclivity see Matroudi, *The Ḥanbalī School*, 105.

[83] Jalāl al-Dīn al-Suyūṭī, *al-Amr bi'l-ittibāʿ wa'l-nahy ʿan al-ibtidāʿ*, ed. Muṣṭafā ʿĀshūr (Cairo, 1987), 139.

[84] The modern word for tap or faucet is *ḥanafiyya*, and it has been suggested that the word evolved from faucets being added to the ablution basin: "If they had taps, they were called *ḥanafiyya*; according to Lane's suggestion, because the Ḥanafīs only permitted ablutions with running water or from a cistern 10 ells broad and deep" (J. Pedersen, "Masdjid," *EI*².).

in fact, makes it considerably easier for Ḥanafīs to escape the state of defilement. Finally, the Mālikī requirements for water are the least exacting, and yet Mālikīs were not immune to *waswās* either, as we shall see. Anxiety about purification was common among adherents of all the legal schools.[85]

The second part of this chapter focuses on how attitudes towards the practices associated with *waswās* shifted among the exemplars of devotional piety, and it may be helpful to reexamine here how the discourse had evolved up through the thirteenth century. The proper forum for discussing the topic of *waswās* had always been in texts aimed at a general readership rather than in *fiqh* texts (where it is mentioned only briefly). It had been addressed by al-Ghazzālī, for example, in his *Iḥyāʾ ʿulūm al-dīn*, which can best be described as a kind of gloss on a legal manual, filled with advice and personal comments as well as hadith, rules of law, ascetic precepts, and Sufi wisdom. To al-Ghazzālī, having doubts about *ṭahāra* was quite normal, and he showed himself to be sympathetic to the victims of *waswās*. For example, speaking of the fear of possible impurities in the water used for ablution, which would invalidate prayer, he notes that this often leads people to seek running water in large amounts. Each of the legal schools has different requirements regarding the amount of water needed to ensure that the impurities it contained are negligible. As a Shāfiʿī, al-Ghazzālī was obligated to describe what his own legal school required, but he writes, "I used to wish that [al-Shāfiʿī's] *madhhab* was like that of Mālik, may God be pleased with him," for the Mālikīs hold that a small amount of water does not become impure unless its qualities have obviously undergone a change. The Shāfiʿīs require more water in order to be certain of its purity, and that creates *waswās*.[86]

But al-Ghazzālī did not understand the problem of *waswās* as being inseparable from matters of purification and prayer. Rather, it was linked to uncertainty (*shubha*) about right and wrong. His examples of *waswās* describe an obsessional kind of doubt that arises in daily decisions about

[85] If anything, it appears to have afflicted Shāfiʿīs most of all, partly for legal reasons, which will be discussed in the next section, but also because of the nature of the sources used in this study. The biographical dictionaries of Damascus covering the late Ayyubid and early Mamluk periods contain far fewer Mālikīs, for example; J. Gilbert asserts that madrasas established in the early Ayyubid period were equally distributed among the four Sunnī *madhhabs*, although she counts more Ḥanafī establishments than Ḥanbalī: Gilbert, "Institutionalization of Muslim Scholarship." Louis Pouzet has similar findings for the period up to 1276: Pouzet, *Damas*, 23–105; chart provided on 426.

[86] al-Ghazzālī, *Iḥyāʾ*, I, 129.

the ethics of the *ḥarām* and *ḥalāl*: One man might fear using a clay cup crafted by a potter who had hit someone; another might be afraid to eat the meat of sheep tended by a shepherd who ate unlawful food.[87] Oddly enough, al-Ghazzālī was forced to address the issue of *waswās* in order to balance his own emphasis elsewhere in the *Iḥyā'* on the importance of circumventing doubt (by avoiding dubious substances and situations) as one aspect of "seeking the licit." The late twelfth- and thirteenth-century examples of the affliction, by contrast, are never described in terms of decisions about *ḥalāl* and *ḥarām*. They consistently relate to the performance of ritual.

Beginning with Ibn al-Jawzī's *Talbīs Iblīs*, *waswās* in ritual acts was treated as wrongful practice in *bid'a* treatises, a trend that continued down to al-Suyūṭī, who in the later fifteenth century devoted two brief paragraphs to condemning *waswās* in *ṭahāra* and *ṣalāt*.[88] Ibn al-Jawzī associated it with several groups of people who repeatedly come under attack in the *Talbīs Iblīs*: uneducated worshippers, extreme ascetics, and ignorant Sufis. The latter appear as show-offs more than anything else: absorbed in their communal life, they are confident that they are doing the right thing. The scholar Ibn 'Aqīl, he says, once visited a Sufi hostel (*ribāṭ*) and was laughed at for using too little water.[89] Likewise, the extreme ascetics sometimes overdo their ablutions so that observers will remark on their great piety, and here his emphasis on doing more than necessary was above all a thinly veiled criticism of overly scrupulous devotees – and jurists in particular.

Ibn Qudāma's tract was the first to deal with *waswās* as a separate topic, and also the first to discuss problems in ritual purity in such depth. By extricating the topic from al-Ghazzālī's general theme of doubt (*shakk*) gone wrong, it began to take on a shape of its own.[90] No longer was *waswās* a mere step beyond scrupulosity: it could be a sign of mental illness or self-punishment, harmful to the body and caused solely by Satan's

[87] Ibid., II, 113. For a fascinating discussion of the terms *shabha* and *shakk* see Robert Brunschvig, "Variations sur le thème du doute dans le fiqh," in *Studi orientalistici in onore di Giorgio Levi Della Vida*, vol. I, Pubblicazioni dell'Istituto per l'Oriente 52 (Rome, 1956), 61–82.

[88] al-Suyūṭī, *al-Amr bi'l-ittibā'*, 139.

[89] These Sufis took for granted the availability of water, thinking it was a laudable way of performing ablutions (*Talbīs Iblīs*, 168).

[90] That is, situations that were perceived as dubious result in *waswās*, but Ibn Qudāma's point is that the doubt itself is wrong, especially in matters where God has offered an easier way (*rukhsa*). Thus to him the problem of *waswās* no longer has to do with making choices in doubtful situations, but rather with conforming to correct practice (*sunna*).

command. In addition, he confronted the issue frontally as an example of *bidʿa*, as the voluntary adoption of habits the Prophet had neither practiced himself nor condoned in others. He says bluntly, "There was not a single *muwaswas* among the Companions of the Prophet." Then, as if anticipating the example of the Prophet's pious Companion ʿAbd Allāh ibn ʿUmar going blind from washing his eyes, he continues, "and if there was a *waswasa* that had merit, it was not preserved [as standard practice]."[91] Rather than successfully quelling the excessive habits of the *muwaswasīn*, his identification of various problem areas merely charted the wide territory in which anxieties could take root. The trend towards overperforming the rituals of *ṭahāra* would continue over the next two centuries even among Ḥanbalīs who were the most consistent critics of the *muwaswasīn*.

Part II: *Waswās* and the World

From the middle of the thirteenth century onwards a startling dichotomy emerges between theoretical discussion of *waswās*, which emphasized its wrongheadedness and devilish origins, and the historical accounts of its victims, who are increasingly and almost without exception praised as scholars, exemplary figures, or holy men. This raises several questions that will guide the discussion that follows. Did a kind of holy *waswās* exist, and if so, when did it emerge? Or was it instead a real form of madness to which the pious were particularly susceptible? And finally, is it possible that a pious person – or a learned author for that matter – would have forgotten the Satanic genealogy of the word *waswās*, particularly in the years after Ibn Qudāma's *Dhamm al-waswās* was written? Whereas prior to the thirteenth century the combination of censure and the possibility of madness resulted in purely negative references to people who had *waswās fīʾl-ṭahāra*, by the early fourteenth century the "affliction" had become a wholly positive attribute in the eyes of a number of authors.[92] This certainly seems to have been the case when al-Jazarī described Umm Muḥammad Fāṭima al-Fāmī, a woman of Bedouin origin

[91] Ibn Qudāma, *Dhamm al-waswās*, 26. He continues, "And if the Prophet noticed *muwaswasīn*, he abhorred them; if ʿUmar noticed them, he would strike them and teach them proper behavior, and if one of the Companions noticed them, he would accuse them of *bidʿa* and hate them."

[92] One rare and interesting case of a positive use of the term prior to 1200 C.E. is Ibn al-Jawzī's description of a friend cited in Ibn Rajab, *Dhayl ʿalā Ṭabaqāt al-Ḥanābila*, I, 333.

whose family had settled in the Ṣāliḥiyya district of Damascus. When she died in 727/1326, prayers were said for her in the nearby mosque of the Muẓaffariyya Madrasa on Mount Qasyūn where she was laid to rest.

> ʿAlam al-Din Ibn al-Birzālī said that her birth was around the year 648. She was a virtuous woman, and she had *waswasa* in *ṭahāra* and *wuḍūʾ*. Her nights were spent reciting litanies. Though she became feeble, she used to be patient in bearing that burden. She transmitted texts with an *ijāza* from Sibṭ al-Salafī and others.[93]

Though authors were not averse to including a person's foibles in a biographical portrait, the way the phrase "*waswasa* in *ṭahāra* and *wuḍūʾ*" is inserted among other laudable practices indicates that it is now a marker for a super-performer of purity rituals. Her suffering is reminiscent of Ibn al-Mannī and other exemplars who refused to let a frail or crippled body get in the way of ritual worship; yet her anxiety about purity and minor ablutions is *not* explained as an illness, nor is it portrayed as a misguided approach to piety. No sympathy was needed, and no condemnation seems to have been implied.

This tended to be the pattern historians and biographers in the fourteenth century would follow when they mentioned the trait of *waswās fīʾl-ṭahāra*.[94] Nowhere can its newfound prestige be seen more clearly than in al-Ṣafadī's updated version of Shaykh al-ʿImād's biography. For the most part al-Ṣafadī follows the loyal account of Ibn Khallikān (where the word *waswās* had not appeared), and there is no mention of Qaḍīb al-Bān or financial transactions. But he borrowed a single element from the negative reports and, blending the two views of Shaykh al-ʿImād, ended up with a man who was "strongly scrupulous and full of *waswasa*: he would not touch a pen until he had washed it."[95] As noted earlier in this chapter,

93 al-Jazarī, *Tārīkh*, II, 202. The nighttime recital of prayer formulae (*wird*) is often associated with Sufi brotherhoods, but it was also a common practice outside those circles. Umm Muḥammad Fāṭima was the daughter of al-Shaykh Aḥmad al-Fāmī, a Bedouin from the Kalbī confederation. If al-Jazarī included an entry for her father, Shaʿfūr, it is not in the years of the *Ḥawādith* published to date.

94 That is, a change occurs in how *waswās* appears in biographies. Some men who witnessed firsthand the behavior of the *muwaswasīn* at this time, such as the traveller Ibn Baṭṭūṭa, responded more equivocally. To him Muḥammad ibn Burhān's performance was perhaps awe-inspiring, but it was neither expressly positive nor negative. This suggests, I think, that authors were beginning to read *waswās* in *ṭahāra* as a sign of true devotion to ritual, but when they considered the details of what was involved, they hesitated to make strong pronouncements or take sides. Ibn Farḥūn's fourteenth-century biographical description of Aḥmad al-Qurashī, discussed above, shows a similar ambivalence.

95 al-Ṣafadī, *al-Wāfī*, V, 292.

when Ibn Kathīr mentioned Ibn al-ʿAjamī's severe anxiety about water, it was in a manner that suggested praise rather than blame: it was twinned with his having chosen the harsh life of an ascetic. Likewise, al-Ṣafadī, offering further details about this Ḥanafī jurist who died in Damascus in 734/1334, says that in addition to his "*waswās fī'l-ṭahāra* and godliness," Ibn al-ʿAjamī also kept himself isolated from people and compiled a guide to the rites of his legal school.[96] This was a scholar who knew the details of what his *madhhab* required, and there is no suggestion that his having *waswās* was at odds with his otherwise good behavior.

The apparent rehabilitation of the term towards the end of the thirteenth century is a fascinating commentary on medieval notions of bodily piety and pious acts, a development not unlike the increasingly positive outlook on the perpetual fast that developed over the same century. By the end of the fourteenth century the rehabilitation was complete, and even the Sufis who had *waswās* were no longer the self-righteous but misguided men Ibn al-Jawzī had made them out to be.[97] If the victims of *waswās* in the twelfth century had typically been well educated, now *waswās* in ritual purity appears even more regularly among the circle of jurists and judges; moreover, when ascetic or ethical scrupulosity and *waswās* overlap, questions of madness or deviation are conspicuously absent.[98] For instance, Khalīl ibn ʿAbd al-Raḥmān al-Qasṭallānī (d. 760/1359), a Mālikī *faqīh* of Mecca, well known for having gone into debt because he gave so liberally to the poor, had "*waswasa fī'l-ṭahāra*, the likes of which cannot be found in any land."[99] Another example from Mecca is ʿĀ'isha Umm Kamāl (d. 810/1408), the daughter of the city's Shāfiʿī qadi, Shihāb al-Dīn Aḥmad ibn Ẓuhayra. She married another qadi and bore him three children, two of whom grew up to be qadis also. Al-Fāsī says she was full of "goodness and worship (*ʿibāda*), and she had great *waswās* in purity."[100] Scrupulosity must have been firmly instilled in

[96] See also Ibn Ḥajar, who says he was *muwaswasan fī'l-ṭahāra* (*Durar*, IV, 28).

[97] For example, Abū Bakr al-Kafarsūsī (d. 802/1400) was a Sufi who followed the *ṭarīqa* of Shaykh ʿAlī al-Banāʾ. At first he took work on farms outside Damascus; then, after memorizing the Qurʾān, he began teaching children. He was said to have been exceedingly scrupulous (*yatawarraʿa*) and to have had doubts in matters of ritual purity: Ibn Ḥajar al-ʿAsqalānī, *Inbāʾ*, II, 118. Compare with Ibn al-Jawzī, *Talbīs Iblīs*, 168.

[98] Ibn Ḥajar makes the ties between legal knowledge, ethical scrupulosity, and *waswās* explicit in a description of ʿAlī al-Ḥabakī, a Shāfiʿī jurist from the Ḥawrān who at the end of his life was a mufti in Damascus: "He practiced *fiqh* with *dīn* and *warʿ*, and he had *waswās* in ritual purity" (*Durar*, III, 30–1); see also Ibn Ḥajar, *Inbāʾ*, I, 226.

[99] Ibn Farḥūn, *Tārīkh al-Madīna*, 113.

[100] al-Fāsī, *al-ʿIqd al-thamīn*, VI, 414.

the children of this family, for her mother was Umm Kulthūm, discussed in Chapter 1, who beat her daughters for leaving the house unveiled.[101] In the following generation the trait of *waswasa* appeared again in Umm Kamāl's nephew, the qadi Aḥmad ibn Muḥammad ibn ʿAbd Allāh Ibn Ẓuhayra (d. 827/1424):

> He was a learned imam, good and godly, upright, scrupulous, blameless and humble, filled with gentleness and fairness.... He was proper in his distribution of the alms tax and charitable donations, spreading them equally among those close [to him] and far removed. He had *waswasa* in purity and prayer. He transmitted hadith, he taught [jurisprudence], and he issued fatwas.[102]

The author, al-Sakhāwī, knew this man personally and describes in detail his many responsibilities as a teacher of law and an administrator of justice. Nestled among these other good qualities, his *waswasa fī'l-ṭahāra wa'l-ṣalāt* affirmed that a scrupulous bodily piety accompanied the scrupulosity he demonstrated in public affairs, such as the distribution of alms. By the beginning of the fifteenth century, then, the phrase was almost hyperbolic, having been stripped of all traces of its devilish genealogy.

In all of these biographical examples, the pairing of *waswās* with another positive feature anchors its reputation as a good trait. How had this come about? It seems likely that a key figure in this shift in perception was Ibn Daqīq al-ʿĪd, who died in the opening years of the fourteenth century, for he was both proof of the successful rehabilitation of the term and the most visible exemplar responsible for making it so. While most authors would praise him unequivocally for his worrying, at least one of them seemed unsure about what to make of it. As with the Ibn Ẓuhayras, *waswās* was present in Ibn Daqīq al-ʿĪd's family tree, according to al-Dhahabī (d. 748/1348), who spoke admiringly of the scholar's intellect and his skill in substantive law and the principles of law. But al-Dhahabī also wrote that "suspicions about water and impurity (*najāsa*) got the better of him."[103] While this information is consonant with al-Subkī's description of the youthful scholar scrubbing his inkpot, quoted at the beginning of this chapter, the tone is rather less optimistic. At first the words sound like a pardon, as though Ibn Daqīq al-ʿĪd

[101] For the mother, Umm Kulthūm, see ibid., VI, 460–1.
[102] al-Sakhāwī, *al-Ḍaw' al-lāmiʿ*, II, 134–5.
[103] Quoted in Ibn Ḥajar, *Durar*, IV, 58.

was not entirely responsible for the worries that built up in him; the progressive nature of his anxiety perhaps evokes the prevailing medieval understanding of illness being caused by the accumulation of harmful substances in the body. By way of explanation al-Dhahabī adds, "Stories are told about that. It is said that his maternal grandfather, the famous shaykh Taqī al-Dīn Mufarraj al-Uṣūlī, used to be severe, outdoing himself even, in purification." If it was a family trait, rather than a pious one, there was little to be done about it. But equally this information could have been intended as a compliment: Ibn Daqīq al-ʿĪd came from good, pious stock and had specific virtues instilled in him from an early age; he had inherited a propensity for rigorous devotion.[104] After all, the author considered this *faqīh* to be "the perfection of scrupulosity" (*tāmm al-waraʿ*), and succumbing to *waswās* was part of what allowed him to be so described. Thus it is al-Dhahabī's early fourteenth-century view of scrupulosity, rather than of *waswās*, that is unequivocal. Like him, certain of his contemporaries continued to avoid endorsing *waswās* as a positive trait, but they stopped well short of condemning it outright.

Quite apart from the way in which authors viewed the problem of *waswās*, the case of Ibn Daqīq al-ʿĪd is valuable as evidence of the evolving behavior associated with it, for his anxiety related neither to the personal pollution caused by bodily functions nor to the perfect performance of rituals. Rather, he feared that his body would become defiled by using sullied water. This apprehension about external sources of impurity and avoiding contamination was to become the trademark of many later examples of *waswās*, and it is a crucial clue explaining why views of scrupulous purity were changing.

The threat of impure substances in water used for ritual purposes shifts the onset of *waswās* to the preliminary stages of purification. In fact, the phrase *waswās fī'l-ṭahāra* had probably always evoked the broadest possible frame of time, starting with the intention to perform ablution, followed by the washing of hands and cleaning of garments, then the performance of the ablutions proper. In legal terminology *ṭahāra* had both a generic meaning and a specific one: it could refer both to symbolic purity and to the procedure of cleaning. In the *Mughnī*, for example, Ibn Qudāma uses the term *ṭahāra* specifically to refer to the preliminary cleaning for prayer, a process he contrasts with *wuḍūʾ* and *ghusl*.[105] What

[104] Al-Subkī's version might be taken as corroborating this interpretation: Ibn Daqīq al-ʿĪd's mother was the first to identify the trait in him as a young boy.

[105] He says that jurists differ over whether the statement of intention (*niyya*) is appropriate for *ṭahāra*, and whether *ṭahāra* is worshipful in the way *wuḍūʾ* and *ghusl* are. Here, it is

this means is that whereas the earlier examples of *waswās* had to do with washing the body sufficiently or making sure one had sufficient contact with water to ensure that purity had been achieved, Ibn Daqīq al-ʿĪd's anxiety related to actual dirtiness and cleanness.

Dirt is not, of course, the correct word for ritually defiling substances. *Najāsāt* are material substances that are capable of invalidating prayer, and they are specifically defined by jurists as filth (*khabath* or *qadhar*) rather than as ordinary dirt. They are also remarkably limited in number, at least in the Qurʾān. The necessity of classifying all natural phenomena into the two categories of filthy and clean was perfectly obvious to the jurists, but over the centuries practical problems defied the easy deployment of that system of classification. These problems show through most clearly in Shāfiʿī substantive law. For instance, unlike the other Sunnī law schools, which consider horse manure and the waste of other domesticated animals to be nondefiling, the Shāfiʿīs deem all animal excrement to be *najāsa*. A walk through the streets of a medieval city was therefore automatically risky; and dirt itself, ordinary dirt, might be replete with unseen impurities. This did not create an epidemic of *waswās* among pious Shāfiʿīs for the simple reason that, as Reinhart has noted, these things are easily washed off; furthermore, imperceptible amounts of *najāsāt* were deemed a negligible threat to purity by all the legal schools.

But when the critique of *waswās* was renewed in the fourteenth century by Ibn Qayyim al-Jawziyya, a Ḥanbalī, and the Shāfiʿī scholar Aḥmad ibn ʿImād al-Aqfahsī who died in 808/1409, it was almost wholly devoted to these external threats.[106] Their *waswās* texts are much longer and more detailed than was Ibn Qudāma's, and almost all of the detail relates to defiling substances. The authors quote from his *Dhamm al-waswās* extensively, sometimes reproducing whole passages, but Ibn Qudāma's focus on ablutions is lost in the flood of new topics. Al-Aqfahsī spent only a few pages detailing problems in *wuḍūʾ*, then devoted almost as much space to the circumstances in which smoke can transmit impurity to clothing.[107] As the focus shifted to fears about tangible impurities (*najāsāt al-ḥissiyya*), even those produced by the worshipper, such as urine, began to be discussed as external sources of defilement rather than as causes of impure

utterly clear that he is speaking of the cleaning process, i.e., the removal of *najāsāt*: Ibn Qudāma, *al-Mughnī*, I, 83.

[106] Al-Aqfahsī was a prolific Shāfiʿī jurist who, like Ibn Qudāma, wrote treatises on issues of contemporary relevance, including wine drinking and the use of hashish.

[107] Ibn ʿImād al-Aqfahsī, *Dafʿ al-ilbās*, 238–9. Smoke was not newly identified as a questionable substance in *fiqh*; he quotes from al-Qamūlī and al-Rāfiʿī in this passage.

status (*ḥadath*). In the broadest sense, Ibn Qayyim's and al-Aqfahsī's volumes were dedicated to issues of cleanliness rather than ritual.

Most of the later historical cases of *waswās fī'l-ṭahāra* also have to do with the preliminary steps of *ṭahāra*, in which cleaning takes place, rather than with ritual performance. This did not mean that anxiety about *wuḍū'* had disappeared, or that the concerns about defilement were new ones. (Shaykh al-ʿImād washing his new garments is an obvious precedent.) Rather, the anxiety was subsumed by a new valorization of cleanliness, and odd things began to happen to *wuḍū'* as a result. A Shāfiʿī jurist from Baalbek, Shams al-Din Muḥammad Ibn al-Majd al-Mūsawī (d. 762/1360–1), provided a famous instance of this:

> He became afflicted with a terrible case of *waswās*, such that whenever he performed the minor ablution, he would throw himself into the fountain of the Ṣāliḥiyya Madrasa in Bayn al-Qaṣrayn – in his clothing! Whether summer or winter, he would submerse himself, claiming that *wuḍū'* could not be complete if this were not done.[108]

Here the purification of body and the purification of garments were fused together in a ritual that was anything but symbolic. Despite his total immersion in water, al-Mūsawī still considered himself to be performing *wuḍū'* and not the full ablution, or *ghusl*. In a departure from the usual pairing of *waswās* with ascetic traits, such as self-mortification or hesitance about social intercourse, the only other information al-Maqrīzī mentions about al-Mūsawī is that "he was delightful company and gave fine lectures. His classes were never tedious." Such an observation is proof of how *waswās* even in its most excessive forms was no longer cause for alarm. Al-Mūsawī's own explanation of his behavior was more a bold exhortation than a defense. No doubt al-Maqrīzī and others saw the absurdity of having wet clothing at the end of *wuḍū'* and included his story because it was so anomalous, but one suspects that they also admired him for his bravado in matters of purity.

Author and Victim: The Case of al-Sallāmī

The approval of *waswās* was by now almost seamless. One author who still indicated a wariness about the subject was Ibn Rāfiʿ al-Sallāmī (d.

[108] al-Maqrīzī, *Sulūk*, IV, 258; Ibn Taghrībirdī's version is similar, but clearly negative: "He was an excellent jurist (*faqīhan fāḍilan*), except that *wasāwis* overcame him." Also omitted is the praise of his lectures (Ibn Taghrībirdī, *al-Nujūm al-zāhira*, XI, 11). His son Muḥammad served as a qadi in Baalbek, Tripoli, and Ḥims (al-Maqrīzī, *Sulūk*, IV, 309).

774/1372), who showed a marked reluctance to attribute the trait to anyone. Where other writers described a certain Damascene Qur'ān scholar and erstwhile muezzin as having a good character and "*waswasa* in matters of water," al-Sallāmī used the phrase "exertion (*ijtihād*) in matters of ritual purity."[109] He had avoided it elsewhere, too, when he wrote that Badr al-Dīn Lu'lu''s grandson in Cairo, Quṭb al-Dīn Ibrāhīm, exhibited "prudence (*iḥtirāz*) in matters of purification and *wuḍū'*."[110]

Al-Sallāmī was a hadith scholar and a Shāfiʿī jurist as well as a historian. Raised in Cairo, he made several trips to Damascus with his father to study and learn hadith; on his fifth trip, this time in the company of the influential jurist Tāj al-Dīn al-Subkī (Ibn Daqīq al-ʿĪd's biographer), he finally settled there. From his twenties until his death at the age of seventy he was a familiar figure in the crowd of Damascene scholars, counting among his colleagues the likes of Ibn Kathīr, al-Ṣafadī, and al-Dhahabī.[111] He had devoted students, several of whom noticed that al-Sallāmī himself had an acute case of *waswās*. Three generations of scholars discussed his problem in turn, beginning with the Aleppan historian Ibn Ḥabīb (d. 779/1379), who was six years younger than al-Sallāmī. They probably met in Damascus when both scholars were in their fifties, if not before. Ibn Ḥabīb remembered him as a supremely cautious hadith scholar who fretted over every precious word he transmitted about the Prophet Muḥammad.

> But he did not worry about nice clothing and food, and in worldly matters he steered clear of anything that seemed dubious or ambiguous

[109] Quoting the testimony of al-Birzalī (whose chronicle ended the year before the subject died), he described a director (*naqīb*) of the Shāmiyya madrasa who died in 737/1337 as being "outstanding among the people of the Qur'ān. His occupation was *fiqh* and he transcribed [many] books of learning. For a while he was the muezzin and substitute imām in the town of Umm al-Ṣāliḥ. He practiced bodily mortification and exertion in matters of ritual purity. He had an outstanding mind and was good company … eloquent in his ingenious witticisms": Ibn Rāfiʿ al-Sallāmī, *Wafayāt*, I, 26. Compare with al-Ṣafadī, *Aʿyān al-ʿaṣr*, V, 342; and Ibn Ḥajar, who attributes the description to "al-Irbilī and others": *Durar*, III, 239–40.

[110] al-Sallamī, *Wafayāt*, I, 57.

[111] They shared many of the same teachers, including al-Birzalī and al-Mizzī; al-Subkī was said to have favored him over Ibn Kathīr. Zayn al-Dīn al-ʿIrāqī, Ibn Ḥajar's teacher, concurred on this point. Ibn Ḥajar attempted a diplomatic intervention here, explaining that Ibn Rāfiʿ better fit the description of a scientist of hadith, because of his extensive travels and his attention to the biographies and qualifications of its transmitters, whereas Ibn Kathīr was more of a specialist in *fiqh* and *tafsīr*. If the two were put together, they would make a perfect whole! (*Inbā'*, I, 49). Al-Sallāmī's most famous work, *al-Wafayāt*, was a continuation of the work of al-Birzalī. See also the informative biography in Ibn Qāḍī Shuhba, *Tārīkh*, III, 421–3.

to him. He kept his contact with people to a minimum. And regarding the purity of his garments and his body, what anxiety he had![112]

Aside from a remarkably succinct statement of how asceticism, ethical scrupulosity, and *waswās* overlap, this description again confirms that the onset of *waswās* could occur well before the acts of the minor ablution proper began. There was ample room for doubts arising from a set of strongly recommended practices that prepared one for ablution, such as washing one's hands *before* dipping them into the water basin or container used for ablutions.[113] The requirement of clean garments, especially for the Shāfiʿīs, was an unforgiving one: not only should a stain or spot of filth be removed, the whole garment should then be washed three times. Al-Nawawī explained the Shāfiʿī approach to clean garments as follows: if the color of a bloodstain remains after scratching and rubbing, it is deemed pure; if the smell of wine persists on a garment but its color vanishes with cleaning, it too is pure. On the one hand, this means that a person can dispense with worry even when his or her human faculties are not satisfied, but, on the other hand, the corollary logic insists that all other strategies must be exhausted first.

The fourteenth-century critics dealt with this form of *waswās* more patiently than their predecessors had with *waswās* in ablutions. Ibn Qayyim al-Jawziyya resurrected one of al-Ghazzālī's arguments about the etiquette of urination. "Shaykh Abū Ḥāmid said: 'It is recommended that a man wet his pudenda (*farj*) and his leggings (*sarawīl*) with water after he urinates, so as to dispel from his soul any *waswasa*.'" Then, should he find some moisture there later, he can reassure himself by saying, "This is from the water I just sprinkled."[114] It was not the act of relieving oneself, a cause of *ḥadath*, that caused worry. As a defiling substance, urine was an external threat to the body and garments even after a person was purified. This form of *waswās* was not portrayed as absurd or delusional, or even as especially deviant. On the contrary, further acts of symbolic purification were prescribed as a solution to worrying about something concrete.

112 Ibn Ḥajar, *Inbāʾ*, I, 48, quoting the historian Ibn Ḥabīb. This was probably Badr al-Dīn al-Ḥasan ibn ʿUmar, the author of the *Dhayl aslāk* (which ends in 1375) and an exact contemporary of Ibn Rāfiʿ; they were both students of Ibn al-Shiḥna (Ibn Ḥajar, *Durar*, II, 17–18).

113 See, for example, al-Nawawī, *Rawḍat al-ṭālibīn*, I, 168–9; Ibn Qudāma, *Mughnī*, I, 80–2.

114 Ibn Qayyim al-Jawziyya, *al-Waswasa*, 28; compare with al-Ghazzālī's longer passage in the *Iḥyāʾ*, I, 131.

These additional acts did not solve the problem for al-Sallāmī. If the line between enthusiasm for purity and *waswās* was for many authors a gray area, it was not so for him. On the contrary, according to Ibn Ḥajar,

> Ibn Rāfiʿ used great precision in what he copied and was always editing and correcting what he composed. He suffered from *waswās* in *ṭahāra* to the point where he weakened his body and ruined his mind and his clothing. He regretted this intensely, but was thus afflicted until the day he died.[115]

Concise and sorrowful, this passage confirms that a painful awareness of doing something wrong sometimes accompanied the doubt, even at a time when *waswās* had become an acceptable trait. His actions signal a preoccupation with how impurity was transmitted to skin and clothing; perhaps he kept away from people partly for this reason. Such an attitude was certainly not without precedent. Much earlier, Shaykh al-ʿAṭṭār of Hamadān (d. 560/1165) was said to have been "severe in matters of *ṭahāra*, never letting people touch so much as his sandal." Shaykh al-ʿAṭṭār avoided human contact not because it was morally defiling, but from fear of tangible – and transmissible – impurities. The difference between him and al-Sallāmī was only one of perception. The informant who described Shaykh al-ʿAṭṭār was one of his students, ʿAbd al-Qādir al-Ruhāwī, who echoed the words Ibn al-Najjār had used to condemn Saʿd Ibn Marzūq, saying, "This is a lapse by a learned man." In other words, he should have known better.[116] Al-Sallāmī did know better but could not help himself.

Al-Sallāmī's problem was widely known and discussed; three separate accounts testify that his body bore the brunt of the worry and his clothing the marks of excessive washing.[117] Like the anxiety about correctly performing *wuḍū'*, fear of *najāsāt* also was a kind of loop: dwelling

115 Ibn Ḥajar al-ʿAsqalānī, *Inbā'*, I, 49. Two of the informants for the biography were al-Sallāmī's students: the historian Ibn Ḥijjī (d. 816/1413) and the historian and hadith expert Zayn al-Dīn ʿAbd al-Raḥīm al-ʿIrāqī (d. 806/1404), about whom see Berkey, *Popular Preaching*, 32–5. Ibn Qāḍī Shuhba was a student of both, Ibn Ḥajar of the latter. Al-Dhahabī has a cursory entry for al-Sallāmī in *al-Muʿjam al-mukhtaṣṣ bi'l-muḥaddithīn* (Ṭā'if, 1988), 229–30; and one on his father, Rāfiʿ ibn Hajras, who was a Sufi as well as a *faqīh* and hadith transmitter. He was born in Ṣamīd, a town near Damascus, and later moved to Cairo (ibid., 98). Ibn Ḥajar says Rāfiʿ was an associate of Ibn Daqīq al-ʿĪd (*Durar*, II, 67).

116 Ibn Rajab, *Dhayl ʿalā Ṭabaqāt al-Ḥanābila*, I, 325.

117 For example, Ibn Qāḍī Shuhba reports one of al-Sallāmī's students (and the author's own teacher) as saying that al-Sallāmī's appearance was "marred" by his *waswās*: Ibn Qādi Shuhba, *Tārīkh*, III, 422.

upon the unseen qualities of water, worrying about how to sufficiently remove a stain, or being hesitant to touch anything for fear of redefiling oneself without knowing it all resulted in repetitive gestures of cleaning. At least in the fourteenth century, the perception of the need for *ṭahāra* did not have to do solely with the "lifting" of the state of *ḥadath*. Men like al-Sallāmī, in scrubbing and otherwise attempting to remove blemishes from their bodies and the garments they wore, aimed to conform perfectly to specific recommendations given to them by jurists such as al-Nawawī.[118] The meaning of their gestures seems mundane when compared with the notion of ablutions as sealing the borders of the body; the removal of *najāsāt* is concerned with material details rather than spiritual preparedness. Furthermore, a number of the offending substances typically mentioned in legal texts – such as wine, the saliva of dogs, menstrual or postpartum blood – could hardly have been encountered by a pious man such as al-Sallāmī every day. In any case, these were neither permanently harmful nor literally dangerous. But al-Sallāmī and others appear to have obeyed the Qurʾānic injunction to "shun filth" just as heartily as they submitted to the command to "purify yourselves."[119]

It was not an illogical outlook, or even an unusual one. Ibn Taghrībirdī, who was not a *muwaswas* as far as we know, recalled his qualms about visiting a Stylite who was greatly venerated in Cairo. Muḥammad al-Maghribī was a *majdhūb*, a man "besotted" with God, who lived inside the city gate of Bāb al-Naṣr under the roof of a vestibule leading into a hostel. "He stayed in that place for years, summer and winter, without budging, on a raised platform of stones. People had great faith in him, and would deliver him food and drink." It seems his other bodily needs were not provided for, however. "When I visited him," Ibn Taghrībirdī says, "I would do so from a distance, for fear of the filth (*najāsa*) that surrounded him."[120] The last phrase might have been a pejorative term for the class of people who flocked to a holy man, but it is much more likely that its meaning is literal, referring to an obvious problem faced by Stylites that even modern historians have skirted. At least in fourteenth-century Cairo, stepping in human waste was a risk one took when visiting them.[121]

118 For example, see al-Nawawī's discussion of the recommendation that the whole garment be washed, and washed a second and third time in *Rawḍat al-ṭālibīn*, I, 138.

119 See Qurʾān 74:1–5 on shunning pollution.

120 Ibn Taghrībirdī, *al-Nujūm al-zāhira*, XVI, 177–8.

121 See Ibn Kathīr's description (*Bidāya*, XIV, 123) of the place where Ibrāhīm al-Muwallah held gatherings.

How pressing a matter the state of defilement was purely depended upon one's outlook. If Ibn Taghrībirdī came home with dirty feet intending to perform prayer, he need only have removed his boots or washed his feet if he were wearing sandals. But although he feared the *najāsa*, and presumably found both a real and a symbolic solution in washing and abluting, his distaste seems to have related even more to the sense of having been around pollution. Even to a person who was only mildly scrupulous, *najāsāt* are not substances that only invalidate prayer, and things to be shunned because the Qur'ān instructs believers to shun them, but additionally because they are or have, over time, become repulsive. Reactions to different kinds of impure matter are not always guided by legal discourse, for the degree to which people might have avoided them finds no equivalent gradation in legal texts. Ibn Qudāma drew attention to this in no uncertain terms when he stated that "there is no distinction between light or heavy *najāsa*."[122]

While many jurists in their *fiqh* texts were busy explaining all the situations one need *not* worry about, elsewhere some of them were devoted to increasing fears about invisible contagion. Just as he had charged bakers with moral responsibilities in preparing bread on clean surfaces and using pure ingredients, the Mālikī jurist Ibn al-Ḥājj described water carriers as being burdened with an even more precious trust, since water had sacred as well as alimentary purposes. It is not only a drink and an ingredient used in cooking, he reminds his readers: "It lifts the state of *ḥadath* and *najāsa*, and it revives the spirit." The pitfalls a *sāqī* might encounter as he fetched water for the Muslim public were many. Waste water from a public bath or a paper factory, facilities that use large amounts of water, could threaten the town's water supply, he says. But even a single individual was capable of having a devastating effect on his environment: "An ignorant person or someone unconcerned with the welfare of his fellow Muslims might urinate beside or even into the water source, such as a river. Then along comes the *sāqī* and collects water to supply the whole town." From there the impurity could find its way into every corner of a city, sullying everything and indeed everyone it touched.

> Their garments and bodies become impure along with the food they bake with it, and their prayers are nullified because of having cleansed themselves with it. Then they will face the inconvenience of cleaning their garments and bodies and returning once again to prayer, and

[122] Ibn Qudāma, *Mughnī*, I, 114.

disposing of their food, and washing their dishes and anything else they had poured water on.[123]

If Ibn al-Ḥājj imagined a city plagued by unseen particles of *najāsāt*, it was hardly an unscientific vision of medieval sanitation. He offered it as a warning in order to jar his readers into watchfulness; at least we may presume he did not expect only *sāqī*s to read this section.

But here lay the crux of the matter: in legal texts, jurists, and especially the Mālikīs, consistently used the argument of mathematical probability to reduce such fears. A small but adequate amount of water that appears pure *is* pure; a single man urinating into a river could not possibly ruin the ability of its water to purify. Yet the fear of a required duty being invalidated citywide was a frightening possibility. Erring on the side of caution was, as always, an appealing solution, and this was precisely why Ibn al-Ḥājj spent pages detailing how the *sāqī*'s individual's duty was a collective one. The best solution, Ibn al-Ḥājj advised, is for the water carrier to go out to collect water at night. And as a backup plan, he urged that the vendor of water who purchased it from the carrier "should similarly be careful lest everyone's prayers be nullified."[124]

The fourteenth-century critics of *waswās* offered no response to Ibn al-Ḥājj's fear-mongering. On the contrary, Ibn Qayyim al-Jawziyya and al-Aqfahsī are, like Ibn al-Ḥājj, insistent about the need for physical purity. In their treatises a new vocabulary was put to use: where *waswās* had formerly been a deviation that was the opposite of correct practice, it now began to be more closely aligned with two other terms relating to scrupulosity, *iḥtirāz* and *iḥtiyāṭ*, both of which mean prudence or caution.[125] What had been a binary opposition between right and wrong now becomes a more finely calibrated scale of behavior: overzealous or overly cautious, extra-scrupulous, prudent, careful, merely correct, lax, and ignorant. Al-Aqfahsī condemned "excessively cautious" Muslims (for instance, those who flee from the mere sight of dogs for fear of being

[123] Ibn al-Ḥājj, *al-Madkhal*, II, 369.

[124] Ibid., II, 369–70. At least in theory, Ibn al-Ḥājj's purpose here was to ensure that the individual did not have to decide whether or not to trust the unseen purity of the water he or she used.

[125] Ibn Qayyim al-Jawziyya, *al-Waswasa*, 52. He says that the *muwaswasīn* would like to call their actions *iḥtiyāṭ* instead of *waswās*, but their excessiveness places them well beyond caution or prudence; see also his concluding remarks on p. 62. Ibn Taymiyya says that with regard to water, even *iḥtiyāṭ*, when no real doubt is involved in a situation, is not encouraged or legitimate (*Majmūʿ fatāwā*, XXI, 56.)

licked), but he also said they were better than those who "take the easy path" and neglect the duty of avoiding *najāsāt*.[126]

One of Ibn Qudāma's chief complaints about *waswās* had been that someone afflicted by it fails to take advantage of God's easing the stringency of certain requirements. The clearest instance he cited, which so perfectly addresses the crux of the matter, involved a woman in the Prophet's time who worried that by walking through muddy streets after having performed the ablution she would become impure again before reaching the mosque. The Prophet's response, after he had ascertained that there was no alternative route for getting there, was that it was fine for her to enter the mosque for prayer without reperforming *wuḍū'*.[127] Despite quoting this very passage and many others, al-Aqfahsī and Ibn Qayyim both argue that prudence and caution are *not* objectionable according to Divine Law; these are proper attitudes that should not be categorized as *waswās*. Indeed, Ibn Qayyim trumpets many instances when jurists have said that acts of worship should be repeated. For example:

> The jurists say, "If the location of a spot of *najāsa* on one's garment is unknown, he is required to wash the entire thing." They also say, "If he has clean garments and some of them become impure, and he has doubts about which ones they are, let him pray again in garment after garment, according to the number of impure substances [he came into contact with]; the extra prayers will replace his worry with certainty." Likewise, they say: "If the vessel used for *ṭahāra* has become doubtful, he should pour out the entire contents and [use sand to] perform *tayammum* [instead]. And likewise, if he is uncertain about the direction of the *qibla*, and he doesn't know in which direction to pray, then he should pray four times ... this will replace his worry with certainty." And they say: "He who forgets one of the daily prayers is required to pray all five prayers [over again]."[128]

He even cites the example of Ibn ʿUmar having gone blind from washing the insides of his eyes as a positive example of scrupulosity; Ibn Qudāma had used it in precisely the opposite way. And finally, Ibn Qayyim concurs with al-Aqfahsī's comment: it is better for the sake of our souls, he concludes, for us to be certain that we have forsworn doubtful things in favor of what is certain and to be overcautious in avoiding *bidʿa* than

[126] Ibn al- ʿImād al-Aqfahsī, *Dafʿ al-ilbās*, 26.
[127] Ibn Qudāma, *Dhamm al-waswās*, 52.
[128] Ibn Qayyim al-Jawziyya, *al-Waswasa*, 9. He supplies many more examples, some taken from the Mālikī school, others from the hadith. *Tayammum* is, again, the substitute ablution performed with clean sand in case of the absence of water.

to take an overly relaxed and easy attitude.[129] Finding certainty through prudence in no way conflicts with the *sharīʿa*, for it is a way of avoiding deviation or *bidʿa*. This validation of doubt brings the discourse back around to al-Ghazzālī's perspective in the eleventh century. As a comment on the changing spirit of medieval Islamic practice, few could be more dramatic than the diverging approaches of Ḥanbalī legal scholars between 1200 and 1400 C.E.

And yet the most vivid historical examples were offered by Shāfiʿīs. An instructive display of how exposure to impurity could become a pressing matter was made by none other than Ibn Daqīq al-ʿĪd, once he had attained the post of Shāfiʿī chief qadi in Cairo. The position required him to meet with the sultan periodically, and on those occasions he would have been expected to humble himself by performing the customary gesture of kissing the ground at the sultan's feet before taking a place on a seat below that of the ruler. According to al-Ṣafadī, in the late 1290s Ibn Daqīq al-ʿĪd was summoned to such a meeting with Sultan Manṣūr Lājīn. When he entered the room and found the sultan sitting on a hassock made of *jūkh*, a type of broadcloth, he went over and sat down next to him on it and then proceeded to carry out his business. Afterwards he returned to his house, where he stripped off all his clothes and washed them.[130]

A deep suspicion of rulers and temporal authorities was a standard attitude – even the correct attitude – of a pious jurist. Self-abasement was one of the main hazards of an encounter with a sovereign and probably why men like Burhān al-Din al-Fazārī refused the post of chief qadi.[131] Later, when people heard about Ibn Daqīq al-ʿĪd's meeting, they exclaimed in horror, "O master, you weren't really sitting on the hassock, were you?" But their horror was not due to fear of the sultan's displeasure. The real hazard was caused by something much more mundane, for al-Ṣafadī affirms that the chief qadi's *waswās* was so severe that "he would not sit on the fabric known as *jūkh* or even approach it." Ibn Daqīq al-ʿĪd explained: "I thought: if I sat below the Sultan, I would be weakening holy law, and the effects of that would never go away. So I sat next to him, then I washed what I wore, and [this other effect] disappeared." The chief qadi had been forced to make a strategic decision between his defense of the *sharīʿa* and his personal purity. What he sacrificed in that

[129] Ibid., 10.
[130] al-Ṣafadī, *Aʿyān al-ʿaṣr*, V, 586.
[131] Ibn Kathīr, *Bidāya*, XIV, 151; for background see Ibn al-Jawzī, *Talbīs Iblīs*, 118.

choice was his own personal purity. But the anecdote was probably made more thrilling because of the strong suggestion that close proximity to the sultan had resulted in him sullying his garments.[132]

The reason why a *jūkh*-covered hassock could be threatening is of special interest, for *jūkh* is certainly not a substance or material mentioned in the Qurʾān. Indeed, the woolen cloth was a product of European manufacture, which only began to be imported to the Middle East during the Crusades. According to a fatwa written by the Shāfiʿī mufti Ibn al-Ṣalāḥ al-Shahrazūrī (d. 643/1245) soon after the fabric first hit the markets of Syria, Muslims in the early thirteenth century had already heard that *jūkh* was manufactured abroad by unbelievers (*kuffār*) using pork suet. Ibn al-Ṣalāḥ's answer was, "If it has not been confirmed that there is *najāsa* in it, then it is not judged to be a *najāsa*."[133] By the end of the same century the imports were available in Cairo, where it is not unlikely that Ibn Daqīq al-ʿĪd's public example had a lasting effect on fashion. The chronicler al-Maqrīzī confirms that in his day, the early decades of the fifteenth century, the *jūkh* market in Cairo was busy selling the fabric, but only as saddle pads, cushion covers, and curtains. Once upon a time, he says, it was the fabric of great men, "but then people began to worry about wearing it," and nowadays the only people seen dressed in *jūkh* are "those returning from the Maghrib or from the land of the foreigners, the people of Alexandria, and some of the common folk of Cairo. Among the chiefs, bigwigs and notables you'll find no one who wears it except when it rains. As soon as the rain stops, they take it off." Conveniently for us, al-Maqrīzī pinpoints a time when it had already fallen from favor, although he never explains why. His father's maternal uncle had been a deputy market inspector in Cairo in the 1330s, and when he showed up one day wearing a new *jūkh*-lined

[132] To understand this, one must refer to al-Qalqashandī's explanation of how the titles given to men who serve the sultan refer to the physical location of the seat one was entitled to sit in: proximity to the sultan was the sign of high position: al-Qalqashandī, *Ṣubḥ al-aʿshā*, V, 493–500. Sultan Lājīn ruled the Mamluk realm for only four years, from 694/1294 to 698/1299, having attained the throne through murder and subterfuge, methods that were by no means uncommon in this period. While he was hated by a significant faction of the amirs, at whose hands he was murdered in his turn, the sources say nothing especially damning about his relations with his subjects. See P. M. Holt, "The Sultanate of al-Manṣūr Lāchīn (696–8/1296–9)," *Bulletin of the School of Oriental and African Studies* 3 (1973).

[133] ʿUthmān ibn ʿAbd al-Raḥmān Ibn al-Ṣalāḥ al-Shahrazūrī, *Fatāwā wa-masāʾil Ibn al-Ṣalāḥ wa'l-tafsīr wa'l-ḥadīth wa'l-uṣūl al-fiqh*, ed. ʿAbd al-Muṭʿī Āmīn Qalajī, 2 vols. (Beirut, 1986), I, 221; the fatwa is also mentioned by Ibn ʿImād al-Aqfahsī, *Dafʿ al-ilbās*, 242.

jacket, his superior made him return it to the seller, saying the fabric was "more appropriate for donkeys."[134]

Conclusion: Triumphant Scrupulosity

Maghen's statement about the reluctance of Sunnī Islam to regard whole categories of persons as defiling remains a valid "law" of purity. But the historical sources clearly indicate that a growing preoccupation with unseen sources of defilement came to admit the possibility of human contagion. Although pigs in the land of unbelievers were the real cause of Ibn Daqīq al-ʿĪd's avoidance of *jūkh*, Sultan Manṣūr Lājīn was, in a sense, the instigator of his state of pollution. For though the ruler was not himself contagious, his own chief qadi nevertheless returned home from the citadel defiled – not in a state of *ḥadath* but still unable to proceed with prayer or apparently other daily activities because of his sullied garments. Thus, in addition to avoiding dubious substances, the scrupulous needed to avoid the kind of people whose lower standards of purity – or indeed cleanliness in the case of Ibn Taghrībirdī's Stylite – made them the bearers of pollution. Carelessness on the part of Stylites, water carriers, the "great unwashed," or even sultans meant that humans were inevitably capable of being polluting. That is, "real" impurity, transmitted in the form of tangible substances, was what many believers now identified as the target of purification; by extension, humans were sometimes drawn into this category of "real" impurity.

In the case of the chief qadi and the sultan, Ibn Daqīq al-ʿĪd's avoidance of *jūkh* made an unsubtle statement about moral hygiene as well. More typically, though, a more ordinary and literal kind of fear was at work. Given Ibn al-Ḥājj's call for alarm far to the west, these sentiments were appearing in a rather wide swath across the Islamic world. Ibn Baṭṭūṭa, for example, registered some surprise when a shaykh in India refused to shake his hand when they were introduced. The man excused himself with a statement of self-abasement, saying, "I am not worthy." But Ibn Baṭṭūṭa noticed that he washed his garments whenever someone so much as touched them.[135] Strange tales of exceptional scrupulosity cannot, by the fourteenth century, be dismissed as embellishments or exaggerations: the rise of scrupulosity-as-cleanliness meant that avoidance became the

[134] al-Maqrīzī, *Khiṭaṭ*, II, 98.
[135] Ibn Baṭṭūṭa, *Riḥlat Ibn Baṭṭūṭa*, II, 322.

watchword of the pious. It affected people in general, and not only the *muwaswasīn*, and its targets were not just people who were visibly sullied. *Al-adnās*, the word that came to describe the masses, was the same term used in discussions of *ṭahāra* referring to blemishes or stains – to things that are defiling. As much as this might be a comment upon the bathing habits of the poorer classes, the example of pious men who avoided them proves that at least some people did indeed think in terms of large categories of threatening human beings.[136]

It must be stressed that the fourteenth-century concern with *najāsāt* was not newly created, nor did it supersede the worry about ablutions. The fourteenth century is thus partly an arbitrary boundary, a period in which shifts in emphasis take shape in ways that are visible in historical and argumentative texts. In this century the duty of being cautious was promoted clearly and in myriad ways, through legal texts and popular treatises – and even more dramatically in the actions of exemplary figures. To the people who lived through either the thirteenth or fourteenth century these shifts were probably imperceptible except to the few authors who tried to intervene, hoping to steer the community in a different direction, or when they made decisions about what word to use for problem of doubts and caution. But by the end of the fourteenth century the separation between the ritual ablutions as symbolic actions and what at least appears to be the more mundane duty of removing filth from one's garments no longer existed for the *muwaswasīn* who, by this point in time, must be called enthusiasts of purity rather than errant practitioners of purity rituals.

While developments in substantive law confirm that this transition occurred gradually and perhaps unintentionally, the explanation for why it occurred at all lies in the possible medieval "readings" of *waswās fī'l ṭahāra*. In the twelfth and early thirteenth centuries it was a departure from correct ritual, a mild form of insanity, or a sign of sycophantic scrupulosity. By the fourteenth century *waswās* was now recast in terms of affliction as triumphant scrupulosity. Having lost one's mind to a holy pursuit was read by others (but not, in an exceptional case, by al-Sallāmī himself) as the ultimate statement of pious devotion rather than as a deviation. This is why al-Ṣafadī, when describing Ibn Daqīq al-ʿĪd's *waswās*, said that he had been "vanquished" by it.[137] As though he had been bested

[136] See, for example, the phrasing in al-Ṣafadī's biography of ʿAbd Allāh Ibn Taymiyya, *Aʿyān al-ʿaṣr*, II, 693.

[137] Ibid., V, 582.

by a worthy opponent, this defeat became the source of Ibn Daqīq al-ʿĪd's own style of heroism. Such a change in perception was also made possible by the rise in the social importance of scrupulosity both as a form of correct practice and as a moral outlook. Indeed, by succumbing to doubts one could gain the moral high ground.

Conclusion

Beyond Transgression, Beyond sunna

What are we to make of the fact that the most high-minded of medieval Muslims began to see deviance as being culturally valid, at least in the specific domain of purity? Considering the prominence of attitudes condoning excess that surfaced in other practices, such as voluntary fasting, it appears that the boundaries of acceptable behavior in devotional piety had already been subtly altered by the mid-thirteenth century, if not earlier. In the past several decades scholarship on Islamic law has begun to emphasize how the legal traditions of Islam are a constantly evolving set of norms rather than an unchanging body of rules. The same is true of piety, which is subject to more profound changes over time. But the two were linked, at least in medieval culture, in several fundamental ways: first of all through the intersection of what the jurists did with their own bodies and the laws they discussed. The changing views of purity in the thirteenth century exemplify precisely this sort of ongoing process. The laws of ritual purity were not fundamentally altered, and yet social conceptions of purity shifted dramatically under the guidance of legal writers and legally minded exemplars.

Second, and in a somewhat similar way, this ongoing discourse with the law was also the purview of certain men who have typically been seen as living outside the law, namely the antinomian holy men of the late medieval period, who were variously described as Sufis or ascetics or *muwallahūn*. The latter were the men who displayed a kind of pious insanity, the "mystic eccentrics" as Pouzet calls them, and they present something of a special case. The first part of this final chapter will focus on the meaning of the *muwallahūn*'s actions in the two areas of purity and fasting. It addresses the issue of religious transgression more generally in order to explain some of the problems involved in defining the scope of devotional piety as it existed by the end of the fourteenth century. The second part, the conclusion proper, draws together the themes of this book as a whole.

Part I: Excessive Piety and Transgression

Reports of extreme social and personal scrupulosity were so common in the thirteenth and fourteenth centuries that for anyone who saw the benefit of having a reputation for godliness, there must have been considerable pressure to adopt ascetic habits and to develop a specialty in a particular practice of worship. The corresponding ideals were reinforced and consistently encouraged through sermons and hortatory texts on asceticism from the twelfth to the fifteenth centuries. In such a climate, what did it mean to not conform? Ascetic ideals and practices could not actually be enforced, of course. In fact, the doggedness of ascetic discourse in medieval texts and the wealth of historical vignettes describing pious exemplars perhaps convey a false image of uniformity in behavior and a sense that there was complete agreement about social values in the Ayyubid and Mamluk periods. Other avenues to fame did continue to be available, and the careers and reputations of those who chose to take them still flourished. One such man was Badr al-Dīn Muḥammad Ibn Baṣkhān, a well-known grammarian and respected shaykh of Qurʾān recitation in Damascus who died in 734/1334. The historian al-Ṣafadī knew him personally and described him in rhymed prose as

> dignified in appearance, displaying open haughtiness and disdain towards people, fine in his dress, nice-smelling ... so elegant was his turban that one would think, from the whiteness of its cloth, it was a dove [perching on his head].... It was widely known that he would not eat meat unless it was well-roasted, nor sweets unless they were made with sugar. And it was said that never in his whole life did he eat an apricot.[1]

Apricots, the delight of most Damascenes and the pride of Syria, were either not sweet enough or too commonplace to please his tastes. Ibn Baṣkhān had even written a poem mocking apricots sold at unaffordable prices, which al-Ṣafadī obligingly supplies. The portrait of this scholar fits well with Michael Chamberlain's description of members of the civilian

[1] al-Ṣafadī, *Aʿyān al-ʿaṣr*, IV, 284–5.

elite of Damascus living in great style and with good taste, not to mention flair.[2] The grammarian had his own list of food prohibitions – frivolous ones perhaps, but uncompromising nonetheless. Ibn Baṣkhān's reasons for not eating apricots and al-Nawawī's rejection of fruit could not have been in more perfect opposition. It was precisely such a contrast that al-Ṣafadī intended the reader to see. He structured the biography so as to call attention to the fact that Ibn Baṣkhān's devotion to a particular set of ideals, those befitting a gourmand and man of letters, matched in its excessiveness the devotion that characterized other breeds of admirable men.[3]

Bucking the trends of the pious exemplars was as satisfying to some members of society as following them was to others. Indeed, an earlier and more scandalous figure who would have horrified Ibn Baṣkhān was the polymath Ibn al-Khashshāb, famous for his expertise in many fields: literature, grammar, philosophy, engineering, hadith, and jurisprudence, although some of his colleagues considered him to be weak in the latter.[4] Ibn al-Khashshāb was a contemporary of the famed twelfth-century ascetic Ibn al-Mannī in Baghdad (discussed in Chapter 1), and like him lived the life of a celibate. But there the similarities ended.

> He was vulgar in his dress, his eating and his drinking. He took neither a wife nor a concubine. It is said that he was a miserly skinflint [even] with himself and used to wear a turban which remained on his head for months at a time until its fringes became soiled from his sweat, blackened, and frayed from filth. Birds used to bombard it with their shit.[5]

A man fond of joking and a devotee of chess, his total disdain for the religious mores of his milieu was discussed by a number of informants, but more with awe than disapproval at the fact that he was in no way affected by the desire for scrupulous purity that distinguished many of his colleagues. He refused, for example, to don a clean turban even after visiting the public bath. Another author says that Ibn al-Khashshāb "paid

[2] Chamberlain, *Knowledge and Social Practice*, 100–3.

[3] Although he seems ill suited to a specialization in Qur'ānic recitation, his expertise is explained by the fact that the Qur'ān's relevance to the fields of philology and grammar was paramount. Studying or teaching the sacred text did not, apparently, automatically place a person among the pious, nor did it preclude an enthusiasm for secular topics or a secular lifestyle.

[4] Ibn Rajab, *Dhayl ʿalā Ṭabaqāt al-Ḥanābila*, I, 318. In this biography Ibn Rajab includes comments made by authorities such as Ibn al-Jawzī, who made the remark about Ibn al-Khashshāb being deficient in his knowledge of law.

[5] Ibid., I, 320. Ibn al-Khashshāb died in 572/1172.

no heed" to what he ate or what he wore, and presumably this means that he was not cautious about impurities in either case.[6] Given his stinginess, indiscriminate eating also suggests a willingness to eat cheap or unpalatable food. In describing these as deliberate habits rather than mere absent-mindedness, the authors create a shadow biography invoking the self-neglect of men such as Ibn al-Mannī and other ascetics. In his refusals Ibn al-Khashshāb was as consistent as any of his more pious colleagues and, like them, unyielding to the point of excess. He was the epitome of neglect.

In both these cases, motifs of avoidance, abstention, or misanthropy, which elsewhere could be signs of exemplary piety were used here to good – and even humorous – effect. Significantly, the two men shared a love of grammar and poetry, and they appear to have consciously reinforced the distinction between those fields (and secular conduct) and the field of religious scholarship (and the piety that accompanied it). No one, for example, seems to have thought that Ibn Baṣkhān was secretly a pious man; his bodily habits so obviously made no claims of piousness. Nor was Ibn al-Khashshāb censured for the behavioral traits mentioned above. On the contrary, upon his death he was said to have assured a friend from beyond the grave that things were going well for him in heaven. When the dreaming man asked him in surprise if God was merciful to the *literati* (the *udabā'*) he replied, "Yes." When asked, "Even if they were negligent?" he replied that after a goodly dose of rebuke, they would be granted grace.[7]

Ibn al-Khashshāb did get into trouble for other reasons, ones that make him a more complicated figure than Ibn Baṣkhān. Despite the fact that he identified himself after death as a literary man, in life he had been involved in religious questions and matters of law, offering opinions on such things as the permissibility of supererogatory prayers on the eve of the first Friday in Rajab, a popular custom he criticized vehemently and refused to take part in.[8] In light of this, his habits in matters of dress and food may be read as relating to – indeed, responding to – piety, rather than ignoring it, and as an explicit rejection of the scrupulosity in matters of etiquette and food purity his colleagues took pride in displaying. He purposefully transgressed the norms of the jurists, and we must assume

6 Ibn Khallikān, *Wafayāt*, III, 103.

7 Ibid.

8 Ibn Rajab, *Dhayl 'alā Ṭabaqāt al-Ḥanābila*, III, 318, quoting Yāqūt. On this controversy see Ukeles, "Innovation or Deviation," chapter 4.

he did this not only as a way of showing how unimportant outward displays of piety were, but also as a protest against conformity.[9]

The line between ascetical humility in matters of dress, on the one hand, and neglectful shabbiness, on the other, was in many ways a rather thin one. After all, owning a single garment and wearing it until it was tattered was a typically ascetic style of dress. Bearing in mind the example of Ibn al-Khashshāb, we may consider how other sorts of "transgressors" made use of confusing messages about purity. Neglecting cleanliness was a trait associated above all with the *muwallahūn*, the pious madmen of the twelfth to fifteenth centuries.[10] Among the first to exhibit this trait – and to be called a *muwallah* because of it – was Qaḍīb al-Bān, who died around 570/1174. According to an early source for his life, Ibn al-Mustawfī's *Tārīkh Irbil*, Qaḍīb al-Bān was reputed to have been raving mad and to have acted in ways contradicting holy law. Well known for the filthy clothing he wore, he was, as one observer put it, "not careful (*lā yaḥtarizu*) about urine on his garments and his legs."[11]

In fact, there is a final twist in the story of the confrontation between Qaḍīb al-Bān and Shaykh al-ʿImād, the Shāfiʿī jurist who was afflicted by *waswās*, which may have been familiar to some medieval readers. A later hagiography of the *muwallah* written by the Sufi author al-Shaṭṭanūfī (d. 713/1313–14) portrays Qaḍīb al-Bān as a miracle-working sage gifted with suprasensory powers, knowledge of the law, and a respectable Sufi genealogy connecting him with the "sober" Sufi al-Junayd, who died in 298/911.[12] Unlike a typical *muwallah*, Qaḍīb al-Bān was not so absorbed in God that he ignored his religious obligations, according to al-Shaṭṭanūfī's informant ʿAbd Allāh al-Mārdīnī. One day al-Mārdīnī was at a madrasa in Mosul where Shaykh al-ʿImād's brother Kamāl al-Dīn and a group of scholars were discussing Qaḍīb al-Bān. Just as they began slandering him, the holy man arrived. After listening to Qaḍīb

[9] It is tempting to see him as a *malāmatī*, a pious person who hides his true nature and seeks out blame in order to demonstrate how God's good opinion is the only one that matters. But *malāmatī* was a label that no longer existed in the twelfth century, at least in historical sources, and none of the informants seem to have viewed Ibn al-Khashshāb in this fashion. For background see Sara Sviri, "Ḥakīm Tirmidhī and the Malāmatī Movement in Early Sufism," in *The Heritage of Sufism, Volume I: Classical Persian Sufism from its Origins to Rumi (700–1300)*, ed. Leonard Lewisohn (Oxford, 1999).

[10] At this time it was also a characteristic of the *majdhūb*, a person "besotted with God," who was a familiar figure in Sufism. The two terms *muwallah* and *majdhūb* were used interchangeably by some authors in the medieval period.

[11] Ibn al-Mustawfī, *Tārīkh Irbil*, I, 371; discussed also by Meri, *The Cult of Saints*, 97–8.

[12] al-Shaṭṭanūfī, *Bahjat al-asrār*, 196–8.

al-Bān's insightful rebuttal of Kamāl al-Dīn, al-Mārdīnī's curiosity was sufficiently aroused that he left the circle of scholars and followed Qaḍīb al-Bān out of the city to a remote spot on the riverbank. There, for two days in a row, the holy man "took off his clothes and washed them in the river and then went and hung the garments on a tree. Then he put them on and prayed until dawn broke."[13] Thus, no less than Shaykh al-ʿImād, this *muwallah* was scrupulous about the cleanliness of his garments and the purity of water used for washing them; the choice of a running river appealed to both of them.

The account also establishes a clear point of conflict between the scholarly brothers (ʿImād al-Dīn and Kamāl al-Dīn) and the holy man who bested them on two occasions within the city of Mosul. Their confrontations were not only about competing ideals of cleanliness but also about competition over religious authority. After all, Qaḍīb al-Bān succeeded in making a convert of the brothers' colleague, al-Mārdīnī.[14] While al-Shaṭṭanūfī might have wished to provide a corrective to earlier reports of the *muwallah*'s filthiness and lunacy, similar themes are found in the earlier accounts as well, all of which identify Qaḍīb al-Bān as a wise Sufi.[15] One of them tells the story of how Qaḍīb al-Bān grew incensed upon hearing that a scholar he had come to visit was busy compromising himself at a meeting with the ruling atabeg of Mosul. He accused the scholar of doing the devil's work, then proceeded to strip off his tattered clothes and, standing naked at the fountain in the courtyard of the house, sprinkled water on his body.[16] This appears to be yet another perfect and highly appropriate performance of a *ṭahāra* ritual: renewing the minor ablution after an outburst of anger is a commendable act.

There were more than a handful of men like Qaḍīb al-Bān in the two following centuries, familiar figures in and around the cities of the Near East, and especially Damascus, who broke the law in various ways. They frequently resided in cemeteries, at garbage heaps or dunghills; some were hermits, others drew crowds of uneducated men and

[13] Ibid., 197.

[14] Compare the account given by al-Shaṭṭanūfī with Sibṭ Ibn al-Jawzī's in *Mirʾāt al-zamān*, 558–9; another important story of his instructing others in moral and physical purity appears in Ṣafī al-Dīn ibn Abī Manṣūr Ibn Ẓāfir, *La Risāla: biographies des maîtres spirituels connus par un cheikh égyptien du VII/XIIIe siècle*, ed. and trans. Denis Gril (Cairo, 1986), 118–19.

[15] In one account he demonstrated his knowledge of the Qurʾān (Ibn al-Mustawfī, *Tārīkh Irbil*, I, 372); Ibn al-ʿAdīm spoke of him as a revered Sufi figure and visited his grave sometime after 617/1220 (Morray, *An Ayyubid Notable*, 37).

[16] Ibn Ẓāfir, *La Risāla*, 118–19; Arabic text, 30; also Dols, *Majnūn*, 407.

women, who mingled freely at their sessions. Many of them neglected ritual duties altogether: they failed to keep up the daily prayers, ate during the day in Ramaḍān, and ignored the required purification of the body and garments. ʿAlī al-Kurdī (d. 622/1225) was known for walking barefoot in excrement and entering mosques without washing, and another *muwallah* named Ḥasan al-Kurdī followed his example a century later. Ibrāhīm al-Shāghūrī, whose funeral in 680/1281 drew masses of people, was "not fearful about *najāsa*," carelessly picking up defiling substances as he let the hems of his garments drag through the filth in alleyways.[17] While each *muwallah* exhibited some unique feature of shocking or nonconformist behavior, as a group they nevertheless lend themselves well to analyses that emphasize this behavior as a common pattern in medieval Islam. Indeed, al-Dhahabī and other medieval authors discussed them as a familiar social type, and in Damascus they had their own cemetery, separate from that of the Sufis. Abū Shāma did not call them by name but identified a common series of practices when he castigated people for "having belief in evil shaykhs who eat during the day in Ramaḍān with no excuse, neglect prayer, and dwell in filth (*al-najāsāt*).[18]

A number of modern scholars have sought to explain the existence of these *muwallahūn*, and to resolve the apparent contradiction between their antinomian behavior and their status as figures revered by the uneducated masses, the political elite, and a good many pious scholars as well.[19] Michael Chamberlain, one of the few authors who has moved beyond merely providing descriptions of these characters, sees their behavior as being aimed at the religious elite (the *ʿulamāʾ* and *aʿyān*), whose dominance, he says, they "lampooned" with impunity. They were famous for "reversing the normal order of things" in deliberately wearing sullied clothing and neglecting other ritual duties. And yet, as Chamberlain points out, there was no attempt to silence or publicly

[17] See Sibṭ Ibn al-Jawzī, *Mirʾāt al-zamān*, 638 on ʿAlī al-Kurdī: "No one had ever seen him pray, and he would go about wearing no sandals, stepping in *najāsāt*, and then come right into the mosque like that." Ḥasan al-Kurdī (d. 724/1324) also went barefoot in the dirty places he frequented (Ibn Kathīr, *Bidāya*, XIV, 120). For the description of Ibrāhīm al-Shāghūrī see Ibn Kathīr, *Bidāya*, XIII, 315.

[18] Abū Shāma, *Kitāb al-Bāʿith*, 100. He was certainly familiar with them, having described ʿAlī al-Kurdī's filthiness in his biographical dictionary (*Tarājim*, 146).

[19] For example, Pouzet, *Damas*, 222–6; Chamberlain, *Knowledge and Social Practice*, 130–3; Geoffroy, *Le soufisme*, ch. 17; Meri, *The Cult of Saints*, 91–100; and Talmon-Heller, *Islamic Piety in Medieval Syria*, chap. 8. Several of the these same Damascene *muwallahūn* appear in Gramlich's *Die Wunder der Freunde Gottes* but with less commentary.

censure them.[20] Explaining this, he argues that despite their transgressions the *muwallahūn* did not actually threaten or seek to weaken the powerful position of the scholars. "By virtue of their pollution" they were ineligible for positions at madrasas, for example, and thus "their clownishness could be tolerated even by very grave men." In fact, he continues, "such reversals, by inverting the normal order, paradoxically often serve to affirm it."[21] In other words, as long as they were on the margins of society, the *muwallahūn* could make almost any statement they wished. Their actions were like those in a shadow play or caricature; the lack of subtlety actually cast social norms associated with the spiritual and geographical center of the city in sharper relief.

Michael Dols has taken a different approach to some of the same characters in medieval Damascus. To begin with, Dols verifies the presence of a long tradition of feigned insanity in Islam, and particularly in Sufism, as an *instructive* rather than a deviant kind of behavior. Under the cloak of madness, transgression became tolerable and, almost through a sleight of hand, important social lessons were imparted to the public. Cultivated madness was "a license to criticize others."[22] Dols also stresses the esteem and awe sometimes bestowed upon the clinically insane as sources of inspiration in the Islamic world over the centuries. Thus we must appreciate the historical tradition of insanity, both natural and cultivated, when approaching the sudden spate of deliberately odd behavior in a place such as thirteenth-century Damascus or fourteenth-century Cairo. The *muwallahūn* spoke to and from within a larger cultural tradition where there was a degree of purposeful uncertainty about the sorts of people who might possess true wisdom.[23]

As for the views of the medieval authors, there was much curiosity but no consensus about these characters. A scholar such as al-Dhahabī reviled the *muwallahūn* for their neglect of prayer, fasting, and purification, but

[20] Chamberlain, *Knowledge and Social Practice*, 132.

[21] Ibid., 133.

[22] Dols, *Majnūn*, 406.

[23] For example, the ninth-century grammarian Mubarrad stopped in a monastery to "listen to the poetry of confined lunatics." As for the wisdom of the *muwallah* and *majdhūb*, their sayings were adapted and popularized by entertainers, teachers, and writers: "Clearly the madman became a literary fiction derived from historical figures" (Dols, *Majnūn*, 390–1). However, despite the compelling analysis of holy fools, Boaz Shoshan has offered an important critique of Dols's overall approach to analyzing medieval insanity in "The State and Madness in Medieval Islam," *International Journal of Middle East Studies* 35, 2 (2003).

al-Yāfiʿī admired them for the same qualities.[24] Others were torn about whether to believe in such figures or not, and indeed some wondered in the course of their writings about how much credence to give them. Muḥammad al-Maghribī, the *majdhūb* Stylite whom Ibn Taghrībirdī visited with such trepidation, had "an attraction to God that was total." But after his death, according to Ibn Taghrībirdī, he was found to have accrued a hoard of gold and silver in the place where he had sat for years.

> This was a strange and marvelous thing. Since there was no doubt about his "attraction" being real, how could he possibly have come by so much wealth? I will tell you something. These mysterious figures always love to accrue money. Probably he too was so inclined, having a nature that is customary among these odd people. But God knows best.[25]

Although the author's interjection creates the distinct impression that the *majdhūb* was a swindler, Ibn Taghrībirdī was certain that the holy man's holiness was real. As Éric Geoffroy has noted, "However resistant the authors may be to this form of mysticism, their inclusions give testimony to the place the ecstatic man has attained in the Islamic city." By way of example, Geoffroy points out that al-Dhahabī's own professor, Ibrāhīm al-Raqqī (d. 703/1304), wrote a fatwa against the Sufi poet Ibn al-ʿArabī but used to visit Sulaymān al-Turkumānī, "humbling himself before this *muwallah* who surrounded himself with dogs and ate during Ramaḍān."[26] It was al-Dhahabī who imparted this information.

Such intimate social contacts between learned jurists and antinomian holy men were so common that the idea of the *muwallahūn*'s marginality in society must be rejected. Furthermore, their role as critics is firmly in keeping with contemporary notions of what pious men ought to do. At

[24] See al-Dhahabī, *ʿIbar*, V, 328, where he says that neglect of prayer, fasting, and purification is common among them, as it is among "monks, rabbis, and epileptics"; Pouzet, *Damas*, 222–3. Compare with al-Yāfiʿī, *Mirʾāt al-jinān*, IV, 253–4.

[25] Ibn Taghrībirdī, *al-Nujūm al-zāhira*, XVI, 178. Dols (*Majnūn*, 406) and Denis Gril (Ibn Ẓāfir, *Le Risāla*, 40) have suggested that at least in the *Risāla* of Ibn Ẓāfir, the difference between a *muwallah* and the more common term *majdhūb* is that the former strives to achieve divine madness, whereas the latter is beset by it. However, the usage often depends upon the author. It is interesting that *majdhūb* was a traditional term for Sufi "fools for God," yet the chroniclers of thirteenth-century Damascus do not indicate that the *muwallahūn* were Sufis. On this issue see also Pouzet, *Damas*, 223. For examples of the *majdhūb* in the Egyptian context see Mayeur-Jaouen, *al-Sayyid Aḥmad al-Badawī*.

[26] Geoffroy, *Le soufisme*, 315.

least in the case of their purity practices, or apparent lack thereof, what the *muwallahūn* appear to have "reversed" were the priorities of the day. Here they did not serve to reinscribe the boundaries of social practice, but rather to vehemently denounce them. Qaḍīb al-Bān's pollution and his private bathing anticipated Ibn al-Jawzī's criticism of *waswās* and also the preoccupation with *najāsāt*. In doing so he invoked legal norms while critiquing pious ones. These eccentrics did, in other words, pose a threat to dominant piety. Religious transgression has a different meaning from ordinary law-breaking because it is a performance, but this does not mean that it fails to threaten.

In many ways, the concepts of reversal and transgression fail us when it comes to explaining the pious messages the *muwallahūn* imparted. To begin with, such concepts force us to compare these figures to a certain kind of Muslim, one who needs to be precisely defined in order for the comparison to work. The pious scholar or jurist at first seems to be the obvious target of these reversals. But the existence of figures such as Ibn al-Khashshāb, with his soiled garments, or even ʿAbd Allāh Ibn Taymiyya, who hid from people and frequented abandoned mosques, suggests that there was not only one horizontal line along which behavior could be charted.[27] The scholars themselves resorted to abnormal or extreme behavior in order to question the typical behavior of their colleagues and the rest of society.[28] There were many kinds of law-abiding Muslims, and in the end it can only be the ostentatious or overly scrupulous performer of ritual acts who represents the polar opposite of the *muwallah* – at least in cases where purity was involved.

According to Ibn Taymiyya, a failure to pray, to fast during Ramaḍān (without excuse), or to pay the alms-tax is punishable by death if there is no show of repentance.[29] Few other jurists treated the issue of enforcing compliance in matters of personal religious duties so plainly, or indeed so harshly, and, since most of the *muwallahūn* were not prosecuted for their misdeeds, one must assume that conformity in these matters was generally

[27] Daphna Ephrat offers some wonderful examples of surprising combinations in pious behavior, such as a Sufi who exhibited extreme caution in matters of food purity but also ate snakes and dung beetles: Daphna Ephrat, *Spiritual Wayfarers, Leaders in Piety: Sufis and the Dissemination of Islam in Medieval Palestine* (Cambridge, Mass., and London, 2008), 147.

[28] Chamberlain, *Knowledge and Social Practice*, 124.

[29] Ibn Taymiyya, *al-Siyāsa al-sharʿiyya fī iṣlāḥ al-rāʿī waʾl-raʿīyya*, ed. ʿAlī Sāmī al-Nashār and Aḥmad Zakī ʿAṭīya (Cairo, 1951), 79–80. This has been translated as *Ibn Taimiyya on Public and Private Law in Islam: Or Public Policy in Islamic Jurisprudence*, trans. Omar A. Farrukh (Beirut, 1966).

considered a private affair. Punishment was left up to God.[30] But it is worth noting that there may be a difference between neglecting cleanliness and other forms of pious transgression – particularly the refusal to participate in fasting, which, for some reason, is more often mentioned in the sources than failing to perform obligatory prayers. There are no historical examples of a person being killed for wearing soiled garments, not surprisingly. This was a sin more worthy of rebuke than punishment partly because, according to many jurists, purification was a duty but not a sacred form of obligatory worship.

Neglecting cleanliness was a practice that permitted the *muwallahūn* to convey messages of social criticism. This was possible because debate about the meaning of *ṭahāra* and the correct performance of its rituals permitted a high degree of individual behavior among pious men and women in general, whose personal expressions of purity were equally capable of conveying broader comments about society. But the obligatory fast of Ramaḍān was a different matter altogether. There were no legal conflicts about how much of it to do, nor did the correct way to perform the fast become an area of personal expression to any significant degree. It did not lend itself well to being used as a form of social critique, and we must look elsewhere for explanations of what it meant not to observe the fast.

The problem is that the pious madmen or eccentrics are mostly silent figures. When Ibn Ḥajar affirmed that a *majdhūb* in Egypt who ate during Ramaḍān was famous for his spiritual insight and his *baraka*, he failed to provide any details about how the man justified his actions.[31] Other examples are similarly brief: ʿAbd Allāh ibn Aybak, a freed slave who died in Cairo in 729/1329, was a well-known *muwallah* who "never spoke to anyone, did not cover his nakedness [sufficiently] and ate during Ramaḍān."[32] Was this shocking behavior itself sufficient cause for veneration? If so, Chamberlain's notion of reversal may indeed apply here. These men may have been, after all, true mystics for whom the outward forms of worship had become meaningless; al-Ḥallāj had set a precedent

30 Communal prayer was in fact a collective duty, but one that was very seldom enforced in Islamic history. On the general view that Muslims should not meddle in other people's affairs see Cook, *Commanding Right and Forbidding Wrong*, 499–500.

31 Ibn Ḥajar, *Inbāʾ*, I, 189–90. This was Masʿūd ibn ʿAbd Allāh al-Mursī al-Aswad (d. 777/1375–6), a man besotted with God (*majdhūb*) "in whom the people had great belief": ibid.

32 Zayn al-Dīn ʿUmar ibn Muẓaffar Ibn al-Wardī, *Tārīkh Ibn al-Wardī*, 2 vols. (Beirut, 1417/1996), II, 282. The text says he did not cover his *ʿawra*, which for men is the area between the waist and the knee.

for this in the late ninth century. Perhaps too they purposely invited society's blame (but seldom received it) in order to reassure themselves of the sincerity of their private acts of devotion to God. The *malāmatī* – a pious person who incurs blame – was a social type identified by Sufi authors in earlier centuries; even then historical examples are quite rare, and the term had dropped out of usage by the medieval period. During the thirteenth and fourteenth centuries, the term was not even used by Sufi historians such as al-Yāfiʿī.[33] When he repeated al-Dhahabī's comments about Sulaymān al-Turkumānī neglecting his ritual duties, he hurried to reassure his readers that similar men such as Qaḍīb al-Bān did in fact pray, just not at times when they could be observed, and when they ate during Ramaḍān, the food never reached their stomachs.[34] Their transgression was in fact a kind of miraculous performance, and therefore not a transgression at all.

Perhaps no one correct answer can explain the regular appearance of the *muwallahūn* during the thirteenth and fourteenth centuries. Considering that they were a familiar part of the human geography of piety in medieval Damascus and Cairo, there must be a logic that links their actions to those of other exemplars. One way of tracing this link is through the sources that describe them. Stories of the pious nearly always have a point or a moral that is meant to be unequivocally clear. (Though whether the moral of each story was constructed by the author or by the holy person as a real actor remains an elusive issue.) Since most accounts of the *muwallahūn* are positive ones, they clearly share a literary context with more "normal" exemplars. In addition, if the moral of a pious biography is usually plain, the plot that leads the reader to it is rarely so simple. An example of this is al-Nawawī's response when asked why he avoided eating fruit. A number of obvious explanations could be expected: fruit was too expensive; it was the food of the rich; he ate only barley bread; he denied himself pleasure in matters of taste. The reason he gave was startlingly different from any that had been heard before, and considerably more complex in terms of its ethics.[35] In Qaḍīb al-Bān's case, his neglect of cleanliness sent a message that was purposely misleading.

[33] Gril, "Saint des villes et saint des champs," 70. Michael Winter places the emergence of a "neo-Malāmatī" movement later in the Mamluk period, citing characters from al-Shaʿranī's biographical writings in the fifteenth century: Winter, *Society and Religion*, 95. See also Sabra, "Illiterate Sufis and Learned Artisans," 156.

[34] al-Yāfiʿī, *Mirʾāt al-jinān*, IV, 253–4. This fits well with al-Mārdīnī's account of the holy man washing his clothes at a secluded spot by the river.

[35] For a discussion of al-Nawawī's refusal see Chapter 3.

Discovering its real meaning was a process that forced observers to learn a lesson about true purity and false piety. Yet the case of eating during the day in Ramaḍān remains frustratingly unreadable from a modern perspective. Is it possible that eating during the day in Ramaḍān had a similar moral that is no longer clear?

Let us suppose for a moment that the *muwallahūn* did have some text in mind, such as a hadith or a clause from Islamic legal discourse. Just as the perpetual fasters had made use of certain hadiths that dispensed with objections raised elsewhere, the *muwallahūn* might have found a principle that grounded their actions as legitimate ones. With a legal justification for not fasting, the *muwallahūn*'s neglect would merely have the outward appearance of being a transgression. Though no such hadith suggests itself in this case, being insane or afflicted with illness are two sound excuses for not fasting. If the *muwallahūn* were "serious" about being possessed by a God-granted insanity, not fasting would highlight how real their *walāh* was. Being absolved of ritual duties made their eccentric madness an official diagnosis. Critics such as Abū Shāma who said they broke the fast "with no excuse" may have been responding to the *muwallahūn*, who used this exception in Islamic law far too freely.

The idea of borrowing or adopting an abnormal state of being for the sake of piety was not unknown. It was common among some of the fasters discussed in Chapter 2, who were enthusiastic about the full and unreserved use of the body in devotional piety. Furthermore, afflictions both pious and physical were the distinguishing mark of many other medieval devotees who gained renown. Cultivating madness achieved the same result: it was the chief source of the *muwallah*'s fame, after all. In fact, given the reverence medieval scholars and ordinary Muslims displayed towards the *muwallahūn*, pious madness was apparently recognized as being one of the most difficult lifestyles, regardless of whether it was a personal choice or a divine blessing.

As a final comment upon the *muwallahūn*, it should be stressed that all the evidence points to their success as exemplars. Though not to the same extent as the jurists, the *muwallahūn* were despite all appearances deeply involved in legal issues. While this shows through most clearly in the case of purity, it is hard to see the neglect of ritual duties as being about anything other than normative notions of what Islamic law dictated: acts of worship were prescribed for ordinary people, and the *muwallahūn* were anything but ordinary. The notion of transgression often functions on the binary distinction between what a typical observer would see as either good or lawful practices and unacceptable or illegal ones. In medieval

Islam the messages were always more complex: beneath the apparent conflict between right and wrong lay the *muwallah*'s source of holiness.

There is another similarity between these figures and other pious exemplars, which suggests that their acts of neglect were a kind of devotional piety more often than a mystical outlook. In any case, evidence of the latter is hard to detect or substantiate in historical sources. For many in the medieval period, legal descriptions of ritual practice explained the very minimum requirements of what a godly person could, or even should, do. This approach to worship accounts for much of the variety in devotional piety, and explains the value placed on individual initiative – and even innovation. For example, commenting upon a hadith in which the Prophet condoned Bilāl's habit of performing two cycles of prayer after every ablution, Abū Shāma asserts that this is an example of a positive innovation in religious practice. While the Prophet did not specially make that part of the *sharīʿa* "by word or by deed," it was permitted because "the door of supererogatory performance (*taṭawwuʿ*) is open except at times that are [expressly] disliked."[36] Being in a state of eccentric delusion or religious insanity is not properly a kind of supererogatory worship, but it was one of the ultimate signs of devotion in medieval culture. This may explain why the *muwallahūn* were routinely left alone, even by those who could not believe in them. The *muwallahūn* granted themselves the right to act in various ways, and when critics reacted to this, it becomes clear that the conflict arose over who had the authority to decide how to proceed with self-defined forms of worship.

Part II: Excessive Piety and the *Sunna*

If we consider the evolution of the theme of transgressive behavior in light of parallel developments in devotional piety, several points of confluence emerge. Medieval authors and other observers conferred accolades upon the exemplars of devotional piety who distinguished themselves in unusual ways. The devotees did not have *complete* freedom to innovate, if only because behavior was regulated by the existence of a core set of practices in which virtually all pious men and women took part, such as voluntary fasting or extra attention to purification. They agreed upon a series of other voluntary practices relating to personal habits in matters of dress, speech, and food, among other things. That is, statements made beyond these areas were surprisingly uncommon, perhaps because

[36] Abū Shāma, *Kitāb al-Bāʿith*, 96.

excellence could only be measured by comparing one person's achievements with those of others. As for asceticism, in the late twelfth century Ibn al-Mannī's overwhelmingly consistent ascetic traits were for the most part indistinguishable from those of much earlier exemplars. By the late fourteenth century excellence in piety seems to have been judged on the basis of one's ability to make much more precise statements of asceticism – as though it were no longer enough to be generically, if extremely, ascetic.

As the various themes in bodily piety, renunciatory asceticism, and ethical ascetic immingled, one begins to find increasing numbers of hybrid characters. For example, Ḥammād al-Ḥalabī, who was born in Aleppo, arrived in Damascus as an adult, where he promptly sequestered himself in a mosque and devoted himself to

> reading the Qurʾān skillfully while facing the *qibla*, in a constant state of ritual purity. He would never accept anything from anyone, for he was perpetually fasting and reciting the Qurʾān. He refused to be called by a name. When he was obliged to say something about his affairs, he would refer to himself [in the third person] and would say: "The faqīr said ..." or "It so happened that the faqīr...." Beneath his overshirt he wore a garment of haircloth. He lived only on things presented to him by companions whose lawful means of gain he could confirm. Ibn Taymiyya had a very high regard for him and acknowledged his righteousness. And that should be enough to convince anyone! His state of exemplary perfection did not cease until he was taken unto God in the month of Shaʿbān 726 [1326 C.E.].[37]

Some early Muslim ascetics had also worn hair shirts; a number of them appear in Ibn al-Jawzī's *Ṣifat al-ṣafwa*, for example, wandering in the hills with no means of income. But the contemporary hair shirt was a dramatic symbol of bodily punishment and degradation: the Mamluk sultan al-Ashraf Shaʿbān was sewn into one before being thrown into a well and left to rot.[38] Wearing this garment voluntarily could only be a sign of private self-humiliation for Ḥammād al-Ḥalabī, especially given that he hid it under his other clothes. The comment about Ibn Taymiyya acknowledges that the mixture presented by this holy man was a strange one. Al-Ḥalabī combined the old and new; devotional practice and voluntary poverty; bodily pain and humble politeness; he was perfectly upright and yet suspiciously irregular. A stamp of approval by a famous and ever-vigilant

[37] Ibn Ḥajar, *Durar*, II, 42.
[38] al-Maqrīzī, *Sulūk*, V, 13.

jurist helped to place this man, who straddled far too many specialities to make sense of, into the general category of "the virtuous."

As al-Ḥalabī's example shows, there were few constraints placed upon the possible uses of the body in medieval Islam. The two main objections raised against excess in devotional piety or bodily asceticism were that overexerting oneself in supererogatory activities could make a person miss the obligatory duties of worship, and the fact that Prophet had not condoned extreme forms of devotion. Yet neither of these caveats had any discernible affect on contemporary practice. Throughout this period piety was not defined in terms of the *sunna* alone, but rather in terms of the broader Islamic legal tradition as it existed in the medieval period. The most typical patterns of behavior in devotional piety arose out of each individual's personalized relationship with Islamic ritual law. And while each ritual was rooted in the precise actions of Muḥammad's own performances, legal debates preserved some sharply different visions about whether to adhere to the minimum requirements of worship or whether to use them merely as a first step. More broadly, since medieval piety was essentially and crucially conceived as a way of being in the world, it was equally defined in terms of moral responsibilities. Certainly wariness and moral uprightness were entirely in keeping with the Prophet's character and his concerns about forming a just society. But the dearth of historical references to direct emulation of the Prophet deserves further comment.[39]

Little has been said in this study about adherence to the *sunna* of the Prophet as a celebrated pattern of pious behavior. Some men and women in the Ayyubid and early Mamluk periods were indeed praised for taking the *sunna* as their watchword, but overall they are surprisingly few in number. Many more, such as Ibn al-Sakrān, were described as "following in the footsteps of the pious forebears," the *salaf*. Already this underscores how a panoply of possible models was available to the medieval exemplars in the hadith literature alone. There they found figures such as Zaynab, who tried to keep herself awake during supererogatory prayer in the mosque by holding onto a rope; ʿAbd Allāh ibn ʿAmr, who begged the Prophet to let him keep fasting; and ʿAbd Allāh ibn ʿUmar, who washed the insides of his eyes.[40] Even though the Prophet did none

39 An interesting example is Ibn al-Jawzī's *Ṣifat al-ṣafwa*, which translates as the "Mark of the Model," that is, the Prophet Muḥammad. Few of the men and women whose lives he recounted were described as following the *sunna*, and many if not most of their practices were considerably more excessive than those of the Prophet.

40 On Zaynab see al-Bukhārī, *Ṣaḥīḥ*, 210, no. 1150.

of these things, and in the first two cases explicitly dictated that such practices cease, these actions became in later centuries part of the wider template of behavior available for emulation.

Though the *sunna* was not often used as a comprehensive set of prescriptions, which, when adhered to exactly, could provide the ultimate protection against the fires of hell, the Prophet's example did affect medieval piety in the profoundest of ways. After all, nearly every pious person studied the hadith, and from its stories drew inspiration. Of the many personal details about the life of the Prophet, it was above all the ascetic model of Muḥammad that pervaded medieval Islamic piety. To take one example from the hadith, ʿUmar wept when he saw the marks left on the Prophet's body by the mat on which he slept.[41] In the late twelfth century Abū ʿUmar Ibn Qudāma emulated this poignant image of suffering and poverty in choosing the same sort of bedding, as did the youthful al-Nawawī a half century later.[42]

In the intervening centuries other deeply ascetic characters only reinforced the importance of this model by embellishing it with their own gestures of sacrifice and renunciation. By the beginning of our period it was not only their practices of worship but their diets, their clothing, and general demeanor that provided endless sources of ascetic inspiration. One scholar, echoing an often-repeated observation about the role of asceticism in Islam, recently remarked that despite the "essentially renunciatory core of the *sunnah*," it was equally possible to "groom" the image of the Prophet into that of a world-embracer. This, he suggests, has caused a fundamental tension in Islam.[43] But – at least in the Arabic-speaking medieval world – there was in fact hardly any tension at all between these two poles of guidance, so dominant was the impact of an unflinching form of asceticism upon piety in general, including that of the devotees, the Sufis, several sultans, the holy fools, devout women, and virtually all of the jurists of medieval Islam.

[41] Ibid., 900, no. 4913. When ʿUmar tried to point out that the Byzantine and Sasanian emperors, Muḥammad's two regional rivals, were living in a style befittting kings whereas the Prophet was destitute, Muḥammad replied that though the emperors took their pleasure in this world, he and ʿUmar would find theirs in the next. The soteriological importance of lying on a mat could not have eluded those later exemplars who copied this act.

[42] On Abū ʿUmar Ibn Qudāma see Abū Shāma, *Tarājim*, 71. Al-Nawawī went even farther: for two years he refused to put anything between his body and the floor on which he slept, according to al-Kutubī, *Fawāt al-wafayāt*, IV, 265.

[43] Karamustafa, *God's Unruly Friends*, 25–6.

Glossary

ʿābid (f. *ʿābida*; pl. *ʿubbād*): devotee, worshipper, a person who practices bodily worship

amir: military commander

baraka: a kind of blessing that comes from a person or object having God-given sanctity

bidʿa: an innovation in religious practice; a practice that is a deviation from correct practice

dār al-ḥadīth: a building devoted to the study, teaching, and oral transmission of the hadith

faqīh (pl. *fuqahāʾ*): a jurist, a legal scholar, an interpreter of Islamic law

faqīr (pl. *fuqarāʾ*): a poor person; someone who has taken a vow of voluntary poverty; a follower of a Sufi group

fiqh: Islamic law, jurisprudence; man-made law – as opposed to ***sharīʿa***

furūʿ al-fiqh: a text on manuals: genre of literature that deals with substantive law

ghusl: the major ablution in which all parts of the body are covered by water .

hadith, the: the collected reports about the Prophet's words and deeds and also (but less often) those of his Companions and family

hadith, a: one of these reports, a single report

ḥalāl: permissible, licit

Ḥanafī: One of four legal schools in Sunnī Islam that grew out of the study circle that formed around the early jurist Abū Ḥanīfa (d. 767 C.E.); also, a member of this school.

Ḥanbalī: one of four legal schools in Sunnī Islam, which grew out of the study circle that formed around the early jurist Aḥmad ibn Ḥanbal (d. 855 C.E.); also, a member of this school.

ḥarām: prohibited

ʿibāda (pl. *ʿibādāt*): an act of required worship

Iblīs: the devil

imam: a prayer leader at a mosque

iqṭāʿ: the right granted to someone to collect revenue from a designated property or piece of land, usually received in return for military service or service to the state

kaffāra: an act of expiation

khānqāh: a meeting house for religious study and devotional practice and a residence for the pious, often Sufis

madhhab (pl. *madhāhib*): the four legal schools of Sunnī Islam that have survived: they grew out of the study circles of jurists in the eighth and early ninth centuries C.E. whose methods and doctrines give each school a distinctive flavor, though on most points of law they agree

majdhūb: a man besotted with God; a holy fool

makrūh: disapproved of

Mālikī: one of four legal schools in Sunnī Islam, which grew out of the study circle that formed around the early jurist Anas ibn Malik (d. 795 C.E.); also, a member of this school

masnūn: strongly recommended, so much so that it is nearly ***sunna***

mufti: a jurisprudent, a jurist qualified to give opinions on points of law

mustaḥabb: not obligatory but considered beneficial

muwallah: similar to a ***majdhūb***; a person whose extreme behavior marks them as pious

nāfila: a supererogatory pious act

najāsa: an impure substance, filth

qadi: a judge

ribāṭ: a small lodge

salaf: the pious forebears from the first few generations of the Islamic era

ṣalāt: ritual prayer, required of Muslims

ṣawm al-dahr: the perpetual fast, fasting every day from dawn to sunset

schools of law: see ***madhhab***

Shāfiʿī: one of four legal schools in Sunnī Islam, which grew out of the study circle that formed around the early jurist al-Shāfiʿī (d. 820 C.E.); also, a member of this school

sharīʿa: God's ideal law; not the same as the actual rules of law agreed upon ("discovered" by human experts, i.e., the jurists.)
shaykh: a man respected for his learning or piety; an elder; a Sufi master
Sufi: a mystic; a member of a Sufi brotherhood
sunna: the exemplary practice of the Prophet Muḥammad and/or the *salaf*; one of the bases for Islamic law
taʿabbud: bodily devotion, supererogatory worship
ṭayyib: permitted, good, delicious
ʿulamaʾ: scholars (sing.: m. *ʿālim*, f. *ʿālima*); collective term for the scholarly elite
waqf: a pious endowment, most often in the form of a religious building such as a mosque
wājib: obligatory, as in obligatory ritual duties such as daily prayer or the fast of Ramaḍān
waraʿ: scrupulosity; ethical cautiousness
zāhid: an ascetic
zāwiya: a small building or cell, often attached to a mosque
zuhd: asceticism, especially renunciatory asceticism

Bibliography

Primary Sources

Abū Shāma, Shihāb al-Dīn ʿAbd al-Raḥmān ibn Ismāʿīl. *Kitāb al-Bāʿith ʿala inkār al-bidaʿ waʾl-ḥawādith*. Edited by Mashhūr Ḥasan Salmān. Riyadh: Dār al-Rāya līʾl-Nashr waʾl-Tawzīʿ, 1410/1990.

Tarājim rijāl al-qarnayn al-sādis waʾl-sābiʿ, al-maʿrūf biʾl-dhayl ʿalāʾl-rawḍatayn. Edited by Muḥammad Zāhid ibn al-Ḥasan al-Kawtharī and ʿIzzat al-ʿAṭṭār al-Ḥusaynī. Cairo: Dār al-Kutub al-Mālikiyya, 1366/1947.

al-ʿAynī, Badr al-Dīn Maḥmūd ibn Aḥmad. *Bināya sharḥ al-Hidāya*. Edited by Ayman Ṣāliḥ Shaʿbān. 13 vols. Beirut: Dār al-Kutub al-ʿIlmiyya, 2000.

Baybars al-Manṣūrī al-Dawādār, *Zubdat al-fikra fī taʾrīkh al-hijra*. Edited by D. S. Richards. Berlin and Beirut: Dār al-Nashr al-Kitāb al-ʿArabī, 1998.

al-Bukhārī, Muḥammad ibn Ismāʿīl. *Ṣaḥīḥ al-Bukhārī*. Beirut: Dār Iḥyāʾ al-Turāth al-ʿArabī, 1422/2001.

Combe, E., J. Sauvaget, and G. Wiet et al., eds. *Répertoire chronologique d'épigraphie arabe*. 18 vols. Cairo: Institut Français d'Archéologie Orientale, 1931–91.

al-Dhahabī, Shams al-Dīn Muḥammad ibn Aḥmad. *al-ʿIbar fī khabar man ghabar*. Edited by Ṣalāḥ al-Dīn Munajjid and Fuʾād Sayyid. 5 vols. Kuwait: Dār al-Maṭbuʿāt waʾl-Nashr, 1960.

Kitāb tadhkirat al-ḥuffāẓ. Edited by Zakarīyā ʿUmayrāt. 5 vols. in 3. Beirut: Dār al-Kutub al-ʿIlmiyya, 1998.

Muʿjam muḥaddithī al-Dhahabī. Edited by Rawḥiyya ʿAbd al-Raḥmān al-Suyūfī. Beirut: Dār al-Kutub al-ʿIlmiyya, 1993.

al-Muʿjam al-mukhtaṣṣ biʾl-muḥaddithīn. Edited by Muḥammad al-Ḥabīb al-Hīla. Ṭāʾif: Maktabat al-Ṣiddīq, 1988.

Muʿjam shuyūkh al-Dhahabī. Edited by Rawḥiyya ʿAbd al-Raḥmān al-Suyūfī. Beirut: Dār al-Kutub al-ʿIlmiyya, 1410/1990.

Tārīkh al-Islām wa-wafayāt al-mashāhīr waʾl-aʿlām. Edited by ʿUmar ʿAbd al-Salām Tadmurī. 53 vols. Beirut: Dār al-Kitāb al-ʿArabī, 1987–2000.

al-Fāsī, Taqī al-Dīn Muḥammad ibn Aḥmad. *al-ʿIqd al-thamīn fī tārīkh al-balad al-amīn*. Edited by Muḥammad ʿAbd al-Qādir Aḥmad ʿAṭā. 7 vols. Beirut: Dār al-Kutub al-ʿIlmiyya, 1998.

al-Fayyūmī, Aḥmad ibn Muḥammad. *Miṣbāḥ al-munīr fī gharīb al-Sharḥ al-kabīr li'l-Rāfiʿī*. 2 vols. in 1. Beirut: Dār al-Kutub al-ʿIlmiyya, 1978.

al-Ghazzālī, Abū Ḥāmid Muḥammad ibn Muḥammad. *Iḥyāʾ ʿulūm al-dīn*. 4 vols. Beirut: Dār al- Iḥyāʾ al-Turāth al-ʿArabī, n.d. [1888].

Marriage and Sexuality in Islam: A Translation of al-Ghazali's Book on the Etiquette of Marriage from the Ihya. Translated by Madelain Farah. Salt Lake City: University of Utah Press, 1984.

al-Wajīz fī fiqh al-Imām al-Shāfiʿī. Edited by ʿAli Muʿawwaḍ and ʿĀdil ʿAbd al-Mawjūd. 2 vols. Beirut: Dār al-Arqam, 1997.

Ḥāfiẓ. *Dīvān ghazalīyāt-i mawlānā Shams al-Dīn Muḥammad Ḥāfiẓ Shīrāzī*. Edited by Khalīl Khaṭīb Rahbar. Tehran: Intishārāt afā ʿAlishah, 1364/1985.

al-Ḥiṣnī, Taqī al-Dīn Abū Bakr ibn Muḥammad. Kitāb al-muʾmināt wa'l-ṣāliḥāt wa'l-ayqāẓ min al-mahlūkāt. Dār al-Kutub al-Miṣriyya MS Taṣawwuf no. 4241. Published as *al-Muʾmināt wa-siyar al-sālikāt*. Edited by Aḥmad Farīd Mizyadī. Beirut: Dār al-Kutub al-ʿIlmiyya, 2010.

Ibn al-ʿAdīm, Kamāl al-Dīn ʿUmar ibn Aḥmad. *Bughyat al-ṭalab fī tārīkh Ḥalab*. Edited by Suhayl Zakkār. 10 vols. Damascus: n.p., 1988–9.

Ibn al-ʿArabī, Muḥyī al-Dīn. *al-Futūḥāt al-Makkiyya*. 4 vols. Beirut: Dār al-Ṣādir, 1988 [1876].

Sufis of Andalusia: The Rūḥ al-Quds and al-Durrat al-Fākhira of Ibn ʿArabī. Translated by R. W. J. Austin. Berkeley: University of California Press, 1971.

Ibn al-Athīr, Majd al-Dīn al-Mubārak ibn Muḥammad. *al-Nihāya fī gharīb al-ḥadīth wa'l-athar*. Edited by Maḥmūd Muḥammad Ṭanāḥī and Ṭāhir Aḥmad al-Zāwī. 5 vols. Qum: Muʾassasat al-Ismāʿīliyān li'l-Ṭibāʿa wa'l-Nashr wa'l-Tawzīʿ, 1364/1985.

Ibn al-ʿAṭṭār, Aḥmad ibn ʿAbd al-Raḥīm. *Dhayl ʿala'l-ʿIbar fī khabar man ʿabar*. Edited by Ṣāliḥ Mahdī ʿAbbās. 2 vols. Beirut: Muʾassasat al-Risāla, 1989.

Ibn al-ʿAṭṭār, ʿAlī ibn Ibrāhīm. *Tuḥfat al-ṭālibīn fī tarjamat al-Imām Muḥyī al-Dīn*. Edited by Abū ʿUbayda Mashhūr ibn Ḥasan al-Salmān. Riyadh: Dār al-Ṣumayʿī, 1414/1994.

Ibn Baṭṭūṭa, Shams al-Dīn Muḥammad. *Riḥlat Ibn Baṭṭūṭa*, 2 vols. in 1. Beirut: Dār al-Sharq al-ʿArabī, n.d. Translated by H. A. R. Gibb from the Arabic text and edited by C. Defrémery and B. R. Sanguinetti as *The Travels of Ibn Baṭṭūṭa A.D. 1325–1354*. 5 vols. Works Issued by the Hakluyt Society, Second Series 110 (vol. I); 117 (vol. II); 141 (vol. III); 178 (vol. IV); 190 (vol. V). Cambridge: Cambridge University Press for the Hakluyt Society, 1958–71.

Ibn Baydakīn al-Turkumānī, Idrīs. *Kitāb al-lumaʿ fī'l-ḥawādith wa'l-bidaʿ*. Edited by Subhi Labib. 2 vols. Cairo: Qiṣm al-Dirāsāt al-Islamiyya, al-Maʿhad al-Almānī li'l-Āthār bi'l-Qāhira/Wiesbaden: Franz Steiner Verlag, 1986.

[Ibn al-Bayṭār, ʿAbd Allāh ibn Aḥmad.] *Traité des simples par Ibn el-Beïthar*. Translated by Lucien Leclerc. 3 vols. Paris: Institut du Monde Arabe, n.d. [1877–83].

Ibn Daqīq al-ʿĪd, Taqī al-Dīn Muḥammad ibn ʿAlī. *Iḥkām al-aḥkām: sharḥ ʿUmdat al-aḥkām*. Edited by Ṭāhā Saʿd and Muṣṭafā al-Hawārī. 2 vols. Cairo: Maktabat ʿĀlam al-Fikr, 1976.

Ibn al-Dawādārī, Abū Bakr ibn ʿAbd Allāh. *Kanz al-Durar wa jāmiʿ al-ghurar*. Edited by Hans Robert Roemer et al. 9 vols. Cairo: Deutsches Archäologisches Institut, 1960–72.

Ibn Farḥūn, ʿAbd Allāh ibn Muḥammad. *Tārīkh al-Madīna al-munawwara (al-musammā Naṣīyat al-mushāwir wa-taʿziyat al-mujāwir)*. Edited by Ḥusayn Muḥammad ʿAlī Shukrī. Beirut: Dār al-Arqam, 2001.

Ibn Farḥūn, Ibrāhīm ibn ʿAlī. *al-Dībāj al-mudhahhab fī maʿrifat aʿyān ʿulamāʾ al-madhhab*. Edited by Muḥammad al-Aḥmadī Abū al-Nūr. 2 vols. Cairo: Dār al-Turāth, 1975.

Ibn al-Fuwaṭī, ʿAbd al-Razzāq ibn Aḥmad (attributed). *Kitāb al-ḥawādith: wa-huwa al-kitāb al-musammā bi'l-Ḥawādith al-jāmiʿa wa'l tajārib al-nāfiʿa wa'l-mansūb li-Ibn al-Fuwaṭī*. Edited by Bashār ʿAwwād Maʿrūf and ʿImād ʿAbd al-Salām Raʾūf. Beirut: Dār al-Gharb al-Islāmī, 1997.

Ibn Ḥajar al-ʿAsqalānī, Shihāb al-Dīn Aḥmad. *al-Durar al-kāmina fī aʿyān al-mīʾa al-thāmina*. Edited by ʿAbd al-Wārith Muḥammad ʿAlī. 4 vols. in 2. Beirut: Dār al-Kutub al-ʿIlmiyya, 1418/1997.

Inbāʾ al-ghumr bi-abnāʾ al-ʿumr. Edited by Muḥammad ʿAbd al-Muʿīd Khān. 7 vols. in 4. Beirut: Dār al-Kutub al-ʿIlmiyya, 1406/1987.

Ibn al-Ḥājj al-ʿAbdarī, Muḥammad. *al-Madkhal*. Edited by Tawfīq Ḥamdān. 4 vols in 2. Beirut: Dār al-Kutub al-ʿIlmiyya, 1415/1995.

Ibn al-ʿImād al-ʿAkarī, ʿAbd al-Ḥayy ibn Aḥmad. *Shadharāt al-dhahab fī akhbār man dhahab*. Edited by ʿAbd al-Qādir Arnāʾūṭ and Maḥmūd Arnāʾūṭ. 8 vols. in 4. Damascus and Beirut: Dār Ibn Kathīr, 1992.

Ibn al-ʿImād al-Aqfahsī, Aḥmad. *Dafʿ al-ilbās ʿan wahm al-waswās (wa yalīhi Ikrām man yaʿīshu bi-taḥrīm al-khamr wa'l-ḥashīsh)*. Edited by Muḥammad Fāris and Masʿūd ʿAbd al-Ḥamīd al-Saʿdanī. Beirut: Dār al-Kutub al-ʿIlmiyya, 1995.

Ibn al-ʿIrāqī, Walī al-Dīn Aḥmad ibn ʿAbd al-Raḥīm. *Dhayl ʿalā'l-ʿIbar fī khabar man ʿabar*. Edited by Ṣāliḥ Mahdī ʿAbbās. 3 vols. Beirut: Muʾassasat al-Risāla, 1409/1989.

Ibn al-Jawzī, Abū'l Faraj ʿAbd al-Raḥmān. *Ṣayd al-khāṭir*. Edited by Muḥammad al-Ghazzālī. Cairo: Dār al-Kutub al-Ḥadītha/Baghdad: Maktabat al-Muthannā, n.d.

Ṣifat al-ṣafwa. Edited by Maḥmūd Fākhūrī. 4 vols. Aleppo: Dār al-Waʿī, 1969–73.

Talbīs Iblīs. Beirut: Dār al-Qalam, n.d. [1966]. Partial translation by D. S. Margoliouth as "The Devil's Delusion of Ibn al-Jauzi," parts 1–3. *Islamic Culture* 10, 1 (January 1936): 20–39; 10, 2 (April 1936): 169–92; 10, 3 (July 1936): 339–68.

Ibn Kathīr, Ismāʿīl ibn ʿUmar. *al-Bidāya wa'l-nihāya*. Edited by Aḥmad Abū Mulḥim et al. 14 vols. in 8. Beirut: Dār al-Kutub al-ʿIlmiyya, 1987.

Ibn Khallikān, Aḥmad ibn Muḥammad. *Wafayāt al-aʿyān wa anbāʾ abnāʾ al-zamān*. Edited by Iḥsān ʿAbbās. 8 vols. Beirut: Dār al-Thaqāfa, 1968–72.

Ibn Manẓūr, Muḥammad ibn Mukarram. *Lisān al-ʿArab*. 7 vols. Beirut: Dār al-Ṣādir, 1987.
Ibn al-Miʿmār, Muḥammad ibn Abī'l Makārim. *Kitāb al-futuwwa*. Edited by Muṣṭafā Jawād et al. Baghdad: Maktabat al-Muthannā, 1958.
Ibn al-Mulaqqin, ʿUmar ibn ʿAlī. *Ṭabaqāt al-awliyāʾ*. Edited by Nūr al-Dīn Shurayba. Cairo: Maktabat al-Khānjī, 1393/1973.
Ibn Munqidh, Usāma. *Kitāb al-iʿtibār*. Edited by Philip K. Hitti. Cairo: Maktabat al-Thaqāfa al-Dīniyya, 1980. Translated by Paul M. Cobb as *The Book of Contemplation: Islam and the Crusades*. London: Penguin, 2008; translated by Philip K. Hitti as *An Arab-Syrian Gentleman and Warrior in the Period of the Crusades: Memoirs of Usāmah ibn-Munqidh*, reprint, Princeton: Princeton University Press, 1987 [1929].
Ibn al-Mustawfī, Sharaf al-Dīn Abū'l-Barakāt Aḥmad. *Tārīkh Irbil: al-musammā Nabāhat al-balad al-khāmil bi-man waradahu min al-amāthil*. Edited by Sāmī ibn al-Sayyid Khammās al-Ṣaqqār. 2 vols. Baghdad: Dār al-Rashīd li'l-Nashr, 1980.
Ibn Qāḍī Shuhba, Abū Bakr ibn Aḥmad. *Ṭabaqāt al-Shāfiʿiyya*. Edited by ʿAbd al-ʿAlīm Khān. 4 vols. Hyderabad-Deccan: Maṭbaʿa Majlis Dāʾirat al-Maʿārif al-ʿUthmāniyya, 1978–80.
Tārīkh Ibn Qāḍī Shuhba. Edited by Adnan Darwich. 4 vols. Damascus: Institut Français de Damas, 1994–7.
Ibn Qayyim al-Jawziyya, Shams al-Dīn Muḥammad. *Iʿlām al-muwaqqiʿīn ʿan Rabb al-ʿĀlimīn*. Edited by Muḥammad ʿAbd al-Salām Ibrāhīm. 4 vols. Beirut: Dār al-Kutub al-ʿIlmiyya, 1414/1993.
The Medicine of the Prophet. Translated by Penelope Johnstone. Cambridge: Islamic Texts Society, 1998.
al-Waswasa. Edited by Aḥmad Sālim Bādawīlān. Riyadh: Dār Ṭawīq li'l-Nashr wa'l-Tawzīʿ, 1415/1994–5.
Ibn Qudāma, Muwaffaq al-Dīn ʿAbd Allāh ibn Aḥmad. *Dhamm al-waswās*. Edited by Muḥammad Khālid al-Kharsa. Damascus: Maktabat al-Fārūq, 1990.
Kitāb al-tawwābīn (Le livre de pénitents). Edited by George Makdisi. Damascus: Institut Français de Damas, 1961.
al-Mughnī. Published with *al-Sharḥ al-kabīr ʿalā matn al-muqniʿ* by Shams al-Dīn ʿAbd al-Raḥmān Ibn Qudāma. 14 vols. Beirut: Dār al-Kutub al-ʿIlmiyya, n.d. [1928].
Ibn Rajab, ʿAbd al-Raḥmān ibn Aḥmad. *Kitāb al-dhayl ʿalā Ṭabaqāt al-Ḥanābila*. 2 vols. Beirut: Dār al-Maʿrifa, [1981].
Ibn Rushd. *The Distinguished Jurist's Primer: Bidāyat al-Mujtahid wa Nihāyat al-Muqtaṣid*. Translated by Imran Ahsan Khan Nyazee. 2 vols. Reading: Garnet, 1994–6.
Ibn al-Ṣalāḥ al-Shahrazūrī, ʿUthmān ibn ʿAbd al-Raḥmān. *Fatāwā wa-masāʾil Ibn al-Ṣalāḥ wa'l-tafsīr wa'l-ḥadīth wa'l-uṣūl al-fiqh*. Edited by ʿAbd al-Muʿṭī Āmīn Qalajī. 2 vols. Beirut: Dār al-Maʿrifa, 1986.
Ibn Shaddād, Muḥammad ibn ʿAlī. *al-Aʿlāq al-khaṭīra fī dhikr umarāʾ al-Shām wa'l-Jazīra*. Edited by Sāmī al-Dahhān. Damascus: Institut Français de Damas, 1956.

Ibn Taghrībirdī, Jamāl al-Dīn Yūsuf. *al-Manhal al-ṣāfī wa'l-mustawfī ba'd al-wāfī*. Edited by Muḥammad Muḥammad Amīn. 10 vols. Cairo: al-Hay'a al-Miṣriyya al-'Āmma lī'l-Kitāb, 1984–present.

al-Nujūm al-zāhira fī mulūk Miṣr wa'l-Qāhira. 16 vols. Cairo: al-Mu'assasa al-Miṣriyya al-'Āmma, 1963–72.

Ibn Taymiyya, Taqī al-Dīn Aḥmad. *Majmū' fatāwā Shaykh al-Islām Aḥmad ibn Taymiyya*. Edited by 'Abd al-Raḥmān ibn Muḥammad ibn Qāsim al-'Āsimī. 35 vols. Riyadh: Maṭābi' al-Riyāḍ, 1381–6/1961 or 62–1966 or 67.

al-Siyāsa al-shar'iyya fī iṣlāḥ al-rā'ī wa'l-ra'īyya. Edited by 'Alī Sāmī al-Nashār and Aḥmad Zakī 'Aṭīya. Cairo: Dār al-Kitāb al-'Arabī, 1951. Translated by Omar A. Farrukh as *Ibn Taimiyya on Public and Private Law in Islam: Or Public Policy in Islamic Jurisprudence*. Beirut: Khayats, 1966.

Ibn Waḥshiyya, Abū Bakr Aḥmad. *Kitāb al-filāḥa al-Nabaṭiyya*. Edited by Tawfiq Fahd. 3 vols. Damascus: Institut Français de Damas, 1993–8.

Ibn al-Wardī, Zayn al-Dīn 'Umar. *Tārīkh Ibn al-Wardī*. 2 vols. Beirut: Dār al-Kutub al-'Ilmiyya, 1417/1996.

Ibn Ẓāfir, Ṣafī al-Dīn ibn Abī'l-Manṣūr. *La Risāla: biographies des maîtres spirituels connus par un cheikh égyptien du VII/XIIIe siècle*. Edited and translated by Denis Gril. Cairo: Institut Français d'Archéologie Orientale, 1986.

al-Iṣfahānī, Abū Nu'aym. *Ḥilyat al-awliyā' wa ṭabaqāt al-aṣfiyā'*. 10 vols. Cairo: Maktabat al-Khānjī/Maktabat al-Ṣa'āda, 1932–8.

Jāmī, 'Abd al-Raḥmān ibn Aḥmad. *Nafaḥāt al-uns*. Edited by Mahdi Tawhidi Pur. Tehran: Sa'dī, 1958.

al-Jazarī, Shams al-Dīn Muḥammad ibn Ibrāhīm. *Tārīkh ḥawādith al-zamān wa-anbā'ihi wa-wafayāt al-akābir wa'l-a'yān min abnā'ihi*. Edited by 'Umar 'Abd al-Salām Tadmurī. 3 vols. Sidon: al-Maktaba al-'Aṣriyya, 1998.

al-Jazīrī, 'Abd al-Raḥmān. *al-Fiqh 'alā'l-madhāhib al-arba'a*. 5 vols. Beirut: Dār Iḥyā' al-Turāth al-'Arabī, n.d.

al-Kazarūnī al-Zubayrī al-Shāfi'ī al-Madanī, Abū'l-Abbās Aḥmad ibn Muḥammad. Kitāb kifāyat al-'ābid. Dār al-Kutub wa'l-Wathā'iq al-Qawmiyya, MS Fiqh Shāf'ī Ṭala'at no. 137.

al-Kutubī, Muḥammad ibn Shākir. *Fawāt al-wafayāt wa'l-dhayl 'alayha*. Edited by Iḥsān 'Abbās. 5 vols. Beirut: Dār al-Ṣādir, n.d.

al-Makkī, Abū Ṭālib Muḥammad ibn 'Alī. *Qūt al-qulūb fī mu'āmalat al-maḥbūb wa-waṣf ṭarīq al-murīd ilā maqām al-tawḥīd*. Edited by Sa'īd Nasīb Makārim. 2 vols. Beirut: Dār al-Ṣādir, 1995.

al-Maqrīzī, Taqī al-Dīn Aḥmad. *Kitāb al-sulūk li-ma'rifa duwal al-mulūk*. Edited by Muḥammad 'Abd al-Qādir 'Aṭā. 8 vols. Beirut: Dar al-Kutub al-'Ilmiyya, 1418/1997.

al-Mawā'iẓ wa'l-i'tibār bi-dhikr al-khiṭaṭ wa'l-āthār (al-ma'rūf bi'l-Khiṭaṭ al-Maqrīziyya). 2 vols. Beirut: Dār Ṣādir, n.d. [1877].

al-Maqqārī al-Tilmasānī, Aḥmad ibn Muḥammad. *Nafḥ al-ṭīb min ghusn al-Andalus al-raṭīb*. Edited by Muḥammad Muḥyī al-Dīn 'Abd al-Ḥamīd. 10 vols. in 5. Cairo: al-Maktaba al-Tijāra al-Kubrā, 1949.

al-Muḥāsibī, al-Ḥārith ibn Asad. *al-Ri'āya li-ḥuqūq Allāh*. Cairo: Dār al-Kutub al-Ḥadītha, 1970.

Muslim ibn al-Ḥajjāj. *Ṣaḥīḥ Muslim*. Beirut: Dār Iḥyā' al-Turāth al-'Arabī, 1420/2000.

Nāṣer-e Khosrow's Book of Travels (Safarnāme). Translated by W. M. Thackston. Albany: Bibliotheca Persica, 1986.

al-Nawawī, Muḥyī al-Dīn Yaḥyā ibn Sharaf. *Fatāwā al-Imām al-Nawawī*. Edited by Maḥmūd al-Arnā'ūṭ. Damascus: Dār al-Fikr, 1419/1999.

al-Majmū': sharḥ al-Muhadhdhab. Edited by Zakarīyā 'Alī Yūsuf et al. 19 vols. Cairo: Maṭba'at al-'Āsima and Maṭba'at al-Imām, 1966–9.

Minhāj al-ṭālibīn. Edited by Aḥmad ibn 'Abd al-'Azīz al-Ḥaddād. 3 vols. Beirut: Dār al-Bashā'ir al-Islāmiyya, 1421/2000.

Rawḍat al-ṭālibīn. Edited by 'Ādil Aḥmad 'Abd al-Mawjūd and 'Alī Muḥammad Mu'awwaḍ. 8 vols. Beirut: Dār al-Kutub al-'Ilmiyya, 1412/1992.

Riyāḍ al-ṣāliḥīn. Beirut: al-Maktab al-Islāmī, 1979. Translated by Muhammad Zafrulla Khan as *Gardens of the Righteous: Riyāḍ al-ṣāliḥīn*. Brooklyn: Olive Branch Press, 1989.

al-Nuwayrī, Shihāb al-Dīn Aḥmad ibn 'Abd Allāh. *Nihāyat al-'arab fī funūn al-adab*. 33 vols. Cairo: Dār al-Kutub al-Miṣriyya, 1923–98.

al-Qalqashandī, Aḥmad ibn 'Alī. *Ṣubḥ al-a'shā fī ṣinā'at al-inshā'*. 14 vols. Cairo: al-Mu'assasa al-Miṣriyya al-'Āmma li'l-Ta'līf wa'l-Tarjuma wa'l-Ṭiba'a wa'l-Nashr, 1964.

al-Qarāfī, Shihāb al-Dīn Aḥmad ibn Idrīs. *al-Dhakhīra*. Edited by Muḥammad Ḥajjī. 14 vols. Cairo: Dār al-Gharb al-Islāmī, 1994.

al-Rāfi'ī, 'Abd al-Karīm ibn Muḥammad. *al-'Azīz sharḥ al-Wajīz al-ma'rūf bi'l-Sharḥ al-kabīr*. Edited by 'Alī Muḥammad Mu'awwa and 'Ādil Aḥmad 'Abd al-Mawjūd. 14 vols. Beirut: Dār al-Kutub al-'Ilmiyya, 1997.

al-Ṣafadī, Ṣalāḥ al-Dīn Khalīl ibn Aybak. *A'yān al-'aṣr wa-a'wān al-naṣr*. Edited by 'Alī Abū Zayd et al. 5 vols. Damascus: Dār al-Fikr, 1997–8.

Kitāb al-wāfī bi'l-wafayāt. Edited by H. Ritter et al. 29 vols. Bibliotheca Islamica Series 6. Wiesbaden and Istanbul: Frank Steiner Verlag, 1962–97.

al-Ṣaghānī, al-Ḥasan ibn Muḥammad. *al-Takmila wa'l-dhayl wa'l-ṣila li-Kitāb Tāj al-lugha wa-ṣiḥāḥ al-'Arabiyya*. Cairo: Maktabat Dār al-Kutub, 1971.

al-Sakhāwī, Shams al-Dīn Muḥammad ibn 'Abd al-Raḥmān. *al-Ḍaw' al-lāmi' li-ahl al-qarn al-tāsi'*. 12 vols in 6. Beirut: Dār Maktabat al-Ḥayā, 1966.

al-Sallāmī, Muḥammad ibn Rāfi'. *al-Wafayāt*. Edited by 'Abd al-Jabbār Zakkār. 2 vols. Damascus: Manshūrāt Wizārat al-Thaqāfa, 1985.

The Sea of Precious Virtues (Baḥr al-Favā'id), a Medieval Islamic Mirror for Princes. Translated by Julie Scott Meisami. Salt Lake City: University of Utah Press, 1991.

al-Sha'rānī, 'Abd al-Wahhāb ibn Aḥmad. *al-Ṭabaqāt al-kubrā*. 2 vols. in 1. Beirut: Dār al-Jīl, 1408/1988.

al-Shaṭṭanūfī, 'Alī ibn Yūsuf. *Bahjat al-asrār wa ma'din al-anwār*. Cairo: n.p., 1304/1887.

al-Shīrāzī, Abū Isḥāq Ibrāhīm Fīrūzābādī. *Kitāb al-Tanbīh fī'l-fiqh al-Shāfi'ī wa-bi-hāmishihi: Tahrīr alfāz al-Tanbīh lī'-Imām Yahya ibn Sharaf al-Nawāwī*. Edited by Ayman Ṣāliḥ Sha'bān. Beirut: Dār al-Kutub al-'Ilmiyya, 1995.

Sibṭ Ibn al-Jawzī, Yūsuf ibn Qizughlī. *Mir'āt al-zamān fī tārīkh al-a'yān*, vol. VIII, part 2. Hyderabad-Deccan: Maṭba'at Majlis Dā'irat al-Ma'ārif al-'Uthmāniyya, 1952.

al-Sijistānī, Abū Dā'ūd. *Sunan Abī Dāwūd*, 5 vols. Beirut: Dār al-Jīl, 1991.

al-Subkī, Tāj al-Dīn 'Abd al-Wahhāb. *Mu'īd al-ni'am wa-mubīd al-niqam (The Restorer of Favours and the Restrainer of Chastisements)*. Edited by David W. Myhrman. London: Luzac, 1908.

Ṭabaqāt al-Shāfi'iyya al-kubrā. Edited by Maḥmūd Muḥammad al-Ṭanāḥī and 'Abd al-Fattāḥ Muḥammad al-Ḥilw. 10 vols. Cairo: Maṭba'at 'Īsā al-Bābī al-Ḥalabī, 1964–76.

al-Subkī, Taqī al-Dīn 'Alī. *Fatāwā al-Subkī*. 2 vols. Beirut: Dār al-Ma'rifa, n.d.

al-Sulamī, Abū 'Abd al-Raḥmān. *Early Sufi Women: Dhikr an-niswa al-muta'abbidāt aṣ-ṣūfiyyāt*. Edited and translated by Rkia Cornell. Louisville: Fons Vitae, 1999.

al-Sulamī, 'Izz al-Dīn 'Abd al-Azīz ibn 'Abd al-Salām. *Fatāwā al-Mawṣiliyya*. Edited by Īyād Khālid al-Ṭabbā'. Damascus: Dār al-Fikr/Beirut: Dār al-Fikr al-Mu'āṣir, 1999.

al-Suyūṭī, Jalāl al-Dīn. *al-Amr bi'l-ittibā' wa'l-nahy 'an al-ibtidā'*. Edited by Muṣṭafā 'Āshūr. Cairo: Maktabat al-Qur'ān, 1987.

al-Udfūwī, Kamāl al-Dīn Ja'far. *al-Ṭāli' al-sa'īd al-jāmi' asmā' nujabā' al-Ṣa'īd*. Edited by Sa'd Muḥammad Ḥasan. Cairo: Dār al-Miṣriyya li'l-Ta'līf wa'l-Tarjama, 1966.

al-Wansharīsī, Aḥmad ibn Yaḥyā. *al-Mi'yār al-mu'rib wa'l-jāmi' al-mughrib 'an fatāwā ahl Ifrīqiyya wa'l-Andalus wa'l-Maghrib*. 13 vols. Rabat: Nashr Wizārat al-Awqāf wa'l-Shu'ūn al-Islāmiyya li'l-Mamlaka al-Maghribiyya, 1981.

al-Yāfi'ī, 'Abd Allāh ibn As'ad. *Mir'āt al-jinān wa-'ibrat al-yaqẓān*. 4 vols. Hyderabad-Deccan: Maṭba'at Dā'irat al-Ma'ārif al-Niẓāmiyya, 1918–20.

al-Yūnīnī, Quṭb al-Dīn Mūsā. *Dhayl Mir'āt al-zamān*. 4 vols. Hyderabad-Deccan: Osmania Publications Bureau, 1374/1954.

Secondary Sources

Abou-Bakr, Omaima. "Teaching the Words of the Prophet: Women Instructors of the Hadith (Fourteenth and Fifteenth Centuries)." *Hawwa* 1, 3 (2003): 306–28.

Addas, Claude. *Ibn Arabī, ou La quête du Soufre Rouge*. Paris: Gallimard, 1989. Translated by Peter Kingsley as *Quest for the Red Sulphur: The Life of Ibn 'Arabī*. Cambridge: Islamic Texts Society, 1993.

'Afīfī, Abū'l-'Alā'. *al-Malāmatiyya wa'l-ṣūfiyya wa'l-ahl al-futuwwa*. Cairo: Dār Iḥyā' al-Kutub al-'Arabiyya, 1364/1945.

Amīn, Muḥammad Muḥammad. *al-Awqāf wa'l-ḥayāt al-ijtimā'iyya fī Miṣr 648–923/1250–1517*. Cairo: Dār al-Nahat al-'Arabiyya, 1980.

'Ankawī, Abdullah. "The Pilgrimage to Mecca in Mamlūk Times." In *Arabian Studies*, edited by R. B. Serjeant and R. L. Bidwell. London: C. Hurst, 1974.

Arberry, A. J. *Sufism: An Account of the Mystics of Islam*. London: Unwin, 1968.

Āṣī, Ḥusayn. *al-Mu'arrikh Abū Shāma wa kitābuhu al-Rawḍatayn fī akhbār al-dawlatayn al-Nūrīyya wa'l-Ṣalāḥiyya*. Beirut: Dār al-Kutub al-'Ilmiyya, 1411/1991.

Benkheira, Mohammed H. "Le commerce conjugal gâte-il le lait maternel?: sexualité, médecine et droit dans le sunnisme ancien." *Arabica* 50, 1 (2003): 1–78.

"Chairs illicites en Islam: essai d'interprétation anthropologique de la notion de *mayta*." *Studia Islamica* 84, 2 (1996): 5–33.

Berkey, Jonathan. "The Mamluks as Muslims: The Military Elite and the Construction of Islam in Medieval Egypt." In *The Mamluks in Egyptian Politics and Society*, edited by Thomas Philipp and Ulrich Haarmann. Cambridge: Cambridge University Press, 1998.

Popular Preaching and Religious Authority in the Medieval Islamic Near East. Seattle: University of Washington Press, 2001.

The Transmission of Knowledge in Medieval Cairo. Princeton: Princeton University Press, 1992.

"Women and Islamic Education in the Mamluk Period." In *Women in Middle Eastern History: Shifting Boundaries in Sex and Gender*, edited by Nikki R. Keddie and Beth Baron. New Haven: Yale University Press, 1991.

Bligh-Abramski, Irit. "The Judiciary (*Qāḍīs*) as a Governmental-Administrative Tool in Early Islam." *Journal of the Social and Economic History of the Orient* 35 (1997): 40–71.

Bonner, Michael. *Aristocratic Violence and Holy War: Studies in the Jihad and the Arab–Byzantine Frontier*. New Haven: American Oriental Society, 1996.

Bori, Caterina. "A New Source for the Biography of Ibn Taymiyya." *Bulletin of the School of Oriental and African Studies* 67 (2004): 321–48.

Bosworth, Clifford. "Some Historical Gleanings from the Section on Symbolic Actions in Qalqašandī's *Ṣubḥ al-Aʿšā*." *Arabica* 10 (1963): 148–53.

Bousquet, G.-H. "La pureté rituelle en Islām: Étude de fiqh et de sociologie religieuse." *Revue de l'histoire des religions* 138 (1950): 53–71.

Broadbridge, Anne F. "Academic Rivalry and the Patronage System in Fifteenth-Century Egypt: al-ʿAynī, al-Maqrīzī, and Ibn Ḥajar al-ʿAsqalānī." *Mamluk Studies Review* 3 (1999): 85–107.

Kingship and Ideology in the Islamic and Mongol Worlds. Cambridge: Cambridge University Press, 2008.

Brown, Peter. *The Body and Society: Men, Women and Sexual Renunciation in Early Christianity*. New York: Columbia University Press, 1988.

Society and the Holy in Late Antiquity. Berkeley and Los Angeles: University of California Press, 1982.

Brunschvig, Robert. "Urbanisme médiéval et droit musulman." *Revue des études islamiques* 15 (1947): 127–55.

"Variations sur le thème du doute dans le fiqh." In *Studi orientalistici in onore di Giorgio Levi Della Vida*, vol. I. Pubblicazioni dell'Istituto per l'Oriente 52. Rome: Istituto per l'Oriente, 1956.

Buitelaar, Marjo. *On Fasting and Feasting: An Ethnographic Study of Ramadan in Morocco*. Oxford and Providence: Berg, 1993.

Bulliet, Richard. *The Patricians of Nishapur: A Study in Medieval Islamic Social History*. Cambridge, Mass.: Harvard University Press, 1972.

Burton, John. "The Qurʾān and the Islamic Practice of *Wuḍūʾ*." *Bulletin of the School of Oriental and African Studies* 51 (1988): 21–58.

Byman, Seymour. "Ritualistic Acts and Compulsive Behavior: The Pattern of Tudor Martyrdom." *American Historical Review* 83, 3 (1978): 625–43.

Bynum, Caroline Walker. *Holy Feast and Holy Fast: The Religious Significance of Food to Medieval Women*. Berkeley: University of California Press, 1987.

Cahen, Claude. "L'évolution de l'iqṭaʿ du IX au XIII siècle: contribution à une histoire comparée des sociétés médiévales." *Annales: économies, sociétés, civilizations* 8 (1953): 23–52.

Calder, Norman. "Ḥinth, birr, tabarrur, taḥannuth: An Inquiry into the Arabic Vocabulary of Vows," *Bulletin of the School of Oriental and African Studies* 51, 2 (1988): 214–39.

"al-Nawawī's Typology of *Muftīs* and its Significance for a General Theory of Islamic Law." *Islamic Law and Society* 3, 2 (1996): 137–64.

Chamberlain, Michael. *Knowledge and Social Practice in Medieval Damascus, 1190–1350*. Cambridge: Cambridge University Press, 1994.

Chapoutot-Remadi, Mounira. "Femmes dans la ville mamlūke." *Journal of the Social and Economic History of the Orient* 38, 2 (1995): 145–64.

Chih, Rachida, and Denis Gril, eds. *Le Saint et son milieu ou: comment lire les sources hagiographiques*. Cahier des annales islamologiques 19. Cairo: Institut Français d'Archéologie Orientale, 2000.

Conermann, Stephan. "Tankiz ibn ʿAbd Allāh al-Ḥusamī al-Nāṣirī (d. 740/1340) as Seen by his Contemporary al-Ṣafadī (d. 764/1363)," *Mamluk Studies Review* 12, 2 (2008): 1–24.

Constable, Giles. "Attitudes Toward Self-inflicted Suffering in the Middle Ages." In *Culture and Spirituality in Medieval Europe*. Variorum Collected Studies Series 541. Aldershot: Variorum, 1986.

Constable, Olivia Remie. *Housing the Stranger in the Mediterranean World: Lodging, Trade, and Travel in Late Antiquity and the Middle Ages*. Cambridge and New York: Cambridge University Press, 2003.

Cook, Michael. *Commanding Right and Forbidding Wrong in Islamic Thought*. Cambridge: Cambridge University Press, 2000.

"Early Islamic Dietary Law." *Jerusalem Studies in Arabic and Islam* 7 (1986): 218–77.

"Magian Cheese: An Archaic Problem in Islamic Law." *Bulletin of the School of Oriental and African Studies* 47 (1984): 449–67.

Cooperson, Michael. *Classical Arabic Biography: The Heirs of the Prophet in the Age of al-Maʾmūn*. Cambridge: Cambridge University Press, 2000.

Cornell, Vincent. "*Faqih* versus *Faqir* in Marinid Morocco: Epistemological Dimensions of a Polemic." In *Islamic Mysticism Contested: Thirteen Centuries of Controversies and Polemics*, edited by Frederick de Jong and Bernd Radtke. Leiden: E. J. Brill, 1999.

Realm of the Saint: Power and Authority in Moroccan Sufism. Austin: University of Texas Press, 1998.

Coulson, N. J. "Doctrine and Practice in Islamic Law: One Aspect of the Problem." *Bulletin of the School of Oriental and African Studies* 18, 2 (1956): 211–14.

de Gaury, Gerald. *The Rulers of Mecca*. New York: Dorset Press, 1991 [1951].

de Jong, Frederick. *Ṭuruq and Ṭuruq-linked Institutions in Nineteenth Century Egypt*. Leiden: E. J. Brill, 1978.

de Jong, Frederick, and Bernd Radtke, eds. *Islamic Mysticism Contested: Thirteen Centuries of Controversies and Polemics*. Leiden: E. J. Brill, 1999.

Denny, Frederick M. "'God's Friends': The Sanctity of Persons in Islam." In *Sainthood: Its Manifestations in World Religions*, edited by Richard Kieckhefer and George D. Bond. Berkeley: University of California Press, 1988.

Diamond, Eliezer. *Holy Men and Hunger Artists: Fasting and Asceticism in Rabbinic Culture*. Oxford and New York: Oxford University Press, 2004.

Dols, Michael. *Majnūn: The Madman in Medieval Islamic Society*. Edited by Diana E. Immisch. New York: Oxford University Press, 1992.

Donaldson, William J. *Sharecropping in the Yemen: A Study in Islamic Theory, Custom and Pragmatism*. Studies in Islamic Law and Society 13. Leiden: E. J. Brill, 2000.

Dozy, Reinhart Pieter Anne. *Dictionnaire détaillé des noms des vêtements chez les Arabes: ouvrage couronne et publié par la Troisième classe de l'Institut royal des Pays-Bas*. Amsterdam: J. Müller, 1845.

Supplément aux dictionnaires arabes. 2 vols. Beirut: Librairie du Liban, 1981 [1881].

Eddé, Anne-Marie. *La principauté ayyoubide d'Alep (579/1183–658/1260)*. Stuttgart: Franz Steiner Verlag, 1999.

Encyclopaedia of Islam. Edited by M. T. Houtsma et al. Leiden: E. J. Brill, 1913–36. (In notes *EI*)

Encyclopaedia of Islam. 2nd ed. Edited by H. A. R. Gibb et al. Leiden: E. J. Brill, 1954–present. (In notes *EI*²)

Encyclopaedia of Islam. 3rd ed. Edited by G. Krämer, D. Matringe, J. Nawas, and E. Rowson. Leiden and Boston: E. J. Brill, 2011. (In notes *EI*³)

Ephrat, Daphna. *A Learned Society in a Period of Transition: The Sunni ʿUlamaʾ of Eleventh-Century Baghdad*. Albany: State University of New York Press, 2000.

Spiritual Wayfarers, Leaders in Piety: Sufis and the Dissemination of Islam in Medieval Palestine. Cambridge, Mass., and London: Harvard Center for Middle Eastern Studies, 2008.

Farah, Caesar E. "Ibn-al-Najjār: A Neglected Historian." *Journal of the American Oriental Society* 84, 3 (July 1964): 220–30.

Feeley-Harnik, Gillian. *The Lord's Table: The Meaning of Food in Early Judaism and Christianity*. Washington, D. C., and London: Smithsonian Institution Press, 1994.

Fernandes, L. *The Evolution of a Sufi Institution in Mamluk Egypt: The Khanqah*. Berlin: Klaus Schwarz Verlag, 1988.

"*Istibdal*: The Game of Exchange and its Impact on the Urbanization of Medieval Cairo." In *The Cairo Heritage: Essays in Honor of Layla Ali Ibrahim*, edited by Doris Behrens Abouseif. Cairo: Cairo University Press, 2000.

"On Conducting the Affairs of the State: A Guideline of the Fourteenth Century." *Annales islamologiques* 24 (1988): 81–91.

"Three Sufi Foundations in a 15th Century Waqfiyya." *Annales islamologiques* 17 (1981): 141–56.

Fierro, Maribel. "Caliphal Authority and Expiation in al-Andalus." In *Islamic Legal Interpretation: Muftis and their Fatwas*, edited by Muhammad Khalid Masud, Brinkley Messick, and David S. Powers. Cambridge, Mass.: Harvard University Press, 1996.

"The Celebration of ʿĀšūrāʾ in Sunnī Islam." In *Proceedings of the 14th Congress of the Union Européenne des Arabisants et Islamisants: Part One. The Arabist: Budapest Studies in Arabic*, no. 13–14, edited by Alexander Fodor. Budapest: Csoma de Kőrös Society, 1995: 193–208.

"The Treatises Against Innovation (kutub al-bidaʿ)." *Der Islam* 69 (1992): 204–46.

Frenkel, Yehoshua. "Agriculture, Land-Tenure and Peasants in Palestine During the Mamluk Period." In *Egypt and Syria in the Fatimid, Ayyubid, and Mamluk Eras III: Proceedings of the 6th, 7th and 8th International Colloquium Organized at the Katholieke Universiteit Leuven in May 1997, 1998, and 1999*, edited by U. Vermeulen and J. van Steenbergen. Orientalia Lovaniensia Analecta 102. Leuven: Uitgeverij Peeters, 2001.

"Awqāf in Mamluk Bilād al-Shām." *Mamluk Studies Review* 13 (2009): 149–66.

Garcin, Jean-Claude. *Espaces, pouvoirs et idéologies de l'Égypte médiévale.* London: Variorum, 1987.

"La méditerranéisation de l'empire mamlouk sous les sultans bahrides." *Revista degli Studi Orientale* 48 (1973–4): 109–16.

Gauvain, Richard. "Ritual Rewards: A Consideration of the Three Recent Approaches to Sunni Purity Law." *Islamic Law and Society* 12, 3 (2005): 333–93.

Geoffroy, Éric. *Le soufisme en Égypte et en Syrie sous les derniers Mamelouks et les premiers Ottomans: Orientations spirituelles et enjeux culturels.* Damascus: Institut Français de Damas, 1995.

Gilbert, J. "Institutionalization of Muslim Scholarship and Professionalization of the ʿUlamāʾ in Medieval Damascus." *Studia Islamica* 52 (1980): 105–34.

Goitein, S. D. *A Mediterranean Society: The Jewish Communities of the Arab World as Portrayed in the Documents of the Cairo Geniza.* 5 vols. Berkeley and Los Angeles: University of California Press, 1967–88.

Studies in Islamic History and Institutions. Leiden: E. J. Brill, 1968.

Goldziher, Ignaz. *Muslim Studies.* Translated by S. M. Stern and C. R. Barber. 2 vols. London: Allen & Unwin, 1967–71.

Graham, William A. "Islam in the Mirror of Ritual." In *Islam's Understanding of Itself*, edited by Richard G. Hovannisian and SperosVryonis, Jr. Malibu: Undena Publications, 1983.

Gramlich, Richard. *Die Wunder der Freunde Gottes: Theologien und Erscheinungsformen des islamischen Heiligenwunders.* Freiburger Islamstudien 11. Wiesbaden: Franz Steiner Verlag, 1987.

Gril, Denis. "Saint des villes et saint des champs: Étude comparée de deux vies de saints d'époque mamelouke." In *Le Saint et son milieu ou: Comment lire les sources hagiographiques*, edited by Rachida Chih and Denis Gril. Cahiers des annales islamologiques 19. Cairo: Institut Français d'Archéologie Orientale, 2000.

Guo, Li. *Early Mamluk Syrian Historiography: al-Yūnīnī's Dhayl Mir'āt al-zamān.* 2 vols. Leiden: E. J. Brill, 1998.

Haarmann, Ulrich. "Arabic in Speech, Turkish in Lineage: Mamluks and their Sons in the Intellectual Life of Fourteenth-Century Egypt and Syria." *Journal of Semitic Studies* 33 (1988): 81–114.

"Auflösung und Bewahrung der klassischen Formen arabischer Geschichtsschreibung in der Zeit der Mamluken." *Zeitschrift der Deutschen Morgenländischen Gesellschaft* 121 (1971): 46–60.

"Joseph's Law: The Careers and Activities of Mamluk Descendants Before the Ottoman Conquest of Egypt." In *The Mamluks in Egyptian Politics and Society*, edited by Thomas Philipp and Ulrich Haarmann. Cambridge: Cambridge University Press, 1998.

al-Ḥajjī, Ḥayāt Nāṣir. *Dirāsāt fī tārīkh salṭanat al-Mamālīk fī Miṣr wa'l-Shām.* Kuwait: Mu'assasat al-Ṣabāḥ wa-Maktabat al-Nahḍa al-ʿArabiyya, 1985.

Hallaq, Wael B. *Authority, Continuity and Change in Islamic Law.* Cambridge: Cambridge University Press, 2001.

"From *Fatwa*s to *Furu*ʿ: Growth and Change in Islamic Substantive Law." *Islamic Law and Society* 1 (February 1994): 17–56.

A History of Islamic Legal Theories: An Introduction to Sunnī uṣūl al-fiqh. Cambridge: Cambridge University Press, 1997.

"Non-Analogical Arguments in Sunni Juridical *Qiyās*." *Arabica* 36, 3 (1989): 286–306.

Hälm, Heinz. *Ägypten nach den mamlukischen Lehensregistern.* Beihefte zum Tübinger Atlas des Vorderen Orients, Series B, Geistewissenschaften no. 38/1–2. Wiesbaden: Reichert Verlag, 1979–82.

al-Harithy, Howyda N. "Female Patronage of Mamluk Architecture in Cairo." *Harvard Middle Eastern and Islamic Review* 1, 2 (1994): 152–74.

Hawting, Gerald. "An Ascetic Vow and an Unseemly Oath." *Bulletin of the School of Oriental and African Studies* 57 (1994): 113–25.

Heidemann, Stefan. "Charity and Piety for the Transformation of Cities: The New Direction in Waqf Policy in Mid-Twelfth Century Syria and Northern Mesopotamia." In *Charity and Giving in Monotheistic Religion*, edited by Miriam Frenkel and Yaacov Lev. Berlin and New York: Walter de Gruyter, 2009.

Die Renaissance der Städte in Nordsyrien und Nordmesopotamien. Leiden, Boston, and Cologne: E. J. Brill, 2002.

Hirschler, Konrad. *Medieval Arabic Historiography: Authors as Actors.* London and New York: Routledge, 2006.

Hoffman, Valerie J. "Eating and Fasting for God in Sufi Tradition," *Journal of the American Academy of Religion* 63, 3 (1995): 465–84.

"Islamic Perspectives on the Human Body: Legal, Social and Spiritual Considerations." In *Embodiment, Morality, and Medicine*, edited by Lisa Sowle Cahill and Margaret A. Farley. Dordrecht: Kluwer Academic Publishers, 1995.

Holt, P. M. "The Sultanate of al-Manṣūr Lāchīn (696–8/1296–9)." *Bulletin of the School of Oriental and African Studies* 3 (1973): 521–32.

Homerin, T. Emil. "Ibn Taimīya's *al-Ṣūfīyah wa-al-fuqarāʾ*." *Arabica* 32 (1985): 219–44.

"Sufis and their Detractors in Mamluk Egypt: A Survey of Protagonists and Institutional Settings." In *Islamic Mysticism Contested: Thirteen Centuries of Controversies and Polemics*, edited by Frederick de Jong and Bernd Radtke. Leiden: E. J. Brill, 1999.

Horii, Satoe. "Reconsideration of Legal Devices (*Ḥiyal*) in Islamic Jurisprudence: The Ḥanafīs and their 'Exits' (*Makhārij*)." *Islamic Law and Society* 9, 3 (2002): 312–57.

Humphreys, R. Stephen. "The Emergence of the Mamluk Army." *Studia Islamica* 45 (1977): 67–99.

"The Emergence of the Mamluk Army (Conclusion)." *Studia Islamica* 46 (1977): 147–82.

From Saladin to the Mongols: The Ayyubids of Damascus, 1193–1260. Albany: State University of New York Press, 1977.

Islamic History: A Framework for Inquiry. Rev. ed. Princeton: Princeton University Press, 1991.

"Women as Patrons of Religious Architecture in Ayyubid Damascus." *Muqarnas* 11 (1994): 35–54.

Hurvitz, Nimrod. "Biographies and Mild Asceticism: A Study of Islamic Moral Imagination." *Studia Islamica* 85 (1997): 41–65.

The Formation of Hanbalism: Piety into Power. London: Routledge, 2002.

Ḥusayn, ʿAlī Ṣāfī. *al-Adab al-ṣūfī fī Miṣr fī al-qarn al-sābiʿ al-hijrī*. Cairo: Dār al-Maʿārif, 1971.

Jackson, Sherman A. "Ibn Taymiyyah on Trial in Damascus." *Journal of Semitic Studies* 39, 1 (1994): 41–85.

Islamic Law and the State: The Constitutional Jurisprudence of Shihāb al-Dīn al-Qarāfī. Leiden: E. J. Brill, 1996.

Jaques, R. Kevin. *Authority, Conflict, and the Transmission of Diversity in Medieval Islamic Law*. Studies in Islamic Law and Society 26. Leiden and Boston: E. J. Brill, 2006.

Johansen, Baber. *Contingency in a Sacred Law: Legal and Ethical Norms in the Muslim Fiqh*. Leiden: E. J. Brill, 1999.

The Islamic Law on Land Tax and Rent: The Peasants' Loss of Property Rights in as Interpreted in the Hanafite Legal Literature of the Mamluk and Ottoman Periods. London: Croom Helm, 1988.

"The Valorization of the Body in Muslim Sunni Law." *Princeton Papers: Interdisciplinary Journal of Middle Eastern Studies* 4 (Spring 1996): 71–112.

Juynboll, G. H. A. "Some Notes on the Earliest Fuqaha of Islam Distilled from Hadith Literature." In *Studies on the Origins and Uses of Islamic Hadith*. London: Variorum Reprints, 1996.

Kafadar, Cemal. *Between Two Worlds: The Construction of the Ottoman State*. Berkeley: University of California Press, 1995.

Kamālī, Mohamed Hashim. *The Principles of Islamic Jurisprudence*. Cambridge: Islamic Texts Society, 1991.

Karamustafa, Ahmet. *God's Unruly Friends: Dervish Groups in the Islamic Later Middle Period, 1200–1500*. Salt Lake City: University of Utah Press, 1994.

Katz, Jonathan. *Dreams, Sufism and Sainthood: The Visionary Career of Muḥammad al-Zawāwī*. Leiden: E. J. Brill, 1996.

Katz, Marion Holmes. *The Birth of the Prophet Muhammad: Devotional Piety in Sunni Islam*. London and New York: Routledge, 2007.

Body of Text: The Emergence of the Sunnī Law of Ritual Purity. Albany: State University of New York Press, 2002.

"The Ḥajj and the Study of Islamic Ritual." *Studia Islamica* 98/99 (2004): 95–129.

"The Study of Islamic Ritual and the Meaning of Wuḍū'." *Der Islam* 82, 1 (2005): 106–45.

Kedar, Benjamin Z. *Crusade and Mission: European Attitudes towards the Muslims*. Princeton: Princeton University Press, 1988.

Kinberg, Leah. "What Is Meant by *Zuhd*." *Studia Islamica* 61 (1985): 27–44.

Kister, M. J. "'Shaʿbān Is My Month': A Study of an Early Tradition." In *Studia Orientalia: Memoriae D. H. Baneth Dedicata*. Jerusalem: Magnes Press, 1979.

Knysh, Alexander. *Ibn ʿArabī in the Later Islamic Tradition: The Making of a Polemical Image in Medieval Islam*. Albany: State University of New York Press, 1999.

Kueny, Kathryn. *The Rhetoric of Sobriety: Wine in Early Islam*. Albany: State University of New York Press, 2001.

Lambton, Ann. "*Awqāf* in Persia: 6th–8th/12th–14th Centuries." *Islamic Law and Society* 4, 3 (1997): 298–318.

Lane, Edward William. *An Arabic–English Lexicon*. 2 vols. London: Williams & Norgate, 1984 [1877] (repr.).

Laoust, Henri. "Ibn Kathīr historien." *Arabica* 2 (1955): 42–88.

Lapidus, Ira. *A History of Islamic Societies*. Cambridge: Cambridge University Press, 1988; 2nd ed. 2002.

"Knowledge, Virtue and Action: The Classical Muslim Conception of *Adab* and the Nature of Religious Fulfillment in Islam." In *Moral Conduct and Authority: The Place of Adab in South Asian Islam*, edited by Barbara Daly Metcalf. Berkeley and Los Angeles: University of California Press, 1984.

Lassner, Jacob. *The Topography of Baghdad in the Early Middle Ages: Text and Studies*. Detroit: Wayne State University Press, 1970.

Leiser, Gary. "The Madrasa and the Islamization of the Middle East: The Case of Egypt." *Journal of the American Research Center in Egypt* 22 (1985): 29–47.

el-Leithy, Tamer. "Sufis, Copts and the Politics of Piety: Moral Regulation in Fourteenth-Century Upper Egypt." In *Le développement du soufisme en Égypte à l'époque mamelouke*, edited by Richard McGregor and Adam Sabra. Cairo: Institut Français d'Archéologie Orientale, 2006.

Lev, Yaacov. "Piety and Political Activism in Twelfth Century Egypt." *Jerusalem Studies in Arabic and Islam* 31 (2006): 289–324.

Levanoni, Amalia. *A Turning Point in Mamluk History: The Third Reign of al-Nāṣir Muḥammad Ibn Qalāwūn*. Leiden: E. J. Brill, 1995.

Little, D. P. "Did Ibn Taymiyya Have a Screw Loose?" *Studia Islamica* 41 (1975): 93–111.

"The Historical and Historiographical Significance of the Detention of Ibn Taymiyya." *International Journal of Middle East Studies* 4, 3 (1973): 311–27.

"The Nature of Khanqahs, Ribats and Zawiyas under the Mamluks." In *Islamic Studies Presented to Charles J. Adams*, edited by Wael Hallaq. Leiden: E. J. Brill, 1991.

"Religion under the Mamluks." *Muslim World* 73 (1983): 165–81.

"al-Ṣafadī as Biographer of his Contemporaries." In *Essays on Islamic Civilization Presented to Niyazi Berkes*, edited by D. P. Little. Leiden: E. J. Brill, 1976.

Lutfi, Huda. "Manners and Customs of Fourteenth Century Cairene Women: Female Anarchy Versus Male Sharʿi Order in Muslim Prescriptive Treatises." In *Women in Middle Eastern History: Shifting Boundaries in Sex and Gender*, edited by Nikki R. Keddie and Beth Baron. New Haven: Yale University Press, 1991.

"al-Sakhāwī's *Kitāb al-nisāʾ* as a Source for the Social and Economic History of Muslim Women during the Fifteenth Century A.D." *Muslim World* 71 (1981): 104–24.

Maghen, Ze'ev. "Close Encounters: Some Preliminary Observations on the Transmission of Impurity in Early Sunnī Jurisprudence." *Islamic Law and Society*, 6, 3 (1999): 348–92.

"First Blood: Purity, Edibility and the Independence of Islamic Jurisprudence." *Der Islam* 81 (2004): 49–95.

"Much Ado About Wuduʾ." *Der Islam* 76 (1999): 205–52.

Virtues of the Flesh: Passion and Purity in Early Islamic Jurisprudence. Leiden and Boston: Brill, 2005.

Mahdi, Muhsin. "The Book and the Master as Poles of Cultural Change in Islam." In *Islam and Cultural Change in the Middle Ages (Fourth Giorgio Levi Della Vida Conference)*, edited by Speros Vryonis. Wiesbaden: Otto Harrassowitz, 1975.

Makdisi, George. "The Hanbali School and Sufism." In *Actas, IV Congresso de Estudos Árabes e Islâmicos, Coimbra-Lisboa: 1 a 8 de setembro de 1968*. Leiden: E. J. Brill, 1971.

Mandaville, Jon E. "Usurious Piety: The Cash Waqf Controversy in the Ottoman Empire." *International Journal of Middle East Studies* 10 (1979): 289–308.

Marín, Manuela. "Retiro y ayuno: Algunas prácticas religiosas de las mujeras andalusías." *al-Qanṭara: Revista de Estudios Árabes* 21, 2 (2000): 471–80.

Martin, Richard C., ed. *Approaches to Islam in Religious Studies*. Tucson: University of Arizona Press, 1985.

Marmon, Shaun E. "Domestic Slavery in the Mamluk Empire: A Preliminary Sketch." In *Slavery in the Islamic Middle East*, edited by Shaun E. Marmon. Princeton: Marcus Wiener, 1999.

Eunuchs and Sacred Boundaries in Islamic Society. New York: Oxford University Press, 1995.

Massignon, Louis. *Essay on the Origins of the Technical Language of Islamic Mysticism*. Translated by Benjamin Clark. Notre Dame, Ind.: University of Notre Dame Press, 1997 [1922].

Massoud, Sami. *The Chronicles and Annalistic Sources of the Early Mamluk Circassian Period*. Leiden and Boston: E. J. Brill, 2007.

Masud, Muhammad Khalid, Brinkley Messick, and David S. Powers, eds. *Islamic Legal Interpretation: Muftis and their Fatwas*. Cambridge, Mass.: Harvard University Press, 1996.

Matroudi, Abdul Hakim I. *The Ḥanbalī School of Law and Ibn Taymiyya: Conflict or Conciliation*. London and New York: Routledge, 2006.

Mayeur-Jaouen, Catherine. "Le cheikh scrupuleux et l'émir généreux à travers les *Aḫlāq matbūliyya de Šaʿrānī*." In *Le saint et son milieu ou: comment lire les sources hagiographique*, edited by Rachida Chih and Denis Gril. Cahier des annales islamologiques 19. Cairo: Institut Français d'Archéologie Orientale, 2000.

al-Sayyid Aḥmad al-Badawī: Un grand saint de l'Islam égyptien. Cairo: Institut Français d'Archéologie Orientale, 1994.

McGregor, Richard. "The Problem of Sufism." *Mamluk Studies Review* 13, 2 (2009): 69–83.

Sanctity and Mysticism in Medieval Egypt: The Wafāʾ Sufi Order and the Legacy of Ibn ʿArabi. Albany: State University of New York Press, 2004.

Meier, Fritz, and Bernd Radtke. *Essays on Islamic Piety and Mysticism*. Translated by John O'Kane. Leiden: E. J. Brill, 1999.

Melchert, Christopher. "Exaggerated Fear in the Early Islamic Renunciant Tradition." *Journal of the Royal Asiatic Society* 21, 3 (2011): 283–300.

The Formation of the Sunni Schools of Law, 9th–10th Centuries. Studies in Islamic Law and Society 4. Leiden: E. J. Brill, 1997.

"The Ḥanābila and the Early Sufis." *Arabica* 48 (2001): 352–67.

"The Piety of the Hadith Folk." *International Journal of Middle East Studies* 34, 3 (2002): 425–39.

"The Transition From Asceticism to Mysticism at the Middle of the Ninth Century C.E." *Studia Islamica* 83 (1996): 51–70.

Memon, Muhammad Umar. *Ibn Taimīya's Struggle Against Popular Religion: With an Annotated translation of his Kitāb iqtiḍāʾ aṣ-ṣirāt al-mustaqīm mukhālafat aṣḥāb al-jahīm*. The Hague: Mouton, 1976.

Meri, Joseph. *The Cult of Saints among Muslims and Jews in Medieval Syria*. Oxford: Oxford University Press, 2002.

Meyerhof, Max. *Studies in Medieval Arabic Medicine: Theory and Practice*. London: Variorum Reprints, 1984.

Michot, Yahya. "Un célibataire endurci et sa maman: Ibn Taymiyya (m. 728/1328) et les femmes." In *La femme dans les civilisations orientales*, edited by C. Cannuyer. Acta Orientalia Belgica 15. Brussels: Société Belge d'Études Orientales, 2001.

Mojaddedi, Jawid A. *The Biographical Tradition in Sufism: The Ṭabaqāt Genre from al-Sulamī to Jāmī*. Richmond: Curzon Press, 2001.

Morray, David. *An Ayyubid Notable and his World: Ibn al-ʿAdīm and Aleppo as Portrayed in his Biographical Dictionary of People Associated with the City*. Leiden: E. J. Brill, 1994.

Mortel, Richard T. "Madrasas in Mecca During the Medieval Period: A Descriptive Study Based on Literary Sources." *Bulletin of the School of Oriental and African Studies* 60, 2 (1997): 236–52.

"*Ribāṭs* in Mecca During the Medieval Period: A Descriptive Study Based on Literary Sources." *Bulletin of the School of Oriental and African Studies* 61, 1 (1998): 29–50.

Mottahedeh, Roy. *Loyalty and Leadership in an Early Islamic Society*. Princeton: Princeton University Press, 1980.

Mouton, Jean-Michel. *Damas et sa principauté sous les Saljoukides et les Bourides (465–549/1076–1154): Vie politique et religieuse*. Cairo: Institut Français d'Archéologie Orientale, 1994.

Murad, Hasan Qasim. "Ibn Taymiya on Trial: A Narrative Account of his Miḥan." *Islamic Studies* 18, 1 (1979): 1–32.

Naguib, Shuruq. "And your Garments Purify: Ṭahāra in the Light of Tafsīr." *Journal of Qur'anic Studies* 9, 1 (2007): 59–77.

al-Naqar, ʿUmar. *The Pilgrimage Tradition in West Africa: An Historical Study with Special Reference to the Nineteenth Century*. Khartoum: Khartoum University Press, 1974.

Nirenberg, David. *Communities of Violence: Persecution of Minorities in the Middle Ages*. Princeton: Princeton University Press, 1996.

O'Malley, Padraig. *Biting at the Grave: The Irish Hunger Strikes and the Politics of Despair*. Boston: Beacon Press, 1990.

Orsi, Robert A. "'Mildred, Is It Fun to be a Cripple?': The Culture of Suffering in Mid-Twentieth-Century American Catholicism." In *Catholic Lives, Contemporary America*, edited by Thomas J. Ferraro. Durham, N.C.: Duke University Press, 1997.

Patton, Douglas. *Badr al-Din Lu'lu': Atabeg of Mosul 1211–1259*. Seattle: University of Washington Press, 1991.

Perlmann, Moshe. "Ibn Qayyim and the Devil." *Studi orientalistici in onore di Giorgio Levi della Vida*. Vol. II. Pubblicazioni dell'Istituto per l'Oriente 52. Rome: Istituto per l'Oriente, 1956.

Peters, Rudolph. "Sharecropping in the Dakhla Oasis: Shariʿa and Customary Law in Ottoman Egypt." In *The Law Applied: Contextualizing the Islamic Shariʿa*. Edited by Peri Bearman, Wolfhart Heinrichs, and Bernard G. Weiss. London and New York: I. B. Tauris, 2008.

Petry, Carl F. *The Civilian Elite of Cairo in the Later Middle Ages*. Princeton: Princeton University Press, 1981.

"Travel Patterns of Medieval Notables in the Near East." *Studia Islamica* 62 (1985): 53–87.

Philipp, Thomas, and Ulrich Haarmann, eds. *The Mamluks in Egyptian Politics and Society*. Cambridge: Cambridge University Press, 1998.

Popper, William. *Egypt and Syria under the Circassian Sultans 1382–1468: Systematic Notes to Ibn Taghri Birdi's Chronicles of Egypt*. 2 vols. University of California Publications in Semitic Philology 15–16. Berkeley: University of California Press, 1955–7.

"Sakhāwī's Criticism of Ibn Taghrī Birdī." In *Studi orientalistici in onore di Giorgio Levi Della Vida*, vol. II. Pubblicazioni dell'Istituto per l'Oriente 52. Rome: Istituto per l'Oriente, 1956.

Porter, Roy. "The Urban and the Rustic in Enlightenment London." In *Nature and Society in Historical Context*, edited by Mikuláš Teich, Roy Porter, and Bo Gustafsson. Cambridge: Cambridge University Press, 1997.

Pouzet, Louis. *Damas aux VII/XIII siècle: Vie et structures religieuses d'une métropole islamique*. Beirut: Dar al-Mashreq, 1988.

"Haḍir ibn Abî Bakr al-Mihrānî (m. 7 mu. 676/11juin 1277) šay du sultan mamelouk Al-Malik aẓ-Ẓâhir Baïbars." *Bulletin d'études orientales* 30 (1978): 173–83.

Powers, David S. *Law, Society and Culture in the Maghrib, 1300–1500*. Cambridge: Cambridge University Press, 2002.

Powers, Paul R. "Interiors, Intentions and the 'Spirituality' of Islamic Ritual Practice." *Journal of the American Academy of Religion* 72, 2 (2004): 426–59.

Rabbat, Nasser. "Representing the Mamluks in Mamluk Historical Writing." In *The Historiography of Islamic Egypt, c. 950–1800*, edited by Hugh Kennedy. Leiden: E. J. Brill, 2000.

Rabie, Hassanein. "The Size and Value of the *Iqṭāʿ* in Egypt 564–741 A.H./1169–1341 A.D." In *Studies in the Economic History of the Middle East From the Rise of Islam to the Present Day*, edited by M. A. Cook. Oxford: Oxford University Press, 1970.

Rapoport, Yossef. "Ibn Taymiyya's Radical Legal Thought: Rationalism, Pluralism and the Primacy of Intention." In *Ibn Taymiyya and his Times*, edited by Shahab Ahmed and Yossef Rapoport. Karachi: Oxford University Press, 2010.

"Legal Diversity in the Age of *Taqlīd*: The Four Chief *Qāḍī*s under the Mamluks." *Islamic Law and Society* 10, 2 (2003): 210–28.

Marriage, Money and Divorce in Medieval Islamic Society. Cambridge: Cambridge University Press, 2005.

"Women and Gender in Mamluk Society: An Overview." *Mamluk Studies Review* 11, 2 (2007): 1–47.

Reinhart, A. Kevin. "Impurity/No Danger." *History of Religions* 30, 1 (1990): 1–24.

"Transcendence and Social Practice: *Muftī*s and *Qādī*s as Religious Interpreters." *Annales islamologiques* 27 (1993): 5–28.

Robinson, Chase. *Islamic Historiography*. Cambridge: Cambridge University Press, 2003.

Rodinson, Maxime. "Recherches sur les documents arabes relatifs à la cuisine." *Revue des études islamiques* 17 (1949): 95–165.

Rodríguez-Mañas, Francisco. "Encore sur la controverse entre soufis et juristes au moyen âge: critiques des mécanismes de financement des confréries soufies." *Arabica* 43 (1996): 406–21.

Rosenthal, Franz. "The Defense of Medicine in the Medieval Muslim World." *Bulletin of the History of Medicine* 43 (1969): 519–32.

A History of Muslim Historiography. Leiden: E. J. Brill, 1968.

Sabra, Adam A. "Illiterate Sufis and Learned Artisans: The Circle of ʿAbd al-Wahhab al-Shaʿrani." In *Le développement du soufisme en Égypte à l'époque mamelouke*, edited by Richard J. McGregor and Adam Sabra. Cairo: Institute Français d'Archéologie Orientale, 2006.

Poverty and Charity in Medieval Islam: Mamluk Egypt, 1250–1517. Cambridge: Cambridge University Press, 2000.
"Public Policy or Private Charity? The Ambivalent Character of Islamic Charitable Endowments." In *Stiftungen in Christentum, Judentum und Islam vor der Moderne: auf der Suche nach ihren Gemeinsamkeiten und Unterschieden in religiosen Grundlagen, praktischen Zwecken und historischen Transformationen*, edited by Michael Borgolte. Berlin: Akademie Verlag, 2005.
"The Rise of a New Class? Land Tenure in Fifteenth-Century Egypt: A Review Article." *Mamluk Studies Review* 8, 2 (2004).
Safran, Janina M. "Rules of Purity and Confessional Boundaries: Maliki Debates about the Pollution of the Christian." *History of Religions* 42, 3 (2003): 197–212.
Saleh, Nabil A. *Unlawful Gain and Legitimate Profit in Islamic Law: Riba, gharar and Islamic Banking*. With additional research by Ahmad Ajaj. 2nd ed. London: Graham & Trotman, 1992.
Sanders, Paula. *Ritual, Politics and the City in Fatimid Cairo*. Albany: State University of New York Press, 1994.
"Robes of Honor in Fatimid Egypt, 969–1171." In *Robes and Honor: The Medieval World of Investiture*, edited by Gavin Hambly and Stewart Gordon. New York: Palgrave, 2001.
Sartain, Elizabeth. *Jalal al-Dīn al-Suyūṭī, Volume I: Biography and Background*. Cambridge: Cambridge University Press, 1975.
Sayeed, Asma. "Women and Hadith Transmission: Two Case Studies from Mamluk Damascus." *Studia Islamica* 95 (2002): 71–94.
Schacht, Joseph. *An Introduction to Islamic Law*. Oxford: Clarendon Press, 1964.
Schimmel, Annemarie. *And Muhammad Is His Messenger*. Chapel Hill: University of North Carolina Press, 1985.
Mystical Dimensions of Islam. Chapel Hill: University of North Carolina Press, 1975.
Serjeant, R. B. "Ḥaram and Ḥawṭah: The Sacred Enclave in Arabia." In *Studies in Arabian History and Civilization*. London: Variorum Reprints, 1981.
Shoshan, Boaz. *Popular Culture in Medieval Cairo*. Cambridge: Cambridge University Press, 1993.
"The State and Madness in Medieval Islam." *International Journal of Middle East Studies* 35, 2 (2003): 329–40.
Singer, Amy. *Constructing Ottoman Beneficence: An Imperial Soup Kitchen in Jerusalem*. Albany: State University of New York Press, 2002.
Stillman, Norman. "Charity and Social Service in Medieval Islam." *Societas* 2 (1975): 105–15.
Stillman, Yedida Kalfon. *Arab Dress from the Dawn of Islam to Modern Times: A Short History*. Edited by Norman A. Stillman. Leiden: E. J. Brill, 2000.
Sviri, Sara. "Ḥakīm Tirmidhī and the Malāmatī Movement Early Sufism." In *The Heritage of Sufism, Volume I: Classical Persian Sufism from its Origins to Rumi (700–1300)*, edited by Leonard Lewisohn. Oxford: Oneworld Publications, 1999.

Swartz, Merlin. *Ibn al-Jawzī's Kitāb al-Quṣṣāṣ wa'l-Mudhakkirīn*. Beirut: Dar al-Machreq, 1986.

Tabbaa, Yasser. *Constructions of Power and Piety in Medieval Aleppo*. University Park: University of Pennsylvania Press, 1997.

Talmon-Heller, Daniella. "*The Cited Tales of the Wondrous Doings of the Shaykhs of the Holy Land* by Ḍiyā' al-Dīn Abū 'Abd Allāh Muḥammad b. 'Abd al-Wāḥid al-Maqdisī (569/1173–643/1245): Text, Translation and Commentary." *Crusades* 1 (2002): 111–54.

Islamic Piety in Medieval Syria: Mosques, Cemeteries and Sermons under the Zangids and Ayyūbids (1146–1260). Jerusalem Studies in Religion and Culture. Leiden: E. J. Brill, 2008.

"Religion in the Public Sphere: Rulers, Scholars, and Commoners in Syria under Zangid and Ayyubid Rule (1150–1260)." In *The Public Sphere in Muslim Societies*, edited by Miriam Hoexter, Shmuel N. Eisenstadt, and Nehemia Levtzion. Albany: State University of New York Press, 2002.

"The Shaykh and the Community: Popular Ḥanbalite Islam in 12th–13th Century Jabal Nablus and Jabal Qasyūn." *Studia Islamica* 79 (1994): 103–20.

Ṭawīl, Tawfīq. *al-Taṣawwuf fi Miṣr ibbāna al 'aṣr al-'Uthmānī*. Cairo: al-Hay'a al-Miṣriyya al-'Āmma li'l-Kitāb, 1988.

Taylor, Christopher. *In the Vicinity of the Righteous: Ziyāra and the Veneration of Muslim Saints in Late Medieval Egypt*. Leiden: E. J. Brill, 1999.

Thibon, Jean-Jacques. "Hiérarchie spirituelle, fonctions du saint et hagiographie dans l'œuvre de Sulamī." In *Le Saint et son milieu ou: comment lire les sources hagiographiques*, edited by Rachida Chih and Denis Gril. Cahiers des annales islamologiques 19. Cairo: Institut Français d'Archéologie Orientale, 2000.

Trimingham, J. Spencer. *The Sufi Orders in Islam*. Oxford: Oxford University Press, 1971.

Tsugitaka, Sato. *State and Rural Society in Medieval Islam: Sultans, Muqta's and Fallahun*. Leiden: E. J. Brill, 1997.

Tucker, William. "Environmental Hazards, Natural Disasters, Economic Loss, and Mortality in Mamluk Syria." *Mamluk Studies Review* 3 (1999): 109–28.

Tyan, Émile. *Histoire de l'organisation judicaire en pays d'Islam*. 2nd ed. Leiden: E. J. Brill, 1960.

Udovitch, Abraham L. *Partnership and Profit in Medieval Islam*. Princeton: Princeton University Press, 1970.

Ukeles, Raquel Margolit. "Innovation or Deviation: Exploring the Boundaries of Islamic Devotional Law." Ph.D. thesis, Harvard University, 2006.

Ullmann, Manfred, *Islamic Medicine*. Translated by Jean Watt. Edinburgh: University of Edinburgh Press, 1974.

'Umar, Aḥmad Mukhtār. "Ibn Manẓūr al-Lughawī: al-'Ālim al-Ḥā'ir bayn Miṣr wa-Lībyā wa-Tūnis." *Revista del Instituto Egipcio de Estudios Islámicos en Madrid* 18 (1974–5): 155–64.

Van Gelder, Geert Jan. *God's Banquet: Food in Classical Arabic Literature*. New York: Columbia University Press, 2000.

Van Leeuwen, Richard. *Waqfs and Urban Structures: The Case of Ottoman Damascus*. Leiden and Boston: E. J. Brill, 1999.

Van Steenbergen, Jo. "Mamluk Elite on the Eve of an-Nāṣir Muḥammad's death (1341): A Look behind the Scenes of Mamluk Politics." *Mamluk Studies Review* 9, 2 (2005): 173–99.

Vigarello, Georges. *Concepts of Cleanliness: Changing Attitudes in France since the Middle Ages*. Translated by Jean Birrell. Cambridge: Cambridge University Press, 1988.

Wagtendonk, K. *Fasting in the Koran*. Leiden: E. J. Brill, 1968.

Waines, David F. "Muslim Piety and Food of the Gods." *al-Qantara* 21, 2 (2000): 411–24.

Wensinck, A. J. "The Refused Dignity." In *A Volume of Oriental Studies Presented to Edward G. Browne ... on his 60th birthday (7 February 1922)*, edited by T. W. Arnold and Reynold A. Nicholson. Cambridge: Cambridge University Press, 1922.

Wheeler, Brannon M. *Mecca and Eden: Ritual, Relics, and Territory in Islam*. Chicago: University of Chicago Press, 2006.

Winter, Michael. *Society and Religion in Early Ottoman Egypt: Studies in the Writings of ʿAbd al-Wahhāb al-Shaʿrānī*. New Brunswick, N.J.: Transaction Books, 1982.

Index

ʿAbd Allāh ibn ʿAmr (Companion of the Prophet), 80, 212
ʿAbd Allāh ibn ʿUmar (Companion of the Prophet), 174, 178, 191, 212
al-ʿAbdarī, Abū ʿAbd Allāh Muḥammad ibn Ḥarīth, 137–8
al-ʿAbdarī, Muḥammad Ibn al-Ḥājj, *see* Ibn al-Ḥājj
ʿābid (f. *ʿābida*; pl. *ʿubbād*: devotee), 1, 22, 23n4, 24n8
ablutions: after anger, 154, 154n23, 202; after experiencing sexual desire, 42n60; in cold water, 34; excessive, 156–7, 164, 165, 166n56, 177; inadequate for cleanliness, 147, 157, 171, 172; major, 54, 148, 157, 163, 165, 174; after menstruation, 54; minor, 145, 147, 147n8, 149, 151, 155–6, 163, 168, 174, 186, 202; at night, 153; for prayer, 94, 153–4, 210; purity of water, 162, 168, 171, 172n73, 175, 176; to reassert control of bodily functions, 147, 149, 188; *see also ghusl*; washing; *wuḍūʾ*
Abū al-Ghanāʾim Muḥammad ibn Muslim, 46
Abū Ḥanīfa, 136
Abū Madyan, 63
Abū Nuʿaym, 52
Abū Shāma, 79, 135, 137, 150, 153, 156, 158, 161, 173, 175n81, 203, 209
adab, *see* etiquette
ʿĀʾisha Umm Kamāl, 180
"al-Akkāl," *see* Muḥammad ibn Khalīl
amirs, 4, 26, 30n24, 45n68, 46, 57, 74n74, 109, 112n47, 116, 120–1, 124n80, 128, 129n93, 129n97, 143
anxiety, *see waswās*
al-Aqfahsī, Aḥmad Ibn ʿImād, 175, 183, 190, 191
asceticism, 5–8, 21–55, 115, 211, 213; abstention from food, 30, 32, 41, 47–8, 65–9, 97, 101, 143; and antinomianism, 13, 197; and bodily discomfort, 25; celibacy, 30, 35–47, 54; clothing and, 25, 29–30, 34, 40, 43, 46, 49, 50, 52–3; conversion to, 23, 44–7; criticism of, 47–50, 89, 89n92, 212; ethical (*waraʿ*), 125–43; and Islamic law, 7, 13; in late medieval culture, 6, 9, 21, 28–35, 42–3, 47; mild, 31, 31n26, 32–3; and modern scholarship, 9–10; in old age, 33–4, 34n32; as proof of piety, 28, 43, 73, 74, 177; reasons for, 30, 126–7; and ritual practices, 84; self-imposed hardship, 29–30, 34, 35, 43, 47–8, 49, 61, 62, 66–7, 68–9, 75, 79, 84; and self-neglect, 13, 199–201; and Sufism, 6–7, 26; women and, 31n25, 40, 46, 49, 51, 115–17; zealous ascetics (*mutazahhidūn*), 36; *see also* mortification of the body; *muwallahūn*; *waraʿ*; *zuhd*
al-Ashraf Barsbāy (Mamluk sultan), 56–7, 62, 69–70, 72, 75
al-Ashraf Shaʿbān (Mamluk sultan), 211
al-ʿAṭṭār of Hamadān, 187
aʿyān (notables), 10, 26, 203

al-ʿAynī, Badr al-Dīn, 169–70; *Bināya sharḥ al-Hidāya*, 170
Ayyubid dynasty, 3–4, 122
Ayyubid period, 2–4, 6, 30–1, 38, 43, 58, 73, 83, 114, 117, 121, 123, 124, 149, 162, 198, 212

al-Badawī, Aḥmad, 17
al-Bālisī, (Shaykh), ʿAlī 143
baraka (blessings), 59n6, 64n22, 100, 109, 109n38, 111, 112n46, 142, 207
al-Baṣrī, Ḥasan, 45n69
Baybars, al-Ẓāhir (Mamluk sultan), 102, 127
Baybars al-Jashnakīr (Mamluk sultan), 109
Baybars al-Manṣūrī al-Dawādār (chronicler), 146
Berkey, Jonathan, 9, 10
bidʿa, *see* innovation
biographical sources, 13–20, 49–50, 91, 150n12, 155–6, 158–9; and ascetic practices, 21–2, 33–4; bias in, 16; dictionaries, 1, 2, 5, 9, 14, 137; hagiography, 16, 17, 50, 51; and Islamic law, 16, 145; negative accounts, 161, 162, 179; obituaries, 15, 17, 86, 87, 88, 145, 150n12; and piety, 16–17, 44; Sufi *ṭabaqāt* literature, 14n26
body: in asceticism, 25–6; *badan*, 89, 89n91, 89n92; and devotional piety, 8, 10, 13, 25, 58; as focus of sacrifice, 25–6, 33; harmed by excessive devotional practices, 85, 89; health of, 86–91; as instrument of worship, 8, 11, 25, 26, 59, 69, 74, 78, 85; *jasad*, 68; and religious authority, 10; in ritual practice, 3, 10, 94; *see also* asceticism; clothing; fasting; modesty; mortification of the body; ritual purity; *waswās*
bread: avoidance of, 67; baking, 133, 140n125; barley bread, 48, 59, 61, 97–8, 208; distribution of bread by ruler, 102; as meal, 32, 89n92, 116, 134; milling, 140–1
al-Bulqīnī, Jalāl al-Dīn ʿAbd al-Raḥmān, 125
al-Buskarī, ʿAbd Allāh, 98, 105
al-Buṣrawī, Ṣafī al-Dīn Abū'l-Qāsim, 116
al-Buṣrawiyya, Umm Yūsuf Fakhriyya, 115–17
al-Bustī, Abū ʿAbd Allāh Muḥammad, 67n32, 67–9, 73, 76, 84
Buyid period, 6n10, 28
al-Buzūrī, 32, 98n5

celibacy, 30, 35–47, 54, 84, 199; condemned, 36, 41n56, 84; and fasting, 83, 84
Chamberlain, Michael, 9, 10, 43, 124, 151, 198, 203–4
charity, 100–13; as *baraka*, 100, 109; from disreputable sources, 107–14, 117–18, 120, 127–8, 131; in the Qurʾān, 98, 103; rejection of, 115, 116, 117–18, 122–3; *see also* pious endowments
Christianity: and the body, 35n34, 58; and excessive piety, 34, 85n80; and fasting, 58, 59–60, 60n8, 64n22; and food, 59n5, 59–60, 106, 106n30; monasticism, 34, 35n35, 37, 85, 205n24
clothing: coarse, worn by ascetics, 25, 29, 30, 34, 40, 43, 46, 49, 50, 211; fine, worn by scholars, 43, 137, 198; and ritual purity, 118–19, 145, 150–1, 151n15, 161, 162, 168, 170, 182, 183, 184, 186, 187, 188, 188n118, 189, 191, 192–3, 194, 195, 202, 203; soiled, 151, 186, 188, 199, 201, 203, 206, 207; women and, 46, 52–3
Companions of the Prophet, 8, 19, 36, 80, 174, 178, 191, 210, 212; and ablutions, 174; Abū Bakr, 117; ʿĀʾisha (wife of the Prophet), 91; Bilāl, 210; as exemplars, 8, 48, 82, 91, 172; and fasting, 60, 62n1, 62–3, 91, 91n97; hadiths concerning, 19, 91n97; Jābir, 157; and marriage, 36; Umar ibn al-Khaṭṭāb (caliph), 178n91, 213; and *waswasa*, 178; *see also* ʿAbd Allāh ibn ʿAmr; ʿAbd Allāh ibn ʿUmar; pious forebears
concubines, 38n44, 38–9; shunned by the pious, 29, 39, 40, 199

devil: Adam and, 145; harm inflicted by, 172, 177–8; Iblīs, 163n48, 164; Satan, 47–8, 145–6, 163; al-Walhān, 163–4; whispering, 47, 145–6, 163; wrongful actions inspired by, 45n69, 166
devotional piety, 7–13, 29–30; and changes in religious culture, 127–8, 178–84, 195–6; excessive, 8, 44–5, 46, 198–213; iron collars, 92, 93; in the late medieval period, 2, 7–8, 212; ostentatious, 30n23,

50n87, 51, 133, 156, 159, 161, 165, 177, 206; pious conversion, 45–6, 47; and subsistence, 117–31; *waswās* as, 167–8, 178–84, 195–6; women and, 11, 51–5; *see also* asceticism; fasting; *muwallahūn*; *nāfila*; ritual purity; *taʿabbud*
al-Dhahabī, Shams al-Dīn Muḥammad ibn Aḥmad, 16, 35, 91, 110, 150, 155, 181, 182, 187n115, 204
divorce, 37, 42, 166, 166n58
Dols, Michael, 204
Douglas, Mary, 147
Dozy, Reinhart, 164

Eddé, Anne-Marie, 6
etiquette (*adab*), 10, 30, 60, 78, 98, 104, 113, 132, 200

al-Fāsī, Taqī al-Dīn Muḥammad ibn Aḥmad, 5, 15, 54, 66, 180
fasting, 6, 59–60, 63–4, 78; ʿĀshūrāʾ, 59, 70; on behalf of someone else, 77–8, 78n59; benefits of, 74–8; and the body, 58–9, 84; breaking a fast, 64, 64n21, 66n29, 94n107, 104, 132; as changing one's physical and moral status, 94, 95–6; by Christians, 58, 59, 59n5; continuous, 62–3, 70; dangers of, 83, 84, 86–7; David's Fast, 80, 83, 92; demeanor during, 78–9; difficulty and duration, 60–78; dispensations for, 66; and hunger, 21, 33, 58, 68; ʿId al-Aḍḥā, 81; ʿĪd al-Fiṭr, 81; *ifṭār*, 63–4, 64n22, 67; by Jews, 59, 59n7, 60; ignoring a fast, 203, 205, 207, 209; literature on, 62; and loss of appetite, 82; making up for, 64, 66, 66n29, 74–5, 75n49, 79n50; obligatory, 56, 57, 60, 64n21, 66; the perpetual fast, 57, 60–1, 78–96; and prayer, 61; prohibited, 81, 82, 90–1; as protection from corruption, 94, 95; during Ramaḍān, 56, 62, 64, 74, 207; reasons for, 57, 72–4, 75, 76–8; refusal to fast, 207; *saḥūr*, 64n22; and sexual intercourse, 64, 64n21; during Shawwāl, 62, 62n15, 75n49, 90n94, 90n95; Sufis and, 73–4; temporary, 68–9, 94; types of food eaten or rejected, 29, 32, 48, 61, 62, 64n22, 65, 65n26, 67–8, 79, 84, 87, 115; visions during, 77; voluntary, 7, 9, 24, 25, 56–96; after a vow, 6, 52n91, 56, 70–1, 93–5; women and, 52n91, 74–5; *see also ṣawm*
Fāṭima (wife of al-Ṣafadī), 54–5, 75
fatwas, 18, 37n40, 64, 64, 64n21, 70–1, 117n60, 127, 141, 193
al-Fayyūmī, Aḥmad ibn Muḥammad, 23, 23n7, 25
al-Fazārī, Burhān al-Dīn, 65n23, 87–8, 106, 192
Fernandes, Leonor, 125
fiqh, *see* law
food, 97–131; attitudes to, 99; and *baraka*, 59n6, 64n22, 100, 109, 111, 142; carrion, 68–9, 114; as charity, 100–13, 132; condiments, 32, 65, 98, 134, 138, 139–40; declared prohibited, 106n30, 134–42, 199; feasts, 97–8, 103–4, 111, 142; and health, 86, 127; hospitality, 98, 100, 106, 143; luxurious, 103, 108, 137, 138n121, 198; in medieval Islamic piety, 59, 59n6, 69; in the Qurʾān, 106, 113; refusal of, 65, 99, 103–7, 108–9, 113, 115, 115n55, 117–18, 123, 125–30, 143, 199; ritualistic behavior and, 25, 139–40; and ritual impurity, 106–7, 113–17, 127–8, 130–1, 140, 142; table fellowship, 103–5, 106, 110–11, 132; unusual diets, 32, 65, 67–9, 84, 98–9, 138, 141, 198–9, 206n27; *see also* asceticism, abstention from food; bread; fasting; fruit; *ḥalāl*; *ḥarām*; meat; *ṭayyib*
fruit, 32, 67, 86, 97, 98, 134, 137, 148, 198, 208; avoidance of, 32, 48, 65, 126, 198–9; fruit trees, 87, 100, 126–7, 135, 136, 141

Geoffroy, Éric, 16, 205
al-Ghazzālī , 35–6, 80, 82, 90, 113, 162, 176–7, 192; *Iḥyāʾ ʿulūm al-dīn* 36, 82–3, 114, 176; *Wajīz fī fiqh al-Imām al-Shāfiʿī*, 81–2; *Wasīṭ*, 150
ghusl (major ablution), 147, 148, 157, 164n52, 171, 173n77
"the Glutton," *see* Muḥammad ibn Khalīl
Gramlich, Richard, 17

ḥadath (impure status), 147n8, 170, 184, 186, 188
hadiths, 19, 51, 51n90; on ablutions, 157, 163, 170, 170n68; on celibacy, 35; on fasting, 62–3, 66, 70, 80, 81, 82; and

food, 113; on isolation, 119; on prayer, 210; on reading the Qurʾān, 85; as source of Islamic law, 19, 20; women and, 51
Ḥāfiẓ (poet), 143
Hajj, *see* Pilgrimage
al-Ḥalabī, Ḥammād, 211–12
al-Ḥallāj, 207–8
ḥalāl (licit), 69, 134; in an ethical sense, 113, 113n48, 114, 114n52, 138, 177; in the Hijaz, 136; *see also ṭayyib*
Ḥanafī *madhhab*: conversion to, 156n28; and fasting, 62n15; and licit food, 136; and water purity, 175n84, 175–6
Ḥanbalī *madhhab*: and ablutions, 145; and financial transactions, 160; and licit food, 136; and *waswās*, 172–8, 192
ḥarām (prohibited), 62n16, 69, 70, 114, 134; in an ethical sense, 115n55, 130–1, 140, 142, 177; in the Hijaz, 134–7, 135n110; meat, 114, 130–1, 136
al-Ḥarīrī, ʿAlī, 16
ḥīla (pl. *ḥiyal*: legal stratagem), 159, 160, 160n44
al-Ḥiṣnī, Taqī al-Dīn, 48, 51, 103–4

ʿibāda (pl. *ʿibādāt*: devotional act), 24, 25, 69, 180
Iblīs, *see* devil
Ibn al-ʿAdīm, 103, *Bughyat al-ṭalab fī tārīkh Ḥalab*, 120
Ibn al-ʿAjamī , 161, 175, 180
Ibn ʿAqīl, 177
Ibn al-ʿArabī, Muḥyī al-Dīn, 205
Ibn al-Athīr, 23n7
Ibn ʿAttāf al-Kurdī, 133
Ibn Baṣkhān, Badr al-Dīn Muḥammad, 198–9, 200
Ibn Baṭṭūṭa, 42, 46–7, 62, 75–6, 89, 96, 97, 99, 119, 119n67, 165, 179n94, 194
Ibn Baydakīn, 146
Ibn al-Burhān, Muḥammad, 165–6, 179n94
Ibn Daqīq al-ʿĪd, Muḥammad ibn ʿAlī, 36, 38, 39n47, 152, 152n19, 181–3, 192, 193, 194, 195–6
Ibn Farḥūn, ʿAbd Allāh ibn Muḥammad, 5, 37, 93, 98, 134, 137–8, 164, 167, 179n94
Ibn Farḥūn, Ibrāhīm ibn ʿAlī, 66–7
Ibn Ḥabīb, 185
Ibn Ḥajar al-ʿAsqalānī, 14, 16, 91, 187, 187n115, 207
Ibn al-Ḥājj, 74, 189–90, 194; *Madkhal*, 140
Ibn Ḥanbal, Aḥmad, 32–3, 38n44, 113, 141n126, 157, 175
Ibn Ḥijjī, 187n115
Ibn Ḥināʾ, Bahāʾ al-Dīn ʿAlī ibn Muḥammad (vizier), 93–4
Ibn Hudaymī , 23n4
Ibn al-ʿIrāqī, 14
Ibn Jamāʿa, Badr al-Dīn, 36
Ibn al-Jawzī , 9, 11, 47–51, 80, 83–4, 85, 86, 89, 91, 157, 165, 167, 172, 174, 206; self-contradictory, 49–51; *Ṣifat al-ṣafwa*, 9, 10, 11, 49, 50, 211; *Talbīs Iblīs*, 49, 50, 52, 83, 84, 162, 177
Ibn Kathīr, Ismāʿīl ibn ʿUmar, 16, 46, 86, 88, 108, 110, 150, 158–9, 160–1, 180
Ibn Khalaf al-Maqdisī, Shihāb al-Dīn Muḥammad, 173–4, 174n79
Ibn Khallikān, 150, 151, 154, 155, 161, 179
Ibn al-Khashshāb, 199–201, 206
Ibn al-Malīḥ, Yūsuf, 123
Ibn al-Mannī, Abū'l-Fatḥ Naṣr, 29–30, 32–3, 39–40, 47, 48, 53–4, 144, 179, 199, 200, 211
Ibn Manẓūr, 22, 23n7, 24; *Lisān al-ʿArab*, 23, 170
Ibn Marzūq, Saʿd ibn ʿUthmān, 144–5, 146, 149, 162, 187
Ibn al-Munajjā al-Tanūkhī, ʿAlī, 99, 110n40
Ibn Munqidh, Usāma, 61, 67, 106n30
Ibn al-Mustawfī, 67, 150n12; *Tārīkh Irbil*, 201
Ibn al-Najjār, 145, 187
Ibn Niẓām al-Mulk, Sulaymān, 45
Ibn Nubāta, Ismāʿīl, 21
Ibn Qāḍī Shuhba, Abū Bakr, 187n115
Ibn al-Qāṣiḥ, Muḥammad al-Akhmīmī, 55
Ibn Qayyim al-Jawziyya, 36–7, 88, 160, 166, 183, 186, 190, 191
Ibn Qiwām, 115n55, 120n69
Ibn Qudāma, Abū ʿUmar, 24n9, 46, 53, 61, 78–80, 85, 95, 153, 157, 213
Ibn Qudāma al-Maqdisī, Muwaffaq al-Dīn, 18, 80, 85, 90, 136, 163, 164, 165, 172, 173, 177, 189, 191; *Dhamm al-waswās*, 163, 173, 183; *Mughnī*, 84, 174, 182

Ibn Rajab, 14, 16, 29n21
Ibn al-Sakrān, Muḥammad, 100–2, 101n12, 126n88, 212
Ibn al-Ṣalāḥ al-Shahrazūrī, Abū ʿUmar ʿUthmān, 135, 135n109, 193
Ibn Shāshīr, Muẓaffar, 73
Ibn Taghrībirdī, 26, 129, 188–9, 194, 205
Ibn Taymiyya, ʿAbd Allāh, 1–2, 6, 8, 12, 13, 206; as Sufi, 1, 1n1
Ibn Taymiyya, Aḥmad, 1, 2, 24, 41, 41n56, 42, 44, 64, 70–1, 80, 115, 160, 206
Ibn Taymiyya, Zayn al-Dīn, 2
Ibn ʿUbaydān, Zayn al-Dīn ʿAbd al-Raḥmān, 86, 88
Ibn ʿUmar, *see* ʿAbd Allah ibn ʿUmar
Ibn Yūnus, ʿImād al-Dīn, *see* Shaykh al-ʿImād
Ibn Yūnus, Kamāl al-Dīn (brother of Shaykh al-ʿImād), 201–2
Ibn al-Zamlakānī, 76–7, 77n55, 77n57
Ibn Ẓuhayra, Aḥmad ibn Muḥammad ibn ʿAbd Allāh (nephew of ʿĀʾisha Umm Kamāl), 181
Ibn Ẓuhayra, Najm al-Dīn Muḥammad, 53
Ibn Ẓuhayra, Shihāb al-Dīn Aḥmad, 53, 180–1
iḥtirāz (prudence, caution), 185, 190
iḥtiyāṭ (prudence, caution), 190, 190n125
ʿImād al-Dīn Muḥammad ibn Yūnus, *see* Shaykh al-ʿImād
impurity: emotional, 154n23; ethical, 106–7, 114, 131, 160, 194; from external substances, 149, 151, 151n14, 170, 181–95, 187; preventative washing, 150–1, 152; ritual impurity, 147–8; and scholarly activity, 152; temporary, 148, 148n9, 149, 154, 183, 188; transmission of, 187, 192–3, 194; in water, 176, 181, 182, 189–90; *see also ḥadath*; *najāsa*; *waswās*
ʿīna/masʾalat al-ʿīna, 159, 160n43, 160n44
innovation (*bidʿa*), 18n40, 74, 135, 178, 191–2, 210; *bidʿa* treatises, 18, 163n48, 177
iqṭāʿ system, 3, 120–1, 121n71; corruption in, 124; gifts for *muqṭaʿ*, 128–9
al-ʿIrāqī, Zayn al-Dīn ʿAbd al-Raḥīm, 187n115
iṣrāf (extravagance), 157
istiʾnāf (repetition), 132, 132n103
al-Jazarī, Shams al-Dīn Muḥammad, 60, 128
al-Jazarī, Taqī al-Dīn, 61
Jerusalem: al-Aqṣā mosque, 71; pious devotees in, 49n81, 115–16
Jews, Judaism and excessive piety, 47n77; and fasting, 58n4, 59, 59n7, 60, 64n22; and ritual impurity, 148; and washing, 162
jūkh, 192, 193–4
al-Junayd, 201
jundī, 45, 120
jurists: as authors, 19; education of, 20; as exemplars of piety, 6, 8, 12–13, 18, 19, 40, 131–3, 197; and food prohibition, 132–3; and *ṭahāra*, 148, 172
al-Juwaynī, ʿAbd Allāh ibn Yūsuf, 39
Juwayriyya (grandmother of al-Fāsī), 66

Kafadar, Cemel, 5
al-Kafarsūsī, Abū Bakr, 180n97
Karamustafa, Ahmet, 5
Katz, Marion, 114, 114n52
al-Kazarūnī, Aḥmad, 90
khabath (filth), 183
al-Khālidī, Isrāʾīl, 54
khalwa (Sufi spiritual retreat), 12, 118n62
khānqāh (lodge), 37n40, 123
al-Kurdī, ʿAlī, 203, 203n17
al-Kurdī, Ḥasan, 118n62
al-Kurdī, Ḥasan, 203, 203n17

Lājīn, *see* al-Malik al-Manṣūr Lājīn
law (*fiqh*), 2, 3, 18, 39, 152, 176, 189; ascetics and, 13; diets and fasting, 65, 66, 70–1, 74, 80, 82, 133–4, 139; and divorce, 166, 166n58; as evolving, 197; *furūʿ al-fiqh*, 18, 19, 70, 133, 137; legal stratagems, 159–60, 160n43; literature on, 3, 18n40, 18–19, 39; and marketplace ethics, 131; in the medieval period, 20; and ritual practices, 16, 19; and ritual purity, 145; study of, 20; women and, 20, 51n90; *see also ḥīla*; *madhhab*, and under individual *madhāhib*
Luʾluʾ, Badr al-Dīn, 185

madhhab (pl. *madhāhib*: school of Islamic law), 18, 20; and ablutions,

171; conversion between, 150, 156; disagreement among (*ikhtilāf*), 136, 137, 159, 171–2; disagreements within, 137; and fasting, 62n15; and water purity, 175–6
madrasas, 9n14, 36, 37n40, 43, 121, 123–4, 124n81, 126, 131, 142–3, 176n85, 204; Ashrafiyya Madrasa, 34; Badhrā'iyya Madrasa, 106; Iqbāliyya Madrasa, 161; Mirjāniyya Madrasa, 124; Muẓaffariyya Madrasa, 179; Niẓāmiyya Madrasa, 45, 123
Maghen, Ze'ev, 148, 194
al-Maghribī, Muḥammad, 188, 205
majdhūb (holy fool), 188, 204n23, 205, 205n25, 207
al-Majūsī, 86
al-Makkī, Abū Ṭālib, 34, 113
makrūh (disapproved of), 62n16, 70, 80, 82
malāmatī (pious person who incurs blame), 208
Mālik ibn Anas, on licit food, 135
al-Malik al-Ashraf Mūsā (Ayyubid sultan), 118, 120, 143
al-Malik al-ʿAzīz, 122
Mālikī *madhhab*: and fasting, 62n15, 75n49; and licit food, 136; and marriage, 39n49; and water purity, 176, 190
al-Malik al-Manṣūr Lājīn (Mamluk sultan), 128, 146, 192, 194
al-Malik al-Muʿaẓẓam (Ayyubid sultan), 103
Mamluk period, 3, 4, 41–2, 58, 73, 83, 117, 124, 128, 149, 162, 198, 212
Mankūtamur, 128
al-Maqrīzī, 92n99, 129, 184, 193
al-Mārdīnī, ʿAbd Allāh, 201–2
al-Mārdīnī, Rabīʿ ibn Maḥmūd, 120, 122n77, 122–3
al-Marrākushī, Mūsā ibn ʿAlī, 65, 134, 136, 139
marriage, 35–42; to control sexual desire, 39, 39n49; in Islamic culture, 36, 38; pious attitudes to, 29, 35–8, 40, 41, 42; for political or social gain, 26, 38; recommended, 36; *see also* divorce
masnūn (valid, of a practice), 70, 81, 82, 90
Mayeur-Jaouen, Catherine, 17
meat, 48, 52, 59, 60n8, 67–9, 108, 113–14, 115, 130–1, 134–8, 141, 198; avoidance of, 32, 65, 98, 130–1, 177
Mecca, 4, 5; endowed properties in, 37n40, 131; mosques in, 34n32, 71; pious devotees in, 53–4, 165, 180–1; pilgrims, 130–1; Sanctuary, 74n47; special dietary restrictions in, 135n110, 135–7, 154; supererogatory devotions in, 42
Medina, 4, 5, 134–7; endowed properties in, 128n91; mosques in, 34n32, 71; Muḥammad in, 12, 14n28, 59, 67, 135, 154; pious devotees in, 37, 65, 66, 92, 92n100, 98, 105–6, 118, 164, 167; Prophet's tomb, 92, 128n91, 135; special dietary restrictions in, 135–7, 154
al-Minūfī, ʿAbd Allāh, 104
miracles, 1, 6, 16, 17, 23n7, 110, 115n55, 158, 174n79, 208
al-Mizzī, Yūsuf, 34, 185n111
moderation, 43–4; God's easing of requirements, 82, 177n90; recommended for the masses, 50; unfashionable, 47
modesty, female 52–4; veiling, 53, 54
mortification of the body: in biographical literature, 33–4; dangers of, 84, 86–7; excessive devotional practices, 86, 92–3; excessive fasting, 6, 69, 74, 84; excessive prayer, 6; fluctuations in, 31–2; hair shirts, 49, 50, 211; poverty, 6; sleeping on a mat, 61, 213n42; by women, 49
al-Mu'ayyad Shaykh, Sultan, 102
Mubarrad, 204n23
Muḥammad, 19; and ablutions, 154n23, 156–7; and asceticism, 213, 213n41; and fasting, 56, 59, 60, 61, 62n18, 62–3, 69–70, 80, 81, 82, 83, 84, 94; as exemplar, 59, 212–13; and food, 48, 89n92; poverty of, 48, 59, 213; and prayer, 210; and other religious communities, 59; and water, 163; as world embracer, 213
Muḥammad ibn Khalīl ("al-Akkāl"/"the Glutton"), 107–13, 127, 142, 143
al-Murshidī, 110, 111–12, 142
al-Mūsawī, Shams al-Din Muḥammad Ibn al-Majd, 184
mustaḥabb (strongly recommended), 90
muwallahūn (sing. *muwallah*: eccentric mystics), 108, 156, 164n50, 197, 201–10; as antinomian, 13, 197, 203, 205–6, 209; and cleanliness, 199–200, 201–2, 203, 207, 208–9; and insanity, 201, 202, 204, 209; and neglect of ritual duties, 13, 203, 204–5; and the religious elite, 203–4; *see also majdhūb*; Qaḍīb al-Bān

muwaswasīn (sing. *muwaswas*: those beset by anxiety about purity), 147, 162, 163, 172, 195; praised, 178

nāfila (pl. *nawāfil*: supererogatory pious act), 24n9, 72, 74, 95, 104, 171, 173
nafs (spirit; "lower self"), 68, 76, 89, 89n91
najāsa (pl. *najāsāt*: polluting substance), 114, 169n65, 170, 173n77, 183, 188–90, 195, 206
najis (impure, of a substance), 114n50, 169n65
nāsik (one who has purged himself of sin), 22–3, 23n4, 24n8, 25
al-Nāṣir Ibn al-ʿAzīz, 45
al-Nāṣir Muḥammad (Mamluk sultan), 26, 28, 37n40, 129
al-Nawawī, 18, 19, 39, 40–1, 42, 43, 64, 65, 80–1, 104, 125–7, 139–40, 142, 159–60, 170, 175, 186, 199, 208, 213, 213n42; *Minhaj al-ṭālibīn*, 90; *Rawḍat al-ṭālibīn*, 80, 171
Nihāya fī gharīb al-ḥadīth, 22
Niṣf Shaʿbān, 77, 111
niyya (intention), 166n57, 168n63, 182n105
Nūr al-Dīn Arslān Shāh, 150, 155

Pilgrimage (hajj), 1, 54, 81; as changing one's physical state, 94, 96; and fasting, 60n9; as focus for piety, 8, 11; *iḥrām*, 94
pious endowments (*waqf* [pl. *awqāf*]), 102, 121–2, 123; administrative corruption in, 121–7, 122n73, 124n80, 142; providing education, 102n15; providing food, 102n15, 105; providing housing, 102n14
pious forebears (*al-salaf*), 34, 66, 101n12, 117n60, 174, 212
Pouzet, Louis, 108, 197
poverty: and charity, 102–3; *fuqarāʾ* (the pious poor), 98, 101n12; of the Prophet, 59; voluntary, 6, 92, 101–2, 116; women and, 102n14
prayer (*ṣalāt*), 94, 177; and ablutions, 210; and fasting, 61; intention to pray, 166, 166n57, 167; interrupted or invalidated, 132, 132n103, 154n23, 166, 166n57, 176, 183, 189; at night, 1, 7, 8, 21, 49, 61, 72, 72n42, 77, 79, 179n93, 202; repetition of, 85, 191; and ritual purity, 94, 151, 168, 169, 182; stuttering during, 167; supererogatory, 200; *wird* (nighttime recital), 179
Prophet, *see* Muḥammad

Qaḍīb al-Bān, 155, 156, 158, 201–2, 206, 208–9
al-Qalqashandī, Aḥmad ibn ʿAlī, 27
al-Qarāfī, 148, 168–9, 171
al-Qaṣṣarī, Abū ʿAbd Allāh, 138–9
al-Qasṭallānī, Khalīl ibn ʿAbd al-Raḥmān, 180
al-Qaysarānī, Shihāb al-Dīn Yaḥyā ibn Ismāʿīl, 44
al-Qazwīnī, Ḥusayn, 50
Qurʾān, 47, 85; and dietary laws, 106, 113, 139; ritual purity and, 152, 152n17, 183; and Satan, 145–6; and whispering, 145–6
al-Qurashī, Aḥmad, 164, 166, 179n94
Quṭb al-Dīn Ibrāhīm (grandson of Badr al-Dīn Luʾluʾ), 185

Rāfiʿ ibn Hajras, 187n115
al-Rāfiʿī, 81–2, 183n107
Ramaḍān, 56, 207; neglecting the fast, 203, 205, 207
al-Rāzī, Fakhr al-Dīn, 25n11
Reinhart, Kevin, 147, 148
rejection of society, 2, 8, 12, 54–5, 116–17, 119–20, 206; celibacy and, 40; and cleanliness, 13, 201; dangers of, 47; and neglect of ritual duties, 13
religious scholars, *see ʿulamāʾ*
ribāṭ (convent, lodge), 29, 123; celibacy in, 36–7, 37n40, 131, 177
ritual purity, 144–96; cautious attitude to, 149, 151–2, 153–4, 155, 168n63, 190–1, 194–5; and cleanliness, 147, 149, 151, 157, 163, 171; degree of individual choice in, 207, 212; and ethical purity, 159–61; as a form of devotional piety, 172; interrupted, 153; and menstruation, 54; neglect of, 199–200, 203, 206–7; and scholarly pursuits, 151–2; symbolic purity, 147, 148–9, 157, 162–3, 168–72; and urination, 186; *see also* ablutions; *muwaswas*; *ṭahāra*; washing; *waswās*; *wuḍūʾ*
rivers: ablutions in, 157, 202; prayer beside, 21, 202; purity of water in, 155, 157, 189–90, 202; drinking water from, 140; washing garments in, 162, 202, 208n34

Robinson, Chase, 14
al-Rūmī, Asad, 167

Sabra, Adam, 102
Ṣadr al-Dīn ibn Naṣr, 72n42, 132
al-Ṣafadī, 1n1, 12, 15, 54, 55, 75, 87, 88, 115, 150, 179, 180, 192, 195, 198–9
al-Sakhāwī, 5, 14, 181
Saladin (Ṣalāḥ al-Dīn), 3, 128n91
Salaf, see pious forebears
ṣāliḥ (virtuous man), 23n40, 24n8
al-Sallāmī, Ibn Rāfiʿ, 184–8, 195
al-Sarrāj, Abū Naṣr, 111
Satan, *see* devil
ṣawm (fasting), 60, 65, 66, 75; *ṣawm al-dahr* (also *al-ṣawm al-dāʾim*), 61, 67, 79, 80, 81, 83, 90, 91, 94, 95; *ṣawm al-taṭawwuʿ*; *ṣawm al-wiṣāl*, 62, 63, 63n20, 65, 75, 96n110
al-Sayfī (amir), 109
Schimmel, Annemarie: and Sufism, 6n10; and *tawakkul*, 101n13
scholarship, 9; and asceticism, 9–10; and bodily piety, 11; and cultural practices, 10, 10n18; women and, 51n90
al-Shāfiʿī, 136, 157, 173n77, 175
Shāfiʿī *madhhab*: on the cleaning of garments, 186; conversion to, 150, 156; and financial transactions, 156, 160, 160n43; and impure substances, 183, 192; and water purity, 172n73, 175, 176
al-Shāghūrī, Ibrāhīm, 203
shakk (doubt), 177
al-Shaʿrānī: *Ṭabaqāt al-kubrā*, 60n8, 140
al-Shaʿrānī, Nūr al-Dīn ʿAlī ibn Aḥmad, 140–2
sharīʿa, 133, 192
al-Shaṭṭanūfī, ʿAlī ibn Yūsuf: *Bahjat al-asrār*, 201
Shaykh al-ʿImād, 150–1, 153, 154–61, 162, 179, 201; *Muḥīṭ*, 150
al-Shīrāzī, 170; *Muhadhdhab*, 150
shubha (uncertainty), 176
Sibṭ Ibn al-Jawzī, 45, 150, 155, 158, 161
slaves, slavery, 44, 133, 155, 207; indication of social status, 38, 43; in Mamluk households, 38; *mamlūks*, 4, 27n15; manumission of, 45, 64n21, 95; pious, 61, 76n53; serf (*ʿabd qinn*), 121; *see also* concubines
al-Subkī, Tāj al-Dīn, 152, 181, 185
al-Subkī, Taqī al-Dīn, 11
Sufis, 7, 26, 26n13; and charity, 100–1, 103, 111; criticized, 177; and dancing, 146; and fasting, 73–4; and hospitality, 100
Sufism, 5–6, 6n10; and asceticism, 5–7, 26; feigned insanity in, 204; and modern scholarship, 5–6, 6n10; and piety, 1, 5, 45; Sufi brotherhoods, 28; *tawakkul*, 101, 118n61
Sulaymān ibn Ḥamza, 41, 42n58
Sulṭān ibn Maḥmūd, 118
sunna (sing. *sunan*: Prophetic tradition), 70n38, 210–13; and ablutions, 157n31, 173; and fasting, 90n94; and medicine, 88n90; neglect of, 82n73, 83, 92n102; and *waswās*, 173, 177
Sunqur al-Qishtimurī, Shams al-Dīn (amir), 128–30
supererogatory worship, 7, 8, 12, 72, 154, 210; jurists and, 12–13; as proof of piety, 28; *taṭawwuʿ*, 66, 210; women and, 52, 55; zealous devotee (*mutaʿabbid*), 22; *see also* fasting, voluntary; *nāfila*; *taʿabbud*; *waswās*
al-Suyūṭī, 175, 177

taʿabbud (bodily devotion), 8, 9, 11, 12, 23–4, 24n9, 25, 33, 42, 49, 96, 118n62, 172, 173, 173n77; *see also* devotional piety
ṭahāra (purity), 145, 148, 149, 150–1, 153, 168, 173, 175, 177, 182n105, 184, 188; *al-adnās* (blemish, stain), 195; meanings of, 168–9, 170–1, 182, 207; misunderstanding of, 162; *naẓāfa* (cleanliness), 170; *ṭāhir* (pure), 168, 171; *ṭahūr* (clean), 171
al-Takrūrī, Qāsim, 92–3, 118
Talmon-Heller, Daniella, 6
Tankiz (amir), 26–8, 27n15, 116, 117, 143
taqwā (piousness), 8, 28
ṭayyib (pl. *ṭayyibāt*: something good, pure), 99, 114n52, 138; *ṭayyib al-maṭʿam*, 99, 130, 134
al-Ṭuraynī, Abū Bakr, 65, 115
al-Turkumānī, Sulaymān, 205, 208
al-Ṭūsī, Naṣīr al-Dīn, 101

ʿubbād, see ʿābid
al-Udfūwī, 5

ʿulamāʾ (religious scholars), 10, 26, 43, 203
ʿUmar ibn ʿAbd al-ʿAzīz (Umayyad caliph), 114n52
Umm Kulthūm (mother of ʿĀʾisha Umm Kamāl), 53–4, 181
urine, urination: on clothing, 186, 201; and ritual impurity, 148n8, 183–4, 186, 189–90; in rivers, 189–90
ʿUthmān (caliph), 91

walking: and exposure to filth, 183, 191, 203; as a form of supererogatory worship, 50, 72; as sign of humility, 29, 30n23, 34
waqf, *see* pious endowments
waraʿ (ethical asceticism, scrupulosity), 115, 144
al-Warghamī, Abū Muḥammad, 66, 67
washing, 147–8; before writing, 150, 151–2; in cold water, 34; excessive, 156–7, 162, 164, 165, 166n56, 172, 188; excessive washing of clothing, 187; of the eyes, 173–4, 178, 191, 212; of garments, 150–1, 184, 186, 188, 192, 194, 202; of limbs, 155, 156, 158, 162, 169–70; neglect of, 13, 52; wasting water, 155–8, 157n34, 162–3, 165, 166, 166n56; and *wuḍūʾ* 147; *see also* ablutions
waswās (pl. *wasāwis*: anxiety about purity), 146–7, 149, 150–94; as anxiety, 145, 146, 147, 151, 152, 158, 161–8, 172, 174, 176, 178, 179, 180, 182–3, 187–8; and the body, 150–78; as caused by insanity, 163–5, 173, 175, 177, 195; criticized, 172–8, 190–1, 206; as a form of piety, 167–8, 178–84, 195–6; inability to complete obligatory rituals, 165–7; as interfering with obligatory duties, 165–6; meanings of, 165; repetitive behavior, 166n59, 166–7, 167n62, 174, 187–8; *waswās fīʾl-ṭahāra/waswasa fīʾl-ṭahāra*, 39n47, 145, 146–7, 150, 152, 153, 154, 161, 163, 165, 166, 168, 171, 172, 173, 174, 179, 182, 184, 195; and water purity, 162, 175–6, 180, 181, 182; *see also* impurity; *najāsa*; ritual purity
wuḍūʾ (minor ablution), 145, 147, 149, 153–4, 157, 165, 171, 173n77, 183; total immersion as, 184

al-Yāfiʿī, 16, 17n36, 111–12, 142, 208
al-Yūnīnī, ʿĪsā ibn Aḥmad, 42
al-Yūnīnī, Quṭb al-Dīn Mūsā, 108; *Dhayl Mirʾāt al-zamān*, 132
al-Yāfiʿī, 205

zāhid (pl. *zuhhād*: ascetic), 1, 22, 24n8, 33; *see also* asceticism
Zangid dynasty, 122, 155
zāwiya (cell), 123
Zaynab Bint al-Wāsiṭī, 79
zuhd (asceticism), 9, 11, 23–4, 25, 31, 32–3, 115

Titles in the Series

POPULAR CULTURE IN MEDIEVAL CAIRO *Boaz Shoshan*

EARLY PHILOSOPHICAL SHIISM: THE ISMAILI NEOPLATONISM OF ABŪ YA'QUB AL-SIJISTĀNI *Paul E. Walker*

INDIAN MERCHANTS IN EURASIAN TRADE, 1600–1750 *Stephen Frederic Dale*

PALESTINIAN PEASANTS AND OTTOMAN OFFICIALS: RURAL ADMINISTRATION AROUND SIXTEENTH-CENTURY JERUSALEM *Amy Singer*

ARABIC HISTORICAL THOUGHT IN THE CLASSICAL PERIOD *Tarif Khalidi*

MONGOLS AND MAMLUKS: THE MAMLUK–ĪLKHĀNID WAR, 1260–1281 *Reuven Amitai-Preiss*

HIERARCHY AND EGALITARIANISM IN ISLAMIC THOUGHT *Louise Marlow*

THE POLITICS OF HOUSEHOLDS IN OTTOMAN EGYPT: THE RISE OF THE QAZDAĞLIS *Jane Hathaway*

COMMODITY AND EXCHANGE IN THE MONGOL EMPIRE: MOSUL, 1540–1834 *Dina Rizk Khoury*

THE MAMLUKS IN EGYPTIAN POLITICS AND SOCIETY *Thomas Philipp and Ulrich Haarmann (eds.)*

THE DELHI SULTANATE: A POLITICAL AND MILITARY HISTORY *Peter Jackson*

EUROPEAN AND ISLAMIC TRADE IN THE EARLY OTTOMAN STATE: THE MERCHANTS OF GENOA AND TURKEY *Kate Fleet*

REINTERPRETING ISLAMIC HISTORIOGRAPHY: HARUN AL-RASHID AND THE NARRATIVE OF THE ʿABBĀSID CALIPHATE *Tayeb El-Hibri*

THE OTTOMAN CITY BETWEEN EAST AND WEST: ALEPPO, IZMIR, AND ISTANBUL *Edhem Eldem, Daniel Goffman, and Bruce Masters*

A MONETARY HISTORY OF THE OTTOMAN EMPIRE *Sevket Pamuk*

THE POLITICS OF TRADE IN SAFAVID IRAN: SILK FOR SILVER, 1600–1730 *Rudolph P. Matthee*

THE IDEA OF IDOLATRY AND THE EMERGENCE OF ISLAM: FROM POLEMIC TO HISTORY *G. R. Hawting*

CLASSICAL ARABIC BIOGRAPHY: THE HEIRS OF THE PROPHETS IN THE AGE OF AL-MA'MŪN *Michael Cooperson*

EMPIRE AND ELITES AFTER THE MUSLIM CONQUEST: THE TRANSFORMATION OF NORTHERN MESOPOTAMIA *Chase F. Robinson*

POVERTY AND CHARITY IN MEDIEVAL ISLAM: MAMLUK EGYPT, 1250–1517 *Adam Sabra*

CHRISTIANS AND JEWS IN THE OTTOMAN ARAB WORLD: THE ROOTS OF SECTARIANISM *Bruce Masters*

CULTURE AND CONQUEST IN MONGOL EURASIA *Thomas T. Allsen*

REVIVAL AND REFORM IN ISLAM: THE LEGACY OF MUHAMMAD AL-SHAWKANI *Bernard Haykel*

TOLERANCE AND COERCION IN ISLAM: INTERFAITH RELATIONS IN THE MUSLIM TRADITION *Yohanan Friedmann*

GUNS FOR THE SULTAN: MILITARY POWER AND THE WEAPONS INDUSTRY IN THE OTTOMAN EMPIRE *Gábor Ágoston*

MARRIAGE, MONEY AND DIVORCE IN MEDIEVAL ISLAMIC SOCIETY *Yossef Rapoport*

THE EMPIRE OF THE QARA KHITAI IN EURASIAN HISTORY: BETWEEN CHINA AND THE ISLAMIC WORLD *Michal Biran*

DOMESTICITY AND POWER IN THE EARLY MUGHAL WORLD *Ruby Lal*